Task/Topic	Menu Selection	
Copy a report	•**R**eports→**C**reate/modify •**C**opy	REPORTS
Copy a table	•**I**nfo→**C**reate/modify •**T**ables→**C**opy	RBDEFINE
Create a command file	•**T**ools→**E**ditor→**N**ew file	RBEDIT
Create a database	•**D**atabases→**C**reate/modify •**C**reate→**N**ew database	CREATE SCHEMA
Create a form	•**F**orms→**C**reate/modify •**C**reate	FORMS
Create a rule	•**I**nfo→**C**reate/modify •**R**ules→**C**reate	RULES
Create a view	•**V**iews→**C**reate/modify	CREATE VIEW
Create an application	•**A**pplications→**C**reate/modify •**C**reate→**N**ew application	EXPRESS
Define rules	•**I**nfo→**C**reate/modify •**R**ules→**C**reate	RULES
Define user access	•**I**nfo→**C**reate/modify •**A**ccess rights	GRANT, REVOKE
Delete a column	•**I**nfo→**C**reate/modify •**T**ables→**M**odify	DROP COLUMN
Delete a file	•**T**ools→**D**isk Management→**E**rase a file	ERASE, DEL
Delete a form	•**F**orms→**C**reate/modify •**D**elete	DROP FORM
Delete a report	•**R**eports→**C**reate/modify •**D**elete	DROP REPORT
Delete a row	•**I**nfo→*tablename* **F9**	DELETE ROWS
Delete a rule	•**I**nfo→**C**reate/modify •**R**ules→**D**elete	DROP RULE
Delete a table	•**I**nfo→**C**reate/modify •**T**ables→**D**elete	DROP TABLE
Delete a view	•**V**iews→**C**reate/modify •**M**anage views→**D**elete	DROP VIEWS
Delete an application	•**A**pplications→**C**reate/modify •**D**elete	DEL, ERASE
Delete multiple rows	•**I**nfo→*tablename* •**E**dit→**D**elete all rows	DELETE ROWS
Detach a dBASE database	•**D**atabases→**d**BASE files→**D**etach file	DETACH
Disconnect a database	•**D**atabases→**D**isconnect database	DISCONNECT
Display data on screen		OUTPUT SCREEN

Continued on back page

Computer users are not all alike.
Neither are SYBEX books.

We know our customers have a variety of needs. They've told us so. And because we've listened, we've developed several distinct types of books to meet the needs of each of our customers. What are you looking for in computer help?

If you're looking for the basics, try the **ABC's** series. You'll find short, unintimidating tutorials and helpful illustrations. For a more visual approach, select **Teach Yourself**, featuring screen-by-screen illustrations of how to use your latest software purchase.

Mastering and **Understanding** titles offer you a step-by-step introduction, plus an in-depth examination of intermediate-level features, to use as you progress.

Our **Up & Running** series is designed for computer-literate consumers who want a no-nonsense overview of new programs. Just 20 basic lessons, and you're on your way.

We also publish two types of reference books. Our **Instant References** provide quick access to each of a program's commands and functions. SYBEX **Encyclopedias** provide a *comprehensive reference* and explanation of all of the commands, features and functions of the subject software.

Sometimes a subject requires a special treatment that our standard series doesn't provide. So you'll find we have titles like **Advanced Techniques, Handbooks, Tips & Tricks**, and others that are specifically tailored to satisfy a unique need.

We carefully select our authors for their in-depth understanding of the software they're writing about, as well as their ability to write clearly and communicate effectively. Each manuscript is thoroughly reviewed by our technical staff to ensure its complete accuracy. Our production department makes sure it's easy to use. All of this adds up to the highest quality books available, consistently appearing on best seller charts worldwide.

You'll find SYBEX publishes a variety of books on every popular software package. Looking for computer help? Help Yourself to SYBEX.

For a complete catalog of our publications:

SYBEX Inc.
2021 Challenger Drive, Alameda, CA 94501
Tel: (415) 523-8233/(800) 227-2346 Telex: 336311
Fax: (415) 523-2373

Understanding
R:BASE
3.1

Understanding R:BASE®
3.1

Alan Simpson
Ron Dragushan

SYBEX®

San Francisco   Paris   Düsseldorf   Soest

Acquisitions Editor: Dianne King
Editor: Peter Weverka
Project Editor: Kathleen Lattinville
Technical Editor: Sharon Crawford
Word Processors: Scott Campbell, Ann Dunn, Lisa Mitchell, Paul Erickson
Chapter Art: Charlotte Carter
Technical Art: Delia Brown
Screen Graphics: Cuong Le
Typesetter: Elizabeth Newman
Proofreaders: Rhonda M. Holmes, Bill Cassel
Indexer: Julie Kawabata
Cover Designer: Thomas Ingalls + Associates
Cover Photographer: Michael Lamotte
Screen reproductions produced by HOTSHOT Graphics.

To Susan
A.S.

To my parents, Sadie and John Dragushan
R.D.

Acknowledgments

Many thanks go to all the people whose skills and talents produced this book. We would especially like to thank Peter Weverka, editor, and Sharon Crawford, technical editor, who were so helpful and a delight to work with. We are also indebted to Charlotte Carter, artist; Rhonda Holmes and Bill Cassel, proofreaders; Elizabeth Newman, typesetter; Scott Campbell, Ann Dunn, Lisa Mitchell, and Paul Erickson, word processing; Delia Brown, technical art; and Cuong Le, screen production. Thanks are also due to Kathleen Lattinville and Richard Mills, who helped shepherd the manuscript through production; and to Jon Strickland, editor, and Maria Mart, proofreader, for their excellent work on the first R:BASE book. Of course, we are also thankful to Dianne King, the acquisitions editor at SYBEX.

Special thanks to literary agents Bill and Cynthia Gladstone for their support.

Sincere thanks to Harley Hahn for his support and encouragement, especially the introductions that created the opportunity for this project.

Contents at a Glance

Table of Contents

Introduction

R:BASE 3.1 IS THE SIXTH VERSION OF THE R:BASE database-management system for microcomputers. Like its predecessors, R:BASE 4000, R:BASE 5000, R:BASE System V, R:BASE for DOS, and R:BASE 3.0, version 3.1 is a powerful, flexible tool for storing, organizing, analyzing, and retrieving information on a microcomputer. The new R:BASE, though, offers significant improvements over its predecessors.

For the beginner, R:BASE 3.1 includes a powerful, better-integrated menu system for managing and analyzing data spontaneously, without any programming. For intermediate and advanced users, R:BASE 3.1 offers a more consistent interface and powerful report, form, and application generators that make it easier to develop customized business systems. The power of the R:BASE language has been made more accessible with the addition of SQL commands. SQL is an emerging standard in the world of relational databases. Learning R:BASE commands will make it easy for you to learn the commands used with many Unix, OS/2, and mainframe databases.

The R:BASE 3.1 user interface and application development tools let you share data directly with dBASE III and dBASE III Plus databases and indexes. Now you can access and update dBASE databases with almost all the same techniques you use with R:BASE tables.

WHO SHOULD READ THIS BOOK

This book is written for the absolute beginner as well as the experienced user who wants to develop sophisticated applications. To encourage rapid learning and complete mastery, this book offers practical examples that let you put R:BASE to work immediately. Once you've learned how to manage data in R:BASE databases, this book will teach you more advanced topics, such as how to develop customized applications. An accounts-receivable system is provided as a practical example.

There are many new features in R:BASE 3.1, so even readers with previous experience in R:BASE System V, R:BASE for DOS, or R:BASE 3.0 can profit from this book. Some of the basic concepts presented in the earlier chapters will seem like "old hat" to experienced R:BASE users. Nevertheless, by reading on, experienced users will find valuable information about tools and techniques new to version 3.1.

THE STRUCTURE OF THIS BOOK

This book is designed as a tutorial as well as a reference. It begins with the simplest and most basic concepts and builds upon acquired knowledge and skills toward complete mastery. We encourage you to consult the table of contents and index whenever you need advice or information about a specific topic. Although this book presents many step-by-step exercises, they are written as a way of explaining and highlighting useful R:BASE techniques and concepts. You do not have to begin at the beginning to make use of this book.

Part I, "Working with a Single Table," discusses all of the basic database-management techniques. These techniques include storing, organizing, analyzing, searching for, and updating information in a database table.

Part II, "Working with Multiple Tables," introduces more advanced techniques for relating data in multiple tables. It shows how to develop effective data-entry and reporting facilities, and perform more complex data analysis.

Part III, "Developing Applications," discusses how to create custom business applications with the R:BASE Application Generator and programming language. All of the material from the previous chapters is applied to the development of a fully customized accounts-receivable system.

Part IV, "Advanced Application Techniques," discusses how to design and create powerful menus to make your applications easier to use. It introduces the CodeLock program, which can make your applications run faster. Here, you'll learn how to interface with other software packages. You'll learn how to produce merge files with common word processing packages, how to upgrade your data and programs from previous versions of R:BASE, and how to access and update dBASE III and dBASE III Plus files directly with R:BASE menus and commands.

An appendix is also included to provide you with tips for installing and customizing R:BASE.

CONVENTIONS USED IN THIS BOOK

This book contains many carefully chosen tutorial exercises to provide you with excellent learning opportunities. To follow along with the exercises, press the keystrokes that appear in boldface. We encourage you to follow along on-line as you progress through the book. A little effort on your part will pay big dividends.

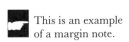 This is an example of a margin note.

From time to time in this book you'll see margin notes side-by-side with the text. A margin note might contain a useful shortcut, a reminder, a reference telling you where to find more detailed information about a subject, or a word definition. Margin notes are meant to complement the information in the main text and exercises.

HARDWARE REQUIREMENTS

To run R:BASE 3.1, you'll need the following software and hardware:

- An IBM PC, AT, PS/2, or 100% compatible computer.

- DOS version 3.1 or higher for most IBM-compatible computers, DOS version 3.2 or higher if you are installing with 3½-inch diskettes, or DOS version 3.3 or higher for an IBM PS/2.

- At least 640K of RAM, with at least 450K available.

- A hard disk with at least 6.5 megabytes (MB) of disk available for installing the R:BASE program files and doing the exercises in this book. You will need 8 MB of disk available to install the tutorial files, sample files, and program files; as well as to do the exercises in this book. These figures include .5 megabytes of disk to hold the results of your exercises.

R:BASE can use any printer and any mouse that works with your system. R:BASE will use extended or expanded memory if you have it, but neither type of memory is required.

R:BASE is not copy-protected, and it can be run directly from any hard disk without the use of a key disk in the floppy drive.

Part I

Working with a Single Table

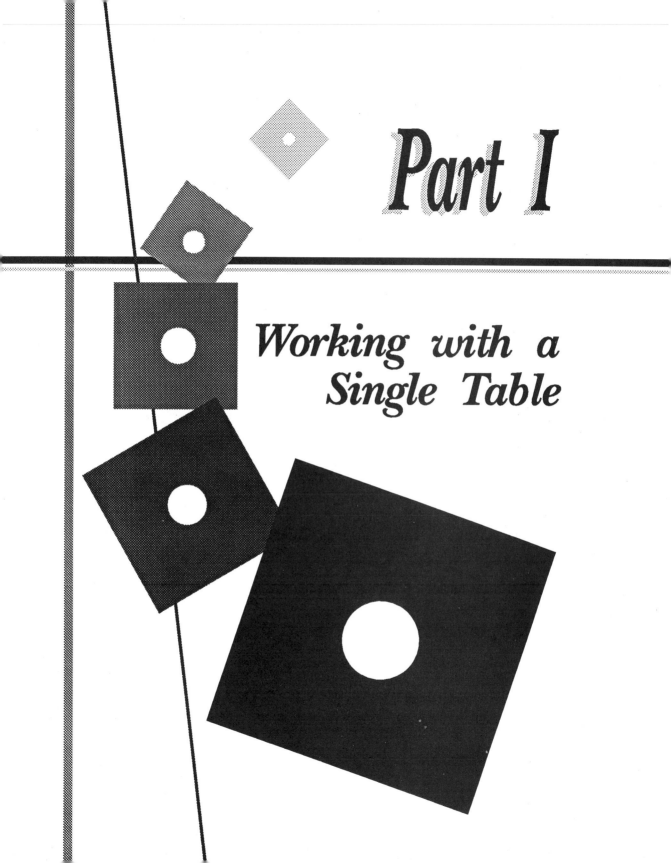

Chapter 1

What Is
a Database?

WHILE THE TERM *DATABASE MANAGEMENT* MAY sound like just another mysterious computer buzzword, managing a database is as commonplace as storing a Manila folder in a file cabinet. Rolodexes, tickler files, file cabinets, and even shoe boxes full of index cards are all databases. They all hold information (data) in an organized fashion. Each time you use one of these databases to look up information, store new information, create a sorted list, calculate numbers, or make changes, you are *managing* the database.

A computer database management system also allows you to store information in an organized way. However, rather than writing the data on paper and storing it in a file drawer, you store the information on a disk, where it is easily accessible through a computer. Once you've stored information, you can easily retrieve it, sort it, search through it, perform calculations, and make changes and additions.

The greatest advantage to using a computer to manage a database is speed. For example, suppose you had a shoe box full of index cards with names and addresses, stored in alphabetical order by name. If you wanted to print mailing labels for all the California residents, sorted in ZIP-code order (for bulk mailing), you'd have quite a bit of work ahead of you. The process could take hours. If this information were stored on a computer instead, your work would be limited to typing a few commands at the keyboard. The time required to pull out all the California residents and put them into ZIP-code order would be two or three seconds. Then you could go to lunch while the computer printed the mailing labels.

Of course, R:BASE can do much more than print mailing labels, as you'll see throughout the coming chapters.

R:BASE DATABASES

An R:BASE database can be a collection of many different types of information. Most of this information is stored in *tables,* which consist of neatly organized rows and columns of information. For example, take a look at the table of names and addresses in Figure 1.1. This table consists of six *columns* of information, labeled Last Name, First Name, Address, City, State, and Zip. The table consists of five *rows* of information, sorted into alphabetical order by last name. An

CUSTOMER TABLE

Last Name	First Name	Address	City	State	Zip
Adams	Anthony	123 A St.	Berkeley	CA	94710
Baker	Betty	345 B St.	New York	NY	12345
Carlson	Marianne	P.O. Box 123	Houston	TX	54321
Carrera	Fred	3211 Fox St.	L.A.	CA	92991
Davis	Julie	671 Alpine Way	Newark	NJ	87654

Figure 1.1: A sample table in a database

R:BASE table can consist of as many as 800 columns and tens of thousands of rows.

Notice how each column in the sample table contains a specific item of information; that is, each last name, first name, address, city, state, and ZIP code occupies a separate column. Generally speaking, when structuring an R:BASE table, you want to break the information into as many separate, meaningful columns as possible, because this gives you the greatest flexibility in managing a database.

For example, notice how the table in Figure 1.2 combines the city, state, and ZIP code into a single column named CSZ. This sample table has some distinct disadvantages compared to the first one. Suppose you wanted to sort this table into ZIP-code order or pull out all the California residents? You couldn't do either operation with this table, because the state and ZIP code are combined within the CSZ column. As you'll see in the many examples throughout this book, it's always a good idea to place each item of information in its own column.

MANAGING A DATABASE

Once you've defined a structure for a table, you need to begin managing it. You may do any of the following tasks:

- Add new information to the table.

- Sort the table into a meaningful order.

Last Name	First Name	Address	CSZ
Adams	Anthony	123 A St.	Berkeley, CA 94710
Baker	Betty	345 B St.	New York, NY 12345
Carlson	Marianne	P.O. Box 123	Houston, TX 54321
Carrera	Fred	3211 Fox St.	L.A., CA 92991
Davis	Julie	671 Alpine Way	Newark, NJ 87654

Figure 1.2: A table with city, state, and ZIP code entries in one column

- Search the table for specific types of information.
- Calculate sums and averages from information in the table.
- Print the information in an organized fashion.
- Edit (change) information in the table.
- Delete superfluous information from the table.

These tasks are no different from those performed with a shoe-box database. However, with the shoe box, you have to do all the labor; with R:BASE managing the table, you just do the thinking and a little typing. R:BASE does all the work—quickly, efficiently, and without errors.

DATABASE DESIGNS

There are many ways to structure or *design* a database. For example, the table in Figure 1.1 is useful for keeping track of basic mailing information. But a business manager using this table might also want to keep track of appointments or credit charges for each of the individuals in the list. In this case, two tables could be used in a database, as shown in Figure 1.3.

This database design keeps track of a *one-to-many* relationship between individuals in the Customer table and charges recorded in the Charges table. For every one customer in the Customer table,

CUSTOMER TABLE

Last Name	First Name	Address	City	State	Zip
Adams	Anthony	123 A St.	Berkeley	CA	94710
Baker	Betty	345 B St.	New York	NY	12345
Carlson	Marianne	P.O. Box 123	Houston	TX	54321
Carrera	Fred	3211 Fox St.	L.A.	CA	92991
Davis	Julie	671 Alpine Way	Newark	NJ	87654

CHARGES TABLE

Last Name	Date	Amount
Adams	6/1/88	123.45
Adams	6/8/88	92.00
Adams	7/8/88	456.78
Davis	6/2/88	99.99
Davis	8/1/88	544.00

Figure 1.3: Two related tables in a database

there may be many rows of charges in the Charges table. The two tables are *related* to one another based on their common Last Name column.

The advantage of the one-to-many design is that it allows you to find basic information quickly, such as the address of Mr. Adams, as well as find and total the charges that he has incurred during any period of time. By breaking the information into two separate tables, you avoid repeating the address, city, state, and ZIP code with every charge transaction that occurs and thereby avoid wasting a lot of disk space (as well as data entry time).

A one-to-many relationship among tables can be used in other settings too. For example, note the structure of the basic inventory database in Figure 1.4. It consists of three tables: Master Inventory, Sales, and Purchases.

MASTER INVENTORY TABLE

Item Number	Item Name	In Stock	Price	Reorder
10001	Apples	100	.45	50
10002	Bananas	150	.65	40
10003	Cherries	50	.39	55

SALES TABLE

Item Number	Units Sold	Date
10001	5	6/1/88
10003	10	6/1/88
10001	5	6/1/88
10001	17	6/1/88

PURCHASES TABLE

Item Number	Units Bought	Date
10003	10	6/1/88
10002	20	6/1/88

Figure 1.4: A sample structure for an inventory database

The Master Inventory table contains a single row for each item in the store (or warehouse). The Sales and Purchases tables record individual sales and purchase transactions. The tables are all related to one another through the Item Number column; that is, each table contains a column for recording the item number. These three tables can provide much business information. For example, through a procedure known as *updating*, R:BASE can instantly recalculate the Master Inventory table to determine the current quantity of any item in stock by using the data in the Sales and Purchases tables.

The sample inventory database structure is sometimes called a *master file-transaction file* relationship. The Master Inventory table keeps track of the status quo of each item in stock, while the two transaction tables, Sales and Purchases, maintain a history of every individual sale or purchase.

LEARNING THE ROPES

Before we get too carried away with database-design theory here, it's a good idea to learn all of the techniques for managing a single table first. Once you've learned to handle one table, you will easily expand your skills to design and manage databases with multiple tables. Beginning with Chapter 2, you'll learn how to create and manage an R:BASE database with a single table. In the process, you'll develop a powerful mailing-list management system.

Chapter 2

Creating Your First Table

IN THIS CHAPTER, YOU'LL LEARN HOW TO CREATE an R:BASE database. If you have R:BASE readily available, you may want to try these examples as you read. If you haven't already done so, you'll need to install R:BASE on your computer first. If you are using a single-user microcomputer, refer to Appendix A at the back of this book. If you intend to use R:BASE on a network, the network manager will need to refer to the *Installation Guide* that comes with the the the R:BASE 3.1 package for installation instructions.

STARTING R:BASE

The first step in using R:BASE is, of course, to start the computer. In most cases, R:BASE will have been installed on your hard disk, drive C. Therefore, to start R:BASE you need to switch to the directory that contains the file that you want to use (using the DOS CD command), then run R:BASE. Follow these steps to run R:BASE now:

If your R:BASE program is installed on a drive other than C, switch to that drive to start R:BASE. For example, if your R:BASE is installed on drive D, type **D:** and press ←⏎.

1. Type **C:** and press ←⏎ to switch to drive C.

2. Type **CD \RBFILES** and press ←⏎ to switch to the directory that R:BASE is stored on.

3. Type **RBASE** and press ←⏎ to run R:BASE.

If all you see is an error message such as "bad command or file name," then one of three things is wrong:

- You spelled RBASE incorrectly (try again).

- You can't access R:BASE because it is not installed on your computer, it is not on the drive you're using, or it requires different start-up instructions on your network. See Appendix A for help, or if you share a computer with co-workers, ask someone how to start R:BASE on your computer.

- The DOS path to the R:BASE directory has not been set. Refer to Appendix A for additional information about modifying your AUTOEXEC.BAT file to set the DOS path for you in the future.

Once R:BASE is running, you'll see the Main menu, which looks like Figure 2.1.

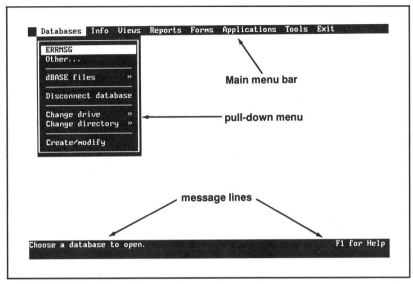

Figure 2.1: The R:BASE Main menu

EXPLORING THE R:BASE MENUS

R:BASE 3.1 is a *menu-driven* program, which means that you use it by selecting options from menus. Across the top of your screen you can see the *Main menu bar,* which displays eight options.

Under Databases, the currently highlighted option in the menu bar, is a *pull-down menu* with choices related to the Databases option. Try moving the highlighter across the top options by pressing the → and ← arrow keys. (If the arrow keys don't work, press the Num Lock key once, and then try again.) Another way to move the highlighter to an option is to hold down the Alt key and press the first letter of a bar option. For example, pressing Alt-F moves the highlighter to the Forms option.

Move the highlighter within a pull-down menu by pressing the ↑ and ↓ arrow keys. You can also type the first letter of an option in a pull-down menu to move the highlighter to that option. To actually select the highlighted option, press ↵ or F2. For example, if you wanted to select Other on the Databases pull-down menu, you would move the highlighter in the menu bar to Databases, then move the highlighter in the box below to Other, and press ↵ or F2.

If you select an option by accident and you want to "back out," you can cancel your selection by pressing the Esc, or Escape, key (aptly named because it lets you "escape" from an incorrect or unfamiliar menu selection).

MAKING MENU SELECTIONS WITH A MOUSE

If a mouse is attached to your computer, you can use it to make selections from the R:BASE menus. With the mouse properly set up, you should see a *mouse pointer* (a highlighted block) on the screen. You can move the pointer around by sliding the mouse across the top of your desk. To highlight an option, position the mouse pointer on it and click the left button.

There are two ways to select a menu option using a mouse, and which one you use depends on whether the mouse pointer is on the option you want to select.

- If the mouse pointer is already on the highlighted option you want to select, click the left mouse button.

- If the mouse pointer is not on the highlighted option, click the right mouse button to select the highlighted option.

In other words, you can select the currently highlighted menu option at any time simply by pressing the right mouse button. Optionally, you can move the mouse pointer to any option and double-click the left mouse button to highlight and immediately select an option. Table 2.1 lists both the keys and mouse buttons you use for navigating the menus. You'll have a chance to try out some of these navigation techniques in the next section.

INVESTIGATING THE MAIN MENU

The R:BASE Main menu lists the major activities you are likely to perform on your database. In summary, these options are:

- Databases lets you create a new database, select an existing database to open or close, modify an existing database, or use dBASE files. The Databases option is discussed later in this chapter.

Table 2.1: Techniques for Highlighting and Selecting Menu Options

KEY NAME	FUNCTION
→ *or* **Tab**	Moves the highlighter to the right on the menu bar. At the rightmost option, moves the highlighter around to the leftmost option.
← *or* **Shift-Tab**	Moves the highlighter to the left on the menu bar. At the leftmost option, moves the highlighter around to the rightmost option.
↓	Moves the highlighter down the pull-down menu. At the last option, moves the highlighter up to the first option.
↑	Moves the highlighter up the pull-down menu. At the first option, moves the highlighter down to the last option.
Home *or* **PgUp**	Moves the highlighter to the first option in the pull-down menu.
End *or* **PgDn**	Moves the highlighter to the last option in the pull-down menu.
↵ *or* **F2**	Selects the currently highlighted menu option.

MOUSE CLICK	DESCRIPTION
Left	If the mouse pointer is on a menu bar or pull-down menu option that is not highlighted, moves the highlighter to that option.
	If the mouse pointer is on a highlighted pull-down menu option, selects that option.
Right	Selects the currently highlighted menu option.

- Info lets you look at or change the data you've stored in a table within an open database. It is discussed in Chapter 3.

- Views lets you look at or change selected data in one or more tables in an open database. This option is discussed in Chapter 10.

- Reports lets you create, use, or change custom reports for displaying your data on the screen or printer. The Reports option is discussed in Chapter 7.

- Forms lets you use, create, or modify custom data-entry forms for entering and changing data. For example, you might use the Forms option to make the screen look exactly like a paper form your company uses. This makes it easier to enter and view data. You can find out more about Forms in Chapter 8.

- Applications lets you use, create, or modify a custom application designed to perform a specific job, such as managing an inventory or a mailing list. This option is discussed in Chapter 15.

- Tools provides options for general file management tasks (often called "housekeeping"), such as backing up a database by making an extra copy, exchanging information with other programs, and temporarily accessing DOS. You'll learn about Tools later in this chapter.

- Exit allows you to exit R:BASE and return to DOS, or leave the R:BASE Main menu and enter R:BASE programming commands at the R> prompt. You will learn how to use both R:BASE menus and R:BASE programming commands later in this book. Exit, meanwhile, is discussed later in this chapter.

As you scroll across the Main menu bar with the ← and → keys, the message line near the lower-left corner of the screen changes to tell you what kinds of options the current pull-down menu offers (see Figure 2.1). As you move the highlighter up and down a pull-down menu with the ↑ and ↓ keys, the message line near the lower-right corner of the screen changes to tell you about the highlighted option.

Now look at the pull-down menus. Notice that some options end with an ellipsis (. . .), some end with a double arrow (»), and some end with nothing at all. The ellipsis and double arrow tell you what will happen when you select the option.

. . .   You will be asked to type in information

»   You will be taken to a *submenu*

If you select an option ending with an ellipsis or a double arrow but you want to return to the pull-down menu, "unselect" the option by pressing Esc.

When you select an option with no ending you will be taken to a different screen with its own menu bar. But you can select Exit to return to the Main menu again.

GETTING ONLINE HELP WITH R:BASE COMMANDS AND FUNCTIONS

Another useful R:BASE feature is the built-in help system. Notice the "F1 for help" message at the lower-right corner of the screen. Press the Help key (F1) at any time and R:BASE will display a *help screen;* a list of explanatory information about the task you are trying to perform.

Some help screens are several pages, or screens, in length. You can read through the screens, taking note of the information they offer, by pressing any key (a prompt at the bottom of the screen reminds you of this). When you see the message "Press any key to continue," it means no more help for the current topic is available. Press any key and you will be taken back to the R:BASE Main menu.

The help screens are *context-sensitive.* This means the help they provide always pertains to whatever you are doing at the moment. For example, if you move the highlighter to the Databases option on the Main menu bar and press the Help key (F1), you'll see a brief description of each menu on the Databases pull-down menu. As you read through other help screens (by pressing any key), you'll see general help screens that summarize techniques for using the help system and navigating the R:BASE menus. Then, you'll be returned to the Main menu.

Keep in mind that help screens are available for all menus, not just the Main menu. So whenever you have a question, simply press the Help key (F1) to see if the help screens can provide an answer. If at any time you want to leave the help screens rather than progressing through a series of screens, just press the Esc key.

CREATING YOUR FIRST DATABASE

It's time to put R:BASE to work and create your first database. As described in Chapter 1, a database is a collection of information, stored in tables, which includes various objects that simplify the process of entering, changing, and viewing your data.

It's a common practice to store each database in its own subdirectory on the hard disk. A *subdirectory*, also called simply a directory, is a place on your hard disk where files are stored. Storing each database on a subdirectory keeps the databases separate and makes it easier to copy them to floppy disks or other computers. To copy a database, you simply issue a command to copy the entire directory. This way you don't have to list the names of all its files when you copy it. So the general procedure is to create a subdirectory and then create the new database in the subdirectory. Exact instructions for creating your first database will appear shortly, but for now, look at the general instructions below. They'll give you a sense of how to create a database in R:BASE.

1. Move the highlighter to **T**ools on the menu bar to access the Tools pull-down menu.

2. Select **D**isk management in the pull-down menu.

3. Select **M**ake directory on the submenu that appears.

4. Enter a valid subdirectory for the new database.

5. Move the highlighter to **D**atabases on the menu bar.

6. Select **C**hange directory from the pull-down menu.

7. Select the name of the directory you just created if it is listed in the submenu that appears. If the new directory is not listed, select **O**ther and enter the directory name.

Only directories in your current directory are listed.

8. With **D**atabases highlighted on the menu bar, move the highlighter to **C**reate/modify and press ←.

9. With **C**reate highlighted on the menu bar of the next menu, and with **N**ew database highlighted on the pull-down menu, press ←.

10. Enter a valid DOS file name for the database.

At this point you'll be taken to a screen where you can create or change individual tables within the database. But before getting onto that topic, let's backtrack and actually create a database named Mail. We'll store it on a subdirectory named RBFILES\LEARN.

CREATING A SUBDIRECTORY

The first thing we need to do is create the subdirectory to store the new database on. Subdirectories are actually a feature of your DOS operating system. Refer to your DOS manual for more information about subdirectories if necessary. But in a nutshell, a subdirectory name can be up to eight characters in length, and it cannot include spaces or punctuation.

To create a subdirectory name such as RBFILES\LEARN, you must have already created the parent directory—RBFILES in this example.

You place a subdirectory "beneath" an existing directory by preceding the subdirectory name with the parent, or higher level, directory name, and a backslash (\). Typically, you define the entire *path* by preceding the directory and subdirectory name with the disk drive name and a backslash. For example, the path

C:\RBFILES\LEARN

refers to the subdirectory named LEARN beneath the directory RBFILES on hard disk drive C. Note that in a pathname you always use backslashes (\) rather than slashes (/), and you never use blank spaces.

Assuming that the R:BASE Main menu is on your screen and you're ready for action, you can follow the steps below to create your RBFILES\LEARN subdirectory.

1. Highlight **T**ools on the Main menu.

2. Select **D**isk management.

You can use some keyboard shortcuts. Press **Alt-T** to highlight Tools, press **D** and ⏎ to select Disk management, and press **M** ⏎ to select Make directory. Or, if you're using a mouse, move the mouse pointer to Tools and click the left button, move the mouse pointer to Disk management and double-click the left button, and move the mouse pointer to Make directory and doulbe-click on the left button.

3. Select **M**ake directory.

4. Type **C:\RBFILES\LEARN** (substitute the appropriate drive name if R:BASE is not stored on drive C) and press ⏎.

If all went well, you'll briefly see the "Working..." message, then be returned to the Main menu. If you hear a beep instead and see a message such as "Unable to create directory," then perhaps you made one of the following errors:

- You typed C:\RBFILES\LEARN incorrectly. (Maybe you typed C:/RBFILES/LEARN or C: \RBFILES\LEARN.) In this case, press any key and start again at step 1.

- You specified the wrong drive and RBFILES does not exist on the drive you specified. For example, suppose R:BASE was stored on disk drive D on a directory named RBFILES. The correct entry would be D:\RBFILES\LEARN rather than C:\RBFILES\LEARN.

- You, or somebody else, already created a subdirectory named \RBFILES\LEARN. In this case all you have to do is make \RBFILES\LEARN the current directory. Proceed with the next section to find out how to do this.

CHANGING TO ANOTHER DIRECTORY

Assuming that you've now created the \RBFILES\LEARN directory, your next step is to make that directory the current directory. Follow these steps to do so:

1. Press **Alt-D** or use the arrow keys or mouse to move the highlighter to the Databases option. The Databases pull-down menu appears on your screen.

2. Select **C**hange directory.

3. Select **LEARN** to switch to your new subdirectory. If LEARN is not in your list, select **O**ther and enter the directory name **C:\RBFILES\LEARN**, and press ⏎.

Usually LEARN is last in the list. You can press the End key to move to the end of a submenu.

If all went well, you should be returned to the Main menu without hearing any beeps or seeing any error messages. To verify that you are now on the RBFILES\LEARN directory, follow these steps:

1. With **D**atabases highlighted on the menu bar, select Change directory from the pull-down menu. You should see LEARN, the name of the current directory, in bright white letters in the middle of the submenu that appears.

2. Press Esc to leave this submenu.

You've created a subdirectory for the new database, and you've made it the current directory. Now you can create your database. With the Databases pull-down menu displayed on your screen,

1. Select **C**reate/modify from the Databases pull-down menu.

2. From the **C**reate pull-down menu, select **N**ew database, as in Figure 2.2.

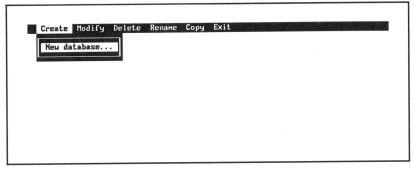

Figure 2.2: The Create pull-down menu

The name you assign to a database can be no longer than seven characters. It can't include any blank spaces or punctuation marks other than the underscore (_) character.

3. You will now see the prompt:

   Enter new database name (1-7 characters)

   Type **MAIL** as the name of the database.

4. Press ⏎.

5. Return to the Main menu by highlighting and selecting **E**xit from the next two menus that appear.

You should be able to see the name of your database, MAIL, inside the Databases pull-down menu, as shown in Figure 2.3.

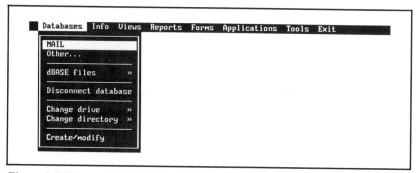

Figure 2.3: The name of the new database, MAIL, on the Databases menu

EXITING R:BASE

Now you have an empty database in which to store tables and other information. But before we add a table to this database, let's discuss how to save your work. It's very important to remember to exit R:BASE (and return to the DOS prompt) before turning off your computer. Otherwise, some of your work might get lost. Exiting R:BASE is a simple task, and you can try it right now.

1. Highlight **E**xit on the Main menu.

2. Select **L**eave R:BASE.

All your work will be saved to disk, and you'll be returned to the DOS prompt. This is really the only safe time to turn off your computer without running the risk of losing some work. When you are ready to use R:BASE again, just type **RBASE** at the DOS prompt and press ◄─┘.

OPENING A DATABASE
YOU'VE ALREADY CREATED

To open an existing R:BASE database, you must first switch to its directory. Let's assume that you exited R:BASE in the preceding section and you are now at the DOS command prompt. Follow these steps to run R:BASE and open the MAIL database that you created on the \RBFILES\LEARN directory:

1. At the DOS prompt, type **RBASE** and press ← to run R:BASE.

2. Select **C**hange directory from the Databases pull-down menu.

3. Select **LEARN** to switch to your new subdirectory. If LEARN is not in your list, then select **O**ther and enter the directory name **C:\RBFILES\LEARN** and press ←.

4. With **D**atabases still highlighted on the menu bar, select **M**AIL, the database you want to use.

Once you've successfully opened a database, you'll see its name in the lower-left corner of the screen. For example, you should now see the name Database: C:..MAIL in the lower-left corner of your screen. To leave room for messages to the right of the database name, the screen shows only two periods (..) rather than the subdirectory name.

CREATING YOUR FIRST TABLE

Data within a database are stored in tables. To create a table within a database, you follow the general steps below. Detailed instructions for creating your first table will appear in a moment, but for now you can get acquainted with how to create tables by studying these instructions. After you've opened the database to which you want to add a table,

1. Highlight **I**nfo on the Main menu.

2. Select **C**reate/modify.

3. Select **C**reate from the **T**ables pull-down menu.

4. Name the table and define the number of columns.

5. Press F2 to save your completed table definition.

    a. Optionally, define rules and access rights for the table.

6. Select **E**xit to return to the Main menu.

Let's go ahead and create a table that stores peoples' names and addresses. This table could be a general mailing list, a customer list, or a list of sales prospects. We'll call this table "Names."

You already opened the MAIL database in the preceding section, so now you can proceed straight to the Info pull-down menu to create your table.

1. Highlight **Info** on the Main menu.

2. Select **C**reate/modify.

A new screen appears with a set of menu options for creating and managing tables, as shown in Figure 2.4. Notice the message line in the lower-left corner of the screen. It tells you that the highlighted Tables pull-down menu can be used to define, change, remove, rename, or copy a table. Meanwhile, the message line in the lower-right corner points out that Create, the currently highlighted option, lets you define a new table.

3. Select **C**reate to create a new table. You'll be taken to a screen for defining your table, as shown in Figure 2.5.

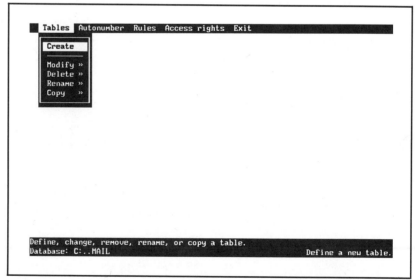

Figure 2.4: The Tables pull-down menu for creating and managing tables

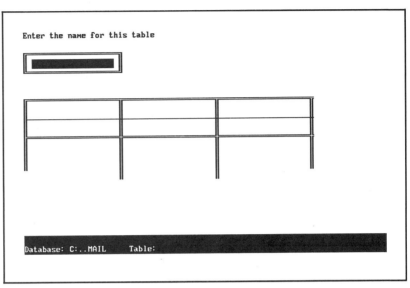

Enter the name for this table

Database: C:..MAIL   Table:

Figure 2.5: Screen for defining a database table

Table names are discussed in more detail in the next section, "Naming Tables and Columns."

4. Your next step is to enter a name for the table. For the current example, type **Names** (using the backspace key to correct errors if necessary), then press ←.

5. Next, you'll be prompted to type in a description of your table. Simply type a plain description that will remind you of the contents of the table when you use it in the future. For this example, type **Names for mailing list database** and press ←.

Now your screen shows the name and description of the table, as in Figure 2.6. The highlighter should be positioned to start entering column descriptions in the table. Notice the message line at the bottom of your screen. It lists the name of the table and the column position of the highlighter.

NAMING TABLES AND COLUMNS

Before we proceed with the creation of this table, let's take a moment to summarize the general rules about table and column names.

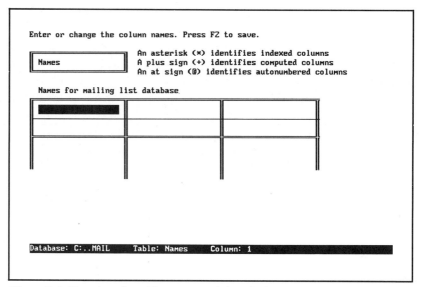

Figure 2.6: Entering the table name and description

- Each table in a database must have a unique name. In other words, no two tables within one database can have the same name.

- Each column within a table must also have a unique name.

- Table names and column names must begin with a letter.

- The names can contain letters and numbers, as well as number signs (#), dollar signs ($), underscore characters (_), and percentage signs (%).

- Names cannot contain blank spaces. To separate words in column or table names, use the underscore character (_).

- Names can be eighteen characters in length, but R:BASE only recognizes the first eight characters. Consequently, the first eight characters must be unique in each name.

The last rule may seem a little confusing. R:BASE lets you assign names eighteen characters in length so that you can have long, descriptive table and column names. For filing purposes, however, R:BASE recognizes only the first eight letters of a name. And because R:BASE only "pays attention" to the first eight letters, you could not have one column named CORPORATE_TAX and another column named CORPORATE_SHARES, for example, in the same table—the first eight letters of both these column names are identical. R:BASE would think you were repeating a column name, which is against the rules since all column names must be unique.

Let's suppose you tried to enter the second column name COR-PORATE_SHARES after defining the column name, CORPO-RATE_TAX. R:BASE would beep and display the "Column name is a duplicate" message. You would then need to change the name of one of the columns. You could change the names to CORP_TAX and CORP_SHARES. These two are not identical names, because their first eight characters are not the same.

DEFINING COLUMNS FOR YOUR TABLE

Don't confuse the underscore character (_) with a hyphen (-). On most keyboards, you type the underscore character by holding down the Shift key and pressing the underscore key.

We'll divide the data to be stored in the Names table into the following columns: L_Name, F_Name, Company, Address, City, State, Zip_Code, and Ent_Date. As you'll see in a moment, you can also assign a description to each column. You also need to define the *type* of data and the maximum *length* of the data to be stored in each column. The types of data used in R:BASE tables are listed in Table 2.2.

Table 2.2: R:BASE Data Types

DATA TYPE	USED TO STORE
TEXT	Any textual information that has no numeric value, such as names and addresses. Maximum length of a TEXT column is 1500 characters.
CURRENCY	Dollar amounts, such as the price of an item or an hourly wage.
INTEGER	Whole numbers that do not have any decimal places. Sometimes used for identification numbers, such as account numbers or part numbers.

Table 2.2: R:BASE Data Types (continued)

DATA TYPE	USED TO STORE
REAL	Numbers that may contain decimal places and have no more than six digits. Used to store numeric quantities such as -123.45 or 6543.2123.
DOUBLE	Very large numbers, outside the range $\pm 9 \times 10^{\pm 37}$. (Generally used only in scientific and engineering applications.)
DATE	Dates, usually displayed in MM/DD/YY format.
TIME	Time, usually displayed in HH:MM:SS format (for example, 12:31:46), in either a 24-hour clock or an AM/PM 12-hour clock.
NOTE	Non-numeric textual information. Maximum length of a NOTE column is 4092 characters.
NUMERIC	Numbers with a lot of digits, where a maximum number of digits as well as where to put the decimal point is specified. Good for storing numbers with a small number of digits that are not used in many calculations.
COMPUTED	A column that receives its value from the computation of other columns. For example, if a table contains two columns named Qty and UntPrice, a COMPUTED column named Total could contain the results of multiplying Qty times UntPrice.

All of the columns in our first table except for Ent_Date will be TEXT data. Ent_Date will be DATE data. Table 2.3 shows the exact structure that we'll use for the Names table.

Notice that we've assigned the Zip_Code column the TEXT data type. This may seem odd at first, since we often think of ZIP codes as numbers; however, they have some characteristics that make them unlike actual numbers. For example, some ZIP codes contain hyphens, such as 94131-2802. Some foreign ZIP codes contain letters and spaces, such as M3H 3A8. Because these examples are not true numbers, R:BASE would not know how to handle these data values if they were entered into a numeric column. In order to play it safe, we've defined the Zip_Code column as TEXT data.

Table 2.3: The Structure for the Names Table

COLUMN NAME	COLUMN DESCRIPTION	TYPE OF DATA	MAXIMUM LENGTH
L_Name	Last Name	TEXT	15
F_Name	First Name	TEXT	15
Company	Company Name	TEXT	20
Address		TEXT	25
City		TEXT	15
State		TEXT	5
Zip_Code	ZIP Code	TEXT	10
Ent_Date	Entry Date	DATE	

Follow the steps below to define the columns for the current table.

1. Type **L_Name** and press ⏎.

2. As the description, type **Last Name** and press ⏎.

3. The menu of data types appears on the screen, as in Figure 2.7. You can use the same menu-selection techniques you've been using till now to select options from this menu. In this case, press ⏎ to select TEXT.

4. A prompt appears asking you to enter a maximum length for this column. Type **15** and press ⏎.

5. The "Do you want this column to be an indexed column?" prompt appears. Indexed columns are used to speed processing in some operations, but are of no concern to us now. Just press ⏎ to select No.

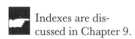 The small ↓ at the lower-right corner of the menu of data types indicates that there are more options below that you can scroll to by using the ↓ key.

Indexes are discussed in Chapter 9.

At this point, the contents of the first column are defined, and the highlighting moves to the second column, as shown in Figure 2.8.

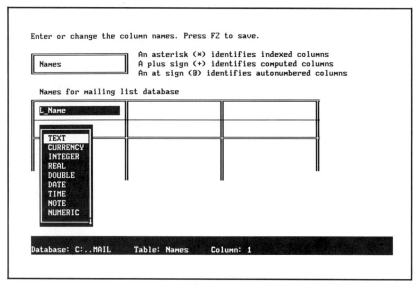

Figure 2.7: Menu of data types

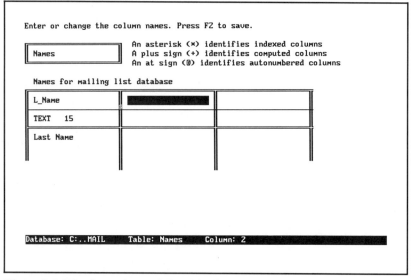

Figure 2.8: The first column defined in the Names table

You can now define the structure of the second column, or you can use the arrow keys to back up and make corrections to the first column. Let's go ahead and define the rest of the columns in this table, using Table 2.3 as a guide. You'll notice in Table 2.3 that there is no column description for Address, City, and State. This is because the column names themselves describe the contents of the columns very well. When you are asked for descriptions of these three columns, simply press ◄┘. The exact steps to follow are summarized below.

1. Type **F_Name** and press ◄┘; type **First Name** and press ◄┘; press ◄┘ to select **TEXT**; enter **15** as the length and press ◄┘; press ◄┘ again to select No to indexing the column.

2. Type **Company** and press ◄┘; type **Company Name** and press ◄┘; press ◄┘ to select **TEXT**; type **20** as the length and press ◄┘; press ◄┘ again to select No to indexing the column.

3. Type **Address** and press ◄┘; press ◄┘ to leave the column description blank; press ◄┘ to select **TEXT**; type **25** and press ◄┘; press ◄┘ again to select No to indexing.

4. Type **City** and press ◄┘; press ◄┘ to leave the column description blank; press ◄┘ to select **TEXT**; type **15** as the width and press ◄┘; press ◄┘ to select No to indexing.

5. Type **State** as the next column name and press ◄┘; press ◄┘ to leave the description blank; press ◄┘ to select **TEXT**; type **5** as the width and press ◄┘; press ◄┘ to select No to indexing.

6. Type **Zip_Code** as the next column name and press ◄┘; type **ZIP Code** as the description and press ◄┘; press ◄┘ to select **TEXT**; type **10** as the length and press ◄┘; press ◄┘ again to select No to indexing.

7. Type **Ent_Date** as the next column name and press ◄┘; type **Entry Date** as the description and press ◄┘; press ↓ until the **DATE** data type is highlighted in the menu and press ◄┘; press ◄┘ to select No to indexing.

Column names will start to scroll off the left edge of the screen as you add more columns. Don't worry, your columns are still there!

You may have noticed while defining the last column, Ent_Date, that you did not need to specify a length. That's because R:BASE uses a predefined length for dates.

At this point, you have defined all of the columns for the Names table, and your screen should look like Figure 2.9. Notice that only the Zip_Code and Ent_Date columns are displayed on the screen and that the columns L_Name, F_Name, Company, Address, City, and State have scrolled off to the left. But you can scroll left and right with the Shift-Tab and Tab keys to view any column you wish.

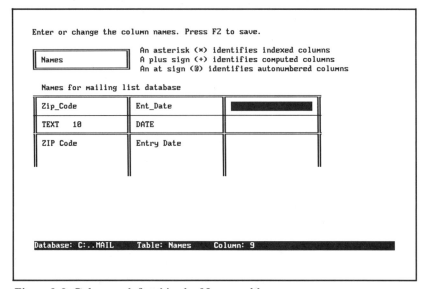

Figure 2.9: Columns defined in the Names table

MAKING CHANGES AND CORRECTIONS TO TABLES

It is easy to make changes and corrections after you've entered column names. The keys that you use to help with table modifications are explained in Table 2.4.

For example, if you accidentally left out the State column name and needed to back up and fill it in, you would use the Tab and Shift-Tab keys to move to the Zip Code column, then press F10 to insert a new column to the left of the Zip Code column. Then you would fill in a new column name and structure as usual.

Table 2.4: Keys Used to Modify Table Structure

KEY NAME	EFFECT
Home	Moves highlighting to the first column
End	Moves highlighting to the last column
←	Moves the cursor to the left through the highlighted area, character by character, then to the prior column if one exists
→	Moves the cursor to the right through the highlighted area, character by character, then to the next column if one exists
Tab	Moves highlighting one column to the right
Shift-Tab	Moves highlighting one column to the left
↵	Defines the structure of the highlighted column
F1	Gets help
Shift-F1	Gets function key descriptions
F9	Deletes the highlighted column
F10	Inserts a new column to the left of the high-lighted position

GETTING HELP WITH FUNCTION KEYS

See the section "Getting Online Help with R:BASE Commands and Functions" earlier in this chapter for more information about the Help function.

Earlier in the chapter you learned a bit about R:BASES's context-sensitive help, which you can access at any time by pressing F1. For example, if you press Help (F1) now, while a column name is highlighted, you'll get help with column names, as shown in Figure 2.10. Press any key to leave the help screen and return to your table.

You can also get help on the role played by the function keys. For example, suppose you needed to insert a column in your table but you could not remember which key lets you insert a column. In this case, you could press Shift-F1, which displays the role of currently active function keys, as shown in Figure 2.11. Notice that the left column (Unshifted) describes what happens when you press the function key by itself. The center column (Shifted) describes what happens when you hold down the Shift key while pressing a function key.

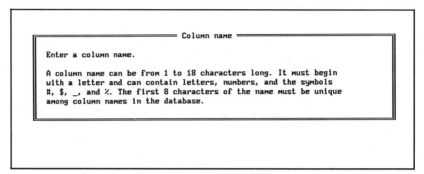

Figure 2.10: A help screen for column names

```
                         Currently Active Function Keys
              Unshifted                 Shifted                 Control

    F1        Help                      Function keys           Script/Key menu
    F2        Do it                     Do it                   End script recording
    F3        Database information      N/A                     N/A
    F4        N/A                       N/A                     N/A
    F5        Reset field               Discard all changes     N/A
    F6        N/A                       N/A                     N/A
    F7        N/A                       N/A                     N/A
    F8        N/A                       N/A                     N/A
    F9        Delete column             N/A                     N/A
    F10       Insert column             N/A                     N/A
```

Figure 2.11: Uses of the function keys when entering a column

The right column (Control) describes what happens when you hold down the Ctrl key while you press the function key. Where an N/A appears, it means the corresponding function key is *not active* and has no function at the current screen.

As examples, you can see that pressing F10 lets you insert a column and pressing F9 lets you delete one (after you leave this help screen, of course). If you can't remember what key to press in a given situation, you might be able to get a quick answer simply by pressing Shift-F1 rather than referring to a book or manual. Press Esc after viewing the Help screen to return to the task at hand.

SAVING THE TABLE STRUCTURE

Once you've defined your table structure and made any necessary corrections, press F2 to save your work—as the top of the screen reminds you. You'll be taken back to the previous menu, where you can add more tables to the current database, make changes to existing tables, or use the Exit option and return to the Main menu. For now, you can exit back to the Main menu by pressing Alt-E or by highlighting the Exit option with your mouse or arrow keys, and then selecting Exit.

You can also high-light the Exit option on a menu bar by pressing Esc.

CHANGING COLUMN SIZE, WIDTH, OR NAMES IN A TABLE

The column names, data types, column widths, and so forth that you define while creating a table are not cast in granite. You can add, change, delete, rename, or resize columns at any time, no matter whether you've added data to the table. You can also add new tables, delete tables, change the name of a table, and so forth. In other words, you are free to add, change, and delete whatever and whenever you want. Making these kinds of changes is called modifying the table structure.

The general steps for modifying the structure of your table are listed below. You'll have a chance to try them out in a hands-on example later on.

Chapters 9 and 10 will provide more in-depth coverage of techniques for modifying and managing table structures.

1. On the R:BASE Main menu, make sure that the database that contains the table you want to modify is open. If it is open, the database name will appear near the lower-left corner of the screen. If you need to open it, highlight **Data**bases on the menu bar and select the name of the database from the pull-down menu.

2. Highlight **I**nfo on the Main menu.

3. Select **C**reate/modify.

If you've selected an option and you want to back up and "unselect" it, press Esc.

At this point you should see the screen that lets you create and modify tables. Below is a summary of the options on this screen. Notice the prompts at the bottom of the screen. They also tell you about the current pull-down menu and the currently highlighted menu option. The options in the Tables pull-down menu are

Create	Creates a new table
Modify	Changes the column definitions or description of any table in the current database (press F2 when done)
Delete	Deletes a table permanently from the current database (use this option with caution, because it permanently erases the table, including all of its contents)
Rename	Changes the name of any table in the database
Copy	Makes a copy of any table in the database

The other options on this menu are

The Autonumber, Rules, and Access Rights options are explored in detail in Chapter 10.

Autonumber	Creates a column that is numbered automatically
Rules	Creates, modifies, deletes, or views current data-entry rules
Access Rights	Restricts access to sensititive data
Exit	Saves any changes, leaves the menu and returns you to the Main menu.

ESTABLISHING RULES

There's an old saying about computers: garbage in, garbage out. This means that if you type a bunch of incorrect or useless data into your database, you're going to get a bunch of incorrect and useless data back when you print it.

One way to minimize the likelihood of putting faulty data into a table is to define *rules* that determine whether or not the data being entered is acceptable. For example, in the case of the Names table, we could establish a rule that prevents the L_Name field or Address field from being left blank. Or, to use another example, you might use rules to make sure that only the current date, valid part numbers, and realistic quantities are entered in a database that stores data for printing invoices.

To give you some experience in how R:BASE handles rules while you are entering or changing data, we'll create a rule for the Names table. This rule will reject any entry in the Ent_Date field that includes a year earlier than 1990. This will help make sure that obviously mistyped dates such as 12/21/09 are rejected.

In order to add a rule to the Names table, you'll need to modify the table first. Don't worry if this topic seems a bit advanced at the moment—we will get deeper into rules later. From the R:BASE Main menu, with the MAIL database open,

Chapter 10 disscusses rules in detail.

1. Highlight **I**nfo on the Main menu.

2. Select **C**reate/modify.

3. Highlight **R**ules on the next menu.

4. Select **C**reate to create a new rule.

5. Select **C**ustom rule from the submenu.

6. Select **S**ucceeds. This tells R:BASE to accept the entry when the user enters a valid date.

7. Select **N**ames (the name of the table that you will be assigning the rule to in this example).

8. In the Where box, tell R:BASE to accept the Entry Date only if it is on or after January 1, 1990. Do this by carefully typing in the following rule:

   Ent_Date > = 01/01/90 OR Ent_Date IS NULL

9. Press ◄┘.

10. In the Message box, type **Entry Date cannot be before 1990**. Your screen should look like Figure 2.12.

11. Press ◄┘.

12. To save your changes and return to the Main menu, highlight and select **E**xit from the menu bar.

Now you've defined a rule for your Names tables, and saved that rule. You'll see the rule in action in the next chapter when you add

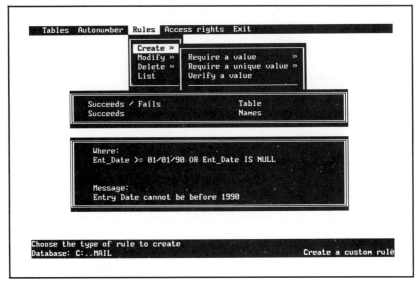

Figure 2.12: Establishing a custom entry-date rule

some new data to the table. For now, let's just briefly discuss the rule itself.

The first part of the rule, Ent_Date > = 01/01/90, specifies that the entry date must be on or after January 1, 1990. (In R:BASE, > = is the symbol for greater-than-or-equal-to.) The second part of this rule, OR Ent_Date IS NULL, specifies that a blank date is also acceptable. Therefore, the rule states that either no date or a date later than or the same as 1/1/90 is acceptable.

If you enter an invalid date into the Names table, R:BASE will reject the entry and display the message you specified, "Entry Date cannot be before 1990."

As mentioned earlier, the only way to ensure that all your work is saved is to exit R:BASE before you turn off your computer. Now that you've created and modified a table, you want to be sure to exit R:BASE before turning off your computer. To do so, select **L**eave R:BASE from the **E**xit pull-down menu. The DOS prompt will appear on the screen.

DATABASE LIMITATIONS

There are a few limitations to the size of an R:BASE database. A single database can have a maximum of eighty tables assigned to it. Each individual table may have a maximum of 80 columns. However, a database also can contain a maximum of 800 columns. Therefore, a database can contain a maximum of ten tables if each contains 80 columns, or twenty tables if each contains 40 columns. This is a very large maximum, and it is unlikely that you will run out of room in an R:BASE database.

NUMBERS stored in Currency columns can take on values in the range $\pm\$99,999,999,999,999.99$. INTEGER column numbers can have values in the range $\pm999,999,999$. REAL columns can accept numbers in the range $\pm1.0 \times 10^{\pm38}$, with six digits accuracy. DOUBLE columns can store numbers in the range $\pm1.0 \times 10^{\pm308}$, with fifteen digits accuracy. NUMERIC columns can store numbers with up to fifteen digits and the decimal point can be positioned within in those digits.

Alphanumeric data stored as text can be up to 1,500 characters long. If longer fields are needed, you can store data in Note fields of up to 4,092 characters.

The maximum number of rows in a table or database is limited only by the maximum file size allowed by your version of DOS, and by the amount of disk storage available on your system.

You have now created your first database, and it's ready to start storing information. Let's move on to the next chapter, where you'll start entering and editing data in the table.

Chapter 3

Entering
and Editing Data

NOW THAT YOU'VE CREATED A DATABASE WITH AN empty table in it, you can start storing information. In this chapter, we'll discuss techniques for opening an existing database, adding new data to it, and changing, or editing, existing data.

If you exited R:BASE in the last chapter (so that the DOS prompt is showing), start R:BASE again. You should see the R:BASE Main menu on the screen.

INTRODUCING COMMAND MODE

Before getting into the specifics of opening a database and adding data to it, let's discuss two alternative techniques for working interactively with a database:

- the R:BASE menus, which display menus of choices; and

- the Command mode, which displays only the symbol R> on the screen.

So far, we have been using the R:BASE menus. The menus are a very powerful and convenient way to use R:BASE, and we will continue to learn more about R:BASE menus. In this chapter, though, we will also begin to learn how to use the Command mode. Since R:BASE programs are just sets of commands, learning Command mode is a good first step toward learning to write programs.

To enter Command mode, follow these steps:

1. Highlight **Exit**.

2. Select **R>** prompt in the pulldown menu.

To go to Command mode, you can also press **Esc**, ↓, and ←. Or, with the mouse, move the pointer to **Exit**, click the left button, move the pointer to the **R>** prompt, and click the left button twice.

The screen will go completely blank except for an R> prompt in the top left-hand corner. The R> prompt tells you that you are in Command mode.

EXPLORING THE PROMPT BY EXAMPLE (PBE) MENUS

To make it easier to learn Command mode, we will start by using the Prompt By Example (PBE) menus, which guide you through the steps in building a command. You access the PBE Main menu by going into Command mode and entering the PROMPT command. To return to Command mode from the PBE Main menu, simply press Esc. To see how this works, follow these steps:

1. Type **PROMPT** next to the R> prompt, and press ◄┘.

2. The Prompt By Example Main menu appears on the screen, as shown in Figure 3.1.

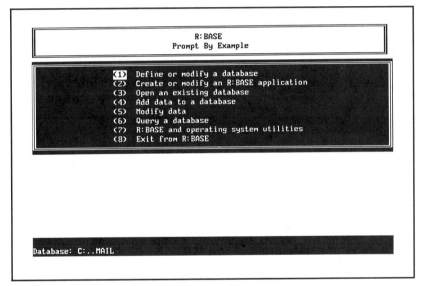

```
                              R:BASE
                         Prompt By Example

             ◄1►  Define or modify a database
             (2)  Create or modify an R:BASE application
             (3)  Open an existing database
             (4)  Add data to a database
             (5)  Modify data
             (6)  Query a database
             (7)  R:BASE and operating system utilities
             (8)  Exit from R:BASE




Database:  C:..MAIL
```

Figure 3.1: The Prompt By Example Main menu

3. Press **Esc** to return to Command mode. The R> prompt appears.

In Command mode, you are not far from the familiar R:BASE Main menu. Return to the Main menu now by typing **MENU** and pressing ◄┘.

OPENING A DATABASE

The first step in using any database is to open it (or connect to it) so that R:BASE has access to it. You can open a database in several different ways, but the easiest way is from the Main menu, like so:

1. Highlight **D**atabases.

2. Select the name of the database you want to open from the list presented in the top of the menu box. In our example, you select **MAIL**. You see the following information on the left side of the bottom status line:

   Database: C:..MAIL

OPENING A DATABASE FROM THE PROMPT BY EXAMPLE MENUS

Now let's use the Prompt By Example (PBE) menus to open the Mail database. Follow these steps to go to the PBE Main menu:

1. Enter Command mode by highlighting **E**xit and selecting R> prompt in the pull-down menu.

2. Type **PROMPT**, and press ⏎.

3. Select option 3, Open an existing database. From the keyboard, you do this either by pressing the ↓ key twice and pressing ⏎, or by pressing **3** on the top row of the keyboard and pressing ⏎. With the mouse, move the mouse pointer on top of option 3 and click the left button twice.

PBE displays a screen, as in Figure 3.2, to help you build an R:BASE command that opens, or connects to, a database. At the top of the screen, above the solid line, you see

   CONNECT _____

This is the CONNECT command, the R:BASE command for opening a database. At this point you are still building a CONNECT command. The underscores (_) that you see to the right of the word "CONNECT" tell you to fill in the next part of this command. Beneath the command you're building is a description of what the CONNECT command does. Take a moment to read this description. Underneath this description is a menu asking you to

   Choose a database; Press F2 if it isn't listed.

Notice the databases to choose from at the bottom of the screen. These are the databases in the current directory. MAIL is the only database name in Figure 3.2, but your screen may show more names.

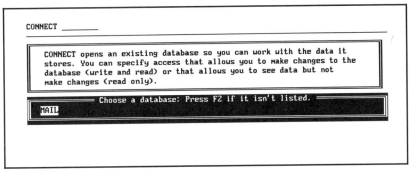

Figure 3.2: PBE instructions for opening, or connecting to, a database

If the database you want to open is on another disk or directory, press F2 and specify the disk and directory along with the database name.

4. Select **MAIL**. The screen displays the command

   CONNECT MAIL _____

   followed by another prompt that asks whether you want to open the database in Write or Read mode.

5. To find out the difference between Write and Read mode, press the Help key (**F1**). You'll see the help screen shown in Figure 3.3. As you can see, opening a database in Write mode lets you add data to the database as well as edit and view data, but Read mode only allows you to view the data.

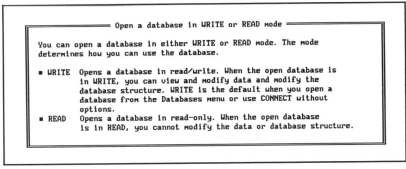

Figure 3.3: A PBE help screen explaining the difference between Write and Read mode

6. Press any key to remove the help screen.

7. Press ⏎ to select **Write**, the default mode.

A *default* command, setting, or mode is one that a computer program activates automatically unless you specify otherwise.

The next Prompt By Example menu displays the revised command, CONNECT MAIL WRITE, that your selection built. Your PBE menu options are now

Execute	Edit	Reset	Help	Exit

8. To execute this CONNECT command, select the **Execute** option. R:BASE displays the message

    ```
    CONNECT MAIL WRITE
    Database exists
    ```

    and instructs you at the bottom of the screen to press any key to continue. Now that you have connected to an existing database, you can continue.

9. Press any key to remove the message and return to the PBE Main menu.

OPENING A DATABASE FROM COMMAND MODE

Let's take a moment to try entering the command to open the Mail database without the aid of the prompts. To return to Command mode, press the **Esc** key. You'll see the R> prompt on your screen.

The command you executed to open the Mail database was CONNECT MAIL WRITE. To perform this same task in Command mode, type the command

    CONNECT MAIL WRITE

next to the R> prompt, and press ⏎. Again, R:BASE will display the "Database exists" message and redisplay the R> prompt so that you can enter more commands.

Help Mode and Syntax Diagrams

Take another moment to type **HELP CONNECT** (and press ⏎) at the R> prompt. What you see on the screen is an example of R:BASE's Command mode help screens, as shown in Figure 3.4.

You might think of HELP as a condensed version of Prompt By Example. Help screens give you basic information about an R:BASE command and display that command's *syntax* diagram. In grammar, "syntax" refers to the proper arrangement of words in a sentence. In the world of computers, however, "syntax" refers to the proper arrangement of terms in a command.

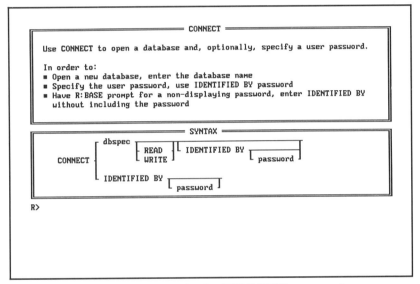

Figure 3.4: R:BASE help screen for the CONNECT command

The CONNECT command, along with many R:BASE commands, is an SQL (Structured Query Language) command. Because it is part of the SQL standard, you might someday be able to transfer applications and databases between R:BASE and other systems that also support SQL.

R:BASE syntax diagrams read from left to right. R:BASE words are shown in uppercase. In the case of the CONNECT command, the words CONNECT, WRITE, READ, and IDENTIFIED BY are R:BASE terms. *Arguments*—or parts of a command that you must supply because they are specific to your database—are shown in lowercase. For example, *dbspec* is a sample argument which stands for the database name. Since *dbspec* is lowercase, you should supply your own argument (the name of your database) in its place. Mandatory parts of a command are displayed along a continuous horizontal axis, while optional parts of a command are shown as spurs off the main left-to-right axis.

With this knowledge, you can deduce that WRITE and READ are optional parts of the CONNECT command. In fact, the help screen for the Write or Read mode (see Figure 3.3) choice tells you that WRITE is the default. That is, if you type CONNECT MAIL, you are in effect typing CONNECT MAIL WRITE.

To illustrate how defaults work, remember what happened when you opened a database from the R:BASE Main menu. You weren't asked whether you wanted Read mode or Write mode. R:BASE assumes that you want to open the database in Write mode—the default—when you open the database from the R:BASE Main menu.

Let's return to the R:BASE Main menu. To do so, type in the **MENU** command and press ←⎯. The familiar R:BASE Main menu will appear on the screen.

CLOSING A DATABASE

R:BASE lets you work with only one database at a time. When you are finished using one database and you want to begin using another one, R:BASE first *closes* (or disconnects from) the first database, updating the disk with any changes you made, before opening the second database. Usually this is automatic—when you have an opened database and you leave R:BASE or open a new database, R:BASE simply closes the database you were working on and returns you to the DOS prompt or opens the new database. However, suppose you wanted to close a database without opening another one, or you were finished using a database but wanted to leave R:BASE running on your computer for someone else to use.

CLOSING A DATABASE FROM THE R:BASE MAIN MENU

You can close a database from the R:BASE Main menu with the Disconnect database option in the Databases pull-down menu. Let's try closing the MAIL database now.

1. Highlight **D**atabases.

2. Select **D**isconnect database.

Notice that the MAIL database no longer appears in the lower-left corner of the screen, since it is no longer the currently open database.

So that you can practice closing the database from Command mode in the next section, open the database again by highlighting **D**atabases and selecting **MAIL**. The lower-left corner of the screen will once again show that the MAIL database is open.

CLOSING A DATABASE FROM COMMAND MODE

From Command mode, you can use the DISCONNECT command to close a database. You can try this out as follows:

1. Highlight **E**xit and select **R>** prompt to go into Command mode.

2. Type **DISCONNECT** and press ↵. R:BASE will display another R> prompt and wait for another command.

3. Type **MENU** and press ↵ to return to the Main menu. The bottom-left corner of the screen does not display the name of the MAIL database, since the MAIL database is no longer open.

4. Highlight **D**atabases and select **MAIL** to open the MAIL database again, preparing for the examples in the next section.

ENTERING DATA IN YOUR TABLES

Now that you've opened the database, you can enter data into it using a variety of techniques. We'll begin with the simplest technique, which is available on the Main menu.

1. Highlight **I**nfo on the R:BASE Main menu.

The message line on the left side of the bottom of the screen tells you that the Info option lets you "Choose a table to look at or edit data." In computer terminology, the term "edit" means to add, delete, or change data. Notice also that the "Names" table is highlighted in the menu box.

2. Since you want to add data to the Names table, select the
    Names table.

R:BASE now displays the prompt

No data exists. Do you want to add an empty row?   Yes   No

This prompt tells you that there is no data in the Names table and
asks if you want to add an empty row.

If you don't have at
least one row in the
table, R:BASE will not
let you edit the table.

3. Select **Yes.**

Now you should see the Edit screen for the Names table, shown in
Figure 3.5. Table 3.1 lists the keys that you can use to help edit this
table. At the bottom of the Edit screen is a status line with some helpful reminders.

- On the left side is the name of the database you have
  opened (MAIL) and the table you are editing (Names).

- On the right side is the word "Edit," which indicates that
  you are in *Edit mode.* In Edit mode, you can make changes
  to the data in the table.

- To the left of the word "Edit" is the message "F4 to Browse."
  This is a reminder that you press the F4 key to go into
  Browse mode. In Browse mode, you can look at the data but
  not make any changes.

Table 3.1: Keys Used with the EDIT Command

KEY NAME	FUNCTION
↑	Moves highlighting up one row
↓	Moves highlighting down one row
Tab	Moves highlighting one column to the right
Shift-Tab	Moves highlighting one column to the left
→	Moves the cursor one character to the right
←	Moves the cursor one character to the left

Table 3.1: Keys Used with the EDIT Command (continued)

KEY NAME	FUNCTION
Ctrl-→	Moves the highlighter to the righthand set of columns when some columns are locked in position
Ctrl-←	Moves the highlighter to the lefthand set of columns when some columns are locked in position
PgUp	Shows the previous screenful of data
PgDn	Shows the next screenful of data
Home	If the cursor is not at the beginning of a field, moves the cursor to the beginning of the field; if the cursor is at the beginning of a field, moves highlighting to the first entry of the first record
End	If the cursor is not at the end of a field, moves the cursor to the end of the field; if the cursor is at the end of a field, moves highlighting to the last entry of the last record
Del	Deletes the character over the cursor
Ins	Toggles between Insert mode (the cursor is a block) and Overtype mode (the cursor is an underline)
F4	Toggles between Browse mode (you can only look at data) and Edit mode (you can change data)
F5	Restores the original contents of the current field
Shift-F5	Deletes the value in a field
F9	Deletes the currently highlighted row

Notice in the table that each column in an empty row contains a zero enclosed by hyphens (–0–). R:BASE uses this group of characters to represent an empty, or null, field which has never had a value put in it. When you want to put your own data in the table, you can

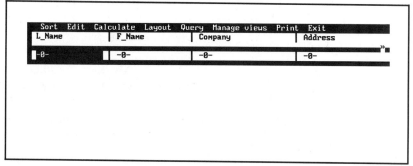

Figure 3.5: Edit screen for the empty Names table

just type over the null characters in each field with your data. To add another row, you press the F10 key. This creates another row with null characters in every column. Since you will add a total of seven rows to our example table, press **F10** six times.

Now let's enter some data. We will store the following information in the first row:

L_Name	Baker
F_Name	Robin
Company	Peach Computers
Address	2311 Coast Hwy.
City	San Diego
State	CA
Zip_Code	92122
Ent_Date	6/15/90

Follow these steps to add this data:

Use the backspace key to correct any errors you make when entering data.

1. Type in **Baker** under L_Name and then press **Tab** to move to the F_Name column.

2. Type in the first name, **Robin**, in the F_Name column, and press **Tab**.

Continue entering data until you've typed in all the information for the first row. Since the state abbreviation is only two characters long, you will have to press the Del key to delete the last hyphen (-) of the null indicator (-0-). When you've finish entering the Ent_Date column and pressing Tab, the highlighter will jump down to the first column in the next row and your screen will look like Figure 3.6.

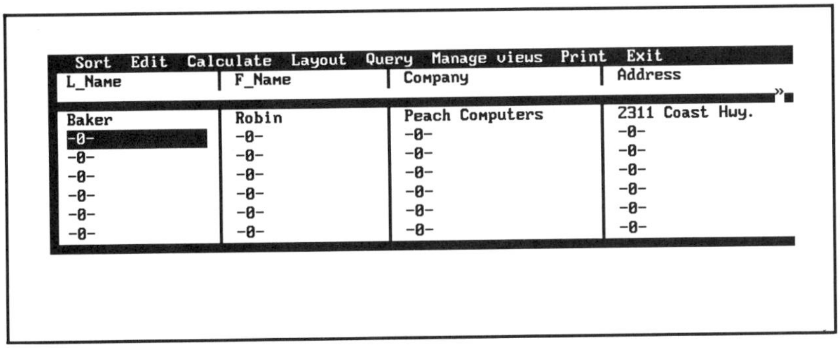

```
  Sort  Edit  Calculate  Layout  Query  Manage views  Print  Exit
  L_Name            F_Name           Company            Address
                                                                      ">■
  Baker             Robin            Peach Computers    2311 Coast Hwy.
  -0-               -0-              -0-                -0-
  -0-               -0-              -0-                -0-
  -0-               -0-              -0-                -0-
  -0-               -0-              -0-                -0-
  -0-               -0-              -0-                -0-
  -0-               -0-              -0-                -0-
```

Figure 3.6: The first row typed in on the screen

If you're following along online, enter the rows below into the table (don't worry about typing errors—you will have an opportunity to fix those later).

Smith, Sandy, Hi Tech Inc., 456 N. Rainbow Dr., Berkeley, CA, 94711, 6/01/90

Jones, Mindy, ABC Co., 123 A St., San Diego, CA, 92122, 6/01/90

Jacobs, Fred, Softex Inc., 410 Hill St., La Jolla, CA, 92345, 6/15/90

Miller, Marie, Zeerox Inc., 234 C St., Los Angeles, CA, 91234, 6/15/90

Adams, Bart, DataSpec Inc., P.O. Box 2890, Malibu, CA, 96543, 6/15/90

Miller, Anne, Golden Gate Inc., 2313 Sixth St., Berkeley, CA, 94711, 6/01/90

When you have finished typing in the data, leave the Edit screen and return to the R:BASE Main menu by highlighting and selecting **Exit** on the menu (press **Esc** and press ◄──┘).

CHECKING IF DATA WAS ENTERED CORRECTLY

You can use the LIST command to verify that R:BASE really did add your data. To use the LIST command, you have to enter Command mode, as follows:

1. Highlight **Exit**.

2. Select **R>** prompt. You should see the R > prompt.

3. Type **LIST** and press ◄──┘.

R:BASE responds by displaying the tables in the Mail database, as shown in Figure 3.7. Notice that there are three tables:

- the Names table you set up in Chapter 2 (on the right side);
- the SYSINFO table; and
- the SYSRULES table.

The Names table, R:BASE says, has eight columns (L_Name, F_Name, Company, Address, City, State, Zip_Code, and Ent_Date) and seven rows. The rows are your data—the seven names and addresses you just entered.

```
R>LIST

  Tables in the Database MAIL

  Name           Columns   Rows    Name          Columns   Rows

  SYSINFO           7        6      Names            8        7
  SYSRULES          4        1
R>
```

Figure 3.7: Finding out about the tables in your database

What about the SYSINFO and SYSRULES tables, though? These are special tables that R:BASE creates and maintains to store information about the database you are creating. The SYSINFO table stores the information you entered about each column when you created the Names table. The SYSRULES table keeps track of any rules you've established.

Try a variation of the LIST command by typing **LIST Names** and pressing ◄┘. Where the LIST command alone gave you an overview of your entire database, LIST followed by a table name gives you the structure of one table only, as shown in Figure 3.8.

```
        Table: Names
        Read Password: No
        Modify Password: No

        Names for mailing list database

        Column definitions
        # Name             Type       Index Expression
        1 L_Name           TEXT    15
                   Last Name
        2 F_Name           TEXT    15
                   First Name
        3 Company          TEXT    20
                   Company Name
        4 Address          TEXT    25
        5 City             TEXT    15
        6 State            TEXT     5
        7 Zip_Code         TEXT    10
                   ZIP Code
        8 Ent_Date         DATE
                   Entry Date

        Current number of rows:      7

    R>
```

Figure 3.8: Getting specific information about the Names table

Your screen contains a good deal of information about the Names table. Beginning from the top, it tells you

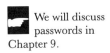 We will discuss passwords in Chapter 9.

- that you haven't established Modify or Read passwords for it;

- the names, data types, lengths, and so on of the columns;

- which columns have a description and need two lines on the screen (with the description displayed on the second line);

- that none of the columns in the Names table has been defined as an index column;

- that no computed fields have been established (notice the lack of data under the headings Index and Expression); and

- that the Names table has seven rows in it.

If you're curious about other variations of the LIST command, type HELP LIST. Otherwise, let's return to the R:BASE Main menu by typing **MENU** at the R> prompt.

EDITING YOUR TABLES

There are many reasons why you might need to edit the Names table. If you misspelled a name, entered the right data in the wrong column, or discovered that some of the people listed in the Names table moved and changed their addresses, you would need to edit the table. There are many commands and techniques for editing a table. We'll start by using the Main menu and then discuss how to edit from the PBE menus and Command mode.

Before you can begin editing a table, the database containing the table needs to be open. In the case of our example, you can verify that the Mail database is already open by seeing if the message on the left side of the status line at the bottom of the screen says "Database: C:..MAIL."

EDITING FROM THE R:BASE MAIN MENU

The fastest way to begin editing a table is to start from the R:BASE Main menu in much the same way that you add data. Follow these steps:

1. Highlight Info on the Main menu.

2. Select Names.

Now you should be looking at the Edit screen for the Names table. The status lines at the bottom of the screen tell you that you are in Browse mode (notice the word "Browse" in the bottom-right corner) and that you can press F4 to edit.

3. Press **F4** now to go into Edit mode, since we want to make changes to this table.

Table 3.1, found earlier in this chapter, lists keys you can use to change data in the Edit screen.

Notice that now the status lines indicate that you are in Edit mode and that you can press F4 to go back into Browse mode. You might also notice that the rows are now in the opposite order in which you entered them. Don't worry about the order of the rows for now. In Chapter 4 you will learn how to use sorting to change the order of the rows in the table in a variety of ways.

Now, let's start with a few simple editing exercises. First, we'll change the ZIP code for Bart Adams from 96543 to 96523.

Although you can use your mouse to move the highlighter on the Edit screen, the keyboard is more convenient for these examples.

1. Press ↓ to move down to the row with Bart Adams in the L_Name column.

2. Press the **Tab** key six times to move the highlighting to the Zip_Code column, as shown in Figure 3.9.

Sort	Edit	Calculate	Layout	Query	Manage views	Print	Exit

	Address	City	State	Zip_Code
te Inc.	2313 Sixth St.	Berkeley	CA	94711
Inc.	P.O. Box 2890	Malibu	CA	96543
c.	234 C St.	Los Angeles	CA	91234
c.	410 Hill Str.	La Jolla	CA	92345
	123 A St.	San Diego	CA	92122
nc.	456 N. Rainbow Dr.	Berkeley	CA	94711
puters	2311 Coast Hwy.	San Diego	CA	92122

Figure 3.9: The Zip_Code column for Bart Adams highlighted

3. Press → three times to move the cursor three spaces to the right. The cursor will appear below the 4 in the 96543 ZIP code.

4. Type the number **2** (using the numbers at the top of the keyboard) to change the 4 to a 2, so the ZIP code reads 96523

Now let's change the Company for Anne Miller from Golden Gate Inc. to Golden Gate Co.

1. Press **Home** twice to move the highlighter back to the top-left corner of the table to see which row Anne Miller is in. Since Anne Miller is in the first row, the highlighter is in the correct row.

2. Press **Tab** twice to move to the Company column. The Company column will be highlighted, as shown in Figure 3.10.

```
    Sort  Edit  Calculate  Layout  Query  Manage views  Print  Exit
    L_Name           F_Name        Company            Address
                                                                    ",

    Miller           Anne          Golden Gate Inc.   2313 Sixth St.
    Adams            Bart          Dataspec Inc.      P.O. Box 2890
    Miller           Marie         Zeerox Inc.        234 C St.
    Jacobs           Fred          Softex Inc.        410 Hill Str.
    Jones            Mindy         ABC Co.            123 A St.
    Smith            Sandy         Hi Tech Inc.       456 N. Rainbow Dr.
    Baker            Robin         Peach Computers    2311 Coast Hwy.
```

Figure 3.10: The Company column for Anne Miller highlighted

3. Press the → key repeatedly, or just hold it down, until the cursor is under the letter I in the word Inc.

4. Type in the letters **Co.**, which gives us

   Golden Gate Co̱.

5. Now we need to delete the extra period. Press the **backspace** key to do so. Now the item reads

   Golden Gate Co̱.

Editing data in this fashion is easy, once you get used to the keystrokes that control the highlighting and the cursor. If there are other errors in your table, try correcting them now. Refer to Table 3.1 earlier in this chapter for a list of the keys to use for editing.

EDIT SCREEN FUNCTIONS FOR MANIPULATING YOUR TABLE

Notice the menu at the top of your screen. This is the Edit screen menu and it offers various ways to manipulate your tables. We will return to the Edit screen menu later on, but for now, here is a brief summary of the choices on this menu.

Sort	Sorts the data to make it easier to make changes to the table. You will learn more about sorting in Chapter 4.
Edit	Provides alternative ways to perform the actions of the function keys, including switching between Edit mode and Browse mode, adding rows, deleting rows, and deleting values. Also deletes all the rows in a table and allows you to change all the values in one column to a single new value.
Calculate	Performs calculations on the columns of your table, such as finding the maximum, minimum, and average values in a column, tallying the number of times each value occurs in a column, displaying cross-tabulations and other groupings. You will learn more about the Calculate command in Chapter 6.
Layout	Changes the layout of the rows and columns on the screen. Allows you to move or hide columns, change column size, lock columns or rows at the edge of the screen, and hide duplicate rows. You will have a chance to try some of these functions later in this chapter.
Query	Reduces the number of rows that are displayed by letting you search for rows that match certain conditions. You will learn more about queries and searching in Chapter 5.
Manage views	Modifies, deletes, renames, or copies views. You will be using views in Chapter 14.

Print   Prints the table on a printer or sends the
             information to a text file on a disk. You will
             be learning about printing and creating text
             files in Chapter 6.

Exit   Saves the changes on your disk and returns
             you to the PBE menu.

To use the Edit menu, press the **Alt** key and you will see that Sort is
highlighted and a box of selections has appeared underneath the
menu bar, as in Figure 3.11.

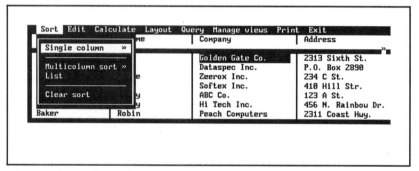

Figure 3.11: Highlighting the Sort option on the Edit screen menu

In computer termi-
nology, a toggle key
is a key you press to
switch back and forth
between functions.

This is a pull-down menu just like the R:BASE Main menu. You
can use the ← and → keys to move the highlighter in the menu bar,
the ↑ and ↓ keys to move the highlighter inside the menu box beneath,
and the ← key to activate the selection. In this instance, the Alt key
is a *toggle key*. Use it to switch back and forth between the menu and
the table. To see how a toggle key works, try pressing the Alt key to go
back to the table, and press it again to go to the menu.

A couple of shortcuts you used with other R:BASE menus also
work with this menu. To jump directly to a selection on the menu bar,
hold down the Alt key and press the first letter of the selection you
want. To jump to the Exit function, press the Esc key.

Moving Around the Edit Screen with Your Mouse

If you have a mouse on your computer and you were able to use it
to make menu selections, then you can also use the mouse on the Edit

screen. Moving the highlighter and making selections on the pull-down menu at the top of the screen requires the same actions as on the R:BASE Main menu. Anytime you want to activate a menu function, move the mouse cursor up to the one you want and press the left mouse button. The menu function you wanted will be highlighted and a menu box of selections will appear below it. To activate the currently selected choice, either press the left mouse button while the mouse cursor is on top of the selection, or press the right mouse button.

You can also use the mouse to move around in the table. To move the highlight to a new field in a table, move the mouse cursor to the field and then press the left mouse button. To move to fields which are not displayed on the screen, place the mouse pointer on the line under the column headings, either on the double arrow head at the left («) or the one on the right side (») of the screen and press the left mouse button. This makes the highlighter tab over one column in the direction of the arrow heads.

A *field* is where a column and row intersect in a table. Each field can hold one piece of data.

CHANGING THE TABLE LAYOUT

Sometimes rearranging the table makes it easier to find the data you want to change on the screen. This is especially true if you have a large table. For example, suppose you want to see two columns on the screen at the same time, but they are far apart in the table. You can rearrange the order of the columns. Or it might be handy to make a long description column shorter so that you can see other columns on the screen at the same time. The Layout function on the Edit screen menu lets you accomplish these and other changes to the layout of the rows and columns.

Moving Columns in a Table

To see an example of how this works, let's move the Ent_Date column between the F_Name and the Company column. If the highlight is on a menu item in the Edit screen menu, press Alt to return to the table.

1. Move the highlighter to any row in the Company column, pressing **Tab** or **Shift-Tab** (or using the mouse) if necessary.

If you make the wrong choice in any menu, you can back up and return to the previous menu by pressing Esc. Then, make the selection you want and continue with your choices.

2. Highlight **Layout** in the menu by pressing **Alt-L** (or using the mouse).

3. Select **Move** column in the pull-down menu. The next menu box that appears lets us choose which columns to move.

4. Select Ent_Date. Notice the check mark (✔) next to Ent_Date in the list.

5. Press **F2** (or the right mouse button) to indicate that you are finished choosing columns to move. At this point, your screen should look like Figure 3.12.

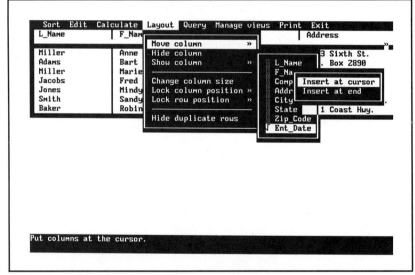

Figure 3.12: Moving the Ent_Date column to the left of the Company column

Now R:BASE is asking you if you want to move the chosen columns to where the cursor is or to the end of the table.

6. Select the **Insert at cursor** option by pressing ↵ or using the mouse. Since we started by making sure the highlighter was placed in the Company column, inserting the Ent_Date column at the cursor will place it exactly where we want it to be, to the left of the Company column. The Ent_Date column now moves ahead of the Company column, as in Figure 3.13.

```
 Sort  Edit  Calculate  Layout  Query  Manage  views  Print  Exit
 L_Name          │ F_Name       │ Ent_Date │ Company         │ Address
                                                                    ➤■
 Miller            Anne           06/01/90   Golden Gate Co.   2313 Six
 Adams             Bart           06/15/90   Dataspec Inc.     P.O. Box
 Miller            Marie          06/15/90   Zeerox Inc.       234 C St
 Jacobs            Fred           06/15/90   Softex Inc.       410 Hill
 Jones             Mindy          06/01/90   ABC Co.           123 A St
 Smith             Sandy          06/01/90   Hi Tech Inc.      456 N. R
 Baker             Robin          06/15/90   Peach Computers   2311 Coa
```

Figure 3.13: The Names table with the Ent_Date column moved

Keeping Columns in View on the Screen

Let's change the layout with another simple example. We can fix the position of the Last Name and First Name columns on the left side of the screen. This way, these columns stay on the screen as you scroll through the other columns in the table.

1. Use the mouse or press **Back-Tab** twice to move the high-lighter to the L_Name column.

2. Highlight Layout in the menu by using the mouse or by pressing **Alt-L**.

3. Select **L**ock column position in the pull-down menu.

4. R:BASE asks where you would like the columns to be locked. Select **L**eft margin since you want the columns locked at the left side of the screen. Now the entire L_Name column is highlighted and a prompt at the bottom of the screen says to

   Move the cursor to paint the area. Press Esc to cancel, Enter when done.

5. Press → to include the F_Name column in the highlighted, or painted, area.

6. Press ↵. The screen should look like Figure 3.14.

Moving the Highlighter across Column Separators

Notice that there is a thick line to the right of the F_Name column. This line separates the first columns from the rest of the columns. If you

```
 Sort  Edit  Calculate  Layout  Query  Manage views  Print  Exit
 L_Name          │ F_Name          │ Ent_Date │ Company          │ Address
─────────────────────────────────────────────────────────────────────────»▪
 Baker            Anne              06/01/90   Golden Gate Co.     2313 Six
 Adams            Bart              06/15/90   Dataspec Inc.       P.O. Box
 Miller           Marie             06/15/90   Zeerox Inc.         234 C St
 Jacobs           Fred              06/15/90   Softex Inc.         410 Hill
 Jones            Mindy             06/01/90   ABC Co.             123 A St
 Smith            Sandy             06/01/90   Hi Tech Inc.        456 N. R
 Baker            Robin             06/15/90   Peach Computers     2311 Coa
```

Figure 3.14: The Names table with the L_Name and F_Name columns fixed
at the left margin

press the Tab key a few times, you will see that the highlighter does not
go past the thick line no matter what. However, moving the highlighter
across the thick line is no problem if you are using a mouse. Simply
move the mouse cursor across the line to the new column and click the
left button. To move to the right of the thick line with the keyboard and
test the column-locking feature, follow these steps:

1. Press **Ctrl-→**. The highlighter is now in the Ent_Date
   column.

2. Press the **Tab** key twice and notice that the L_Name and
   F_Name columns stay on the left side of the screen. Meanwhile, the remaining columns scroll on the right side of the
   screen.

3. Press **Ctrl-←** to move the highlighter back to the left side of
   the thick line.

The Names table certainly looks different from when you started
using the Layout function. You might be wondering if the table still
has the same format on the disk. Changing the layout of the Edit
screen does not change the way the data is stored on the disk. In the
Names table, the columns are still stored in the same order on
the disk; only the appearance of the table on the Edit screen has
changed. In the next section, you'll find out how to make these
changes a permanent feature of the Edit screen by using a feature
called the Layout setting. Unless you have changed the Layout setting, the next time you look at the Names table in the Edit screen, the

screen will have the same layout as it did before you used the Layout function on the Edit menu.

Save the editing changes you just made by highlighting and selecting **Exit** (press **Esc** and press ◄┘). You are now back at the R:BASE Main menu.

MAKING LAYOUT CHANGES PERMANENT

The Settings menu is discussed in detail in Chapter 6.

You can use the Settings menu to tell R:BASE that you would like to keep the layout changes you made on the Edit screen. Let's test this feature with the following small example. Starting from the Main menu,

1. Highlight **Tools** and select **Settings** to display the Settings menu.

2. Highlight **Settings** and select **Layout**. The current value of the Layout setting (OFF) is displayed under Current. You can select ON or OFF under the words "Set to."

3. Select **ON**. This turns on the Layout saving feature.

4. Highlight and select **Exit** to return to the Main menu.

5. Highlight **Info** and select **Names** to display the Names table on the Edit screen.

6. To lock the L_Name column on the left side of the screen, highlight **Layout**, select **Lock column position**, select **Left margin**, and press ◄┘.

7. Highlight and select **Exit** to leave the Edit screen.

8. Highlight **Info** and select **Names** to display the Names table on the Edit screen again. Notice how the L_Name column is still locked at the left side of the screen.

9. Unlock the L_Name column by highlighting **Layout**, selecting **Lock column position**, and selecting **Clear**.

10. Highlight and select **Exit** to leave the Edit screen. Now let's return the Layout setting to the OFF default.

11. Highlight **Tools** and select **Settings** to display the Settings menu.

12. Highlight **Settings** and select **Layout**. The current value of the Layout setting is now ON.

13. Select **OFF**. This turns off the Layout saving feature.

14. Highlight and select **E**xit to return to the Main menu.

EDITING FROM THE PROMPT BY EXAMPLE MENUS

The PBE menus (and the programming commands that you build with them) provide a lot of flexibility in the way that you begin an editing session. We have seen how to modify the layout of the Edit screen by using the Layout function on the top menu bar. It is also possible to use an R:BASE command that specifies a particular layout to use when the Edit screen is displayed.

To go into the PBE Main menu, highlight **E**xit, select **R >** prompt in the menu box, type **PROMPT**, and press ◄——. Now you are ready to begin editing from the PBE Main menu.

You can use the mouse to make selections on PBE menus. However, when you have finished choosing several items from a list, you cannot click the right mouse button as you can on the R:BASE Main menu. You have to press F2.

1. Select option **5**, Modify data from the menu. This displays the instructions and options shown in Figure 3.15. For general editing, you'll want to choose the EDIT command.

```
Modify data
────────────────────────────────────────────────────────────
  ┌────────────────────────────────────────────────────────┐
  │ Several commands modify data values in a database.       │
  │ AUTONUM  Defines a column as an autonumbering column and, optionally, │
  │          numbers existing rows in a table.               │
  │ DELETE   Deletes rows from a table.                      │
  │ DROP     Removes a column, table, view, form, report, or index from │
  │          a database.                                     │
  │ EDIT     Allows changes using a table display or a form. │
  │ UPDATE   Changes values in a column. The new value can be a single │
  │          value or the result of an expression.           │
  └────────────────────────────────────────────────────────┘
  ╔══════════════════ Choose a command ══════════════════╗
  ║ AUTONUM   DELETE    DROP     EDIT     UPDATE          ║
  ╚═══════════════════════════════════════════════════════╝




  Database: C:..MAIL
```

Figure 3.15: Options for editing a database

2. Select **EDIT**. You are then given the option of tabular editing or editing with a custom form.

3. Select **T**abular Edit, since the Names table doesn't have any special data-entry forms set up for it yet. Now you are asked whether you want to see all rows, or only distinct rows.

4. Because we want to edit all rows, select **A**ll rows. Now you are asked to choose which table to edit.

5. Select the **N**ames table, since Names is the only table in the database. The next screen lets you select particular columns to edit.

6. Select the (All) option so that you have access to all the columns.

You are given the chance to limit the number of rows displayed on the screen by searching the database for rows which meet specific criteria. We'll discuss searching in Chapter 5, but for now, we'll ignore this option.

7. Press **F2**, since you want to have access to all of the rows.

8. The next screen gives you a chance to display the data in sorted order. Again, press **F2** to skip this option.

When you are done, the top of the screen displays the command line you've created, EDIT ALL FROM Names, along with your current options,

Execute	Edit	Reset	Help	Exit

The command line tells R:BASE to display all the columns in the Names table on the Edit screen so that you can make changes. When you select **E**xecute to execute the command, you'll see the data appear as in Figure 3.16. (As you would expect, you could achieve the same result by entering the EDIT ALL FROM Names command at the R > command prompt.)

```
  ┌─────────────────────────────────────────────────────────────────┐
  │ ┌─────────────────────────────────────────────────────────────┐ │
  │ │ Sort  Edit  Calculate  Layout  Query  Manage views  Print  Exit │
  │ │ L_Name          │ F_Name        │ Company           │ Address    │
  │ │                 │               │                   │         "■ │
  │ │ Miller          │ Anne          │ Golden Gate Co.   │ 2313 Sixth St. │
  │ │ Adams           │ Bart          │ Dataspec Inc.     │ P.O. Box 2890 │
  │ │ Miller          │ Marie         │ Zeerox Inc.       │ 234 C St. │
  │ │ Jacobs          │ Fred          │ Softex Inc.       │ 410 Hill Str. │
  │ │ Jones           │ Mindy         │ ABC Co.           │ 123 A St. │
  │ │ Smith           │ Sandy         │ Hi Tech Inc.      │ 456 N. Rainbow Dr. │
  │ │ Baker           │ Robin         │ Peach Computers   │ 2311 Coast Hwy. │
  │ └─────────────────────────────────────────────────────────────┘ │
  │                                                                   │
  │                                                                   │
  └─────────────────────────────────────────────────────────────────┘
```

Figure 3.16: Edit screen for the Names table, ready for changes

Notice that this screen is exactly the same screen that you saw
when you used the Info option on the R:BASE Main menu, except
that you are placed immediately in Edit mode. (Note the word
"Edit" in the bottom right-hand corner of the status line.) Also, the
layout of the rows and columns is back to the same layout that you
started with before you used the Layout option on the Edit screen
menu in the last exercise. Of course, this doesn't mean that the editing changes you made to the data are gone—Anne Miller's Company has changed to "Golden Gate Co." and the ZIP Code for Bart
Adams has changed to 96523.

DISPLAYING SELECTED COLUMNS USING THE PBE MENUS

Using the EDIT command, you can also choose to display just certain columns in the Edit screen. Suppose you wanted to check the
accuracy of the ZIP codes in the table. For this editing task, you
would need to see only the Address, City, State, and Zip_Code
columns. You would have no need to see the first or last name, the
company name, or the entry date. To display specific columns only,
in this case the Address, City, State, and Zip_Code columns, follow
these steps:

1. Select **Exit** in the Edit screen menu by pressing **Esc** and ◄──┘
   or by using the mouse. You are now back at the PBE Modify data menu.

2. Select **EDIT** on the PBE menus.

3. Select **Tabular Edit**.

4. Select **All** rows.

5. Select **Names**, as before. Now you are asked to

   Select columns to display—Press F2 when done

6. Begin by selecting **Address**.

If you choose the wrong column for display, correct your error by choosing the Reset option.

   Your choice, Address, is displayed under the menu box on the left side of the screen. Meanwhile, the Address choice is removed from the menu box. Notice also that a new choice, Reset, is added to the menu box. If you make a mistake and choose the wrong column, you can start over by choosing the Reset option.

7. Now select **City**, then **State**, and then **Zip_Code**. Notice that as each one is chosen it is moved from the menu box to the list underneath the box.

8. Press **F2**.

You cannot use the mouse for steps 8 and 9.

9. For the next two menus, press **F2** as before. Now the command at the top of the screen is

   EDIT Address City State Zip_Code FROM Names

   and the current options are

Execute	Edit	Reset	Help	Exit

You can see the difference between this command and the command for editing all rows that you executed in the last exercise. Here, instead of the word ALL following EDIT, there is a list of columns to include in the command.

10. Select **Execute** to execute the command you've constructed. You will see the Edit screen as shown in Figure 3.17. This screen is very easy to work with because all the columns fit on the screen.

DELETING ROWS FROM A TABLE

If you wanted to take someone off your mailing list, you would have to delete his or her row from the Names table. Once again, the

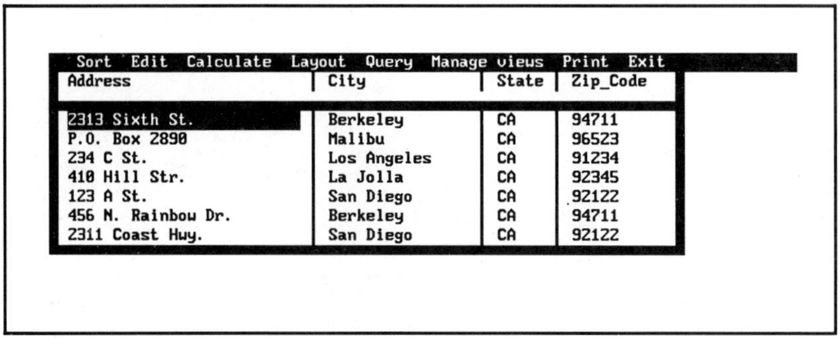

Figure 3.17: Selecting only the Address, City, State, and Zip_Code columns for display

simplest way to accomplish this is to use the Edit screen. For our example, let's delete the fourth row of the Names table, the one that contains information about Fred Jacobs. To leave the Edit screen you are in now, highlight and select **Exit** to return to the Modify data menu. Next, press **Esc** to return to the PBE Main menu, and press **Esc** again to return to Command mode. Now the R > prompt should be showing. Follow the steps below to go into the Edit screen for the Names table using Command mode.

1. Enter the command

   EDIT ALL FROM Names

   and press ◀━ to display the Edit screen with all rows and columns.

2. Move the highlighter down to the fourth row, which contains the data for Fred Jacobs.

3. Delete this row by highlighting **E**dit in the menu and selecting **D**elete row from the pull-down menu.

> You could also delete this row by pressing F9.

4. R:BASE now confirms that you really want to delete this row. Select **Y**es. The row you wanted to delete disappears.

TESTING YOUR DATA-ENTRY RULES

In Chapter 2 you set up a rule so that no dates could be entered in the Names table unless they were after the beginning of 1990. To test this rule, we will now try to break it.

You should still be in the Edit screen for the Names table. Move the highlight to the first row in the Ent_Date column. Type in **12/15/86** and press the tab key. Surprise! Here's what happens:

- R:BASE keeps the highlighter in the Ent_Date column.

- It beeps at you.

- It displays your error message.

- It makes sure that you don't save this incorrect data in the database.

If you press a key to remove the error message and then try pressing Alt or Esc or using the mouse, you will get the error message again. The only way to leave this field is to provide a value that meets the condition specified in the rule. If a column has an error, you can't move the highlighter to the Exit option on the top menu bar.

To correct the error, you could type in any valid value, such as 12/15/90, but let's restore the original value that was in this field. To do this, press **F5** to make the original value of 06/01/90 reappear in the field. To save the changes you made in the table, highlight and select **E**xit in the top menu bar to return to the R > Command mode prompt.

EXITING R:BASE

You have now added some rows to your database and you've edited, or changed, some items of information on an Edit screen you accessed by way of the Info option on the R:BASE Main menu and the Modify data option on the PBE menu. Whenever you make changes to your data, you must exit from R:BASE and return to the operating system prompt before you turn off or reboot your machine.

There are two procedures for exiting R:BASE:

- In Command mode, you can exit from R:BASE by typing the EXIT command and pressing ←⎯; or

- You can enter the MENU command and press ←⎯ to return to the R:BASE Main menu, from which you highlight Exit and select Leave R:BASE.

In this chapter, we've touched on the fundamentals of working interactively with a database, focusing on the techniques for entering and editing data in a table. In the next chapter, we'll look at how you can sort that data in a variety of different ways.

Chapter 4

Sorting Your Data for Easy Use

IN THIS CHAPTER WE'LL DISCUSS TECHNIQUES FOR displaying data in sorted order. *Sort* means to arrange data according to a criterion you choose. For example, you can sort the rows in a database alphabetically by name, in ZIP-code order for bulk mailing, in chronological order, or in numerical order. Your sorts can be in ascending order, such as A to Z in alphabetical sorts, smallest to largest in numerical sorts, or earliest to latest in date sorts. Optionally, sorts can be in descending order, for example, Z to A, largest to smallest, or latest to earliest. Furthermore, you can combine sort orders to achieve "sorts within sorts."

We'll begin working more with the R:BASE Command mode (indicated by the R > prompt) in this chapter. While the Prompt By Example mode is certainly adequate for building command lines in R:BASE, it's a good idea to practice entering commands at the R > prompt. You may eventually want to learn to program in the R:BASE programming language; and even if you don't, the Command mode is a bit faster than the Prompt mode.

If you've exited R:BASE since the last chapter, enter the command that starts R:BASE on your system.

SORTING FROM THE PROMPT BY EXAMPLE MENUS

We saw in the last chapter that the EDIT command allows you to select columns to sort the table on (although we skipped over the Sort option then). Actually, several different commands in R:BASE allow you to specify sort orders. In this chapter, we'll discuss sorting with the EDIT command and the SELECT command. The SELECT command only displays the data on the screen; it does not allow you to make changes. Nonetheless, the SELECT command is useful for getting a quick view of your database. SELECT is also one of the R:BASE commands that supports the SQL standard.

Suppose that you want to see a list of all the rows on your database, sorted into alphabetical order by last name. To start, bring up the PBE Main menu. Do this by highlighting **Exit**, selecting **R** > prompt, and pressing ◀┘ to go into Command mode. Next, enter the PROMPT command. Then choose option **6**, Query a database. You will be presented with the menu in Figure 4.1. In this example, we'll use the SELECT command to view data.

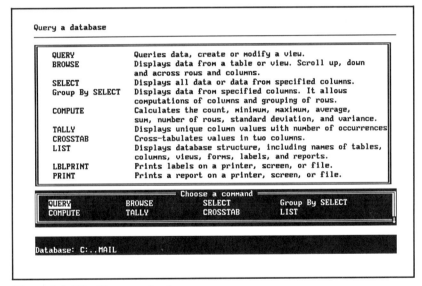 Remember that you can use the mouse to make selections on the PBE menus.

1. Choose the **S**ELECT option. R:BASE will ask for the name of the table to display. (If you haven't opened the Mail database yet, you'll be prompted to do so now.)

2. Select **N**ames. R:BASE asks if you want all rows or only distinct rows displayed.

3. Select **A**LL rows. R:BASE will ask you to choose the columns to display.

```
Query a database

    QUERY            Queries data, create or modify a view.
    BROWSE           Displays data from a table or view. Scroll up, down
                     and across rows and columns.
    SELECT           Displays all data or data from specified columns.
    Group By SELECT  Displays data from specified columns. It allows
                     computations of columns and grouping of rows.
    COMPUTE          Calculates the count, minimum, maximum, average,
                     sum, number of rows, standard deviation, and variance.
    TALLY            Displays unique column values with number of occurrences
    CROSSTAB         Cross-tabulates values in two columns.
    LIST             Displays database structure, including names of tables,
                     columns, views, forms, labels, and reports.
    LBLPRINT         Prints labels on a printer, screen, or file.
    PRINT            Prints a report on a printer, screen, or file.

══════════════════════ Choose a command ══════════════════════
 QUERY          BROWSE         SELECT          Group By SELECT
 COMPUTE        TALLY          CROSSTAB        LIST

Database: C:..MAIL
```

Figure 4.1: The Query a database menu

4. Select (ALL) columns. R:BASE then displays a screen for searching the database for rows which meet specific criteria (a topic we'll discuss in the next chapter).

5. Press **F2** to bypass this screen and make R:BASE display a screen for selecting columns to sort on, as shown in Figure 4.2. This screen tells you to "select columns to order rows" at the top. It is used for selecting columns to sort by.

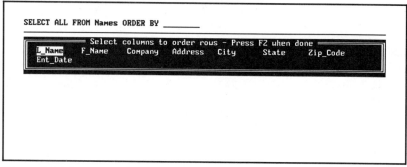

Figure 4.2: The screen for specifying columns to sort by

6. Select the **L**_Name column, since you want to display the data in alphabetical order by last name. R:BASE asks if you want the data sorted in Ascending order (A to Z) or Descending order (Z to A).

7. Select **A**scending. R:BASE then gives you the opportunity to select more sort columns.

8. Press **F2** to finish choosing sort columns.

Now you have built the following command, displayed at the top of your screen:

> Choose (Reset) to start over if you choose the wrong column for sorting.

SELECT ALL FROM Names ORDER BY L_Name

and you are presented with the following PBE options:

Execute   Edit   Reset   Help   Exit

The command tells R:BASE to display all the columns from the Names table, sorted on the L_Name column.

9. Select **E**xecute to execute the command. R:BASE displays as many columns as will fit on the screen, sorted by last name, as shown in Figure 4.3.

SPECIFYING TABLE COLUMNS FOR DISPLAY

The SELECT command displays only as many columns as will fit on the screen; therefore, you probably will not be able to see all your data. Just as you chose particular columns for the EDIT command in Chapter 3, you can specify which columns to display with a SELECT command. You can even specify the order (from left to right) that they will appear on the screen. Let's look at an example and sort the rows in descending order by date. Follow these steps:

1. Press any key to return to the Query a database menu.

2. Choose the **SELECT** command.

3. Select the **N**ames table.

4. Select **ALL** rows for display. R:BASE shows a menu for selecting columns to display, as in Figure 4.4.

5. To display the entry date in the leftmost column, select Ent_Date.

```
SELECT ALL FROM Names ORDER BY L_Name
  L_Name            F_Name            Company            Address
  ---------------   ---------------   ---------------    -------------------------
  Adams             Bart              DataSpec Inc.      P.O. Box 2898
  Baker             Robin             Peach Computers    2311 Coast Hwy.
  Jones             Mindy             ABC Co.            123 A St.
  Miller            Anne              Golden Gate Co.    2313 Sixth St.
  Miller            Marie             Zeerox Inc.        234 C St.
  Smith             Sandy             Hi Tech Inc.       456 N. Rainbow Dr.
```

Figure 4.3: The Names table sorted by last name

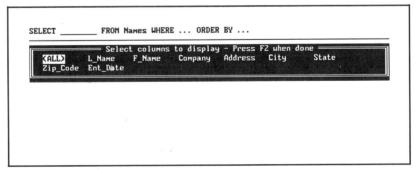

Figure 4.4: The menu for selecting columns to display

6. To display the L_Name column next, select **L_Name**.

7. To display the F_Name column, select **F_Name**.

The names of the columns you selected are removed from the box containing the menu and appear below the menu on the screen, as follows:

Ent_Date   L_Name   F_Name

8. Press **F2** to indicate that you're finished selecting columns to display.

9. The screen for entering search criteria appears. Press **F2** to bypass it.

10. The screen for choosing sort columns appears (see Figure 4.2). In this example, select **Ent_Date**, then select **Descending**, and then press **F2** to finish choosing sort columns.

Now the command line reads

SELECT Ent_Date L_Name F_Name FROM Names ORDER +
+ > BY Ent_Date DESC

Note the plus sign (+) at the end of the first and the beginning of the second line above. R:BASE uses the plus sign to indicate that a command continues on the next line. Although your screen has enough room to display the entire command on one line, this page doesn't. We've adopted R:BASE's conventions by using the plus and plus-and-greater than (+ >) symbols to show the continuation of a command on the starting and continuing lines, respectively.

The command that we've constructed tells R:BASE to display the Ent_Date, L_Name, and F_Name columns from the Names table, sorted by Ent_Date in descending (DESC) order.

11. Select **Execute**. The data appear on the screen accordingly, as in Figure 4.5.

12. Press any key when you are finished viewing the data.

```
SELECT Ent_Date L_Name F_Name FROM Names ORDER BY Ent_Date DESC
Ent_Date L_Name           F_Name
-------- ---------------- ----------------
06/15/90 Miller           Marie
06/15/90 Adams            Bart
06/15/90 Baker            Robin
06/01/90 Miller           Anne
06/01/90 Smith            Sandy
06/01/90 Jones            Mindy
```

Figure 4.5: Selected columns from the Names table sorted in descending date order

So far, you've sorted the Names table by a single column only. On a very large table, this type of single-column sort would probably not produce the result that you had in mind. For example, suppose you had a table with 1000 names in it, and you decided to sort them into alphabetical order by last name. There might be six Smiths, listed in totally random order by first name, as follows:

    Smith,   Norma

    Smith,   Alan D.

    Smith,   Jake

    Smith,   Rudolph

    Smith,   Sam

    Smith,   Anne

You probably would want the data sorted by last name, and within common last names, sorted by first name, as in the following list:

    Smith,   Alan D.

    Smith,   Anne

    Smith,   Jake

    Smith,   Norma

    Smith,   Rudolph

    Smith,   Sam

You can easily handle this kind of situation, which is called a *secondary sort,* by listing multiple column names in the ORDER BY clause. Where more than one column name is listed, the additional columns act as tie-breakers for the immediately preceding column.

PERFORMING SORTS WITHIN SORTS

To perform sorts within sorts, you merely need to select multiple sorting columns, in order from most important to least important. For example, suppose you want to display the Names database sorted by last name, and within common last names, you want the rows sorted by first name. In this case, you need to select L_Name as the first sort column and F_Name as the second sort column. Let's work through an example.

> If you make the wrong choice on a PBE menu, just press Esc to go back to the previous choice or menu. Then make the correct choice and continue.

1. From the PBE Query a database menu, choose **SELECT**, Names, **ALL**, (ALL), and then press **F2** as before.

2. From the Sort columns menu (see Figure 4.2), select **L**_Name and **A**scending order. This makes L_Name the primary sorting column.

3. Select **F**_Name and **A**scending order. Now F_Name is the secondary sorting column. The columns you selected for sorting are displayed below the menu, as follows:

   L_Name   F_Name

4. Press **F2** to finish selecting sort columns. The command you've built reads

   SELECT ALL FROM Names ORDER BY L_Name F_Name

This command tells R:BASE to display all the columns from the Names table, sorted by last name and then by first name within identical last names.

5. Choose **E**xecute from the menu on your screen, and R:BASE displays your data (see Figure 4.3). Notice that Anne Miller comes before Marie Miller.

The Names table is too small to demonstrate the full range of sorts within sorts. Suffice it to say that you can sort up to ten columns, which gives you tremendous flexibility in defining sort orders even in very large tables. (The only restriction on R:BASE sorts is that you can't sort on a column that has a NOTE data type.) We'll see more examples of sorts within sorts later in the chapter, but first we'll discuss a shortcut for displaying table data in sorted order.

SORTING WITH THE SELECT COMMAND

You've probably noticed that the commands that your menu selections have produced have all had a similar format, or syntax, in computer jargon. That syntax is

> SELECT column display list FROM table name ORDER +
> + > BY column sort list

where *column display list* is the name of the column or columns to display (or the ALL operator to display all columns); *table name* is the name of the table containing the columns, and *column sort list* is the name of the column (or columns) to sort by. You can enter commands directly from the R > prompt using this same syntax.

For example, suppose you want to see the Names table sorted into ZIP-code order, and furthermore, you want to see the Zip_Code, City, L_Name, and F_Name columns on the screen. To type in the appropriate command directly at the R > prompt,

1. Press any key to remove the display from the SELECT command.

2. Press **Esc** twice to leave PBE mode, so that the R > prompt appears on the screen.

3. Type in the command

> SELECT Zip_Code City L_Name F_Name FROM Names +
> + > ORDER BY Zip_Code

You may not have to enter the + sign in your command. If the command you type is too long, R:BASE puts a + at the end of the first line and a + > at the start of the next line automatically.

and press ↵. Remember, you can type the entire command on one line. However, if you choose to type it in on two lines, as we have, you don't have to type the + > on the second line. R:BASE does it for you. When you're done, the appropriate columns, in ZIP-code order, appear on the screen.

You may have noticed that in the commands created with the PBE menus and those you have been typing, some words are spelled in uppercase letters and other words are spelled with just the first letter in uppercase. The all-uppercase words are special R:BASE words that are always spelled exactly the same way, regardless of which database or table you are using. The words that have only the first letter in uppercase are names that you make up, like the names of your databases, tables, or columns. Having the special R:BASE words spelled in uppercase letters makes it easier to identify them in a command. However, you don't have to use any uppercase words when you are typing commands unless you want to. In the example above, you would get the same results if you typed the command:

```
select zip_code city l_name f_name from names order +
+ > by zip_code
```

Suppose you want to display all the columns in alphabetical order by company. To do so, you would type in the command

```
SELECT ALL FROM Names ORDER BY Company
```

and press ◄─┘. R:BASE would display the table in alphabetical order by company name.

When typing in long commands directly at the R > prompt, you continue a command from one line to the next by ending the first line with a plus sign (+). After pressing ◄─┘, you simply continue typing the command on the next line, which will begin with a + > prompt. However, you don't need to worry about explicitly typing the plus sign, since R:BASE will do this for you automatically if you just keep typing. Because a computer screen can accommodate more characters per line than a page of this book, you should be careful in entering sample commands. Your plus sign will often fall in a different place from the plus sign in this book.

In another example, the SELECT command below tells R:BASE to display the City, L_Name, and F_Name columns from the Names table, sorted by city, by last name within each city, and by first name within each last name (within each city):

```
SELECT City L_Name F_Name FROM Names ORDER BY +
+ > City L_Name F_Name
```

The data are displayed in alphabetical order across all three columns, as shown in Figure 4.6.

Now let's display the data in chronological order by entry date, with common dates sorted alphabetically by last and first name.

SELECT Ent_Date L_Name F_Name FROM Names ORDER +
+ > BY Ent_Date L_Name F_Name

This produces the listing shown in Figure 4.7.

```
R>SELECT City L_Name F_Name FROM Names ORDER BY City L_Name F_Name
City             L_Name           F_Name
---------------  ---------------  ---------------
Berkeley         Miller           Anne
Berkeley         Smith            Sandy
Los Angeles      Miller           Marie
Malibu           Adams            Bart
San Diego        Baker            Robin
San Diego        Jones            Mindy
R>
```

Figure 4.6: The Names table sorted by city and last and first name

```
R>SELECT Ent_Date L_Name F_Name FROM Names ORDER BY Ent_Date L_Name F_Name
Ent_Date L_Name           F_Name
-------- ---------------  ---------------
06/01/90 Jones            Mindy
06/01/90 Miller           Anne
06/01/90 Smith            Sandy
06/15/90 Adams            Bart
06/15/90 Baker            Robin
06/15/90 Miller           Marie
R>
```

Figure 4.7: Data listed chronologically and alphabetically

Any column can be sorted in descending order by placing the DESC option after the column name. For example, to sort the Names table in descending alphabetical order by last name, enter the command

SELECT ALL FROM Names ORDER BY L_Name DESC

You can mix and match ascending and descending sorts. For example, the command below displays data in descending chronological order and ascending alphabetical order:

SELECT Ent_Date L_Name FROM Names ORDER BY +
+ > Ent_Date DESC L_Name

This display is shown in Figure 4.8.

```
R>SELECT Ent_Date L_Name FROM Names ORDER BY Ent_Date DESC L_Name
  Ent_Date L_Name
  -------- ----------------
  06/15/90 Adams
  06/15/90 Baker
  06/15/90 Miller
  06/01/90 Jones
  06/01/90 Miller
  06/01/90 Smith
R>
```

Figure 4.8: The Names table sorted in descending date and ascending name order

Again, our sample table is too small to show the full power of R:BASE sorting. But suppose you had a table listing salespersons' last names, first names, sales amounts, and dates of sales. You could display the data in chronological order by date, and within common dates, alphabetical order by name, and within common names, descending order of sales amounts, using the command

SELECT ALL FROM Sales ORDER BY S_Date L_Name +
+ > F_Name Amount DESC

The result might look like this:

06/01/90	Adams	Andy	$999.99
06/01/90	Adams	Andy	$89.90
06/01/90	Adams	Andy	$1.23

06/01/90	Miller	Mike	$1000.00
06/01/90	Miller	Mike	$987.65
06/01/90	Miller	Nancy	$1234.56
06/01/90	Miller	Nancy	$899.00
06/02/90	Adams	Andy	$1200.00
06/02/90	Adams	Andy	$888.99

SORTING WITH THE EDIT COMMAND

Recall that in the last chapter when you selected the Modify data and EDIT commands from the PBE menus, R:BASE displayed a screen for selecting sort orders—the same screen, in fact, that the SELECT command displays. You can specify a sort order for the Edit screen in the same way that you specify a sort order for the SELECT command.

You can access the Edit screen directly from the R > prompt, using the EDIT command and the same syntax as the SELECT command. For example, to put the Names table into alphabetical order by last name on the Edit screen, you could enter the command

EDIT ALL FROM Names ORDER BY L_Name

The Edit screen would display all data in alphabetical order by last name.

Presorting the data in an Edit screen can make it easier to find specific items in a large table. You can specify columns with the EDIT command, along with a sort order. The command below presorts the Names table into descending chronological order and displays the L_Name, F_Name, and Ent_Date columns for editing, as shown in Figure 4.9:

EDIT Ent_Date L_Name F_Name FROM Names ORDER BY +
+ > Ent_Date DESC

Sort	Edit	Calculate	Layout	Query	Manage	views	Print	Exit

Ent_Date	L_Name	F_Name
06/15/90	Miller	Marie
06/15/90	Adams	Bart
06/15/90	Baker	Robin
06/01/90	Miller	Anne
06/01/90	Smith	Sandy
06/01/90	Jones	Mindy

Figure 4.9: The Edit screen sorted and limited to three columns

SORTING ON THE EDIT SCREEN

You can also sort the rows in the Edit screen by using the Sort command on the top menu bar. Like the Layout function, the Sort function only changes the appearance of the table on the Edit screen; the order of the rows in the table on the disk is not affected. However, unlike the Layout function, the results of the Sort function cannot be made permanent by changing the Layout setting to ON.

Let's see how the Sort menu function works. If necessary, return to Command mode (highlight and select Exit if you are in an Edit screen). Then type the command

> **EDIT ALL FROM Names**

and press ←⎯⎯. You now see the Edit screen for the Names table, with all columns included.

For our first example, let's say you are looking for someone who works at a particular company. To find this person, you want to sort the rows by the Company column. To tell R:BASE which column you would like to sort,

1. Move the highlighter to the Company column.

2. Highlight **S**ort on the menu. The pull-down menu under the Sort function allows you to choose between Single column and Multicolumn sorts.

3. Select **S**ingle column, since you want to sort on only one column.

The final piece of information R:BASE needs is whether to sort in ascending or descending order. With Ascending highlighted, your screen should look like Figure 4.10.

4. Select Ascending now, and the rows on your screen will be displayed sorted by the Company column, as in Figure 4.11.

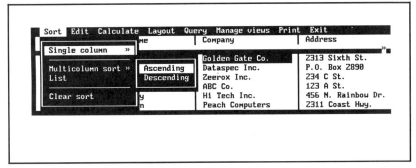

Figure 4.10: Sorting by the Company column, in ascending order

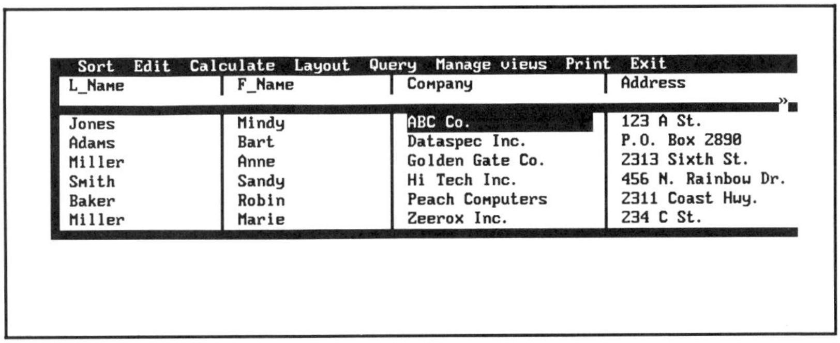

Figure 4.11: The Edit screen, sorted in Company order

Suppose that later in your editing you want to see the rows sorted first by last name and then by first name as a secondary sort (a sort within a sort). Because you can use the Sort menu function, you don't have to leave the Edit screen to accomplish this. Follow these steps:

1. Highlight Sort.

2. Select Multicolumn sort, because you want to sort on more than one column.

R:BASE asks you to choose which columns and which sort types (ascending or descending) you would like. If you look at this menu, you'll notice that the Company column is already chosen with ascending sort type even though you haven't made any choices yet. The reason for this is that R:BASE keeps track of the last sort you did to remind you of how the table is currently sorted.

3. Since you don't want to sort on the Company column this time, select **C**ompany. The check mark (✔) beside Company disappears.

4. Select **L_Name** as the new column to sort on. The submenu beside L_Name asks you to choose the sort type.

5. Select **A**scending. A *1* and an *A* appear to the left of L_Name in the menu. The *1* tells you that the sort on the L_Name column is the primary (first) sort. The *A* is to let you know that the sort will be ascending.

6. Select **F_**Name as the next sort column.

7. Select **A**scending. A *2* and an *A* appear to the left of F_Name. This indicates that the sort on the F_Name column is the secondary sort (used only to break ties in the first sort) and that the sort on this column will be ascending. You have finished choosing your columns and sort types, and your screen should look like Figure 4.12.

8. Press **F2** and your Edit screen will reappear with the rows sorted by last and then first name, as in Figure 4.13.

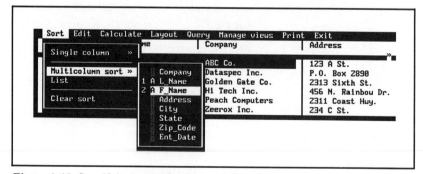

Figure 4.12: Specifying a sort by last and then first name

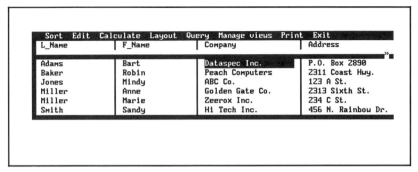

Figure 4.13: The Edit screen, sorted by last and then first name

9. Highlight and select **E**xit to finish with this Edit screen and return to the R > prompt.

Being able to sort the rows on the Edit screen is helpful. Still, sometimes specifying sorts directly in the EDIT command is useful—in spite of the fact that an EDIT (or SELECT) command can include five to ten ORDER BY columns and be awkward to handle. Before you attempt any exceptionally long commands, you should know how to handle them, as well as some common errors that might occur.

MODIFYING PROMPT MODE COMMANDS

When building command lines through the PBE menu selections, you probably will not make errors very often, because PBE "knows" the correct syntax for all the R:BASE commands. However, you may occasionally change your mind about menu selections you've made when you see the final command on your screen. For example, say you had constructed the following command:

SELECT ALL FROM Names ORDER BY L_Name F_Name

The following PBE options will be displayed below this command line:

Execute   Edit   Reset   Help   Exit

As you know, the Execute option sends commands to R:BASE to be processed immediately. The other options from the PBE menu are summarized here:

Edit   Moves the cursor up to the command line at the top of the screen, and allows you to make changes to the command. You can use the Ins key to toggle between Insert and Overtype mode and the Del key to delete a character. Pressing F2 returns to the PBE Execute/Edit/Reset/Help/Exit menu.

Reset   Returns you to the first menu selection you made for the command, and allows you to reselect menu items for the command.

Help   Displays helpful information and options for using the command.

Exit   Abandons the command line altogether and returns you to the PBE menu in which you chose the command.

More often than not, you'll be able to choose Execute to process the command line immediately. When entering your own command lines at the R> prompt, however, you will be more likely to make mistakes. (The advantage of entering commands at the R> prompt is that it is faster; the disadvantage is that doing so requires some familiarity with the syntax of the commands.) The most common errors when entering commands at the R> prompt are discussed in the next section.

CORRECTING MISTAKES MADE AT THE R> PROMPT

Unless you are a truly superb typist, you're likely to get error messages from time to time as you work with R:BASE, particularly with longer commands. No need to worry, you can't do any harm by typing in an invalid command. The worst that will happen is that the computer will beep and display a message. For example, typing in the command

SELECT ALL FROM Bananas

causes the computer to beep and R:BASE to display the following message:

–ERROR– Bananas is an undefined table

which means that there is no table named Bananas in the open database. Perhaps you've misspelled the table name, or you've forgotten to open the database containing the table. To review the table names, use the LIST TABLES command to display the names of all the tables in the open database.

Another common error is to enter a command such as

SELECT ALL FROM Names ORDER BY LastName F_Name

R:BASE displays the message

–ERROR– Column LastName not found

indicating that there is no LastName column in the table. The actual column name is L_Name.

Some errors are caused by incorrect syntax. For example, if you type in the command

LIST THE TABLES

R:BASE would display the message

–ERROR– Syntax is incorrect for the command

and, as a helping hand, would display the syntax diagram, shown in Figure 4.14.

VIEWS are discussed in Chapter 14. CURSORS are discussed in Chapter 16.

The syntax chart in Figure 4.14 shows that the LIST command can stand alone or be followed by ALL, COLUMNS, CURSORS, DATABASES, FORMS, LABELS, REPORTS, RULES, TABLES or VIEWS. Furthermore, LIST TABLES can either stand

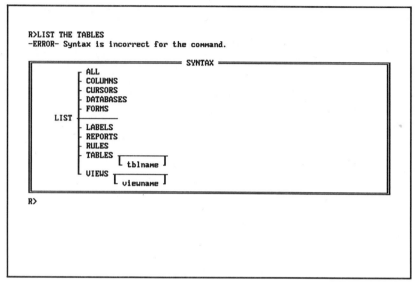

Figure 4.14: The syntax diagram for the LIST command

alone, or be followed by *tblname,* the name of a table in the currently open database. Similarly, LIST VIEWS can stand by itself or be followed by *viewname,* the name of a view in the currently open database. Our syntax error occurred because we included the word "THE," which cannot be used in the LIST command.

Sometimes, R:BASE knows that a command is wrong but not where the error is. For example, entering the command

SELECT ALL FROM Names BY L_Name

results in the less informative error message

–ERROR– Syntax error

with no syntax diagram presented. In these cases, you can always use the HELP command to get information on the command as well as the syntax diagram.

Fortunately, you don't have to type in an entire command from scratch just because of a simple error. R:BASE remembers your command, even after displaying the error message. You can use the following keys to bring back the command line and correct the errors in it:

End *or* Ctrl-→   Recalls the entire command.

→   Brings back one character from the line.

Tab   Recalls the previous command ten characters at a time.

Ins   Toggles between Insert (the cursor is a block) and Overtype (the cursor is an underline) mode.

Del   Deletes the character at the cursor.

PgUp   Recalls previous commands, the most recent one first.

PgDn   Recalls subsequent commands when used after PgUp; otherwise recalls the oldest command stored in the command buffer.

For example, suppose you enter the command

    SELECT ALL FROM Names ORDER BY L_Nam F_Name

R:BASE rejects the line because it can't find the L_Nam column. To correct the error (change L_Nam to L_Name), press the → key repeatedly to bring back all characters up to the error, as below:

    SELECT ALL FROM Names ORDER BY L_Nam_

Next, press the **Ins** key to go into Insert mode. The cursor changes into a block. Type the missing *e* and press the **Ins** key again to make the cursor return to an underline. The line should look like this:

    SELECT ALL FROM Names ORDER BY L_Name_

Now you can recall the rest of the line either by holding down the Ctrl key and pressing → or by tapping the End key. The entire line appears on the screen, as follows:

    SELECT ALL FROM Names ORDER BY L_Name F_Name_

Press ← to execute the command.

CH. 4

As previously mentioned, you can also press PgUp to bring back the previous command you typed. If you have been following along with the above exercise, you could press **PgUp** twice to bring back the command with the error

SELECT ALL FROM Names ORDER BY L_Nam F_Name

Then press ← to position the cursor at the end of L_Nam, as follows:

SELECT ALL FROM Names ORDER BY L_Nam_F_Name

Now press the **Ins** key to go into Insert mode, changing the cursor into a block. Type the missing *e*, press **Ins** again, and the line looks complete as follows:

SELECT ALL FROM Names ORDER BY L_Name_F_Name

But don't press ↵ just yet! When you are editing commands, R:BASE assumes that you want to end the line where you leave the cursor. If you pressed ↵ now, R:BASE would erase the rest of the command to the right of the cursor and execute the following command:

SELECT ALL FROM Names ORDER BY L_Name

In order to execute the entire command, move the cursor to the end of the command by repeatedly pressing → or by pressing End. Now press ↵ to execute the command.

Getting Database Information

In order to correct the error you were working with above, you have to remember how you spelled the last name column. If you can't remember how to spell the name of a table or column, you can

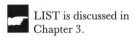
LIST is discussed in Chapter 3.

- type **LIST** to see a list of all the tables in your database; or
- type **LIST** *table name* to see all the columns in a specific table.

R:BASE provides a third way to remind yourself of the names of tables and columns (as well as variables, views, forms, and reports, which we'll be discussing in future chapters). This third way is particularly handy when you are correcting an error in a command. Follow these steps:

1. Press **PgUp** three times to bring back the command that you entered with an "L_Nam" error.

2. Press ← to move the cursor to the *L* at the beginning of L_Nam.

3. Press **Ins**, making the cursor into a blinking block, so that the new column name you enter does not type over the command that follows the cursor.

4. Press **F3** to bring up the Database Information screen (Figure 4.15).

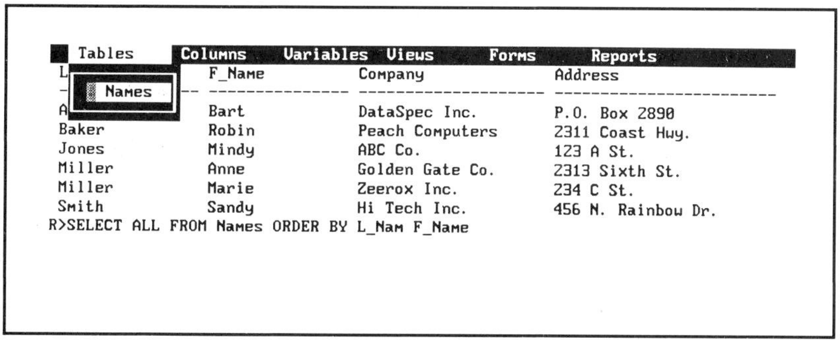

```
  Tables     Columns    Variables  Views     Forms       Reports
             F_Name       Company             Address
   Names    -- --------------- -------------------- -----------------------
 A           Bart        DataSpec Inc.       P.O. Box 2890
Baker        Robin       Peach Computers     2311 Coast Hwy.
Jones        Mindy       ABC Co.             123 A St.
Miller       Anne        Golden Gate Co.     2313 Sixth St.
Miller       Marie       Zeerox Inc.         234 C St.
Smith        Sandy       Hi Tech Inc.        456 N. Rainbow Dr.
R>SELECT ALL FROM Names ORDER BY L_Nam F_Name
```

Figure 4.15: The Database Information screen with information on the Mail database

Under the Tables choice on the menu bar, you see a pull-down menu with a list of all the tables in the Mail database, which in this case is just the Names table.

5. Highlight **Columns**, since you are interested in finding the name of a column. You see another pull-down menu containing Names.

6. Select **Names**. A submenu appears with a list of columns in the Names table.

7. Select **L_Name**, since this is the name of the column you want.

A check mark (✔) appears to the left of L_Name. If you wanted to add other column names to your command, you could select other column names by putting a check mark beside them.

8. Press **F2** to indicate that you are finished making your choices.

You see that L_Name has been inserted into the command line, as follows:

SELECT ALL FROM Names ORDER BY L_Name L_Nam F_Name

with the cursor flashing over the first letter of L_Nam.

9. Press **Ins** to leave Insert mode.

10. Press **Del** six times to remove the incorrectly spelled L_Nam (as well as the extra space).

11. Now, with the command corrected, press **End** to move the cursor to the end of the command line.

12. Press ◄── to execute the command.

Just about anytime you are in an R:BASE menu or in Command mode and you would like information about the database you have opened, you can press F3 to bring up the Database Information menu. Even if you don't have to enter the names of tables, columns, variables, views, forms, or reports on the screen, you can look at the names in the menu and then press Esc to return to the screen you were working on without making any selections.

ABBREVIATING COMMANDS

Another way to deal with long commands is to use abbreviations. Most R:BASE commands can be trimmed down to only the first three letters. For example, the command line

SELECT ALL FROM Names ORDER BY L_Name F_Name +
+ > Ent_Date DESC

can be abbreviated to

SEL ALL FRO Names ORD BY L_Name F_Name Ent_Date +
+ > DESC

Keep in mind that you can't abbreviate your own table names, column names, and so on. You also can't abbreviate DESC, used to indicate a descending sort. However, you can use column numbers rather than their names in column lists, as long as you include a number sign (#). For example, the rather lengthy command

SELECT Ent_Date L_Name F_Name Address FROM Names +
+ > ORDER BY Ent_Date DESC L_Name F_Name

can be abbreviated

SEL #8 #1 #2 #4 FROM Names ORD BY #8 DESC #1 #2

since Ent_Date is column number 8 in the Names table, L_Name is column number 1, and so on. From the R > prompt, you can use the LIST command, along with the table name (for example, LIST Names), to see column numbers. For purposes of clarity, we'll continue to use the longer versions of commands throughout this book.

SORTING AND THE PROJECT COMMAND

You may have noticed that the original order of data in the Names table is unaffected by the ORDER BY clause. To verify this, type

SELECT ALL FROM Names

and press ◄─┘. You see that the data is still in the original order.

One of the characteristics of a relational database is that the order of rows, or records, in your tables is irrelevant. Why, you ask? Because by using commands like SELECT, you can arrange to have the rows displayed (or printed) in any order you need on the spur of the moment.

However, you may prefer to have your data sorted in a particular order so you don't have to use the ORDER BY clause. The easiest way to do this is to use R:BASE's PROJECT command. At the R> prompt, type

HELP PROJECT

and press ◄─┘. Your screen should look like Figure 4.16.

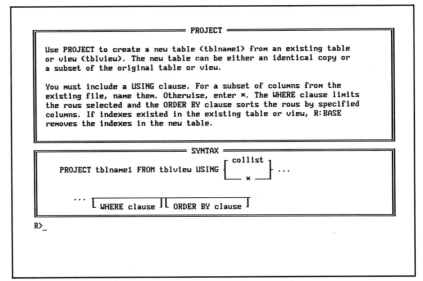

Figure 4.16: Help screen for the PROJECT command

This syntax diagram is broken into two parts because it is too wide to be displayed on the screen in one piece. The three dots to the right of the top part and the three dots to the left of the bottom part mean that the bottom part is a continuation of the top one. The PROJECT command is extremely useful for creating table backups and subscts of existing tables, and it can also be used to create a new table that is the same as an existing one, except for the order of the rows.

As an example, type the following at the R > prompt:

PROJECT SortName FROM Names USING * ORDER BY +
+ > L_Name

R:BASE should respond with a comforting message telling you that a successful PROJECT was accomplished, and that the new table has six rows in it.

To verify that the new table (called SortName) does indeed contain the same data as the Names table, but in alphabetical order by last name, type

SELECT ALL FROM SortName

> You'll learn more about PROJECT and other relational commands in Chapter 14.

The data should be displayed in the same order as they were in Figure 4.3. At this point, of course, the Mail database has two tables in it with redundant data. Generally, you would want to delete one of the tables by using the DROP TABLE command. If you have created the SortName table, go ahead and delete it by typing

DROP TABLE SortName

and pressing ◄──┘. R:BASE will ask you if you are sure you want to remove this table. Choose **Y**es to remove the SortName table. You've just issued one of R:BASE's six relational commands, which are generally used to combine data from different tables.

In this chapter you've learned numerous commands and techniques for displaying data in a table in sorted order. You've also learned more about entering commands at the R > prompt without the aid of the PBE mode. In the next chapter we'll discuss techniques for searching, or filtering, a table.

Chapter 5

Finding the Data
You Need

IN THIS CHAPTER, WE'LL DISCUSS TECHNIQUES FOR searching, *filtering,* and *querying* a table. When you filter a table, you access only those rows that meet specific search criteria. For example, from the Names table you might want to list everyone who has an entry date of June 1, 1990, or perhaps everyone who has an entry date in the first quarter of 1990. Alternatively, you might want to list all the individuals who live in a certain city or work for a certain company.

There is no limit to the ways that you can filter a table. Furthermore, you can mix sorting and searching criteria however you wish. For example, suppose you needed to send a form letter to all the individuals listed in a table who work for ABC Company in California. You could easily pull these individuals out of the table, sorted in ZIP-code order, so that you could get the benefits of bulk mailing.

SEARCHING ON THE EDIT SCREEN

As we mentioned in Chapter 4, one of the options in the top menu bar of the Edit screen is Query. This option allows you to reduce the number of rows displayed in the Edit screen so that only rows that meet certain conditions are displayed.

Suppose there were over a thousand names in the Names table, and you wanted to edit a row for an individual named Miller. If you did not use the Query option, you would need to scroll through many rows on the Edit screen to locate the appropriate row to edit. However, you could limit the Edit screen to displaying only rows with the last name of Miller.

Let's try it. First, make sure that the Mail database is open. Next, go to the Main menu and bring up the Edit screen for the Names table by highlighting **Info** and selecting **Names**. Now we are ready to perform a search or query.

1. Highlight **Q**uery and a pull-down menu appears, as shown in Figure 5.1.

2. Select **S**how Query screen, the first red-and-black (or black) choice on the menu. Now you see the Query screen, shown in Figure 5.2.

Some of the choices on the Query pull-down menu will appear in white, not the red and black you have seen on color screens or the black on monochrome screens. The white choices are not available now, but are included to remind you that at another time you will be able to choose them. When you move the highlighter, either with the arrow keys or the mouse, it will only move to the red-and-black choices on color screens or the black choices on monochrome screens in the pull-down menu.

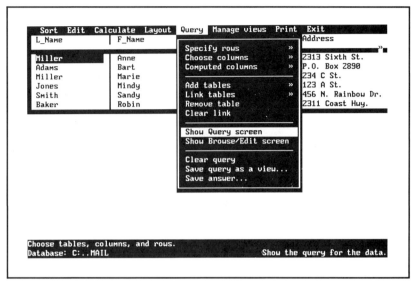

Figure 5.1: The Query pull-down menu on the Edit screen

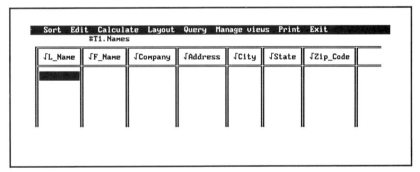

Figure 5.2: The Query screen for the Names table

3. The cursor is now in a column with the heading ↙L_Name. Press ↵, and you see a menu with several operators for performing the search, as shown in Figure 5.3.

Notice the small arrow pointing down in the lower-right corner of the menu box. This arrow means that there are more choices (in the down direction) than you can scroll to on the screen.

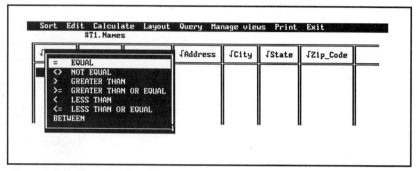

Figure 5.3: Menu for choosing a search operator

Using the mouse, you can look at operators above or below the seven displayed on the screen by selecting the up- or down-pointing arrow. Since this only moves the list up or down one choice at a time, the PgUp and PgDn keys are much faster at scrolling the list up or down.

4. Press **PgDn** to look at the seven new operators, with the highlighter on NOT BETWEEN. Now there are two arrows, one in the upper-right corner pointing to the first seven choices you saw and one in the lower-right corner pointing to more choices below.

5. Press **PgDn** again to look at the choices below. Now there is an arrow in the upper-right corner but not in the lower-right one, so you know you are at the bottom of the list of operators. We'll discuss these operators throughout the chapter.

6. Press **Home** to return to the top of the list (Figure 5.3) and select = EQUAL. R:BASE now displays a box in which you are asked to

   Enter a comparison value for : =

R:BASE is asking you for a name to search for in the L_Name column.

7. Type **Miller** and press ←┘. Under the ✓L_Name column, your condition is displayed as

   = 'Miller'

How to use single quotes (') is discussed later in this chapter under the heading "Comparing Columns in Searches."

R:BASE has added the single quotes (') to indicate that Miller is the value to search for, and not the name of another column in the Names table. We will discuss when to use single quotes later in this chapter. For now, you don't need to worry about single quotes because R:BASE will add them when they are required.

8. Press **F2** to execute this query. The Edit screen displays only rows with Miller in the Last Name column.

The Query option affects what you see on the Edit screen but not the data stored in the table. Of course, you could make any changes you wish to the Millers' data and those changes would be reflected in the table on the disk. And at any point, you could choose Exit from the top menu and return to the R:BASE Main menu.

SEARCHING FOR DATA
THAT MEETS SEVERAL CONDITIONS

Let's look at another example, this time using multiple search criteria. Suppose our table had ten thousand names on it, and of those about one hundred had the last name Miller. If you wanted to look up Anne Miller's address, specifying Miller for the search would still leave you with a hundred names to search through. To make this search easier, you could search for rows with the last name Miller and the first name Anne. Let's work through this example.

1. Highlight **Q**uery, since we are going to try another Query example.

2. Select **S**how Query screen to return to the Query screen. It still has the condition = 'Miller' in the ✔L_Name column, so you only have to add the condition that the first name be Anne.

3. Move the highlighter to the column with the heading ✔F_Name.

4. Press ⏎ to bring up the menu of conditions.

5. Select = EQUAL by pressing ⏎ again.

6. Type in **Anne** for the comparison value, and press ⏎. You now see = 'Anne' in the column headed ✔F_Name.

7. Press **F2** to see the Edit screen with just Anne Miller.

Now let's remove the conditions that you used in your last search. To do this, you have to go back to the Query screen by highlighting **Q**uery and choosing **S**how Query screen. The highlighter should be in the ⊬F_Name column where you left it. Before we remove the conditions you used for your last search, let's see if you can use a function key to remove these conditions. Press **Shift-F1** to see the R:BASE function key descriptions, as shown in Figure 5.4.

```
                    Currently Active Function Keys
            Unshifted              Shifted              Control

    F1      Help                   Function keys        Script/Key menu
    F2      Do it                  Do it                End script recording
    F3      Database information   Show query command   Browse/Edit screen
    F4      N/A                    Zoom                 N/A
    F5      Clear a condition      Clear table conditions N/A
    F6      Toggle one column      Toggle all columns   N/A
    F7      N/A                    Previous table       N/A
    F8      N/A                    Next table           N/A
    F9      Remove table           Clear column condition Delete Link
    F10     Add table              Add an either-or     Add Link
```

Figure 5.4: Function keys for use in the Query screen

The entry for F5 reads "Clear a condition," so this key would clear the condition in the ⊬F_Name column you are in. However, the entry for Shift-F5, "Clear table conditions," says this key combination would clear all the conditions in the table. This sounds perfect for our needs. First, press any key to finish looking at the function key descriptions. Press **Shift-F5** to clear all the conditions. The Query screen now looks the same as it did when you first displayed it, with no conditions specified.

You might expect that you could press F2 now and see all rows displayed on the Edit screen, since there are no conditions specified on the Query screen. Press **F2** to find out. Now only the row for Anne Miller is displayed on the Edit screen. Although pressing Shift-F5 is convenient for clearing all the conditions on the Query screen, Version 3.1 of R:BASE will not show you all rows on the Edit screen if the only change you made to the Query screen was to clear all of the conditions by pressing Shift-F5. However, if you make other changes to the Query screen, such as adding another condition, R:BASE will make the rows on the Edit screen match the conditions on the Query screen. If you wanted to display all rows on the Edit screen, you could accomplish this in other ways besides pressing Shift-F5 on the Query screen. One way is to remove each condition from the Query screen by moving the highlighter to each condition and pressing F5. By pressing F2 next, all rows would be displayed on the Edit screen. Perhaps the makers of R:BASE will change the Shift-F5 function key on the Query screen in a future release of R:BASE so that it works as you would expect it to. To prepare for the next example, return to the Query screen by pressing **Ctrl-F3**.

EXPLORING THE FEATURES OF THE QUERY OPTION

Now let's go back to the Query option on the top menu bar and find out what the other selections in the pull-down menu under Query (see Figure 5.1) do. Highlight **Q**uery again. Notice that only the Show Query screen option is displayed in white (making it currently unavailable). Right now, you don't need the Show Query screen option since you are already on the Query screen.

SELECTING SPECIFIC ROWS FOR DISPLAY

The first option under Query is Specify rows. Using this option, you can determine which rows are displayed on the Edit screen. Select **S**pecify rows and a menu box appears with the following choices, as shown in Figure 5.5:

You can also modify a condition by placing the highlighter on the condition and pressing ←. A box containing the operator and a value for the current condition appears. Make changes to the operator and value using the cursor control keys, backspace key, etc.

Add condition — allows you to add a condition to the current column. (You will be asked to choose an operator and enter a value.) If conditions are in this column already, R:BASE adds the new condition after the others. Choosing this option is the same as pressing ← when the highlighter is in an empty field in a column.

Modify condition — allows you to change the condition that the highlighter is on. (You are first asked to choose an operator and then asked to enter a value.)

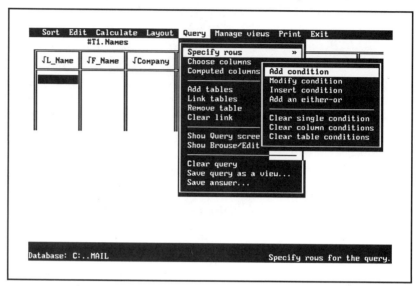

Figure 5.5: Menu box for selecting specific rows for display

Insert condition	allows you to insert a condition just above the condition where the highlighter is placed. This option is useful when you want to make sure that the conditions are evaluated in a certain order.
Add an either–or	allows you to start a second set of conditions for selecting rows. Either the row can match the existing set of conditions or the new set for it to be displayed on the Edit screen.
Clear single condition	removes the condition that the highlighter is on.
Clear column conditions	removes all of the conditions in the column where the highlighter is.
Clear table conditions	removes all of the conditions in the entire Query screen.

Alternatively, you can clear a single condition by pressing F5, clear column conditions by pressing Shift-F9, or clear table conditions by pressing Shift-F5. See Figure 5.4 for details on function keys you can use in the Query screen.

Let's try some exercises with these selections. To return to the Query table, press **Esc** and then **Alt**. The highlighter should now be back in the ⌐L_Name column.

In a previous example, you found all of the Millers by making "Miller" the comparison value in the ✓L_Name column. Let's find the rows that have Jones in the Last Name column as well. To start, enter the condition that the last name has to be Miller.

1. Press ↩ to bring up the menu box of operators.

2. Press ↩ to choose = EQUAL.

3. Type in **Miller**, and then press ↩ to finish specifying the condition. Adding a new condition to this column requires a different approach from simply pressing ↩. Try pressing ↩ now, and you will be presented with the condition = 'Miller' in a box ready to be edited, as in Figure 5.6.

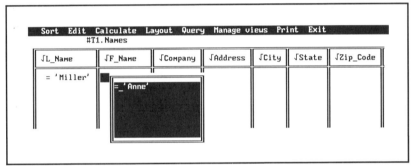

Figure 5.6: The first condition displayed on the screen, ready for editing

4. Press ↩ without making any changes to our existing condition.

5. Highlight **Query**.

6. Select **S**pecify rows.

7. Select **A**dd condition.

8. Select = EQUAL from the menu of operators.

9. Type in **Jones** and press ↩ to make it the comparison value.

Instead of activating the Query option on the menu, you could add a new condition in step 5 by moving down one row and pressing ↩. This is an easier way, but it doesn't give you any practice in using the Query option.

Now there are two query conditions in the last name column. At this point, by pressing a function key, we can take advantage of a feature of the Query screen that shows the command that R:BASE is building up, similar to the one we saw in the PBE menus. To find out which function key to use,

    a. Press **Shift-F1**. The list of function keys available in the Query screen appears (see Figure 5.4). Notice that pressing Shift-F3 will activate the Show query command.

    b. Press any key to remove the function key descriptions.

10. Press **Shift-F3**. A box appears showing a SELECT command with the conditions you set up, as in Figure 5.7.

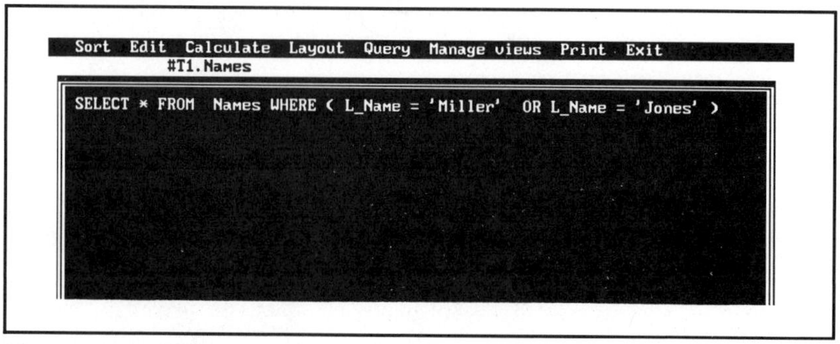

```
 Sort  Edit  Calculate  Layout  Query  Manage views  Print  Exit
       #T1.Names

 SELECT * FROM  Names WHERE ( L_Name = 'Miller'  OR L_Name = 'Jones' )
```

Figure 5.7: A SELECT query command for searching for Millers and Joneses

You could enter this very same SELECT command at the R> prompt and it would find the same rows that the Edit screen will display. Of course, entering the SELECT command at the R> prompt displays the information, but it doesn't give you the opportunity to scroll through or change the information as the Edit screen does.

11. Press any key to finish looking at the SELECT query command.

12. Press **F2**. The Edit screen displays the Millers and the Joneses in your database table.

Let's return to the Query screen for another example. You have seen that you can go to the Query screen by choosing the Show Query screen option in the pull-down menu under the Query option in the menu bar. However, there is also a function key for this purpose. Press **Shift-F1** to display the description of available function keys, shown in Figure 5.8. You can see that Ctrl-F3 takes you to the

Query screen. Press any key to remove the function key descriptions and then press **Ctrl-F3**.

If the Names table were very large, then you might want to narrow your search down to even fewer rows on the Edit screen. Say, for example, that you only wanted to see those rows for Miller and Jones that were entered on June 1, 1990. Follow these steps to add this condition to the Query screen:

1. Press **Ctrl-→** to move to the ✓Ent_Date column.

2. Press ◄— to add a condition.

3. Select the = EQUAL operator.

4. Type in **06/01/90** for the comparison value (and press ◄—).

5. Press **Shift-F3** to look at the Query command, which is shown in Figure 5.9.

```
                    Currently Active Function Keys
          Unshifted                 Shifted               Control
                                    ─────────             ─────────
    F1    Help                      Function keys         Script/Key menu
    F2    Do it                     Do it                 End script recording
    F3    Database information      N/A                   Query screen
    F4    Browse/Edit toggle        Zoom                  N/A
    F5    Reset field               N/A                   N/A
    F6    Mark data                 N/A                   N/A
    F7    Previous row              N/A                   Copy marked data
    F8    Next row                  N/A                   Move column
    F9    Delete row                Clear whole field     Clear to end of field
    F10   Insert row                N/A                   N/A
```

Figure 5.8: Functions keys for use in the Edit screen

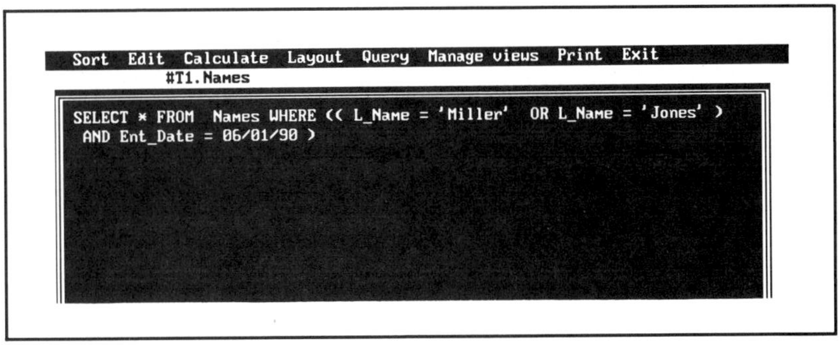

```
 Sort  Edit  Calculate  Layout  Query  Manage views  Print  Exit
       #T1.Names

 SELECT * FROM  Names WHERE (( L_Name = 'Miller'  OR L_Name = 'Jones' )
 AND Ent_Date = 06/01/90 )
```

Figure 5.9: Query command to display Millers and Joneses with the entry date of 06/01/90

We will learn more about how to use parentheses in WHERE clauses later in this chapter under the heading "Using Parentheses in WHERE Clauses."

R:BASE interprets this query command as follows: the row will be included if the last name is either Miller or Jones and the entry date is 06/01/90. Notice the two sets of parentheses in the WHERE clause. The extra set indicates that the conditions L_Name = 'Miller' and L_Name = 'Jones' are checked first. Then the condition Ent_Date = 06/01/90 is checked.

6. Press any key to finish looking at the Query command.

7. Press **F2** to see the Edit screen corresponding to this Query command. Now two rows are displayed, one for Jones and one for Anne Miller. The row for Marie Miller was not chosen because the entry date for her row is not 06/01/90.

In a previous example, when you were looking for Anne Miller's row, you placed the = 'Miller' condition in one column (✔L_Name) and the = 'Anne' condition in a different one (✔F_Name). You saw that when there are two conditions, each in a different column, both have to be true for the row to be selected and displayed in the Edit screen. You also learned that when there are two or more conditions in the *same* column, only one condition has to be true for the row to be selected. But suppose you were looking for rows where either the last name is Miller or the first name is Robin. In this case, you would have two search conditions, each in a different column, but only one condition would have to be true for the row to be selected. To set up a search query where only one of the columns has to be true and match a search condition, you can use the Add an either–or option. Follow these steps:

1. Press **Ctrl-F3** to return to the Query screen.

2. Press **Shift-F5** to remove all of the conditions on the Query screen.

3. Press ↵ twice to choose = EQUAL, and type **Miller** and press ↵ again to place the condition = 'Miller' in the ✔L_Name column.

4. Move the highlighter to the ✔F_Name column.

5. Highlight **Q**uery in the menu.

6. Select **S**pecify rows.
7. Select the **A**dd an either–or option. At this point you see the familiar operator selection box.
8. Select the = EQUAL operator.
9. Type in **Robin** and press ↵ to provide the comparison value. This time, R:BASE displays a dashed line to separate the condition you just entered from the first condition, as shown in Figure 5.10.
10. Press **Shift-F3** to see the Query command corresponding to these conditions, as shown in Figure 5.11. Here, the Query command will select a row if either the last name is Miller or the first name is Robin, just as we wanted.

Sort Edit Calculate Layout Query Manage views Print Exit
#T1.Names
√L_Name
√F_Name
√Company
√Address
√City
√State
= 'Miller'
= 'Robin'

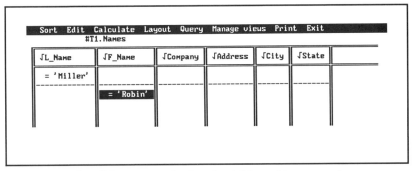

Figure 5.10: Conditions entered using the Add an either–or option

Sort Edit Calculate Layout Query Manage views Print Exit
#T1.Names
SELECT * FROM Names WHERE (L_Name = 'Miller' OR F_Name = 'Robin')

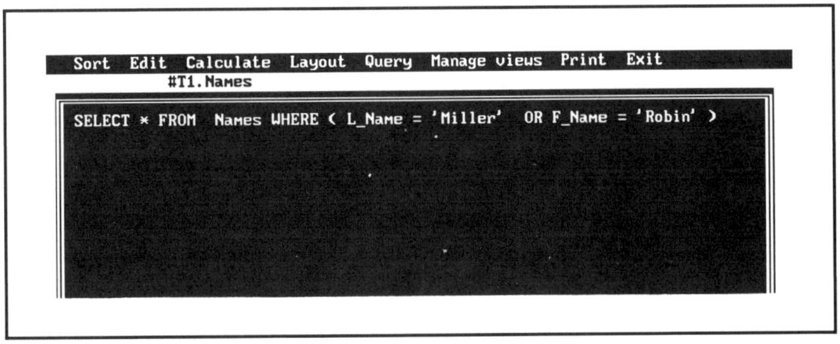

Figure 5.11: The Query command corresponding to the either–or conditions in Figure 5.10

11. Press any key to remove the Query command.

12. Press **F2**. You now see both Millers on the Edit screen, as well as Robin Baker.

We have seen how to use the Specify rows option under the Query option pull-down menu to search for rows that match specified conditions. To look at the other selections under Query, return to the Query screen by pressing **Ctrl-F3** and clear all of the conditions in the table by pressing **Shift-F5**.

SELECTING SPECIFIC COLUMNS FOR DISPLAY

The next selection below the Specify rows option in the Query pull-down menu (see Figure 5.1) is Choose columns. This option allows you to choose columns for display on the Edit screen. You have already seen how to display columns using R:BASE commands and the Layout option on the Edit screen menu. R:BASE gives you the capability to change both the rows and the columns on the Query screen so that you can perform both chores in one place and display your work in the Edit screen.

Look at the column headings on the Query screen. If a column name has a check mark (✔) in front of it, then it will be displayed on the Edit screen. Follow these steps to see how to remove or add check marks and so tell R:BASE which columns to display:

1. Highlight **Q**uery on the menu bar.

2. Select **C**hoose columns in the pull-down menu. In the selection box which is now displayed, you are presented with two choices, select/unselect and select/unselect all.

   • Select/unselect changes the current column—the column containing the highlighter—from selected to not selected or vice versa. This option either removes the check mark from the current column heading if it has a check mark, or displays a check mark if there is none. (You can perform this command directly from the keyboard by pressing F6.)

- Select/unselect all either unselects *all* of the columns in the table, or selects all of them. (You can perform this command directly from the keyboard by pressing Shift-F6.)

3. Let's try unselecting the L_Name column. With the highlighter in the L_Name column, choose **S**elect/unselect. The check mark in the heading of the L_Name column disappears.

4. Press **F2** and the Edit screen will be displayed without the L_Name column.

5. Press **Ctrl-F3** to return to the Query screen.

6. Now, to see how to select or unselect a column directly from the keyboard, press **F6**. You will see the check mark reappear in front of L_Name.

7. Press **F2** to see the Edit screen.

Where is the L_Name column? R:BASE put it at the right-hand side of the table, following all of the other columns.

8. Press **End** twice and you will see that the L_Name column has been placed to the right of the Ent_Date column.

You could move the L_Name column back to the left-hand end of the table with the Move column option in the pull-down menu under Layout.

1. Move the highlighter back to the F_Name column.

2. Highlight **L**ayout and select **M**ove column.

3. Select **L**_Name and press **F2**.

4. Select **I**nsert at cursor.

The Query screen is a very powerful tool for finding and editing data in a large table. As you would expect, there are also R:BASE commands you can use to select rows to display or edit. In previous chapters, we passed by some of these options when we skipped the

Don't forget, you can check the function keys that are active on the Query screen by pressing Shift-F1. (Figure 5.4 also lists these keys.)

Pressing **End** twice is a fast way to move the highlighter to the bottom-right corner of the table.

Pressing **Home** twice is a fast way to move the highlighter back to the top-left corner F_Name column.

PBE menus related to the searching options. Now we will use the PBE menus to do some searching and then try entering the R:BASE commands directly.

SEARCHING FROM THE PROMPT BY EXAMPLE MENU

When you display or edit data using the Query a database or Modify data options on the Prompt By Example (PBE) Main menu, the last screen to appear before the final command is displayed allows you to specify criteria for filtering the database. We haven't put this screen to use in previous chapters, so let's work through some exercises now.

On the Query screen, you created a query for searching for only the Millers on the Edit screen. Let's see how to search for the Millers by creating an Edit command using the PBE menus. First, let's go to the PBE Main menu:

1. Highlight and select **E**xit to leave the Edit screen.

2. Highlight **E**xit.

3. Select **R>** prompt to go to Command mode.

4. Type **PROMPT** and press ↵ to display the PBE Main menu.

5. Choose option **5**, Modify data.

6. Choose **E**DIT from the next menu.

7. Choose **T**abular Edit.

8. Choose **A**ll rows to have access to all rows (as opposed to just distinct rows).

9. Choose **N**ames as the table to edit.

10. Choose **(ALL)** to have access to all columns. The screen that appears (Figure 5.12) lets you specify searching criteria.

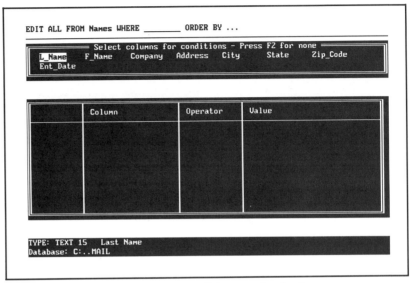

Figure 5.12: The PBE screen for specifying search criteria

11. In this case, we want to search for individuals with the last name Miller. Select **L_Name** as the column to search on.

A menu appears over the top of the screen displaying a list of operators for performing the search. This list contains the same operators you saw on the Query screen (see Figure 5.3), although the operators on your screen are displayed in two columns. Notice the downward arrow in the lower-right corner of the box. This arrow means that you can display more choices in the menu by pressing the ↓ or PgDn keys.

> If you are using a mouse, you can display more choices in the operator's menu by selecting the down arrow in the lower-right corner of the box or the up arrow in the upper-right corner.

12. Choose = EQUAL. The cursor moves to the Value column and a prompt appears in the lower-right corner of the screen asking you to

    Enter a comparison value

13. Type in **Miller** and press ⏎. The screen displays a prompt and some menu choices:

    Choose an operator to combine conditions or choose (Done).
    AND   OR   AND NOT   OR NOT   (Done)

14. Choose (Done).

15. Press **F2** to bypass the next screen. R:BASE displays the screen for entering sorting criteria. The command you've built appears on the screen:

EDIT ALL FROM Names WHERE L_Name = 'Miller'

This command tells R:BASE to display all the columns from the Names table on the Edit screen, but only those rows that have Miller in the L_Name column. Select **E**xecute to execute the command, and the Millers appear on the Edit screen.

Before leaving the Edit screen, let's look at this a bit further. Press **Ctrl-F3** to display the Query screen. Notice = 'Miller' in the L_Name column, just as if you had entered this criterion on the Query screen. Now press **Shift-F3** and you will see the Query command

SELECT * FROM Names WHERE (L_Name = 'Miller')

In the EDIT and SELECT commands, an asterisk (*) can be used in place of the word ALL.

which looks very much like the EDIT command you used to display the Edit screen. The asterisk (*) can be used in lieu of the word ALL. Now press any key to return to the Query screen. Next, highlight and select **E**xit to return to the Modify data menu.

Searching for Data that Meets Several Criteria

As you did on the Query screen, you can use multiple search criteria. Let's use the PBE menus to construct a SELECT command that displays only the row for Anne Miller. To make a SELECT command, you have to return to the PBE Main menu. Follow these steps:

1. Press **Esc**.

2. Choose option **6**, Query a database.

3. Choose the **SELECT** command.

4. Choose the **N**ames table.

5. Choose **ALL** (not just DISTINCT) rows.

6. Choose (ALL) columns.

7. Choose the **L**_Name column when the search criterion screen appears.

8. Choose the = EQUAL operator.

9. Type in **Miller** (and press ←) to specify that the last name has to be Miller. The menu box appears with the prompt

   Choose an operator to combine conditions or choose (Done).

10. Select the **AND** option.

11. Select **F**_Name.

12. Choose = EQUAL as the operator.

13. Enter **Anne** as the comparison value (and press ←). Your screen will look like Figure 5.13.

14. Choose (Done) to finish entering the search criteria.

15. Press **F2** to bypass the sort criteria screen. The command you just created appears:

    SELECT ALL FROM Names WHERE L_Name = 'Miller' +
    + > AND F_Name = 'Anne'

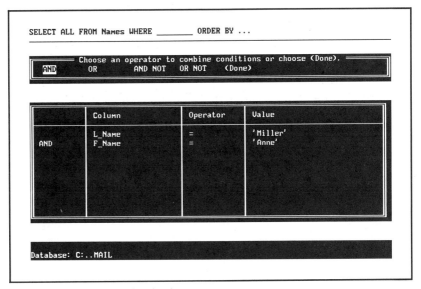

Figure 5.13: PBE search criteria screen

R:BASE displays the one column from the Names table that has Miller in the L_Name column and Anne in the F_Name column.

16. Choose Execute to execute the command.

17. Press any key when you are finished viewing the data.

SEARCHING FROM THE R> PROMPT

As we continue our discussion of searching techniques, we'll start presenting commands as they would be entered at the R> prompt. You can type them in as displayed, or use PBE mode to build them. Press the **Esc** key twice to leave PBE and get to the R> prompt.

SPECIFYING COLUMN WIDTHS

Before we go any further, let's take advantage of R:BASE's Help function to examine the SELECT command in more detail. If you type

    HELP SELECT

at the R> prompt, you'll see a screen with a general discussion of the SELECT command. Press any key, and you'll see another screen which describes variations of the SELECT command. The next two screens show the SELECT command's syntax, as in Figures 5.14 and 5.15.

Although the syntax diagram looks fairly complicated, most uses of SELECT will involve straightforward syntax as you have seen in the Query command on the Query screen. To display all rows from a table, you would enter the command

    SELECT ALL FROM table name

Or you could enter an asterisk (*) in place of the word ALL. Since we're working on the Names table, type

    SELECT ALL FROM Names

Your output should display all six rows in the table.

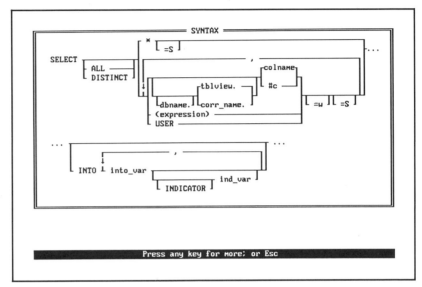

Figure 5.14: The first help screen for the syntax of the SELECT command

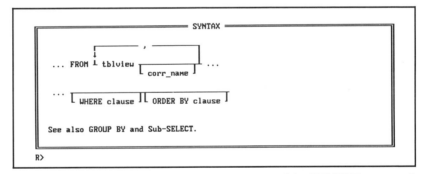

Figure 5.15: The second help screen for the syntax of the SELECT command

The problem with this display is that we only see the first four columns. Furthermore, unlike EDIT, SELECT doesn't allow us to scroll back and forth through the columns. In the last chapter, we built commands that displayed only some of the columns; that's one way to deal with the problem of not being able to see the desired data. However, there's another option that can be very useful. Take another look at the syntax diagram in Figure 5.14, and note the = w

CH. 5

In case you're curi-
ous about the = S
option next to the = w
option, it stands for
"Sum." You'll learn
more about it in the next
chapter.

option to the right of *colname*. When you tell R:BASE which columns
to display, you can also specify the width of the individual screen
fields in which the columns are displayed. For example, you could
enter

SELECT Ent_Date F_Name = 10 L_Name = 10 Company = 10 +
+ > Address = 15 City = 10 State FROM Names

in order to display more data on one screen. Note that R:BASE doesn't
simply truncate the data to fit your specifications; any data that runs
over the specified width is wrapped around, as in Figure 5.16.

```
R>SELECT Ent_Date F_Name=10 L_Name=10 Company=10 +
+> Address=15 City=10 State FROM Names
Ent_Date F_Name     L_Name     Company    Address          City        State
-------- ---------- ---------- ---------- ---------------- ----------  -----
06/01/90 Anne       Miller     Golden     2313 Sixth St.   Berkeley    CA
                               Gate Co.
06/15/90 Bart       Adams      DataSpec   P.O. Box 2890    Malibu      CA
                               Inc.
06/15/90 Marie      Miller     Zeerox     234 C St.        Los         CA
                               Inc.                        Angeles
06/01/90 Mindy      Jones      ABC Co.    123 A St.        San Diego   CA
06/01/90 Sandy      Smith      Hi Tech    456 N. Rainbow   Berkeley    CA
                               Inc.       Dr.
06/15/90 Robin      Baker      Peach      2311 Coast       San Diego   CA
                               Computers  Hwy.
R>
```

Figure 5.16: Specifying the width of column displays

HOW TO USE THE WHERE CLAUSE

You've probably noticed that several of the searches you've performed using the Query screen, the EDIT command, and the
SELECT command included the keyword WHERE, followed by
the search condition:

WHERE L_Name = 'Miller' AND F_Name = 'Anne'

For the rest of this chapter, we'll discuss numerous searching techniques that you can use with the WHERE clause.

The WHERE clause can be used with both the SELECT and EDIT commands, as well as with several other commands that we'll discuss later. In its simplest form, the WHERE clause contains

- a column name,

- the equal sign (=), and

- the search value.

You have seen that the following command displays all the Millers:

SELECT ALL FROM Names WHERE L_Name = 'Miller'

You can, as you have seen, specify that only certain columns be displayed. For example, to see the dates and names of people whose entry dates are June 1, 1990, you would enter the command

SELECT Ent_Date L_Name F_Name FROM Names WHERE +
+> Ent_Date = '6/1/90'

You can still specify sort orders by using the ORDER BY clause either before or after the WHERE clause. For example, to display Berkeley residents in alphabetical order by name, you could enter either of these commands:

SELECT City L_Name F_Name Company FROM Names +
+> ORDER BY L_Name F_Name WHERE City = 'Berkeley'

SELECT City L_Name F_Name Company FROM Names +
+> WHERE City = 'Berkeley' ORDER BY L_Name F_Name

Either way, the screen displays Berkeley residents in alphabetical order by name, as in Figure 5.17.

So far, our search commands have only used the equals operator (=). However, you might remember that the Search Operator menu on the Query screen and the PBE menus had many more operators. These additional logical operators greatly expand your searching capabilities.

```
R>SELECT City L_Name F_Name Company FROM Names +
+>WHERE City = 'Berkeley' ORDER BY L_Name F_Name
City              L_Name            F_Name            Company
----------------  ----------------  ----------------  --------------------
Berkeley          Miller            Anne              Golden Gate Co.
Berkeley          Smith             Sandy             Hi Tech Inc.
R>
```

Figure 5.17: Berkeley residents displayed in alphabetical order

Table 5.1 shows several operators you can use with the WHERE clause. Note that the operator and symbol can be used interchangeably. For example, LE is equivalent to the less-than-or-equal-to sign ($<=$).

Suppose that you wanted a listing of all the individuals whose last names begin with the letters A through M. You could enter the command

SELECT ALL FROM Names WHERE L_Name < 'N'

This would produce the display shown in Figure 5.18.

```
R>SELECT ALL FROM Names WHERE L_Name < 'N'
L_Name            F_Name            Company               Address
----------------  ----------------  --------------------  --------------------------
Miller            Anne              Golden Gate Co.       2313 Sixth St.
Adams             Bart              DataSpec Inc.         P.O. Box 2890
Miller            Marie             Zeerox Inc.           234 C St.
Jones             Mindy             ABC Co.               123 A St.
Baker             Robin             Peach Computers       2311 Coast Hwy.
R>
```

Figure 5.18: Individuals with last names beginning with A through M

To display individuals with names beginning with the letters N through Z, you could enter the command

SELECT ALL FROM Names WHERE L_Name > = 'N'

Suppose you wanted to display everyone *except* Berkeley residents on your tables. You could use the not-equal operator, as below:

SELECT ALL FROM Names WHERE City < > 'Berkeley'

To display these same individuals in alphabetical order and show the city on the screen, you could use the command

SELECT L_Name F_Name City FROM Names ORDER BY +
+ > L_Name F_Name WHERE City NE 'Berkeley'

The CONTAINS, NOT CONTAINS, LIKE, and NOT LIKE work only with TEXT and NOTE fields. The rest work with any kind of data.

Most of the WHERE clause operators listed in Table 5.1 work with any type of data. For example, to display people whose entry dates are later than June 1, 1990, you could enter the command

SELECT Ent_Date L_Name F_Name FROM Names WHERE +
+ > Ent_Date > '6/1/90'

Table 5.1: WHERE Clause Operators

OPERATOR	SYMBOL	DEFINITION
EQ	=	Equals
NE	< >	Not equal to
GT	>	Greater than
GE	> =	Greater than or equal to
LT	<	Less than
LE	< =	Less than or equal to
CONTAINS *'string'*		Includes a specific string of characters*
NOT CONTAINS *'string'*		Does not include a specific string of characters*
EXISTS		Column contains data
FAILS		Column doesn't contain data
BETWEEN *value1* and *value2*		Greater than or equal to *value1* and less than or equal to *value2*

Table 5.1: WHERE Clause Operators (continued)

OPERATOR	SYMBOL	DEFINITION
NOT BETWEEN *value1* and *value2*		Less than *value1* or greater than *value2*
LIKE *'string'*		Column equals *'string'* *
NOT LIKE *'string'*		Column does not equal *'string'* *
IN (*valuelist* or SELECT *clause*)		Value of column exists in selected rows. When used with another SELECT, referred to as a *subselect.*
NOT IN (*valuelist* or SELECT clause)		Value of column does not exist in selected rows
IS NULL		Value of column is null, as it doesn't contain data
IS NOT NULL		Value of column contains data

*'*string*' can contain the R:BASE wildcard characters % and _.

Suppose you wanted to pull out only those people in the 92111 ZIP-code area. Furthermore, you wanted them displayed alphabetically by last and first names. You could use the command

```
SELECT Zip_Code L_Name F_Name City FROM Names +
+> WHERE Zip_Code = '92111' ORDER BY L_Name F_Name
```

If you wanted to send something to all the people in the ZIP-code range 92000 to 99999, you could filter out the appropriate data using this command:

```
SELECT ALL FROM Names WHERE Zip_Code BETWEEN +
+> '92000' AND '99999'
```

SEARCHING FOR EMBEDDED DATA

Here's a tricky one for you. Suppose you want to list everyone in the Names table with an address on Rainbow Drive. If you enter either of the commands

    SELECT ALL FROM Names WHERE Address = 'Rainbow'

    SELECT ALL FROM Names WHERE Address LIKE 'Rainbow'

R:BASE displays the message

    –WARNING– No rows exist or satisfy the specified clause

indicating that nobody's address equals "Rainbow." But we know that at least one row contains an address on Rainbow. Even so, R:BASE is correct—the address 456 N. Rainbow Dr. does not equal Rainbow. However, that address contains the word *Rainbow*. In this example, we need to use the CONTAINS operator, as follows:

    SELECT ALL FROM Names WHERE Address +
    + > CONTAINS 'Rainbow'

This command displays the data we want, the record of Sandy Smith, who lives at 456 N. Rainbow Dr.

The CONTAINS operator can only be used with TEXT and NOTE columns, which means that you cannot use a WHERE clause like

    WHERE Ent_Date CONTAINS '90'

or

    WHERE Ent_Date CONTAINS '6/'

because Ent_Date is a DATE data type. However, you can pull out ranges of data such as these using the BETWEEN or the AND and OR operators.

Another very useful feature is that you can use the percent sign (%) and underscore (_) wildcard characters to narrow down a search that inlcudes the LIKE or NOT LIKE operator. These wildcards also appear to work fine with the CONTAINS and NOT CONTAINS operators, although the R:BASE manuals do not mention this. The percent sign wildcard is similar to the asterisk (*) used in DOS commands: it will match any number of characters to the end of the field. The underscore wildcard performs the same wildcard function as the question mark (?) in DOS commands: it matches any individual character in that position. For example, a command such as

SELECT ALL FROM Names WHERE F_Name LIKE 'Sm_th'

will find Smith, Smoth, Smeth, Smyth, and so on, but not Smythe or Smooth. On the other hand, the command

SELECT ALL FROM Names WHERE L_Name CONTAINS 'Sm%th'

will find all the names listed above (including Smooth). And, since the last command includes the CONTAINS operator, it would find Smithers and McSmith as well.

CHECKING FOR THE PRESENCE OR ABSENCE OF DATA

Database users frequently need to verify that data exists in a given column. For example, you may want to be sure every person in the Names table has a last name before you use the names for mailing labels. To do this, you could establish a rule that forces data entry into a given field. You could also use the SELECT command with the operators IS NULL or IS NOT NULL. In R:BASE, null is usually represented by a zero enclosed by hyphens (–0–). Let's say that you're concerned that some of the records in the Names table don't have ZIP codes. A fast way to check this would be to type

Null is a term used in the database world to indicate an absence of data.

SELECT L_Name F_Name Zip_Code FROM Names WHERE +
+ > Zip_Code IS NULL

R:BASE would respond with a message telling you that none of the rows in the Names table satisfy the WHERE clause. Why? Because all your records have ZIP codes.

The IS NOT NULL operator is often used to locate data with a certain value quickly. For example, imagine that the Names table has a column called VIP that contains either a *Y* or nothing. You could quickly find VIPs by giving a command such as

SELECT ALL FROM Names WHERE VIP IS NOT NULL

LOCATING ROWS BY POSITION

R:BASE provides three additional WHERE clause operators that help you locate data by row position. These operators are explained in Table 5.2. Although row position is generally insignificant in a relational database, using the COUNT and LIMIT operators can sometimes be handy.

Table 5.2: WHERE Clause Operators Used to Locate Rows by Position

OPERATOR	EFFECT
COUNT *operator n*	Finds row(s) starting with *n,* where *operator* can be = , < >, <, < = , >, > = , **EQ, NE, LT, LE, GT**, or **GE**
COUNT EQ LAST	Finds the last row
LIMIT EQ *n*	Finds the first *n* rows only

For example, if you are interrupted during data entry and want to see where you left off, you can type

SELECT ALL FROM Names WHERE COUNT EQ LAST

If you only want to see the first three records in the Names table, you can type

SELECT ALL FROM Names WHERE LIMIT = 3

If you want to see all records after the first four, you can enter

SELECT ALL FROM Names WHERE COUNT > 4

HELP FOR YOUR SPELLING

An undocumented feature of R:BASE is the SOUNDS operator. If you're not sure of the spelling of a data item, you can use this operator. For example, suppose you want to find someone whose name you think is Mary, but might be Mari, Marie, or something similar. You can type

> SELECT ALL FROM Names WHERE F_Name SOUNDS 'Mary'

R:BASE would respond with the record for Marie Miller.

Another way to approach the problem would be to use the IN operator. IN can be followed either by another SELECT to find matches within a subset of your table, or by a list of possible matches. For example, if you aren't sure whether someone's first name is Mary, Marie, or Marianne, you could enter

> SELECT ALL FROM Names WHERE F_Name IN (Mary, +
> + > Marie, Marianne)

Don't confuse the IN operator with the CONTAINS operator. In the above command, a row is only displayed if the first name is exactly equal to Mary, Marie, or Marianne.

AND OPERATORS AND OR OPERATORS

As you have seen in previous examples, you can specify multiple criteria in a WHERE clause by using the AND and OR operators. AND and OR belong to a larger group, sometimes called *logical* or *Boolean* operators, that also includes AND NOT, OR NOT, and some other terms not used in R:BASE. Let's practice using these operators in Command mode. Suppose you wanted a listing of Berkeley residents whose entry dates are June 1, 1990. The command below would display them for you:

> SELECT ALL FROM Names WHERE Ent_Date = '6/1/90' +
> + > AND City = 'Berkeley'

You might want a display with these same data listed in alphabetical order by last name, showing only the entry date, name, and address. You could enter the command

```
SELECT Ent_Date L_Name F_Name Address FROM Names +
+ > ORDER BY L_Name F_Name +
+ > WHERE Ent_Date = '6/1/90' AND City = 'Berkeley'
```

Suppose you wanted a listing of everyone whose entry date is in the month of June; in other words, in the range of June 1 to June 30. You could enter the command

```
SELECT ALL FROM Names WHERE Ent_Date > = '6/1/90' +
+ > AND Ent_Date < = '6/30/90'
```

or the command

```
SELECT ALL FROM Names WHERE Ent_Date BETWEEN +
+ > '6/1/90' AND '6/30/90'
```

to display these rows.

To put that same display in chronological order and show only date, name, and company, you could use the following command:

```
SELECT Ent_Date L_Name F_Name Company FROM Names +
+ > ORDER BY Ent_Date WHERE Ent_Date > = '6/01/90' +
+ > AND Ent_Date < = '6/30/90'
```

Now, suppose you want to send something to everyone who lives on the 2300 block, or higher, of Sixth Street. Piece of cake, right? The command is

```
SELECT ALL FROM Names WHERE Address > = '2300' +
+ > AND Address CONTAINS 'Sixth'
```

If you wanted to pull out all the people whose last names begin with the letters J through M, you could enter either

```
SELECT ALL FROM Names WHERE L_Name > = 'J' AND +
+ > L_Name < 'N'
```

or

```
SELECT ALL FROM Names WHERE L_Name BETWEEN 'J' +
+ > AND 'N'
```

The AND operator is good for locating specific information to edit. For example, suppose you need to change Marie Miller's address. You could enter the command

EDIT ALL FROM Names WHERE L_Name = 'Miller' AND +
+> F_Name = 'Marie'

This would display Marie's record on the Edit screen, as shown in Figure 5.19.

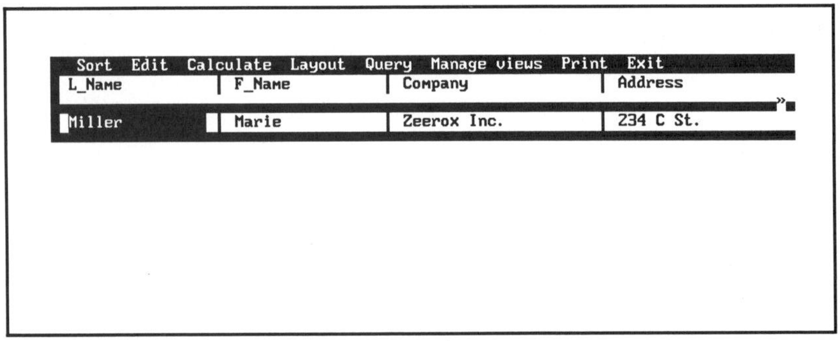

Figure 5.19: The Edit screen with only Marie Miller's record

Suppose you wanted to send something to both San Diego and Los Angeles residents. You could use the OR operator to perform both searches at once, as in the command below:

SELECT ALL FROM Names WHERE City = 'San Diego' OR +
+> City = 'Los Angeles'

Sometimes you have to think a little before performing a search. For example, had we used the command

SELECT ALL FROM Names WHERE City = 'San Diego' +
+> AND City = 'Los Angeles'

no rows would have been displayed, because it's impossible for a row to have both San Diego and Los Angeles in the City column at the same time.

Reversing the situation, the command

    SELECT ALL FROM Names WHERE City = 'San Diego' +
    + > AND State = 'CA'

displays all San Diego, California residents. However, the command

    SELECT ALL FROM Names WHERE City = 'San Diego' OR +
    + > State = 'CA'

displays all California residents, regardless of city, and all San Diego residents, regardless of state (which is probably not what you had in mind).

With the OR operator, only one of the searching criteria needs to be true for the command to display the data. Hence, the OR operator generally broadens the result of the search. The AND operator, however, requires that both criteria be met, which generally narrows the result of the search.

A common mistake that people make when performing AND and OR searches is attempting to use English syntax rather than R:BASE syntax. An example would be to use a command like

    SELECT ALL FROM Names WHERE Zip_Code > = '92000' +
    + > AND < = '92999'

> Be sure to use complete expressions on both sides of the AND and OR operators.

> An *operand* is a column or value acted on by an operator—the items to the left and right of an operator.

Reading that in English, it looks like you're trying to pull out all the ZIP codes between 92000 and 92999. However, that's not what it says to R:BASE. In R:BASE syntax, both criteria must be complete expressions. Zip_Code > = 92000 is a complete expression, but < = 92999 is not. The computer will wonder what < = 92999 means, and it will display an error message. To avoid problems, be sure to use complete expressions on both sides of the AND and OR operators, but this does not mean you can only use a single AND or OR. You can specify as many conditions as you wish, as long as you don't exceed R:BASE's command line limit: five thousand characters, a total of 402 items, or a total of 50 operators and operands! For example, the command

    SELECT ALL FROM Names WHERE City = 'San Diego' +
    + > AND State = 'CA' AND Ent_Date > = 06/01/90 AND +

```
+ > Ent_Date < = 06/30/90 AND L_Name > = 'G' AND +
+ > L_Name < 'Q'
```

is perfectly okay. You'll get San Diego, California, residents with entry dates in June whose last names begin with the letters G through P.

USING PARENTHESES IN WHERE CLAUSES

Sometimes, combining AND and OR conditions in a single WHERE clause can produce unexpected results. If you have both AND and OR conditions in the same command, R:BASE checks conditions connected with AND before checking conditions connected with OR. For example, if you give the command

```
SELECT Zip_Code L_Name F_Name FROM Names WHERE +
+ > Zip_Code > '92000' AND L_Name > = 'M' OR +
+ > F_Name > = 'M'
```

hoping to display all records in which the ZIP code is greater than 92000 and either the first or last name starts with the letter M or higher, you'll be disappointed. What you'll get are all instances where both the ZIP is greater than 92000 and the last name starts with M or higher, and then all other records in which the first name starts with M or higher, regardless of what the ZIP code is. In other words, R:BASE has interpreted the WHERE clause as follows:

[Zip_Code > '92000'   OR [F_Name > = 'M']
AND L_Name > = 'M']

[Both of these are true]   or [this is true]

To pull out the records you are looking for, you have to group your search criteria using parentheses. For example, you could enter

```
SELECT Zip_Code L_Name F_Name FROM Names WHERE +
+ > Zip_Code > '92000' AND (L_Name > = 'M' OR +
+ > F_Name > = 'M')
```

R:BASE would then interpret the WHERE clause as follows:

[Zip_Code > '92000'] AND [L_Name > = 'M' OR
                                                    F_Name > = 'M']

[This must be true]   and [either of these is true]

See "Selecting Specific Rows for Display" earlier in this chapter for information on the use of conditions with the Query command.

You have seen, on the Query screen, how to use parentheses in a Query command when more than two conditions are combined in the query. If you are not sure how R:BASE will interpret a query, put parentheses in the query to tell R:BASE precisely how you want the conditions to be grouped. If you add extra parentheses to be sure that the query will do what you intend, R:BASE will not give you an error message. For example, the above command could be written with extra parentheses without changing the meaning of the WHERE clause:

```
SELECT Zip_Code L_Name F_Name FROM Names WHERE +
+ > (Zip_Code > '92000') AND ((L_Name > = 'M') OR +
+ > (F_Name > = 'M'))
```

It may take you a few trial-and-error runs to get these more complex searches down. Be sure to check the results of a search visually if you are in doubt about the accuracy of your WHERE clause.

MAKING R:BASE SEARCH FOR UPPER- AND LOWERCASE LETTERS

R:BASE normally makes no distinction between uppercase and lowercase letters when searching a table. For example, the command

```
SELECT ALL FROM Names WHERE L_Name = 'miller'
```

will produce exactly the same results as the command

```
SELECT ALL FROM Names WHERE L_Name = 'Miller'
```

But perhaps you would like R:BASE to be *case-sensitive*. In other words, you would like the program to take into account uppercase and lowercase distinctions. If so, you can enter the command

SET CASE ON

at the R > prompt. With the CASE option on, the command

SELECT ALL FROM Names WHERE L_Name = 'MILLER'

would not display any data from the Names table, because you entered all the last names with only the first letter capitalized.

To return to "normal" searches, in which R:BASE ignores uppercase and lowercase distinctions, enter the command

SET CASE OFF

at the R > prompt.

You can check the current status of the CASE option from the R > prompt at any time by entering the command

SHOW

You'll see the current status of many other settings as well, which we'll discuss throughout the book.

COMPARING COLUMNS IN SEARCHES

You can also compare the contents of two columns to perform a search. For example, suppose you had a table that contained Gross Sales and Salary columns for salespeople. You might want to display all those individuals whose salaries are greater than their gross sales.

In our hypothetical Sales table, you could find all the individuals whose salaries were greater than their gross sales using the command

SELECT ALL FROM Sales WHERE Salary > G_Sales

Notice that G_Sales does not have single quotes around it. Because G_Sales is not enclosed in quotes, R:BASE knows that this must be a column in the Sales table. Any value, other than a number

R:BASE assumes that all values other than numbers or dates, if they don't have quote marks around them, are columns.

or a date, which does not have quotes around it is assumed to be a column. If you enter the command

SELECT ALL FROM Names WHERE L_Name = Miller

you will get an error telling you that Miller is not a column in the Names table. But you could use the command

SELECT ALL FROM Names WHERE Ent_Date > 6/10/90

R:BASE knows that Ent_Date is a DATE column so it is expecting the value for this condition to be a date. As well, a column can't be called "6/10/90" since the name of a column has to start with a letter. Similarly, if you had a Customers table with a numeric column called Num_Orders which had the number of orders a customer had placed, you could use the command

SELECT ALL FROM Customers WHERE Num_Orders > 5

to find all customers who had placed more than 5 orders.

To see how to compare two columns in the Names table, let's compare the contents of the F_Name and L_Name columns. The command

SELECT ALL FROM Names WHERE F_Name > = L_Name

will display all the individuals whose first names are alphabetically greater than or equal to their last names. The command

SELECT ALL FROM Names WHERE F_Name < = L_Name

will display those whose first names are alphabetically less than or equal to their last names.

Although these examples aren't particularly useful, comparing columns containing numeric, date, or time data can be very useful. For example, suppose you had a Credit table which contained the columns Climit and Currbal. You could find out which accounts had exceeded their credit limits by typing

SELECT ALL FROM Credit WHERE Climit < Currbal

Or perhaps you have a Rentals table with columns for Duedate and Returndate. To find items returned after they were due, you could type

SELECT ALL FROM Rentals WHERE Returndate > Duedate

When you enter a value which is not a date or a number on the Query screen, R:BASE automatically surrounds the value with single quotes ('). This makes it difficult to enter a condition on the Query screen that compares two columns, since this type of condition cannot have any single quotes in it. To compare two columns on the Query screen, you have to

1. Add a condition in which the second column name is entered as the comparison value.

2. Place the highlighter on the condition you just added and press ◄— to modify the condition.

3. Edit the condition to remove the single quotes and then press ◄—.

GLOBAL EDITS WITH THE WHERE CLAUSE

You've already learned how to use the WHERE clause to limit the amount of data displayed on the screen during the edits. The WHERE clause can also be used with the UPDATE and DELETE commands to perform *global edits*.

A global edit is one that is performed throughout the entire table (or database) with a single command. For example, suppose you have 5000 entries in the Names table. Eventually, you learn that in some cases the city Los Angeles is stored as L.A. and in other cases it is spelled out. This little inconsistency is causing you problems because you always need to include two options, such as

WHERE City = 'Los Angeles' OR City = 'L.A.'

in your WHERE clauses. The solution to this problem is to make them consistent.

You could go into the Edit screen and change each L.A. to Los Angeles by retyping it. Or you could perform a global edit to change all of them to Los Angeles with a single command. Obviously, the latter is more convenient.

The UPDATE command allows you to perform just this sort of global edit. The general syntax for the UPDATE command can be seen by typing

HELP UPDATE

at the R> prompt. The second help screen displays the syntax as shown in Figure 5.20.

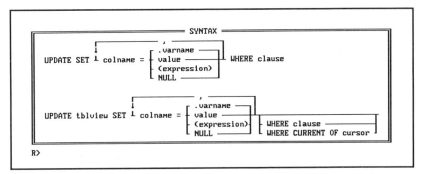

Figure 5.20: The help screen for the UPDATE command showing the command syntax

So, in a hypothetical table named MaiList, you might try to change each L.A. to Los Angeles by entering the command

UPDATE MaiList SET City = 'Los Angeles' WHERE City = 'L.A.'

You must be careful when using this command, though. It has a high "whoops" factor, which means that by the time you finish saying "whoops," the damage is done. For example, suppose you had entered the command

UPDATE MaiList SET City = 'Los Angeles' WHERE City > = 'L'

The greater than or equal to (> =) operator in this WHERE clause tells R:BASE to put Los Angeles in the City column of every row in the table that contains a city starting with the letter L through Z. If there were originally 500 cities that met this criterion, there would now be 500 Los Angeles cities in their place, whether they were originally Las Vegas, Madrid, or Seattle. The bad news is that you cannot reverse this command. You'd have to reenter all the cities through the Edit screen. So be careful!

For practice, you can safely try it out on the Names table. From the R> prompt, enter the command

UPDATE Names SET City = 'S.D.' WHERE City = 'San Diego'

R:BASE will display this message:

Columns have been updated in 2 row(s) in Names

If you then enter the command

SELECT City FROM Names

you'll see that all of the San Diego cities have been changed to S.D.

In this case, we can reverse the global edit by simply changing all S.D. data back to San Diego. Do so now by entering the command

UPDATE Names SET City = 'San Diego' WHERE City = 'S.D.'

If you view the City column again, you'll see that the name "San Diego" has returned.

You can also update several columns with one UPDATE command if you need to. For example, let's say that the Names table consists mainly of people who live in Los Angeles. To ease the burden of data entry, you entered LA instead of Los Angeles in the City column and left the State column empty, with only the null value (-0-) there. However, now you need to print mailing labels, and so you need to have both "Los Angeles" and "CA" spelled out in each record. Although you could use two separate UPDATE commands to do this, a single one would suffice:

UPDATE Names SET City = 'Los Angeles', State = 'CA' +
+> WHERE City = 'LA' AND State IS NULL

Also, remember that you can use column numbers instead of column names in R:BASE commands, as in

UPDATE Names SET #5 = 'Los Angeles', #6 = 'CA' +
+ > WHERE #5 = 'LA' AND #6 IS NULL

R:BASE would change both columns in any row that met the criteria specified by the WHERE clause—no matter which version of the command you used.

You can also globally delete rows from a table, but we won't try this with the Names table—we need those data for future experiments. The general syntax for global deletions is the following:

DELETE ROWS FROM table name WHERE condition(s)

Referring back to our hypothetical Sales table, which contains salespersons' salaries and gross sales, you could use the command

DELETE ROWS FROM Sales WHERE Salary > G_Sales

which would instantly eliminate all those whose salaries were greater than their gross sales. Assuming that five people met this unfortunate criterion (and fate), R:BASE would display the message

5 row(s) have been deleted from SALES

Remember, R:BASE actually puts the symbol -0- in empty columns, rather than leaving them blank. The -0- symbol is referred to as the null value.

If you ever wanted to delete all the rows from the Names table that did not contain either a last name or company value, you could use the command

DELETE ROWS FROM Names WHERE L_Name IS NULL AND +
+ > Company IS NULL

SELECT, DISTINCT, AND GROUP BY OPTIONS

The SELECT command includes two special options that are worth discussing at this point. The DISTINCT option allows you to filter out repetitious data, and the GROUP BY option is particularly useful in performing statistical calculations for groups of selected columns.

Let's look at the DISTINCT option first. On the first syntax screen for the SELECT command (see Figure 5.14), the DISTINCT option is placed right after the word SELECT. This option is useful when you do not want to see duplicates. For example, suppose in the sample Sales table you wanted to see which salespeople had made sales in the first three days of June. Assuming the Sales table had columns called Emp# (employee number), Transamt (transaction amount), and Trandate (transaction date), you could type

> SELECT Emp# FROM Sales ORDER BY Emp# WHERE +
> + > Trandate BETWEEN 6/1/90 AND 6/3/90

using R:BASE's traditional SELECT command. However, you'd have to wade through multiple sales for some of the salespeople, making the visual display less than ideal.

By using the DISTINCT option of the SELECT command, you would only have to type

> SELECT DISTINCT Emp# FROM Sales WHERE Trandate +
> + > BETWEEN 6/1/90 AND 6/3/90

You wouldn't have to include the ORDER BY clause, since SELECT DISTINCT automatically sorts for you. In the syntax diagram for the SELECT command, there is a down arrow which means that you can specify more than one column to be distinct. For example, if you wanted to see if your sales force each had at least one sale per day, you could modify the above command to include Trandate:

> SELECT DISTINCT Emp#, Trandate FROM Sales WHERE +
> + > Trandate BETWEEN 6/1/90 AND 6/3/90

In order to see a simple implementation of the command with the Mail database, you could type

> SELECT DISTINCT L_Name FROM Names

and see that Miller is only listed once.

The GROUP BY option for the SELECT command is extremely powerful when you need to perform statistical calculations on your data. To see the syntax of the GROUP BY option, type HELP

GROUP BY. This displays eight help screens, which review the SELECT command and then expand on the GROUP BY and related options. As in Figure 5.21, the third help screen shows the syntax of the GROUP BY option.

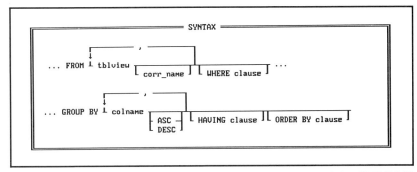

Figure 5.21: The syntax for the GROUP BY option of the SELECT command

Looking at our hypothetical Sales table, there are some interesting uses of the GROUP BY option. For example, suppose you wanted to see total sales by salesperson. You could type

SELECT Emp# SUM Transamt FROM Sales GROUP BY Emp#

The result would be a list of employees followed by their total sales. The GROUP BY option for the SELECT command, like the DISTINCT option, sorts automatically, but in this case based on the column or columns specified in the GROUP BY clause. The ability to generate ad hoc subtotals is a feature generally associated only with complex reports.

In this chapter, we've discussed many techniques for specifying search criteria with the WHERE clause. Because we are working with our small Names table, we could not experiment with the full range of search options. If we had more columns on our sample table, we could do more filtering. For example, had we included a Title column (for Mr., Ms., and so forth), we could have searched for all the doctors by using a

WHERE Title = 'Dr.'

clause. Or, had we included a Job Title (J_Title) column, we could have pulled out all the company presidents and vice presidents by using a

   WHERE J_Title CONTAINS 'Pres'

clause. In a Phone column, we could use a

   WHERE Phone CONTAINS '(415)'

clause to pull out everyone in the 415 area code. There seem to be no limitations to the types of searches that you can perform.

   In the next chapter, we'll discuss techniques for displaying information from an R:BASE table.

Chapter 6

Performing Calculations and Displaying Data

IN THIS CHAPTER, WE'LL DISCUSS SOME TECHNIQUES for displaying R:BASE data, including printing out information on a printer and storing it in a separate file. You'll also discover how to control various display characteristics, such as column widths, page lengths, colors, and date and time formats. Then we'll change gears. You'll set up another small database with some numeric information in it so you can experiment with some of the R:BASE commands that help you to analyze data. Finally, you'll take another look at R:BASE's operating system commands and learn how to back up your database.

To get started with the sample exercises in this chapter, run R:BASE in the usual fashion, open the Mail database, and then go to Command mode by highlighting Exit and selecting **R >** prompt.

DIRECTING OUTPUT TO THE PRINTER, THE SCREEN, OR A FILE

Output is information and data that the computer produces for your use. It might be displayed on the screen, printed by the printer, or transferred to a file stored on disk.

So far, we've displayed the results of all SELECT commands on the screen. The OUTPUT command allows you to print data on a printer or to save the data in a separate file that you can print later. Options for the OUTPUT command are the following:

OUTPUT SCREEN	Data are displayed on the screen.
OUTPUT PRINTER	Data are displayed on the printer.
OUTPUT *d:filename.ext*	Data are stored on a file. (*d:filename.ext* stands for any file name. The *d:* stands for a letter and colon specifying a disk drive.)

The WITH clause allows you to combine OUTPUT options. For example, the command OUTPUT SCREEN WITH PRINTER displays data on both the screen and printer. The command OUTPUT C:MyReport.txt WITH BOTH stores a copy of the output on a file named MyReport.txt on drive C, and also displays the data on both the screen and printer.

The general procedure for using the OUTPUT command is as follows (we'll provide exact instructions when you try some examples later):

1. Enter an OUTPUT command to direct the output to the printer, to a file, or to both the printer and a file.

2. Enter one or more commands to display information. The information will be directed to the places identified in the OUTPUT command you entered in step 1.

3. Enter an OUTPUT command canceling output to the printer or file and sending it instead to the screen only.

SENDING OUTPUT TO THE PRINTER

If you have a printer handy, you can try printing all the information in the Names table. At the R > prompt,

1. Type **OUTPUT SCREEN WITH PRINTER** and press ◄─┘.

2. Type **SELECT ALL FROM Names ORDER BY L_Name F_Name** and press ◄─┘. This command displays the first four columns of the table (all that will fit) on the screen and prints them as well.

3. Enter the command

   SELECT City State Zip_Code Ent_Date FROM Names +
   + > ORDER BY L_Name F_Name

   and press ◄─┘. This command displays the rest of the columns on the screen and prints them.

4. Type **NEWPAGE** and press ◄─┘ to eject the printed page and clear the screen. Figure 6.1 shows a printout of the Names table.

5. Type **OUTPUT SCREEN** to disconnect from the printer and return to normal screen display.

In this example, we used two SELECT commands to print the information because all eight columns would not fit on the screen or

If your printer doesn't print what you see on the screen, see the following section, "Solving Printer Problems."

```
L_Name            F_Name              Company             Address
---------------   ---------------     ----------------    -------------------
Adams             Bart                DataSpec Inc.       P.O. Box 2890
Baker             Robin               Peach Computers     2311 Coast Hwy.
Jones             Mindy               ABC Co.             123 A St.
Miller            Anne                Golden Gate Co.     2313 Sixth St.
Miller            Marie               Zeerox Inc.         234 C St.
Smith             Sandy               Hi Tech Inc.        456 N. Rainbow Dr.
City              State     Zip_Code  Ent_Date
---------------   --------  --------- --------
Malibu            CA        96523     06/15/90
San Diego         CA        92122     06/15/90
San Diego         CA        92122     06/01/90
Berkeley          CA        94711     06/01/90
Los Angeles       CA        91234     06/15/90
Berkeley          CA        94711     06/01/90
```

Figure 6.1: A printout of the Names table

printed page. Later on, you'll see how to reformat the columns and print them all with one SELECT command.

SOLVING PRINTER PROBLEMS

This is a good time to learn what to do if you have problems with your printer. One of the most common printer problems is that the output from the SELECT command appears on your screen but isn't printed. When this happens,

- make sure your printer is turned on.

- make sure you typed OUTPUT SCREEN WITH PRINTER correctly at the R > prompt.

- press the Print Screen key (labeled PrtSc on some keyboards). If what is on your screen still isn't printed, check the manual that came with your printer to make sure your printer is properly set up and connected to your computer.

Another common problem is that R:BASE displays only the first line of output on the screen. In this case,

- make sure the printer is not out of paper.

- make sure the printer is "on-line," or "selected." If you are in doubt, press the on-line (or select) button on the printer. Most printers have a light or display indicating whether they are on-line.

Of course, another common printer problem is that the printer prints gibberish. When this happens,

- Press the Print Screen key (labeled PrtSc on some keyboards). If your printer still doesn't print the material on your screen, check the manual that came with your printer to make sure it is properly set up and connected to your computer.

- Check Appendix A to make sure that R:BASE has been properly set up to print to your printer.

Perhaps none of these suggestions helps you solve your printing problem. If so, call a colleague or support person for help. R:BASE's support number is (206) 649-9551.

SENDING OUTPUT TO A FILE

Besides directing the output of R:BASE commands to the screen and printer, you can send the output to disk files. This has many uses. For example, placing your output in a file allows you to include R:BASE tables in word processed documents. Also, with your output placed in a file, you can use a *print spooler* (such as the DOS PRINT.COM program). A print spooler takes output intended for the printer and writes it temporarily in a file. Your output stays in the file until the printer is ready to print it. Meanwhile, because the output is being stored in a print spooler file and your computer does not have to deal with it, you can use your computer for other tasks; you don't have to wait until the file is done printing.

In this example, we'll store the Names table displayed on the screen in a file named MyReport.txt. From the R> prompt,

1. Type **OUTPUT MyReport.txt WITH SCREEN** and press ←⏎.

2. Type the command

    ```
    SELECT L_Name F_Name City Zip_Code FROM Names +
    + > ORDER BY L_Name F_Name
    ```

    and press ←⏎.

3. Type **OUTPUT SCREEN** and press ←⏎.

You can verify that the file exists by using the TYPE command at the R> prompt. Enter the command

TYPE MyReport.txt

and press ◄─┘. You'll see the contents of the MyReport.txt file on the screen, as shown in Figure 6.2.

```
R>OUTPUT MyReport.txt WITH SCREEN
R>SELECT L_Name F_Name City Zip_Code FROM Names ORDER BY +
+> L_Name F_Name
  L_Name            F_Name            City              Zip_Code
  ---------------   ---------------   ---------------   ---------
  Adams             Bart              Malibu            96523
  Baker             Robin             San Diego         92122
  Jones             Mindy             San Diego         92122
  Miller            Anne              Berkeley          94711
  Miller            Marie             Los Angeles       91234
  Smith             Sandy             Berkeley          94711
R>OUTPUT SCREEN
R>TYPE MyReport.txt
  L_Name            F_Name            City              Zip_Code
  ---------------   ---------------   ---------------   ---------
  Adams             Bart              Malibu            96523
  Baker             Robin             San Diego         92122
  Jones             Mindy             San Diego         92122
  Miller            Anne              Berkeley          94711
  Miller            Marie             Los Angeles       91234
  Smith             Sandy             Berkeley          94711
R>
```

Figure 6.2: The contents of the MyReport.txt file

When naming these text files with the OUTPUT command, you can specify a directory and pathname as well. For example, the command

OUTPUT C:\WP\MyReport.txt

stores output from subsequent commands to the MyReport.txt file in the WP directory on drive C.

SENDING OUTPUT FROM THE EDIT SCREEN

You can also obtain output from the table when it is displayed on the Edit screen. On the menu bar at the top of the Edit screen is an option called Print. You can use this option to print out data on the printer or save data in a text file. When you are printing from the Edit screen, you can choose which rows and columns you want printed by going to the Query screen first. In fact, unless you tell R:BASE which columns and rows to display on the Query screen, the Print option displays the entire table.

The general procedure to produce output from the Edit screen is to first decide whether you want to display all rows and columns. If you do, don't bother going to the Query screen. But if you want to display some columns, leave the check mark (✔) next to each column on the Query screen you want displayed and remove the check mark next to the other columns. Likewise, if you want to display some rows, enter conditions to indicate which rows you want displayed in the output. Next, select the Print option in the menu bar and tell R:BASE whether you want the output to go to the printer or to a file. If the output is going to a file, enter the name of the file to receive the output.

For this next exercise, let's prepare output with the first and last name, company and city of all of the people in our Names table who live in Berkeley. We'll both print this information and place it in a file. At the R> prompt, type **EDIT ALL FROM Names** (and press ◄┘) to display the Edit screen. Then follow these steps to output this information using the Edit screen:

Remember that you can use the mouse to select items from the menu and to move the highlighter.

1. Press **Ctrl-F3** to go to the Query screen.

2. Press **Tab** three times to move to the Address column; and press **F6** to remove the check mark from the Address column.

3. Press **Tab** twice to move to the State column; and press **F6** to remove the check mark from the State column.

4. Press **Tab** to move to the Zip_Code column; and press **F6** to remove the check mark from the Zip_Code column.

5. Press **Tab** to move to the Ent_Date column; and press **F6** to remove the check mark from the Ent_Date column.

6. Press **Back-Tab** (hold down the **Shift** key and press **Tab**) three times to move to the City column; press ◄┘ to enter a condition; press ◄┘ to select = EQUAL; type **Berkeley** and press ◄┘.

On the Query screen, when you select one of the options in the pull-down menu under Print, the Edit screen is automatically displayed with the results of the query.

If you have trouble getting your printer to work, see "Solving Printer Problems."

7. Highlight **P**rint on the menu.

8. Select **P**rint on the pull-down menu (if you have a printer available) to print the output.

   a. If you printed the output on your printer, highlight **P**rint again on the menu.

9. Select **C**reate text file on the pull-down menu. At the "Enter output file name" prompt, type **MyReport.txt** and press ←.

10. Since you created the file MyReport.txt in a previous exercise, R:BASE tells you that this file exists and asks you if you want to overwrite it. Select **Y**es and press ←.

If you chose Print in step 8 above, you will be able to see your output. It should look like Figure 6.3.

```
L_Name            F_Name            Company               City
--------------    --------------    --------------------  ---------------
Miller            Anne              Golden Gate Co.       Berkeley
Smith             Sandy             Hi Tech Inc.          Berkeley
```

Figure 6.3: A printout with the name and company of Names table Berkeley residents

As before, let's use the R:BASE TYPE command to verify that the MyReport.txt file has this same data. Highlight and select **E**xit on the menu to leave the Edit screen. Next, enter the command

TYPE MyReport.txt

and press ←. Your screen should display the same information as Figure 6.3.

Changes you make to the Edit screen with the Layout menu option are not sent to the printer. To change the layout of table printouts, you must specify the changes on the Query screen.

You saw in Chapter 3 that you can use the Layout menu option to hide columns and move columns around. You might think that this would be a convenient way to customize the appearance of a table for printing. Unfortunately, changes to the appearance of the Edit screen made with the Layout menu option will *not* appear in printouts when you use the Print menu option to send output to the printer or to a file. Only changes made using the Query screen will be reflected in your printouts.

In the next section, you will see more ways to control the format of information to the printer or to a file with the OUTPUT command.

CONTROLLING TABLE DISPLAY CHARACTERISTICS

R:BASE SELECT commands for preparing information for printing or for placing it in a file have many uses. For example, you might want to change the length and width of each page. This way, your tables will fit the size of paper you are using and fulfill the requirements for placing the information in a file. To control page length and width, you use the SET WIDTH and SET LINES commands or the R:BASE Settings menu. You can also control the width of individual columns with the SELECT command.

CONTROLLING PAGE LENGTH

When displaying large tables, R:BASE will pause after printing 20 lines of text in order to accommodate a typical screen display. If you are sending a SELECT command to the printer, you'll see a new *header line*—which defines the columns being displayed—printed every 20 lines. You can change this 20-line setting in either of two ways: by issuing the SET LINES command when you are in Command mode or by using the R:BASE Settings menu, which is displayed with the SET command.

To see how page length works in R:BASE, let's issue a SET LINES command to change the page length to five lines. With a five-line page length, R:BASE will start a new page after printing five lines. At the R > prompt, follow these steps to change the page length:

1. Type **SET LINES 5** and press ←.

2. Type **OUTPUT MyReport.txt WITH SCREEN** and press ←.

3. Type **SELECT L_Name F_Name FROM Names** and press ←.

4. When the message "More output follows. Press Esc to quit, any key to continue" appears, press ←.

5. Type **OUTPUT SCREEN** and press ←.

6. Type **SET LINES 20** and press ←.

7. Type **TYPE MyReport.txt** and press ←.

Your screen should look like Figure 6.4. Notice the header line appearing every five lines.

```
    L_Name           F_Name
    ---------------  ---------------
    Miller           Anne
    Adams            Bart
    Miller           Marie
More output follows.  Press Esc to quit, any key to continue.
    L_Name           F_Name
    ---------------  ---------------
    Jones            Mindy
    Smith            Sandy
    Baker            Robin
R>OUTPUT SCREEN
R>SET LINES 20
R>TYPE MyReport.txt
    L_Name           F_Name
    ---------------  ---------------
    Miller           Anne
    Adams            Bart
    Miller           Marie
    L_Name           F_Name
    ---------------  ---------------
    Jones            Mindy
    Smith            Sandy
    Baker            Robin
R>
```

Figure 6.4: Changing the page length with the SET LINES command

The standard 8½-by-11-inch sheet of paper holds 66 lines of text per page. Because tables look better when they fill out the printed page, it is a good idea to print a new header line every 66 lines. For our next exercise, let's use the R:BASE Settings menu to change the page length to 66 lines.

1. Type **SET** and press ← to display the Settings menu.

2. With **C**onfiguration highlighted, select **L**ines. Notice the current page length of 20 displayed beside the "Current" prompt.

You access the Settings menu from the Main menu by highlighting Tools and selecting Settings. This method of accessing the Settings menu is explained in the next section of this chapter.

3. Type **66** beside the "Set to" prompt. Take a look at your screen—it should look like Figure 6.5.

4. Press ◄—⌐.

5. Select **Exit** to leave the Settings menu.

If the Names table had more than 66 rows, we could print it using OUTPUT and SELECT commands and the headings would appear only once at the top of each page.

Figure 6.5: Changing the page length with the Settings menu

CONTROLLING PAGE WIDTH

R:BASE normally displays as much data from each row as will fit in 79 characters. You can change this to a maximum of 256 or a minimum of 40 characters using the SET WIDTH command. For example, if your printer accepts wide paper, the command (entered at the R > prompt) SET WIDTH 132 will take advantage of the full paper width.

Let's see what happens when we set the width to 132 characters and display the data in the Names table with a SELECT command.

1. Type **SET WIDTH 132** and press ←┘.

2. Type **SELECT ALL FROM Names** and press ←┘.

Notice that setting the width to 132 characters causes each row to wrap around the screen, as in Figure 6.6.

```
R>SET WIDTH 132
R>SELECT ALL FROM Names
 L_Name           F_Name            Company               Address
 City             State   Zip_Code  Ent_Date
 ----------------  --------  ----------  --------  --------------------------
 ----------------  --------  ----------  --------
 Miller           Anne              Golden Gate Co.       2313 Sixth St.
 Berkeley         CA      94711       06/01/90
 Adams            Bart              Dataspec Inc.         P.O. Box 2890
 Malibu           CA      96523       06/15/90
 Miller           Marie             Zeerox Inc.           234 C St.
 Los Angeles      CA      91234       06/15/90
 Jones            Mindy             ABC Co.               123 A St.
 San Diego        CA      92122       06/01/90
 Smith            Sandy             Hi Tech Inc.          456 N. Rainbow Dr.
 Berkeley         CA      94711       06/01/90
 Baker            Robin             Peach Computers       2311 Coast Hwy.
 San Diego        CA      92122       06/15/90
 R>
```

Figure 6.6: A screen display of the Names table with 132-character width

Many dot-matrix printers come with a compressed print option. This option allows you to print more columns across the page. In fact, you will have to put your printer into Compressed Print mode in order to take advantage of a command such as SET WIDTH 132 if you are using narrow (8½-inch wide) paper or SET WIDTH 240 if you are using wide (14-inch) paper.

The SET WIDTH command will also affect displays stored on files. For example, to store the Names table in a file with each row fitting on one line, you would issue a command like SET WIDTH 132.

You can also change the page width from the Settings menu. Let's use the Settings menu to change the page width back to 79 characters. However, this time we'll access the Settings menu from the

Main menu. Return to the Main menu with the MENU command and try the following steps:

1. Highlight **T**ools and select **S**ettings.
2. With **C**onfiguration highlighted, select **W**idth. Notice that the current page width of 132 is displayed beside the "Current" prompt.
3. Type **79** beside the "Set to" prompt, press **Del** to erase the 2, and press ◄━┘.
4. Highlight and select **E**xit to return to the Main menu.

CONTROLLING COLUMN WIDTHS

Figure 5.14 in the last chapter shows the syntax diagram of the SELECT command.

As you saw in Chapter 5, you can specify the widths of individual columns by using the SELECT command, followed by the column name, an equal sign (=), and the number of spaces that you want in the column. You may want to review the syntax diagram for the SELECT command by typing HELP SELECT at the R > prompt. Controlling column width with the SELECT command is very useful when you are trying to fit a lot of information onto a printed page. To review this feature, return to Command mode by highlighting **E**xit and selecting **R** > prompt. Now enter the following command:

```
SELECT L_Name = 9 F_Name = 9 Company = 10 Address = 12  +
+> City = 12 State = 2 Zip_Code = 5 Ent_Date = 8 FROM Names  +
+> SORTED BY L_Name F_Name
```

Be sure to press ◄━┘ when you're done. Your screen should look like Figure 6.7. Note how R:BASE fits all the columns onto an 80-column screen (or an 8½-inch wide page) by using more vertical space.

COLOR DISPLAYS

If you have a mono-chrome monitor, you can't display the color palette to change screen colors. In Chapters 13 and 15, you'll see how to set colors for custom forms and custom menus.

If you have a color monitor, you can use the SET COLOR command to establish any combination of colors on the screen that you wish. Let's experiment with screen colors. At the R > prompt, type **SET COLOR** and press ◄━┘. Your screen will display a palette of options for both foreground and background colors. Use the arrow

```
R>SELECT L_Name=9 F_Name=9 Company=10 Address=12 +
+> City=12 State=2 Zip_Code=5 Ent_Date=8 FROM Names +
+> SORTED BY L_Name F_Name
   L_Name    F_Name    Company    Address       City          St Zip_C Ent_Date
   --------- --------- ---------- ------------- ------------- -- ----- --------
 - Adams     Bart      DataSpec   P.O. Box      Malibu        CA 96523 06/15/90
                       Inc.       2890
   Baker     Robin     Peach      2311 Coast    San Diego     CA 92122 06/15/90
                       Computers  Hwy.
   Jones     Mindy     ABC Co.    123 A St.     San Diego     CA 92122 06/01/90
   Miller    Anne      Golden     2313 Sixth    Berkeley      CA 94711 06/01/90
                       Gate Co.   St.
   Miller    Marie     Zeerox     234 C St.     Los Angeles   CA 91234 06/15/90
                       Inc.
   Smith     Sandy     Hi Tech    456 N.        Berkeley      CA 94711 06/01/90
                       Inc.       Rainbow Dr.
   R>
```

Figure 6.7: The Names table displayed with column widths specified

keys (the mouse doesn't work on this screen) to move the cursor to the color that you want for the foreground, and then press ◄┘ to choose that color. Notice that the foreground parts of the screen, the text and the boxes around the colors, change to the color you have chosen. Press the → key to move to the background color options, move the cursor to the color that you want, and press ◄┘ again. This time, the background areas of the screen change to the background color you chose. You can experiment with the foreground and background colors until the screen has the colors you want. Once you find colors you like, activate these colors by pressing F2. You'll be returned to the R> prompt, and the colors that you selected will remain in effect for the duration of the session. If you decide that you don't want to change the colors, press the Esc key. You will see the R> prompt and the colors on your screen will be the ones you had before you looked at the color selection screen.

Of course, you can also set the screen colors from the Settings menu. With the Settings menu displayed, highlight Configuration, select Change colors, and simply choose your screen colors.

CLEARING THE SCREEN

To clear existing data from the screen, type either the CLS command or the NEWPAGE command after the R > prompt, and press ←. Note that this only erases the screen display and has no effect on information in the database.

DATE DISPLAYS

R:BASE typically displays the date in MM/DD/YY format. You can alter the format of date displays using the SET DATE command and any of the options below:

MM	Displays the month as a number, 01 through 12
MMM	Displays the month as a three-letter abbreviation, Jan through Dec
MMM +	Displays the month spelled out, January through December
DD	Displays the day as a number, 01 through 31
WWW	Displays the day of the week as a three-letter abbreviation, Sun through Sat
WWW +	Displays the day of the week spelled out, Sunday through Saturday
YY	Displays the year as a two-digit number, 91
YYYY	Displays the year as a four-digit number, 1991
CC	Allows dates for the B.C. range to be entered

You can also use other characters, such as commas and colons, in dates. When setting a date format, enter the command SET DATE FORMAT followed by the appropriate format in single quotes ('). As an example, let's set the date format to display dates in 'February 01, 1991' format. At the R > prompt, follow these steps:

1. Type **SET DATE FORMAT 'MMM + DD, YYYY'** and press ←.

2. Type **SELECT Ent_Date FROM Names** and press ←.

Figure 6.8 shows the results, with dates listed in MMM + DD, YYYY format. Examples of other formats are listed below:

FORMAT	*EXAMPLE*
WWW: MMM DD, YYYY	Fri: Feb 01, 1991
MMM + DD YYYY (WWW +)	February 01 1991 (Friday)
MM/YY	02/91
YY-MMM-DD	91-Feb-01
MMM + DD	February 01

```
R>SET DATE FORMAT 'MMM+ DD, YYYY'
R>SELECT Ent_Date FROM Names
 Ent_Date
 -------------------
 June 01, 1990
 June 15, 1990
 June 15, 1990
 June 01, 1990
 June 01, 1990
 June 15, 1990
R>
```

Figure 6.8: Names table dates displayed in MMM + DD, YYYY format

You can specify the sequence in which the month, day, and year of dates will be entered by using the command SET DATE SEQUENCE. For example, entering the commands

    SET DATE SEQUENCE 'MMDDYY'
    SET DATE FORMAT 'YY-MMM-DD'

allows you to enter dates in MM/DD/YY sequence, but displays them in 91-Feb-01 format.

When entering two-digit year dates (YY) into a database, R:BASE assumes that you mean this century. For example, if you use YY for the year in the SET DATE sequence, and you enter 90 as the year, R:BASE assumes that you mean 1990. To enter dates in other centuries, use a four-digit format (YYYY) in the SET DATE

SEQUENCE command and in the entered date as well. For example, you could enter the command

SET DATE SEQUENCE 'MM/DD/YYYY'

and then enter the date

6/1/1842

However, if you have a date sequence with YYYY, then you have to enter all four digits of the year. With the date sequence set to MM/DD/YYYY, if you enter a date as 6/1/91, R:BASE will think you mean June 1 of the year 91 A.D.!

If you need to use B.C. dates, include CC in the date format, as in the following command:

SET DATE SEQUENCE 'MM/DD/YYYY CC'

To enter a B.C. date, add the letters BC to your entry; for example,

6/1/3000 BC

To enter an A.D. date into a database field, just enter the date without any letters, as follows:

6/1/1990

If you use a date sequence with YYYY in order to enter dates such as 06/03/1891, then you must make sure that the date format also has YYYY. Without the four-digit year date, no one will know which century your are referring to. For example, suppose you had set the date sequence and format with the following commands:

SET DATE SEQUENCE 'MMDDYYYY'
SET DATE FORMAT 'MMM + DD/YY'

If you entered the date 06/03/1891, it would be stored in the database as June 3, 1891 but it would be displayed as June 3/91—in other words, as June 3, 1991. In this example, the date format could be set to 'MMM + DD, YYYY', which would cause the full year to be displayed.

An easy way to make sure that dates displayed will match the dates that are entered is to set the date sequence and format to equivalent values. For example, suppose you set the date sequence and format as

SET DATE FORMAT 'WWW + : MMM + DD, YYYY'
SET DATE SEQUENCE 'MMDDYY'

This way, you would not have to enter the weekday and month spelled out or the comma before the year. You can enter the date in any format you wish as long as the order of month, day, and year matches the order in the date sequence. (The weekday is always calculated automatically from the date, so you never need to type it in yourself.) You could enter dates into a date field using any of the formats below, since each follows the same sequence of month, day, and year.

Feb 1 1991
2/1/1991
2-1-1991
February 01, 1991

A variation of the SET DATE command allows you to set the date format and sequence to equivalent values in one command. Although this feature is not mentioned in the manuals, you can type SET DATE *value*, where *value* is the format and sequence you want to use. For example, you could type the command

SET DATE 'WWW+: MMM+ DD, YYYY'

to set both the date format to the value 'WWW + : MMM + DD, YYYY', and the date sequence to 'MMDDYYYY'.

You can also change the way dates are entered and displayed from the Settings menu. From the Settings menu, you don't have to include single quote marks (') when you are typing in the format or sequence. Let's try using the Settings menu to change the date input sequence to MMDDYY and the date output format to MM/DD/YY. First, bring up the Settings menu by typing **SET** and pressing ◄┘. Then, follow these steps to change the date format and sequence:

1. Highlight **F**ormat.

2. Select the **D**ate output format option.

3. Beside the "Set to" prompt, type **MM/DD/YY** and press ←.

4. With Format still highlighted, select the **D**ate input sequence option.

5. Beside the "Set to" prompt, type **MMDDYY** and press ←.

6. Leave the Settings menu and return to Command mode by highlighting and selecting **E**xit.

TIME FORMATS

Even though we did not include a column with the TIME data type in this database, now is a good time to discuss R:BASE time formats, since they follow the same basic style as date formats. The command to define the sequence of hours, minutes, and seconds for entering times into a database is SET TIME SEQUENCE followed by the sequence of characters. The command for displaying times is SET TIME FORMAT followed by the time format. Use the commands below to enter and display times in HH:MM:SS AM/PM format:

```
SET TIME SEQUENCE 'HHMMSS AP'
SET TIME FORMAT 'HH:MM:SS AP'
```

The symbols to use in time formats are listed below:

HH   Hours as a two-digit number, 01 through 24

MM   Minutes as a two-digit number, 00 through 60

SS   Seconds as a two-digit number, 00 through 60

AP   A.M. *or* P.M. displayed

If you do not set your own time format, R:BASE uses the format HH:MM:SS, wherein the time is displayed on a 24-hour clock in the format HH:MM:SS. For example, 2:30 in the afternoon is displayed as 14:30:00. Examples of the time 2:30:15 P.M. displayed in several different formats are listed below:

HH:MM:SS	14:30:15
HH:MM:SS AP	2:30:15 PM
HH:MM AP	2:30 PM
SS Seconds	15 Seconds

Similar to the date sequence, the time input sequence only determines the order of the hours, minutes and seconds.

As you would expect, you can also change the time format, output format or input sequence from the Settings menu. Simply highlight Format, select either the Time output format option or the Time input sequence option, and type in the new format. Be sure to press ◄─┘ when you're finished.

VIEWING SETTINGS

As you saw in Chapter 5, you can use the SHOW command to get a quick review of various settings you've established for your database, including the CASE setting. Let's review this command. At the R > prompt, enter the command **SHOW** and press ◄─┘. You will find the settings for the date and time as well as the page length and width on the first screen displayed. Later we'll discuss some of the additional settings displayed. When you are finished looking at the first screen, you can press ◄─┘ twice or press Esc to return to the R > prompt.

ZIPPING IN AND OUT OF R:BASE

Changing the R:BASE environment settings gives you a great deal of flexibility in working with your database, as you have just seen. The ZIP command provides you with yet another tool, allowing you to run external programs without really leaving R:BASE.

For example, let's assume that you have just completed some major data entry and want to back up your database onto a floppy disk. However, you don't have any formatted disks ready to receive the database files (we'll find out more about the DOS files that make up each database later in this chapter). What can you do? One approach would be to leave R:BASE, enter the subdirectory on your hard disk that contains the DOS commands, and format a floppy disk. Then you could use another DOS command to copy the database files from the \RBFILES\LEARN subdirectory onto the floppy. If you wanted to continue working in R:BASE, you'd have to start R:BASE all over again.

Another possibility would be to use R:BASE's ZIP command by typing

ZIP *directory name*\FORMAT A:

and pressing ◄┘. Here, *directory name* is the name of the subdirectory that contains your DOS programs. You could execute the FORMAT command and return automatically to the R> prompt where you left off.

Find out how much memory is available to your computer at any given time by typing CHKDSK at the R> prompt.

There are some limitations to the use of the ZIP command. Your system has to have enough available memory to run the external program you want to use. Similarly, you shouldn't run memory-resident programs using the ZIP command, because they may overwrite part of the R:BASE program in your system's RAM. You can, however, use most memory-resident programs with R:BASE simply by running them before you start R:BASE.

You'll learn how to create command files with RBEDIT in Chapter 16. You can access the RBEDIT program from the R:BASE Main menu by entering the RBEDIT command at the R> prompt, or by entering RBEDIT as a DOS command.

What if you want to run a longer program from within R:BASE? You can do that, too, by using an alternative form of the ZIP command: ZIP ROLLOUT. R:BASE comes with a program called RBEDIT that you can use to create command files. If you type

ZIP RBEDIT

R:BASE will tell you the program is too big to fit in memory. However, if you type

ZIP ROLLOUT RBEDIT

RBEDIT will probably run. If you are following along with this example, select **E**xit from the RDEBIT menu file to return to R:BASE. If you need to run a program via its batch file, you'll have to modify the ZIP command by adding COMMAND /C and then change directories before you can do so. For example, to run WP.BAT in your root directory to start your word processing program, you would type

```
CHDIR \
ZIP ROLLOUT COMMAND /C WP
```

Don't forget to change back to the RBFILES\LEARN subdirectory when you return to R:BASE.

If you wanted to run several DOS programs in a row, you could use the command

```
ZIP ROLLOUT COMMAND
```

This leaves you at the DOS prompt, where you can run as many programs as you like. Of course, any programs you run must still fit in the memory available. To return to R:BASE at the point where you left off, you have to type the command

```
EXIT
```

and press ←⎯. As mentioned above, if you have changed the default directory, change it back to RBFILES\LEARN so that R:BASE can find all your files.

An option on the R:BASE Main menu provides the same function as the command ZIP ROLLOUT COMMAND. On the Main menu, highlight Tools and select Access to DOS. To return to the R:BASE Main menu, type **EXIT** and press ←⎯.

LETTING R:BASE DO YOUR MATH FOR YOU

In order to begin exploring some of R:BASE's mathematical capabilities, we need to create a new database with numeric data in it. Imagine that you're the sales manager of a car dealership. Naturally, you want to keep track of sales, not only for given time periods, but also by salesperson. You decide to set up a simple database called

"Sales" containing a table called "CSales". CSales (for car sales) contains the following columns:

NAME	DESCRIPTION	TYPE	LENGTH
SName	Salesperson's Name	TEXT	10
SDate	Sale Date	DATE	
Amount		CURRENCY	

See if you can remember how to create a new database. Follow the steps below to create the Sales database and the CSales table, and to define the SName column.

1. Type **MENU** and press ◄── to return to the R:BASE Main menu.

2. Highlight **D**atabases.

3. Select **C**reate/modify.

4. With **C**reate highlighted, select **N**ew database.

5. When prompted for the database name, type **SALES** and press ◄──.

6. With **T**ables highlighted, select **C**reate.

7. Type **CSales** and press ◄── to fill in the table name.

8. Type **Car Sales** and press ◄── when asked to provide the description.

9. Type **SName** and press ◄──.

10. Type **Salesperson's Name** and press ◄──.

11. Select **TEXT**.

12. Type **10** and press ◄──.

13. Select **N**o for indexing.

Now fill in the rest of the column specifications as you did in Chapter 2. When you finish, your screen will look like Figure 6.9.

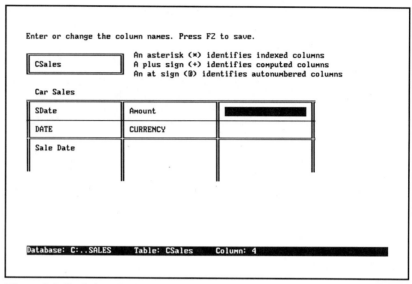

Figure 6.9: Defining the Sales database

Once you've defined the CSales table, press **F2** once and then highlight and select **E**xit twice to return to the R:BASE Main menu. Now we are going to add the following data to the table:

Smith	6/4/90	14350
Jones	6/4/90	6349
Smith	6/4/90	8999
Smith	6/5/90	21000
Jones	6/5/90	24999

Using the techniques you learned in Chapter 3, follow these steps to prepare to enter this data:

1. Highlight **I**nfo.

2. Select **C**Sales.

3. Select **Y**es when asked if you want to add an empty row.

4. Press **F10** four times to add four more empty rows to the table.

You do not have to enter dollar signs or commas in the Amount column—it has been assigned the CURRENCY data type. Amounts will be displayed automatically in dollar-and-cents format, with commas as appropriate.

Now enter the data listed above. When you have entered all the data, highlight and select **E**xit to return to the R:BASE Main menu. Let's examine our data by listing a SELECT command:

1. Highlight **E**xit and select **R** > prompt to go into Command mode.

2. Type the command **SELECT ALL FROM CSales** and press ←.

CALCULATING SUMS WITH THE SELECT COMMAND

Let's say you want to know what total sales are. To do this, you'll need to enter the following command from the R > prompt:

    SELECT ALL = S FROM CSales

and press ←. R:BASE displays the same data as before, but this time with the total sales ($75,697.00) displayed at the bottom of the list under the Amount column data. The = S tells R:BASE to calculate the sum of the data for you. If CSales had additional numeric columns, their sums would also be displayed.

There are situations where a table has several numeric columns, but you are only interested in seeing totals for some of them. In that case, you can use the SELECT command in the form

    SELECT SName Amount = S FROM CSales

specifying = S only for the columns where sums are desired.

You can, of course, use ORDER BY and WHERE clauses to ask more specific questions. If you only wanted to know total sales for June 4th, you could type

    SELECT ALL = S FROM CSales WHERE SDate = '6/4/90'

PERFORMING COMPLEX CALCULATIONS

Totals are extremely useful, but what about other calculations? Maybe you want to find an average or the largest sale in a given period. For cases like these, R:BASE provides the COMPUTE command. For a quick introduction to the COMPUTE command, let's try out a simple version of this command which is available on the Edit screen menu.

Follow these steps to see a demonstration of the COMPUTE function on the Edit screen:

1. From the R> prompt, type **EDIT ALL FROM CSales** and press ◄━━┘. This brings up the Edit screen for the CSales table.

2. Highlight **C**alculate.

3. Select **C**ompute from the pull-down menu.

4. Select **A**mount from the submenu.

R:BASE performs the requested calculations on the Amount column, and displays a screen like the one in Figure 6.10.

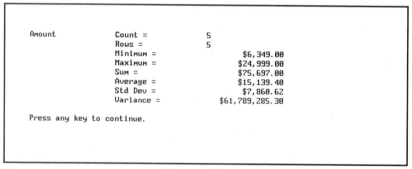

Figure 6.10: Calculations available with the COMPUTE menu option on the Edit screen

You may wonder about some of the items on your screen. Why does R:BASE bother to distinguish between COUNT and ROWS, for example? If you had null entries for the Amount column in some of your rows, ROWS would be a larger number than COUNT, since COUNT only reports the number of entries that are not null. R:BASE's calculations of average, maximum, and minimum sales amounts are straightforward; and notice that a sum is provided here as well. Furthermore, if you need to know about standard deviations and variances, R:BASE provides them quickly and easily.

PERFORMING CALCULATIONS WITH THE COMPUTE COMMAND

You can request the same calculations in Command mode that we just saw on the Edit screen. Press any key to leave the calculation results and return to the Edit screen. Now return to Command mode by highlighting and selecting the **E**xit option. To see the same information that you saw on the Edit screen, type

COMPUTE ALL Amount FROM CSales

and press ◄─┘.

The COMPUTE command is more flexible than its Edit screen counterpart in that you can choose to display only one of the eight calculations that the COMPUTE command on the Edit screen displays. To display just one calculation, replace the word ALL with the name of the calculation. For example, type the following command to display the maximum amount in the CSales table:

COMPUTE MAXIMUM Amount FROM CSales

The following command would display the sum of the values in the Amount column:

COMPUTE SUM Amount FROM CSales

To perform just one calculation with the COMPUTE command, you follow the the word COMPUTE with the name of one of the eight *calculations* available—COUNT, ROWS, MINIMUM, MAXIMUM, SUM, AVERAGE, STDEV, or VARIANCE. However, there are a couple of oddities to note when formulating COMPUTE commands. Although the command COMPUTE AVERAGE seems to work just fine to compute the average of a column, the R:BASE documentation suggests that you use the command COMPUTE AVG instead. For example, to compute the average of the values in the Amount column, you would either enter the command

COMPUTE AVERAGE Amount FROM CSales

or the command

COMPUTE AVG Amount FROM CSales

Another oddity has to do with the COMPUTE STDEV command, which is used to calculate standard deviation. To compute the standard deviation of the Amount column in the CSales table, you would use the following command:

COMPUTE STDEV Amount FROM CSales

Notice, in Figure 6.10, that STDEV is listed as STD DEV instead.

USING THE TALLY COMMAND

Let's say you want to know how many sales each of your salespeople has made. One way to do that would be to issue the SELECT command many times, each time limiting it to an individual salesperson, and then physically count the number of rows on the screen (or screens). Clearly, this would not be feasible if you had a large database. Another way would be to use R:BASE's COMPUTE command, as in

COMPUTE COUNT SName FROM CSales WHERE +
+ > SName = 'Smith'

for each salesperson. This would save you the chore of manually counting the rows on the screen, but you would still have to enter the command for each salesperson.

Fortunately, we can turn to the TALLY command. As you have seen with other commands, TALLY is accessible either from the Edit screen (by highlighting Calculate on the menu and selecting Tally in the pull-down menu) or directly from the R > prompt. Let's see how the TALLY command could be used in our example. At the R > prompt, type the command

TALLY SName FROM CSales

and press ◄┘. R:BASE responds with the information you wanted: Smith has made three sales, while Jones has made only two. If you substitute SDate for SName, you'll see how many sales were made on each day.

The TALLY command counts the occurrences of identical data for the column you specify. For example, if you tally CSales by Amount, you'll see that there's only one occurrence of each amount—in other words, no two sales were for the exact same amount. TALLY is extremely useful when you have a table containing items that all have unique identification codes of some type. If you have a table with invoices, for example, no two rows should have the same invoice number. Using the TALLY command, you can quickly verify that each invoice number is unique.

USING CROSSTAB FOR COMPLEX SEARCHES AND CALCULATIONS

CROSSTAB is another R:BASE command that lets you do sophisticated data analysis. CROSSTAB is used primarily to find unique pairs of values from two columns, but you can also have calculations done on the columns you specify. Let's experiment. Say you want to cross-tabulate salespeople with sales dates. First, type the command

CROSSTAB SName BY SDate FROM CSales

and you will see the number of rows which match each date-person combination. For another example of this command, type

CROSSTAB SDate BY SName FROM CSales

and you see that you have some control over how the results are displayed. The values from the first column you list will be displayed horizontally along the top of the screen. Note that CROSSTAB automatically sorts your data in ascending order.

If you're less interested in tabulations than in sums or averages, you can modify the command using a variation of the command's syntax. For example, if you type

CROSSTAB SUM Amount BY SName FROM CSales

you'll see a table that displays total sales by salesperson.

One further variation on the above command would be to ask R:BASE to display the sum of the daily sales for each salesperson. You could do that by entering

CROSSTAB SUM Amount FOR SName BY SDate FROM CSales

The results, shown in Figure 6.11, give a clear picture of daily sales activity.

The CROSSTAB function is also available on the Edit screen in the pull-down menu under the Calculate option. Let's try out this feature.

1. Type **EDIT ALL FROM CSales** and press ← to bring up the Edit screen for the CSales table.

```
R>CROSSTAB SUM Amount FOR SName BY SDate FROM CSales
SDate    ¦ Jones           Smith           (Total)
-------- ¦ --------------- --------------- ---------------
06/04/90 ¦      $6,349.00     $23,349.00      $29,698.00
06/05/90 ¦     $24,999.00     $21,000.00      $45,999.00
-------- ¦ --------------- --------------- ---------------
         ¦     $31,348.00     $44,349.00      $75,697.00
R>       ¦
```

Figure 6.11: Total daily sales by salesperson, displayed with CROSSTAB

2. Highlight Calculate.

3. Select Crosstab.

4. Select SName as the column to display horizontally across the top of the table of results.

5. Select SDate as the column to display vertically down the left side of the table of results.

6. Select SUM as the calculation to perform for each entry in the results table.

7. Move the highlighter down to Amount. Your screen should look like Figure 6.12. Now press ← (or select Amount with your mouse) to display the table of results, which should look very similar to Figure 6.11.

8. Press any key to return to the Edit screen.

9. Highlight and select Exit to return to Command mode.

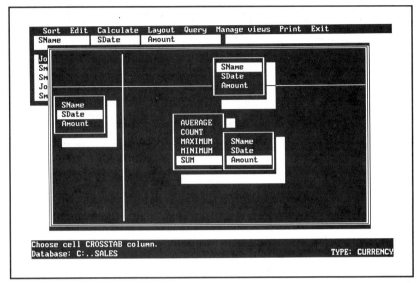

Figure 6.12: Calculating total daily sales by salesperson on the Edit screen

Before we leave the subject of data analysis, you may want to experiment with the GROUP BY option of the SELECT command, which was discussed in Chapter 5. The small database presented here gives you a better base for exploration than the Mail database did.

EXECUTING OPERATING SYSTEM COMMANDS DIRECTLY FROM R:BASE

R:BASE includes about a dozen operating system commands that you can execute directly from R:BASE. We'll take a look at these commands in this section.

For many of these commands, equivalent functions are available from the R:BASE Main menu. The general procedure for executing one of these commands from the R:BASE Main menu is to highlight Tools on the menu, select Disk management on the pull-down menu, select the appropriate option from the Disk management submenu, and complete the specification of the task to perform by selecting options or typing in any further information that R:BASE requests.

Listing Files DIR displays a list of the files in the current directory. You can display the contents of other directories or other drives by providing the appropriate pathname, as in DIR A: or DIR \RBFILES.

On the Disk management submenu, the List files option is equivalent to the DIR command. Let's try using the R:BASE menus to look at a list of all of the database files in the current subdirectory. For this exercise,

1. Type **MENU** and press ← to bring up the R:BASE Main menu.

2. Highlight **T**ools.

3. Select **D**isk management to bring up the Disk management submenu.

4. Select **L**ist files from the submenu.

The parent directory precedes the current directory in the path name. Since \RBFILES\LEARN is the current directory, \RBFILES is the parent directory.

You are now presented with a submenu asking you to choose which files you would like to list. We will choose the first option in the submenu, Other, because it allows us to specify which files we want to list. The second option, Current directory, would list all files in the current directory. You can't choose the third option, LEARN. It is displayed in white to remind you of the name of the current directory. The last option, Parent directory, would display all files in the parent directory \RBFILES.

5. Select **O**ther from the next submenu.

6. When the prompt asking you to "Enter the directory name" appears, type ***.RBF** and press ←.

You can use the asterisk wildcard character (*) in DOS commands and equivalent R:BASE commands.

This command displays all files in the \RBFILES\LEARN directory that have the extension .RBF. You should see the names of several files displayed, along with the size of each file and the date and time it was last modified. The three files SALES1.RBF, SALES2.RBF, and SALES3.RBF make up the Sales database. Similarly, the files MAIL1.RBF, MAIL2.RBF, and MAIL3.RBF make up the Mail database.

Changing Directories You can use the CHDIR or CD command to change the current directory. In Chapter 2, you used the equivalent option to this command, Change directory, on the Disk management submenu.

Changing Active Drives To change the active drive, you can enter the CHDRV command followed by the drive letter. Of course, you can also simply type the drive letter and a colon (:), as you would do in DOS. On the management submenu, you would use the Change drive option to change active drives.

Use the asterisk (*) and question mark (?) wildcards only when specifying file names in DOS commands and their R:BASE equivalents. Don't confuse them with the percentage sign (%) and underscore (_) wildcards used in the WHERE clause of R:BASE SELECT commands. See Chapter 5 for a discussion of WHERE clause wildcards.

Create a Directory If you need to create a directory, you can use the MKDIR (or MD) command. In Chapter 2, you made the LEARN directory using the Make directory option on the Disk management submenu. To remove a directory, you can use the RMDIR (RD) command or the Remove directory option on the Disk management submenu.

Copying and Renaming Files R:BASE's COPY command works much like DOS's COPY command. You can use the asterisk (*) and question mark (?) wildcard characters to designate files to be copied. Be careful, however, if you want to use COPY to make a backup of your database and you want the backup database to have a different name. For example, if you type

    COPY SALES?.RBF S?.RBF

you'll only end up with one file for the S database. When file names for the original and backup database files are different lengths, copy each file separately. Similar care should be taken when renaming files with the RENAME command. On the Disk management menu, the Copy a file option provides a similar function to the COPY command and the Rename a file option is equivalent to the RENAME command.

Deleting Files You can use ERASE to delete entire files. R:BASE will not, however, let you delete the database files of the currently open database. If you want to erase all traces of the currently open

CH. 6

database, close it first (you can do that by opening another database or by typing DISCONNECT at the R> prompt), and then type something like

ERASE *dbname*?.RBF

The question mark (?) beside *dbname* in this command ensures that R:BASE will delete all the files in the database. For example, if you had an inventory database called INVENT, the command ERASE INVENT?.RBF would delete INVENT1.RBF, INVENT2.RBF, and INVENT3.RBF.

where *dbname* is the name of the database to be erased. You can also include paths in the ERASE command. As you might expect, the equivalent option to the ERASE command on the Disk management submenu is the Erase a file option.

Clearing the Screen The CLS command can be used like R:BASE's NEWPAGE command for clearing the screen. If you have issued an OUTPUT command to begin sending output to your printer, the NEWPAGE command tells the printer to go to the top of the next page. There are no equivalent Database management submenu options.

Display an ASCII File TYPE, like its DOS counterpart, can be used to display the contents of an ASCII file. On the Database management submenu, you can perform this function with the Show a file option.

Checking Disks Several other R:BASE commands work much, but not exactly, like their DOS counterparts. The R:BASE CHKDSK command displays only the total and available number of bytes of memory and disk space. The R:BASE command does not display the amount of disk space used for hidden files, directories, user files, and bad sectors. Also, R:BASE's CHKDSK does not support the optional parameters /F and /V, available from the DOS command.

If you want to find out about disk utilization on a drive that isn't the active drive, you can use CHKDSK in the form

CHKDSK *d:*

where *d:* is the drive in question.

To perform the CHKDSK function on the Disk management submenu, choose the Check disk option.

BACKING UP YOUR DATABASE

The R:BASE BACKUP and RESTORE commands, as well as options on the R:BASE menus, perform similar functions to the DOS commands of the same name. However, the R:BASE functions are optimized for use with R:BASE databases, and allow you to back up an entire database or just parts of it. The easiest way to back up a database, of course, is to copy all three .RBF files onto a floppy disk. But if your database is too large to fit onto a floppy disk, you'll be glad to know that BACKUP and RESTORE can span multiple floppy disks.

How do you use the R:BASE backup functions? Let's say you have a database on your hard disk and want to back it up onto a floppy disk in drive A. The floppy should be formatted, but otherwise empty.

First, let's try using the BACKUP command to back up the Sales database onto a floppy disk. At the R> prompt,

1. Type **CONNECT SALES** and press ↵ to make sure that the Sales database is open.

2. Place a floppy disk in drive A.

3. Type **OUTPUT A:SALES.BAK** and press ↵.

4. Type **BACKUP ALL** and press ↵.

5. Type **OUTPUT SCREEN** and press ↵.

6. Remove the floppy disk from drive A.

The command you issued in step 3 redirected R:BASE's output to the file called SALES.BAK on drive A. You could have chosen any legal DOS file name in lieu of SALES.BAK. The command in step 4 told R:BASE to back up the entire database into the SALES.BAK file. If more than one floppy is required, R:BASE will prompt you to supply additional ones. When the backup is completed, the last OUTPUT command redirects R:BASE's output back to the screen.

The R:BASE menu function to backup a database is just as easy to use. Let's try using the R:BASE menus to make a backup of the Mail database onto the same floppy disk that you used in the previous example. Return to the Main menu now by typing **MENU** and pressing ↵.

1. With **D**atabases highlighted, select **M**ail to open the Mail database.

2. Place the floppy disk in drive A.

3. Highlight **T**ools.

4. Select the **B**ack up database option.

5. Type **A:MAIL.BAK** (and press ←┘) when prompted to enter the backup file name.

6. When prompted to press any key to continued, press a key to return to the menu.

7. Remove the floppy disk from drive A.

When you use the BACKUP command or the Back up database option, you should remember three things. First, be sure to have enough blank, formatted floppy disks to accommodate your database. Second, don't be worried if the backed-up database seems very small. The total byte size of your backup may be one fifth the size of the original database. Third, be sure the R:BASE environment setting NULL is set to its default (–0–) when you use BACKUP.

If you later need to restore a database, how do you do it? Just as with BACKUP, there is both an R:BASE RESTORE command and a Restore function on the R:BASE menus to restore a database that you have backed up. If you have backed up the entire database and need to restore it, make sure you have removed or renamed any database with the same name from the current directory. Then, to use the RESTORE command, you would type the

RESTORE *d:filename.ext*

command from the R > prompt. To restore the Sales database, you would type

RESTORE A:SALES.BAK

If the backup spans more than one disk, you'll be prompted to replace one floppy disk with the next one.

You can initiate the same process from the R:BASE menus by highlighting Tools, selecting Maintenance from the pull-down menu, and then selecting Restore from the submenu that appears. You can use these backup and restore functions to move a database from one machine to another one.

Remember, the backup and restore functions are used primarily to back up a large database that can't fit onto a single floppy disk. The copy functions will be faster if your database files can fit onto a single floppy disk.

In this chapter we've discussed techniques for managing R:BASE displays using the SET command. You've discovered how to zip in and out of R:BASE if you need to. We've also explored some of the ways to harness R:BASE's power to perform calculations and help you analyze data. We'll continue this discussion in Chapter 11 when we talk about SuperMath functions. Finally, we've talked about the R:BASE commands that work like DOS commands, and we've shown you several ways to back up an R:BASE database. In the next chapter, we'll learn how to use R:BASE's powerful Report Generator.

Chapter 7

Creating
Custom Reports
and Labels

IN THIS CHAPTER, WE'LL DISCUSS TECHNIQUES FOR generating reports based on your R:BASE database. You'll learn how to set up and modify a formatted report and also to print mailing labels. To follow along with the examples in this chapter, start R:BASE so that you see the R:BASE Main menu and then open the Mail database.

CREATING CUSTOMIZED REPORTS

R:BASE includes a Report Generator that allows you to create customized reports with headers, footers, totals, subtotals, and modified column displays. In this section, we'll experiment with reports and develop a mailing-list report for the Names table, similar to the one shown in Figure 7.1.

```
                         MAILING LIST DIRECTORY

          July 31, 1990                                      Page: 1

          Adams, Bart              DataSpec Inc.          Jun 15, 1990
            P.O. Box 2890          Malibu, CA 96523

          Baker, Robin            Peach Computers        Jun 15, 1990
            2311 Coast Hwy.        San Diego, CA 92122

          Jones, Mindy            ABC Co.                Jun 1, 1990
            123 A St.             San Diego, CA 92122

          Miller, Anne            Golden Gate Co.        Jun 1, 1990
            2313 Sixth St.        Berkeley, CA 94711

          Miller, Marie           Zeerox Inc.            Jun 15, 1990
            234 C St.             Los Angeles, CA 91234

          Smith, Sandy            Hi Tech Inc.           Jun 1, 1990
            456 N. Rainbow Dr.    Berkeley, CA 94711
```

Figure 7.1: A mailing list report for the Names table

Developing a report can be broken down into nine steps:

1. Design the report on paper, marking headers, footers, and detail (the body of the report).

2. Determine variables for the report on paper (information that is to be included in the report but does not come directly from the table).

3. Start the Report Generator, name the report, and identify the associated table to display the Report Layout screen.

4. Define report variables in the Report Layout screen.

5. Enter the report headers, footers, and any other text.

6. Locate the report columns and variables.

7. Save and preview the report, making adjustments to the format if necessary.

8. Leave the Report Generator.

9. Print the report.

Each of these steps is discussed in detail below.

STEP 1: DESIGN THE REPORT

The first step in developing a report is to jot down on paper a rough draft of how you want each printed page to look. Note the headers that appear at the top of each page, footers that appear at the bottom of each page, and the detail lines (the main body of the report where rows from the table are displayed). Figure 7.2 shows a sample rough draft.

STEP 2: PLAN THE REPORT VARIABLES

Report variables are any type of information that does not come directly from a database table, excluding headers and footers. Page numbers, dates, totals, and subtotals are all variables. Special characters that you want to insert into a column, such as commas, can be defined as variables as well.

Therefore, in our mailing-list report, the person's name is a variable that combines the last name, a comma, and the first name with extraneous blanks removed, as in *Miller, Marie*. The City, State, and ZIP Code columns are also combined, as in *San Diego, CA 92122*. Jot down brief names for each of the following variables (but do not use spaces in the variable names):

PgNo	=	Page number
RepDate	=	Report date
Comma	=	','

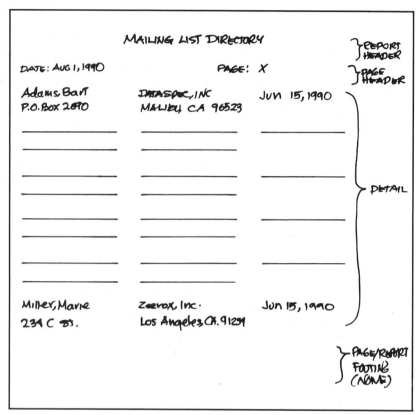

Figure 7.2: A rough draft of a report on paper

> FullName = Last and first names, separated by a comma
>
> FullCSZ = City, State, and ZIP code with a comma inserted after city

Once you've jotted down this information, you can go on-line and develop the report format.

STEP 3: START THE REPORT GENERATOR

Starting the report generator to create a new report involves four substeps: display the Report Generator menu; choose the type of report to create; provide a name and description for the report; and provide additional information, such as the name of the table supplying the data.

Displaying the Report Generator Menu You can choose between two different methods to display the Report Generator menu. From the R:BASE Main menu, you can highlight Reports and select Create/modify. Alternatively, from the R:BASE R> prompt, you can type the REPORTS command and press ←.

Let's start from the R:BASE Main menu. Highlight **R**eports and select **C**reate/modify. You should see the Report Generator menu, as shown in Figure 7.3. (If you have not yet opened the Mail database, you will be given an opportunity to do so before the menu is displayed.) As you can see from the functions in the menu bar, the Report Generator menu allows you to create new reports as well as modify, delete, rename, copy, and list existing reports.

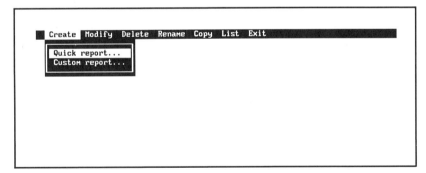

Figure 7.3: The Report Generator menu

The Quick Report option is discussed later in this chapter in the section called "Shortcuts for Creating Reports."

Choosing the Type of Report Since you want to create a report, you will be choosing the Create option in the menu. Below Create, a pull-down menu provides two options: Quick report and Custom report. The Quick report option makes it easy to create a report in one of two standard formats. Since our report does not use one of these standard formats, we will choose the Custom report option. Highlight the **C**ustom report option now and press ←.

Providing a Report Name and Description You are now asked to enter a new report name and description. For this example, type the name **Director** (short for Directory) and press ◄┘. Next, type in a description, **Mailing List Directory From Names Table**, and press ◄┘.

Providing Additional Information   The next piece of information R:BASE needs is the name of the table that will supply the data for your report. Press ◄┘ to choose the Names table, and R:BASE will display the Report Layout screen, as shown in Figure 7.4. This is your clean slate for creating your report format. Now you can begin to design the actual report format.

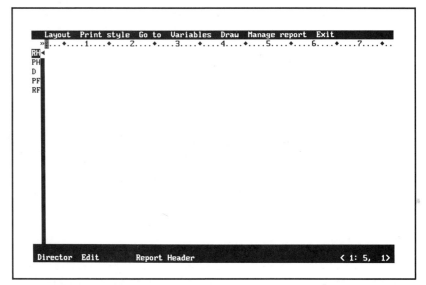

Figure 7.4: The Report Layout screen

STEP 4: DEFINE VARIABLES IN THE REPORT LAYOUT SCREEN

Defining variables to use in a report involves three steps: highlighting Variables, selecting Define, and typing in the definition of the variable. To define a variable you use the formula *Variable = Expression*, where *Variable* is the name of the variable you are defining and *Expression* defines the contents of the variable.

Let's see how this works by defining the PgNo (page number) variable first.

As you might
expect, you can use
the mouse to move the
cursor on the Report
Layout screen and make
menu selections.

1. Highlight **V**ariables and select **D**efine.
2. Type **PgNo** = .**#PAGE** and press ◄—.

.#PAGE is a code that can be used to display page numbers in reports. If you see the message "-ERROR-Syntax is incorrect for the command" at the bottom of the screen, then you made a typing mistake when you entered the definition. Simply press any key and you will have an opportunity to start over and correct your mistake.

Next, define the RepDate (report date) variable using these steps:

1. Highlight **V**ariables and select **D**efine.
2. Type **RepDate** = .**#DATE** and press ◄—.

The code .#DATE gives you the system date you entered when you started your computer. Note that you can also include the time of day on a report using the code .#TIME (but we won't do so in this example). Like .#DATE, .#TIME uses the system time.

Define the Comma variable next using the following steps:

1. Highlight **V**ariables and select **D**efine.
2. Type **Comma** = ',' and press ◄—.

Next we'll define the FullName variable, which contains the last name, a comma, and the first name. To join TEXT data, you can use either of two operators:

   &   Joins two items of text, placing a blank space between them.

   +   Joins two items of text without a blank space.

Since you want to place the comma right next to the last name, with a space after the comma and then the first name, you can define the FullName variable as follows:

FullName = (L_Name + .Comma & F_Name)

This expression will print all the names in the following format:

Miller, Anne

Without using the plus sign variable (+) to join the two parts of the name, Anne Miller's name would be printed like this:

Miller   Anne

Chapter 11 explains more about using parentheses and variables in expressions.

Why is there a period in front of the comma variable and why is the expression to the right of the equal sign enclosed in parentheses? The period helps R:BASE to evaluate Comma as a variable and not a column from the table. As for the parentheses, putting parentheses around an expression helps R:BASE to evaluate the expression correctly.

Follow these steps to define the FullName variable:

1. Highlight **Variables** and select **Define**.

2. Type **FullName = (L_Name + .Comma & F_Name)** and press ⏎.

We would like to display the city, state, and ZIP code in the format

San Diego, CA 92345

We'll use the variable FullCSZ for this format, which requires the following definition:

FullCSZ = (City + .Comma & State & Zip_Code)

Follow the same steps you used to define the FullName variable to define the FullCSZ variable.

Don't worry if you are feeling uncomfortable with this discussion of variables and expressions. Chapters 10 and 11 go into these topics in greater detail.

To make sure that all three variables have been defined correctly, highlight **Variables** and select **List**. You'll see all the variable names and their expressions on the screen, as in Figure 7.5. Notice that R:BASE automatically places the type of data (DATE, INTEGER, or TEXT) that the variable contains to the left of each variable name. You need not concern yourself with these data types yet. Press **Esc** when you are finished looking at the variable definitions to go back to the Report Layout screen. If you were creating a very complex report format with more variable definitions than could be displayed on the screen, you could press the PgDn or PgUp key to move down or up in the list.

| Layout | Print style | Go to | Variables | Draw | Manage report | Exit |

```
P    1: INTEGER   : PgNo        = .#PAGE
D    2: DATE      : RepDate     = .#DATE
P    3: TEXT      : Comma       = ','
R    4: TEXT      : FullName    = (L_Name + .Comma & F_Name)
     5: TEXT      : FullCSZ     = (City + .Comma & State & Zip_Code)
```

Figure 7.5: The list of report variables and their expressions

MAKING CORRECTIONS TO VARIABLES

If you discover an error in an expression, you can correct it by highlighting Variables and selecting Modify. Next, select the variable to be corrected, and R:BASE will present you with the current definition in a box beneath a prompt that says "Define expression." Modify any part of the definition you want and press ← when you are done.

If you misspelled a variable name, you could use the above technique to correct the spelling. However, correcting the spelling of a variable name only creates a new variable with the right spelling—it does not delete the misspelled variable. To delete the misspelled variable, highlight Variables and select Delete. From the submenu, select the variable you wish to delete. When you are asked to

Choose "Yes" to confirm delete. Yes No

choose Yes to delete the variable.

Now you are ready to design the layout of the report. If Variables is still highlighted on the menu, press **Alt** to return the cursor to the top-left corner of the screen below the menu bar.

STEP 5: ENTER THE REPORT TEXT

A report can have three types of headers and three types of footers, as summarized below:

SYMBOL	NAME	TYPE
RH	Report header	Displayed once at the top of the report
PH	Page header	Displayed once at the top of each page
H1...H10	Break header	Appears at the top of each group in a report (used in reports containing subtotals)
F1...F10	Break footer	Appears at the bottom of each group in a report (used in reports containing subtotals)
PF	Page footer	Displayed at the bottom of each page
RF	Report footer	Displayed at the bottom of the report

Because the symbol for each report section is only two characters long, H0 appears instead of H10, and F0 appears instead of F10.

A symbol for each type of header and footer will appear highlighted in the far-left margin of the screen. Notice on your screen that R:BASE has supplied you with a "starter kit"—a report header line, a page header line, a detail line, a page footer line, and a report footer line. Learning to specify, insert, and delete header and footer types can be tricky (although it's easy once you get used to it). Before you develop the Mailing List Directory report, take a moment to review the keys that you can use while designing a report format, as shown in Table 7.1. Of course, you can also use the mouse to move the cursor around the screen and make menu selections.

Table 7.1: Keys to Use When Creating Reports

KEY	FUNCTION
F1	Brings up a help screen.
Shift-F1	Brings up function key descriptions.

Table 7.1: Keys to Use When Creating Reports (continued)

KEY	FUNCTION
F3	Displays database information (useful for remembering which tables, columns, and variables are available).
F6	Places a column or variable on the report.
F7	Moves the cursor to the previous section.
F8	Moves the cursor to the next section.
F9	Deletes the current line, if the current line is empty.
Shift-F9	Removes a column or variable from the report.
F10	Inserts a blank line above the current line.
Shift-F10	Inserts a blank line below the current line.
↑	Moves the cursor up one line.
↓	Moves the cursor down one line.
→	Moves the cursor to the right one character.
←	Moves the cursor to the left one character.
Ctrl-→	Moves the cursor to the furthest-right screen column.
Ctrl-←	Moves the cursor to screen column number 1.
↵	Moves the cursor to the beginning of the next line.
Ins	Toggles between Insert mode (where the cursor is a block) and Overtype mode (where the cursor is an underline).
Del	Deletes the character at the cursor position.
Tab	Moves the cursor ten spaces to the right.
Shift-Tab	Moves the cursor ten spaces to the left.
Home	Moves the cursor to the upper-left corner of the report format.
End	Moves the cursor to the bottom-right corner of the report format.

CH. 7

Break headers and footers are explained in Chapter 12.

Let's add a report header that consists of the words "Mailing List Directory" with a blank line beneath. We'll also add a page header that shows the date the report was printed and the page number.

The cursor is now to the right of the RH (report header) symbol. The bottom-right corner of the screen displays the indicator, which says < 1: 5, 1 >. This shows the current row position of the cursor (1), the number of rows in the report format (5), and the current column position of the cursor (1). Which column the cursor is in is also indicated at the top of the screen, where a grey block shows the cursor position on a ruler line.

To fill in the heading MAILING LIST DIRECTORY centered as the report header, press → until the cursor reaches column 25 (the indicator will read < 1: 5, 25 > and the grey block will be on the diamond at position 25 in the ruler line). Then type

MAILING LIST DIRECTORY

By pressing Shift-F1, you can see a description of active function keys for whatever task you are trying to perform in R:BASE.

Now we want to add another RH (report header) line to insert a blank line beneath this heading. Fortunately, there is a function key for this purpose. Pressing F10 inserts a line before, and pressing Shift-F10 inserts a line after, the current line on the Report Layout screen. We want to insert a line after the current line, so press **Shift-F10**. You now see a new blank line with the symbol RH at the left margin. Notice that both of the RH symbols at the left margin of the screen are highlighted. This is because the cursor is still in the RH section.

To begin the page header, we want to move to the beginning of the next line, which has the PH symbol at the left side. To move to the beginning of the next line, press ←. Notice that the PH symbol is now highlighted at the left side of the screen. On this line, press the **spacebar** once and type the word

Date:

Press → until the cursor reaches column 58 (the indicator will read < 3: 6, 58 >). Type in the word

Page:

Press **Shift-F10** to create another blank line. This one will also be a PH line and will serve as a blank line in the page header.

Now your screen should look like Figure 7.6, with two sections on the screen containing information: RH (report header) and PH (page header). Next, we'll begin placing variable data (items from the Names table and report variables) on the report.

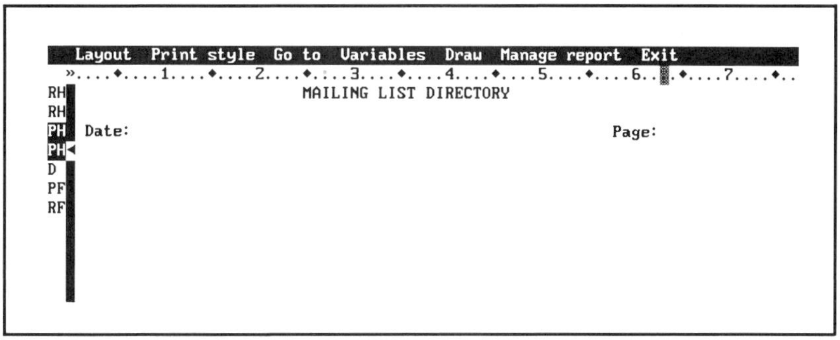

Figure 7.6: A report header and page header on the Report Layout screen

STEP 6: LOCATE COLUMN AND VARIABLE POSITIONS

To place (or *locate*) a table column name or report variable on the report format, you either press the F6 key or use the Layout option on the menu. The general procedure for placing a table column or variable is to first move the cursor where you want the table column or variable to begin. Next, you have a choice to make. You can either

- highlight Layout on the menu bar and begin choosing the appropriate options to select the column or variable you want; or

- press F6 and either choose from menus or type in the name of the column or variable you want.

When a prompt appears at the bottom of the screen asking you to

Move cursor to start location and press S

press **S**—your cursor is already at the start location. A highlighted box will appear on the screen showing an initial size for the column or variable, and R:BASE will ask you to set the length of the field.

Although you can use a mouse to show where a field starts and ends, it's much easier to use the keyboard—you can refer to the position indicator at the bottom of the screen as you adjust the position of the field.

Chapter 12 details how you can use the wrap-around feature to display data in a single field in several lines of a report.

- If the field is not a TEXT or NOTE field, R:BASE will prompt you to "Move cursor to end and press E." Here you have the option of pressing ← or → to lengthen or shorten the field. When you're done, press E.

- If you are entering a TEXT or NOTE field, R:BASE will prompt you to "Move cursor to end and press E or W." R:BASE starts TEXT and NOTE fields with a length of 2 characters. If the field is a column from the table and you want to make it as wide as the defined length of the column, press Ctrl-→. As above, you can use ← and → to change the width if necessary. Then either press E to mark the end of the field, or W to define the end and allow R:BASE to wrap around the data.

R:BASE next asks, "Do you want to add a picture format?" Choose **No**. The *picture format* feature allows you to control how the table column or variable is printed on the final report. We will discuss picture formats in detail in Chapter 12.

Let's get started laying out our report. To place the report date (RepDate) variable in the page heading, follow these steps:

1. Move the cursor to the right of *Date:* (< 3: 7, 8 > on the position indicator).

2. Press **F6** to display the Column or variable name prompt.

3. Press ↵ to bring up the Columns and Variables menu.

4. Highlight **V**ariables and select **RepDate**.

5. Press **S**, since the cursor is already at the start location.

6. Press **E**. (The length displayed is 30 characters, the maximum width for a date. This is a good length for the date stamp.)

7. Choose **No** when asked if you want to add a picture format.

Instead of using the menus in steps 3 and 4, you could just type the name of the variable or column at the "Column or Variable name" prompt.

Next, place the PgNo variable, using the following steps:

1. Move the cursor to the right of *Page:* (< 3: 7, 64 > on the position indicator).

2. Press **F6**.

3. Type **PgNo** and press ↵.

4. Press **S**.

5. Press ← seven times to allow 3 digits for the page number, a maximum of 999.

6. Press **E**.

7. Choose **N**o when asked if you want to add a picture format. Your screen should look like Figure 7.7.

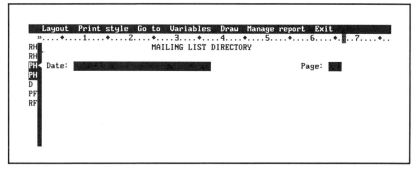

Figure 7.7: The completed report heading and page heading

Now we need to place the table columns on the report format. But these do not belong in a header or footer, because headers and footers only appear once on each page or once in the entire report. Instead, we'll place the table column names in a *detail* section of the report.

THE DETAIL SECTION OF THE REPORT

The detail section displays data repeatedly on a page. In fact, it is generally repeated once for each row in the table. To move into the detail section (which has the letter *D* at the left margin of the screen), press ↵ twice. The letter *D* is now highlighted and the cursor is at the beginning of that line.

First, let's place the FullName variable (which, as you'll recall, displays the L_Name and F_Name columns from the database table) in column 2 of this line. Since the last and first names can each be as long as 15 characters, and because the FullName variable also contains a comma and a space, the FullName variable can be up to 32 characters long. This time, let's use the Layout option on the menu bar to place the FullName variable.

1. Move the cursor to column 2 of the detail row (with the position indicator at < 5: 7, 2>).

2. Highlight **Layout** and select **Variables**.

3. Select **FullName** in the submenu.

4. Press **S**.

5. Move the cursor to column 33 (position indicator < 5: 7, 33>).

6. Press **E**.

7. Choose **No** when asked if you want to add a picture format.

Now let's fill out the rest of the detail section:

1. To place the Company in column 36 and provide a length of 20 characters, move the cursor to column 36 of the detail row (position indicator < 5: 7, 36>); press **F6**; type **Company** and press ◄─┘; press **S**; press **Ctrl-→** to move the cursor to column 55 (position indicator < 5: 7, 55>); press **E**; and choose **No** when asked if you want to add a picture format.

2. To place the Ent_Date column at column 59 of the report, press → to move the indicator to column 59 (position indicator < 5: 7, 59>); press **F6**; type **Ent_Date** and press ◄─┘; press **S**; move the cursor back to column 74 (position indicator < 5: 7, 74>); press **E**; and choose **No** when asked if you want to add a picture format.

3. Most of the report seems to have disappeared from the screen. Press **Ctrl-←** to move the cursor back to column 1.

4. Create another detail line by pressing **Shift-F10**.

5. To place the Address column, move the cursor to column 5 (position indicator < 6: 8, 5>); press **F6**; type **Address** and press ◄─┘; press **S**; press **Ctrl-→** to move the cursor to

column 29 (position indicator < 6: 8, 29>); press **E**; and choose **N**o when asked if you want to add a picture format.

6. Place the FullCSZ variable beginning in column 36 and ending in column 74 using similar steps to those above.

7. Insert a blank line between names printed in the directory by pressing **Shift-F10**. This creates another detail line.

Now you are finished laying out the detail section of the report. However, you still have the page footer (PF) section and the report footer (RF) section. They were provided for you by R:BASE initially, but you do not need them. Follow these steps to remove these lines:

1. Press ← to move to the PF section. The letters *PF* will be highlighted at the left margin and the position indicator will be at < 8: 9, 1>).

2. Press **F9** to delete the PF section. Now the cursor is in the RF section with the position indicator at < 8: 8, 1>.

3. Press **F9** to delete the RF section.

At this point, you'll have highlighted blocks showing the locations of the column names and variables on the screen, as in Figure 7.8. Now that the report format is laid out, you can preview it.

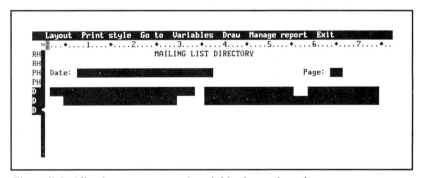

Figure 7.8: All column names and variables located on the screen

STEP 7: SAVE AND PREVIEW THE REPORT

R:BASE automati-
cally saves your
report before it shows you
a preview.

When you preview a report, R:BASE saves the report on disk and then either displays the first few rows on the screen or prints them. Let's try previewing our report on the screen. To do this, highlight **M**anage report and select the **P**review to screen option. You now have a chance to see the report prepared with data from your table, as shown in Figure 7.9. This report looks like our design except that the dates are displayed with month numbers instead of month names. Later in this chapter, you will use the SET DATE FORMAT command to adjust the date format. When you have finished looking at the report, press any key to return to the Report Layout screen. If the report did not look the way you wanted, you could make changes now and save the report again on disk.

```
                         Mailing List Directory

        Date: 09/16/90                                  Page:   1

        Miller, Anne                 Golden Gate Co.      06/01/90
           2313 Sixth St.            Berkeley, CA 94711

        Adams, Bart                  DataSpec Inc.        06/15/90
           P.O. Box 2890             Malibu, CA 96523

        Miller, Marie                Zeerox Inc.          06/15/90
           234 C St.                 Los Angeles, CA 91234

        Jones, Mindy                 ABC Co.              06/01/90
           123 A St.                 San Diego, CA 92122

        Smith, Sandy                 Hi Tech Inc.         06/01/90
           456 N. Rainbow Dr.        Berkeley, CA 94711

        Baker, Robin                 Peach Computers      06/15/90
           2311 Coast Hwy.           San Diego, CA 92122

        Press any key to continue
```

Figure 7.9: Previewing the report on the screen

Under the Manage report option on the menu bar is another option that allows you to preview the report to the printer. Seeing a preview of your report on the screen is fast and convenient, but it doesn't allow you to preview the special features that your printer provides. You can't view these special features on the screen. In Chapter 12 you will learn how to use the special features of your printer to enhance the appearance of reports.

You have the option to save the Report Layout screen at any time without previewing the report. To do this, highlight **M**anage report and select **S**ave changes. After a momentary pause, the report will be stored safely on the hard disk.

STEP 8: LEAVE THE REPORT GENERATOR

Now let's leave the Report Layout screen by highlighting and selecting **E**xit. If you try to leave the Report Layout screen after you made changes and you didn't save them, R:BASE will give you yet another opportunity to save your changes before leaving the Report Layout screen. Since you have not made any changes to the report since the last time you saved it, R:BASE does not ask you whether you want to discard your changes.

STEP 9: PRINT THE REPORT

As you have seen with many R:BASE features, you can print the Mailing List Directory from the R:BASE Main menu or in Command mode at the R > prompt. The general procedure for printing a report from the R:BASE Main menu is to first choose the report you want to print, as follows:

Remember that R:BASE displays the name of the database which is currently open in the bottom-left corner of the screen. To open a database from the Main menu, highlight Databases and select the database you want to open.

- Make sure the database is open that contains the report you want to print; and

- Highlight Reports and select the name of the report you want to print.

From the submenu that appears, specify sorting and searching details and where you want to send the report output. To sort the information before it is printed,

- Select Quick sort;

- Select the columns to sort on, from most important to least important, including whether you want an Ascending or Descending sort; and

- Press F2 when you are finished.

To search for certain rows to include in the report using straightforward search conditions,

- Select Quick select;
- For each column that you want to search, select the column, select a comparison operator, type in a comparison value and press ◄─┘; and
- Select (Done) when you are finished entering conditions.

If you want to enter more conditions, select a logical connection such as AND, OR, AND NOT, or OR NOT.

To search for certain rows to include in the report using more complicated search conditions,

- Select Enter WHERE clause;
- Type in the conditions you want the row to satisfy in order to be included in the report; and
- Press ◄─┘.

If you don't specify where the output should go, it will be sent to the printer.

To specify where you want the output to go,

- Select Print to;
- Choose one or more places to send the output of this report: to send it to the printer, select Printer; to send it to a file, select Create text file, type in the name of the file, and press ◄─┘; to display it on the screen, select Show on screen.
- Press F2 when you are finished specifying where to send the report output.

Press F2 to start the report.

Let's try printing the Mailing List Directory report we just created. To get ready for this example, return to the R:BASE Main menu by highlighting and selecting **Exit**. Let's produce a directory on the screen of all people in Berkeley, sorted by last and first name.

1. Verify that the Mail database is open by glancing in the bottom-left corner of the screen. You should see Database: C:..Mail on the status line.

2. Highlight **R**eports and select **D**irector.

3. Select **Q**uick sort.

4. Select **L_Name** and select **A**scending.

5. Select **F_Name** and select **A**scending.

6. Press **F2** to finish specifying the sort instructions.

7. Select **Q**uick select.

8. Select **C**ity, select = EQUAL, type **Berkeley**, and press ⏎.

9. Select (Done).

10. Select **P**rint to.

11. Select **S**how on screen.

12. Press **F2** to finish specifying where to send the output.

13. Press **F2** to start the report.

When the report finishes, press any key to return to the R:BASE Main menu.

Printing in Command Mode at the R> Prompt

You can also print reports using the PRINT command. To try this command, highlight **E**xit and select **R>** prompt to go to the R> prompt now.

To see the format of the PRINT command, type HELP PRINT and press ⏎. At the bottom of the help screen, under SYNTAX (Figure 7.10), it tells you that the report name must follow the PRINT command. This help screen also tells you, if you want to search for and print rows that meet certain conditions, to follow the report name with a WHERE clause. It also tells you that if you want the rows to be sorted before being printed, include an ORDER BY clause at the end of the command.

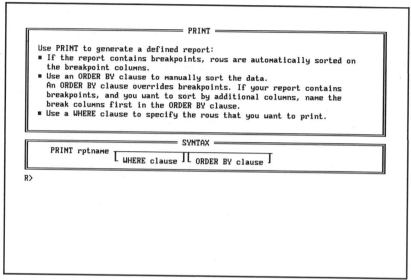

Figure 7.10: A help screen showing the format of the PRINT command

Let's try some examples. To display the Mailing List Directory sorted by last and first names, you could enter the command

PRINT Director ORDER BY L_Name F_Name

The report will appear on the screen, as shown in Figure 7.11.

The date format on your screen may be different from the one in Figure 7.11, depending on the last date output format you established in the exercises in Chapter 6.

To print out the report on the printer, enter

OUTPUT PRINTER
PRINT Director ORDER BY L_Name F_Name

After the report is printed, you can enter the command

NEWPAGE

to eject the report from the printer. Then enter the command

OUTPUT SCREEN

to disconnect from the printer.

```
R>PRINT Director ORDER BY L_Name F_Name
                    MAILING LIST DIRECTORY

    Date: 11/01/90                                    Page:   1

    Adams, Bart                    Dataspec Inc.          06/15/90
        P.O. Box 2890              Malibu, CA 96523

    Baker, Robin                   Peach Computers        06/15/90
        2311 Coast Hwy.            San Diego, CA 92122

    Jones, Mindy                   ABC Co.                06/01/90
        123 A St.                  San Diego, CA 92122

    Miller, Anne                   Golden Gate Co.        06/01/90
        2313 Sixth St.            Berkeley, CA 94711

    Miller, Marie                  Zeerox Inc.            06/15/90
        234 C St.                 Los Angeles, CA 91234

    Smith, Sandy                   Hi Tech Inc.           06/01/90
        456 N. Rainbow Dr.        Berkeley, CA 94711

    R>
```

Figure 7.11: The Director report displayed on the screen

You can also send a copy of the report to a disk file by preceding the PRINT command with an OUTPUT *d:filename.ext* command.

To print a report with only certain rows from the Names table, include a WHERE clause in addition to the ORDER BY clause, as below:

```
PRINT Director ORDER BY L_Name F_Name WHERE +
+ > City = 'San Diego'
```

Before we leave the PRINT command, let's use the following SET DATE FORMAT command to change the output format for dates to the Jan 1, 1991 format. To see the dates in this format, try the following commands:

```
SET DATE FORMAT 'MMM DD, YYYY'
PRINT Director ORDER BY L_Name F_Name
```

PRINTING ON SINGLE SHEETS

When printing long reports on the printer, you can use either continuous form (tractor-fed) paper or single sheets. For continuous form, use the OUTPUT PRINTER option before entering the PRINT command. For single sheets, use the command

OUTPUT PRINTER WITH SCREEN

before entering the PRINT command. R:BASE will print out one page at a time and wait for you to tell it to print the next page.

SHORTCUTS FOR CREATING REPORTS

In the Director report, we created variables for displaying the page number and date. We did this as an exercise to see different types of variables in action. However, R:BASE offers predefined variables for the page number, date, and the time. There are two ways to place one of these predefined variables on your report layout. One way is to highlight Layout on the menu bar and choose the appropriate selection (Page number, Time stamp, or Date stamp) in the pull-down menu. Another way to locate a predefined variable is to press F6 and type in or choose the variable name (#PAGE, #TIME, or #DATE). In the next section, when you create a quick report, you will see how predefined variables work.

Creating Quick Reports

You may recall when you started the Report Generator, earlier in the chapter, that you had the choice of Quick report or Custom report. For the sample report you created, you chose the Custom report option.

When you choose the Quick report option, R:BASE produces a "rough draft" of the report and then lets you refine it. This option can save you time when your report is one of the two standard styles, *column-wise* or *row-wise*. The reports we produced in the last chapter with the SELECT command were column-wise reports. In a column-wise report, each line corresponds to one row in the table, and the values are printed in columns, each column under a heading. In row-wise reports, each value appears on a separate line, usually next to a row header. Row-wise reports are useful when there is too much data to be printed across one line on the page. Figure 7.12 shows a row-wise report of the Names table.

```
Last Name:    Adams
First Name:   Bart
Company:      DataSpec Inc.
Address:      P.O. Box 2890
City:         Malibu
State:        CA
ZIP Code:     96523
Entry Date:   06/15/90

Last Name:    Baker
First Name:   Robin
Company:      Peach Computers
Address:      2311 Coast Hwy.
City:         San Diego
State:        CA
ZIP Code:     92122
Entry Date:   06/15/90
```

Figure 7.12: A row-wise report of the Names table

Once you've chosen the Quick report option, the general procedure for creating a report is very similar to the one you used with the Custom report option. However, there are some differences. First, after you've chosen a table to supply information for your report, you will be asked to select columns to be included in the rough draft. After you've selected the columns, you will be asked to choose an orientation for the report, either Column-wise or Row-wise. And after you've selected an orientation, you will be presented with a rough draft of your report. This rough draft will have only a page heading and a detail section.

- In column-wise reports, the rough draft comprises a page header, column headers, and a detail section with the values placed across one row.

- In row-wise reports, the rough draft comprises three empty page header lines and one detail line for each table column. The name of each table column appears to the left of its corresponding column value.

You can customize the rough draft of the report just as if you had entered the rough draft and you were creating a custom report.

Let's try an example. We'll use the quick report feature to create a detailed report that lists all of the fields in each row of the table. Ours will be a row-wise report similar to the one in Figure 7.12. We'll follow the same nine steps to construct this report that we followed to create the Mailing List Directory.

To review the nine steps used to create the Mailing List Directory report, turn to "Creating Customized Reports" at the start of this chapter.

Step 1: Design the Report As usual, begin by sketching out a rough draft of your details report. Note where you want the date, the page numbers, and the detail lines to be. Figure 7.13 shows a rough draft of the Mailing List Details report.

Figure 7.13: Rough draft of the Mailing List Details report on paper

Step 2: Plan the Report Variables We can use predefined variables for the page number and report date. Therefore, we don't have to define any report variables for this report.

Remember that you can press Shift-F1 to get a list of the function keys currently available on any screen.

Step 3: Start the Report Generator From the R > prompt, start the Report Generator by typing **REPORTS** and pressing ◄┘. Next, highlight **C**reate and select **Q**uick report. To enter the name of the report, type **MLDetail** and press ◄┘. Type **Mailing List Details** and press ◀━━┘ to enter the description of the report. Select the **N**ames table and press **Shift-F6** to select all table columns to be included in the rough draft. Finally, press **F2** to finish selecting table columns, and select **R**ow-wise.

The rough draft of your report should look like Figure 7.14.

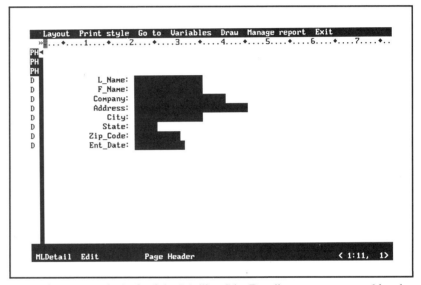

Figure 7.14: Rough draft of the Mailing List Details report generated by the Quick Report feature

Step 4: Define Variables in the Report Layout Screen For this report, we don't have to define any report variables. We can use predefined variables for the date and page number, which are the only variables we need.

Step 5: Enter the Report Text The quick report feature saves us some time in this step because, in row-wise reports, the column names are used for row headers. Of course, we still have to fix the row headers if we abbreviated column names, and we also have to enter the text for the page header. To enter the page header,

1. Move to column 2 in line 1 (position < 1:11, 2>) and type **Date:**.

2. Move to column 25 in line 1 (position < 1:11, 25>) and type **MAILING LIST DETAILS**.

3. Move to column 50 in line 1 (position < 1:11, 50>) and type **Page:**.

4. Press ←┘ to move to the beginning of line 2 (position < 2:11, 1>), and press **F9** to delete a page header line.

To fix up the row header in the detail section,

5. Move to column 10 in line 3 (position < 3:10, 10>), type **Last**, and press the **spacebar** to change the row header from L_Name to Last Name.

6. Move to column 9 in line 4 (position < 4:10, 9>), type **First**, and press the **spacebar** to change the row header from F_Name to First Name.

7. Move to column 11 in line 9 (position < 9:10, 11>), type **ZIP**, and press the **spacebar** to change the row header from Zip_Code to ZIP Code.

8. Move to column 9 in line 10 (position <10:10, 9>), type **Entry**, and press the **spacebar** to change the row header from Ent_Date to Entry Date.

9. Press **Shift-F10** to create a blank line at the end of the detail section. This enters a blank line between the information corresponding to each table row.

Step 6: Place Column and Variable Positions With the quick report feature, we also save time in this step because the table columns have already been placed in the detail section. To place the variables in the page header,

1. Move to column 8 in line 1 (position < 1:11, 8>), highlight **Layout**, and select **Date** stamp.

2. Press **S**.

3. Move to column 18 in line 1 (position < 1:11, 18>), and press **E**.

4. Choose **No** when asked if you want to add a picture format.

5. Move to column 56 in line 1 (position < 1:11, 56>), high-light **L**ayout, and select **P**age number.

6. Press **S**.

7. Move to column 58 in line 1 (position < 1:11, 58>) and press **E**.

8. Choose **No** when asked if you want to add a picture format.

Step 7: Preview the Report and Make Any Necessary Changes You can preview the report to the screen by highlighting **M**anage report and selecting **P**review to screen. When R:BASE has finished displaying the report, your screen should look like Figure 7.15. If you have been following along with all of the examples in this chapter, you will notice a surprise in your report: a line of stars appears in the Entry Date field. R:BASE prints stars in a field when it is not wide enough to contain the information you want to print. Earlier in this chapter, we set the date output format to MMM DD, YYYY—in other words, to 12 characters. But we made all of the date fields 11 characters long. To widen the date fields in your report to 12 characters, first press any key to remove the preview report, then follow the steps below.

1. Move to row 1, column 8 (position < 1:11, 8>), press **F6**, and select **Y**es to tell R:BASE that you want to relocate the field.

2. Press **S** to start the field in the same location.

3. Move to row 1, column 19 (position < 1:11, 19>), press **E**, and choose **No** when asked if you want to add a picture format.

4. Move to row 10, column 21 (position <10:11, 21>), press **F6**, and select **Y**es to tell R:BASE that you want to relocate the field.

5. Press **S** to start the field in the same location.

```
            City: San Diego
           State: CA
        ZIP Code: 92122
      Entry Date: ×××××××××××

       Last Name: Smith
      First Name: Sandy
         Company: Hi Tech Inc.
         Address: 456 N. Rainbow Dr.
            City: Berkeley
           State: CA
        ZIP Code: 94711
      Entry Date: ×××××××××××

       Last Name: Baker
      First Name: Robin
         Company: Peach Computers
         Address: 2311 Coast Hwy.
            City: San Diego
           State: CA
        ZIP Code: 92122
      Entry Date: ×××××××××××

 Press any key to continue
```

Figure 7.15: Previewing a quick report to the screen

6. Move to row 10, column 32 (position <10:11, 32>), press **E**, and choose **No** when asked if you want to add a picture format.

Now try previewing the report again and you should see that the dates appear as entered.

Step 8: Leave the Report Generator   To leave the Report Layout screen, highlight and select **Exit**. If you previewed (and saved) the report just before leaving the Report Layout screen, you have saved your changes already and R:BASE will not ask if you want to save them again. Once you leave the Report Layout screen, you'll see the Report Generator menu. To return to the R > prompt, highlight and select **Exit** again.

Step 9: Print the Report   At the R > prompt, print the report sorted by name on the printer as follows:

1. Type **OUTPUT PRINTER** and press ←┘.

2. Type **PRINT MLDetail ORDER BY L_Name F_Name** and press ←┘.

3. Type **NEWPAGE** and press ←⏎.

4. Type **OUTPUT SCREEN** and press ←⏎.

Your printed report should look like Figure 7.16.

```
       Date: Jul 24, 1990      MAILING LIST DETAILS    Page:   1

   Last Name: Adams
  First Name: Bart
     Company: DataSpec Inc.
     Address: P.O. Box 2890
        City: Malibu
       State: CA
    ZIP Code: 96523
  Entry Date: Jun 15, 1990

   Last Name: Baker
  First Name: Robin
     Company: Peach Computers
     Address: 2311 Coast Hwy.
        City: San Diego
       State: CA
    ZIP Code: 92122
  Entry Date: Jun 15, 1990

   Last Name: Jones
  First Name: Mindy
     Company: ABC Co.
     Address: 123 A St.
        City: San Diego
       State: CA
    ZIP Code: 92122
  Entry Date: Jun 01, 1990
```

Figure 7.16: The printed MLDetail report

MAKING CHANGES TO YOUR REPORT

As you saw when we were creating the Mailing List Details report in the previous section, you may want (or need) to make changes to a report format after previewing it. It is very easy to fix minor problems *before* leaving the Report Layout screen—and you can also change a report *after* you have left this screen. To display the Report Layout screen and change a report, use any of the following three techniques:

- From the R:BASE Main menu, highlight Reports and select Create/modify to display the Report Generator menu. Next, highlight Modify and select the report you wish to modify.

- From the R > prompt, type REPORTS and press ← to display the Report Generator menu. After that, highlight Modify and select the report you wish to modify.

- From the R > prompt, type REPORTS *repname*, where *repname* is the name of the report you wish to modify.

Once your report format is on the Report Layout screen, use the keys listed in Table 7.1 and the options on the menu bar to add, change, or delete text, variables, and column names on the report form.

RELOCATING VARIABLES AND COLUMN NAMES

We will be discussing picture formats in Chapter 12.

You can change the length or location of a variable or column name. First, move the cursor inside the highlighted block representing the variable or column name and press F6. You could also highlight Layout and select Variables if you were changing the size or location of a variable, or Data fields if you were changing the size or location of a column name. Select **Yes** when R:BASE asks, "Do you want to relocate the field?" Move the cursor where you want the field to start and press **S**. Next, move the cursor to where you want the field to end and press **E**. When R:BASE asks, "Do you want to add a picture format?" select Yes if you want a picture format. Select No if you do not. In our examples, we have been choosing No.

DELETING VARIABLES AND COLUMN POSITIONS

To remove a located column name or variable from the report format, move the cursor inside the highlighted block representing the variable or column name. Next, either press Shift-F9 or highlight Layout and select Clear field.

How to delete a variable is discussed earlier in this chapter under the heading "Making Corrections to Variables."

This method of removing a variable from the report format, however, does not delete the variable definition. Earlier in this chapter you saw how to delete a variable definition with the Delete option under Variables on the menu bar. If the variable has been placed on the report, then deleting the variable's definition will also remove the variable from the report format.

REORDERING VARIABLES

Variables must be defined in the order that they are created. For example, the two expressions below are out of order because the Comma variable is defined *after* it is used in the FullCSZ variable:

1. FullCSZ = City + Comma & State & Zip_Code
2. Comma = ','

To change the order of the variable definitions, highlight Variables, select Change order, and select the variable with the definition you want to move. When R:BASE asks you to enter the new position, type in the number of the new position you want the variable to have, and press ◄─┘.

CHANGING VARIABLE DEFINITIONS

Changing the definition of a variable from the Variables menu is discussed in the section of this chapter called "Making Corrections to Variables."

Earlier in this chapter, you learned how to change the definition of a variable with the Modify option under Variables. Remember that when you modify the name of the variable (on the left side of the equals sign), R:BASE creates a new variable definition with the new name you have entered. The old variable definition is not deleted.

PRINTING MAILING LABELS

Printing mailing labels is just like printing a special kind of report. R:BASE has special facilities for creating and printing mailing labels that are very much like those provided for creating and printing reports. However, the label facilities offer several features which take into account the special characteristics of labels:

- Labels don't have headers and footers like most reports, only detail lines.

- Blank lines don't usually appear in the middle of a label.

- Often labels are lined up in more than one column across the page, which means that more than one label is printed at a time.

Designing and printing mailing labels is similar to designing and printing reports. There are nine steps.

1. Design the label on paper and decide what type of label stock to use.

2. Determine any variables for the label on paper.

3. Start the Label Generator, identify the table from which the addresses come, and name the label program.

4. Set the label size and number of columns to match the label stock you are using.

5. Define any variables on the Label Layout screen.

6. Place the label columns and variables, as well as any text.

7. Save and preview the labels, making adjustments to the format if necessary.

8. Leave the Label Generator.

9. Print the labels.

Let's do an example in which we create a label program and print some labels. We'll create a label program to print the labels illustrated in Figure 7.17. Our sample program will print on a common size label stock, with the labels $^{15}/_{16}$-inches high, $3^{1}/_{2}$-inches wide, and with the labels side-by-side in two columns on the page.

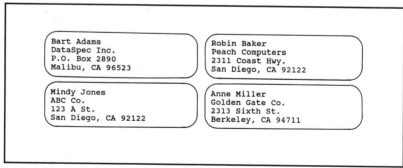

Figure 7.17: Mailing labels for the Names table

STEP 1: DESIGN THE LABEL
AND CHOOSE THE LABEL STOCK

Jot down a rough draft of how you want the printed labels to look. Plan carefully how many lines you want each label to have, and what information should be on each line. Figure 7.18 shows a sample rough draft of the labels.

Figure 7.18: Rough draft of the labels

To choose the label stock, we need to decide the minimum size for each label. Most printers print 6 lines per inch vertically, and at least 10 characters per inch horizontally.

In choosing the height of the labels, note that each label has to hold four detail lines. Assuming 6 lines per inch, this means that the distance between the top of one label and the top of the label below it should be a minimum of $5/6$-inches to allow for four lines of detail and one blank line to cover the little space between labels.

In choosing the width of the labels, we have to make sure that the longest line can fit. Our longest line is the last one, which lists the city (up to 15 characters), a comma and a space, the state (up to 5 characters), a space, and the ZIP code (up to 10 characters). The maximum length for this line is 33 characters, which would be 3.3 inches long at 10 characters per inch.

Our labels can easily fit on a very common label stock—$15/16$-inches high and $3^1/2$-inches wide. In order to print the labels faster, and to make them more convenient to use, let's print them on two columns side-by-side on the page.

STEP 2: PLAN THE LABEL VARIABLES

The first line of each label will combine two columns from the Names table, F_Name and L_Name. The Company and Address columns will work fine by themselves, but the last line combines three columns: City, State, and Zip. Therefore, we will need a couple of variables for these labels:

FullName	=	First and last names
FullCSZ	=	City, state, and ZIP code with a comma inserted after city

STEP 3: START THE LABEL GENERATOR

To start the Label Generator and create a new label program, display the Label Generator menu, choose the table that will supply the data, and provide a name and description for the label program. These steps are described below.

Displaying the Label Generator Menu There are two methods for displaying the Label Generator menu. From the R:BASE Main menu, highlight Reports, select Labels, and then select Create/modify from the submenu displayed. Alternatively, from the R > prompt you can type the RBLABELS command and press ←⏎.

If you have not yet opened your database, you will be given an opportunity to do so before the Label Generator menu is displayed.

Let's start from the R:BASE Main menu. After you have highlighted **R**eports, selected **L**abels, and then selected **C**reate/modify, you should see the Label Generator menu, which looks very similar to the Report Generator menu (see Figure 7.3).

As you can see from the functions in the menu bar, this menu allows you to create new label programs as well as modify, delete, rename, copy, and list existing label programs.

Choose the Table Supplying the Data Under the Create option on the menu bar, you select the table that will be providing most or all of the information printed on the label. For our example, select the Names table.

Providing the Label Program Name and Description You are now asked to enter a new label name and description. For this example, type the name **Nameslbl** and press ←⎯. Then type in the description **Labels for the Names Table** and press ←⎯.

STEP 4: SET THE LABEL SIZE AND NUMBER OF COLUMNS

R:BASE now displays the Label Layout screen, as shown in Figure 7.19. Notice the solid vertical line at column 36 that indicates that only 35 columns are available for a label. Also, notice that a highlighted *D* appears beside the beginning of the first five lines only. This tells you that any information placed below the first five lines will not be printed on the label. Of course, only detail lines are provided on the Label Layout screen, since header and footer lines are not required.

When you first display the Label Layout screen, the screen is set up for labels that are $^{15}/_{16}$-inches high and $3^{1}/_{2}$-inches wide, with a single column of labels going down the page. If your label stock is

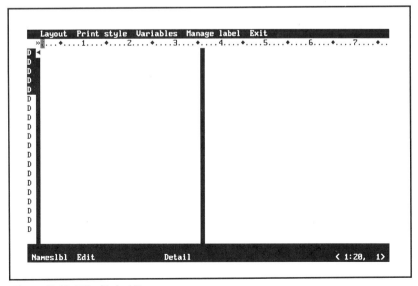

Figure 7.19: The Label Layout screen

A *template* is a complete description—with specifications—of a label stock. Each standard mailing label template in R:BASE has a predefined label size, number of columns, number of rows, and label location.

different from this default, you can specify the size of each label and the number of label columns placed side-by-side on a page. The general procedure for specifying this information is, first, to choose the label template closest to the label stock you will use. R:BASE provides fourteen templates that correspond to fourteen common label stocks. If one of the fourteen standard templates does not match the label stock you are using, you can adjust the size of the labels and the arrangement of the labels on a page.

We decided on a label stock $^{15}/_{16}$-inches high and $3^{1}/_{2}$-inches wide, with two columns per page. Since we want two label columns across the page rather than the default of one column, let's set the label size and number of columns.

1. Highlight **Layout** and select **Size template**.

2. Select $3\text{-}^{1}/_{2} \times {}^{15}/_{16} \times 2$.

Since the $3\text{-}^{1}/_{2} \times {}^{15}/_{16} \times 2$ template matches our requirements exactly, we do not need to customize the label dimensions. However, just to see what is involved in adjusting label dimensions, highlight **Layout** and select **Dimensions** to bring up the Label Dimensions screen, as shown in Figure 7.20. This screen lets you set label dimensions to those of the labels you want to use. Below is a description of the specifications you can make from this screen.

Label width	Sets the width in characters. In our example we have $3^{1}/_{2}''$ (or 3.5″) labels. Assuming our printer prints 10 characters per inch, our labels must be 35 characters wide.
Label height	Sets the height in lines. Our labels are $^{15}/_{16}$-inches high. Assuming we can print 6 lines per inch, each label can accommodate a maximum of 5 lines.
Labels across page	Sets the number of columns. In our example, we want two columns of labels across the page.
Spaces between labels	Sets the horizontal distance between labels, in characters. A value of 1 character is

probably accurate since labels are usually placed very close to one another on a page.

Lines after label	Sets the vertical distance between labels on the page. In our example, a value of 1 line here will account for the small space between one label and the label below it on the page.
Left margin, Top margin, Labels down page	Sets the left margin in characters, the top margin in lines, and the number of rows of labels on a page. These three parameters are almost always set to zero, since you usually start printing labels at the top-left corner of a page and continue with no empty space between pages. However, if you have unusual label stock with an empty border around the edge of a page, you can change these parameters.

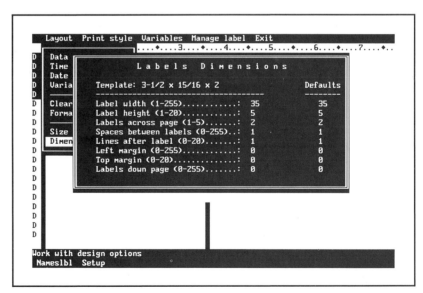

Figure 7.20: The Label Dimensions screen

For each parameter, the minimum and maximum allowable values are enclosed in parentheses. Once you've adjusted the values on this screen, press F2. Since you are not making any changes to these parameters, press **Esc** to return to the Label Layout screen.

STEP 5: DEFINE VARIABLES IN THE LABEL LAYOUT SCREEN

Defining variables to use in a label program involves the same procedure as in a report. To define the FullName variable,

1. Highlight **Variables** and select **Define**.
2. Type **FullName = (F_Name & L_Name)** and press ←.

Next, define the FullCSZ variable.

1. Highlight **Variables** and select **Define**.
2. Type **FullCSZ = (City + ',' & State & Zip_Code)** and press ←.

Note that we avoided having to define the Comma variable by placing a comma enclosed by single quotes (',') directly in the expression.

As on the Report Layout screen, you can list, modify, delete, and change the order of the variables you have defined by highlighting Variables and making the appropriate selection—List, Modify, Delete, or Change order—in the pull-down menu beneath.

STEP 6: LOCATE TABLE COLUMNS, VARIABLES, AND TEXT

We are now ready to specify where the information will be placed on the label. We will be laying out the label with

- the FullName variable placed on the first line from column 2 to column 32,
- the Company column placed on the second line from column 2 to column 21,

- the Address column placed on the third line from column 2 to column 26, and

- the FullCSZ variable placed on the fourth line from column 2 to column 34.

The procedure for placing the columns, variables, and text on the label is very similar to the one used in the Report Layout screen. See if you can remember the steps involved in laying out this information. Refer to the following steps if you get stuck.

1. Move to column 2 in line 1 (position < 1:20, 2>), highlight **Layout**, and select **Variables**.

2. Select **FullName** and press **S**.

3. Move to column 32 in line 1 (position < 1:20, 32>), press **E**, and choose **N**o when asked if you want to add a picture format.

4. Move to column 2 in line 2 (position < 2:20, 2>), highlight **Layout**, and select **D**ata fields.

To save time, you could use this shortcut: press ← and then → to move easily to column 2 in line 2.

5. Select **C**ompany and press **S**.

6. Move to column 21 in line 2 (position < 2:20, 21>), press **E**, and choose **N**o when asked if you want to add a picture format.

Remember, you can press Ctrl-→ to move to the end of a TEXT field table column.

7. Move to column 2 in line 3 (position < 3:20, 2>), press **F6**, type **Address**, and press ←.

8. Press **S**.

9. Move to column 26 in line 3 (position < 3:20, 26>), press **E**, and choose **N**o when asked if you want to add a picture format.

10. Move to column 2 in line 4 (position < 4:20, 2>), press **F6**, type **FullCSZ**, and press ←.

11. Press **S**.

12. Move to column 34 in line 4 (position < 4:20, 34>), press **E**, and choose **N**o when asked if you want to add a picture format.

When you are finished laying out the fields on the label, your screen should look like Figure 7.21. You are now ready to preview the labels.

STEP 7: SAVE AND PREVIEW THE LABELS

By saving and previewing the labels, you can spot any problems and make corrections before you leave the Label Layout screen. To save the labels and preview them, highlight **M**anage label and select **P**review to screen. When you're finished previewing the labels, press any key to return to the Label Layout screen.

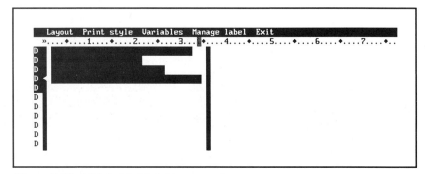

Figure 7.21: All label fields laid out on the screen

From the Label Layout screen, there are three ways of saving your label format:

- When you preview the labels, the label format is saved automatically.

- Highlight Manage label and select Save changes.

- When you leave the Label Layout screen, provided you have made changes since the last time you saved the layout, you are given the opportunity to save your changes.

STEP 8: LEAVE THE LABEL GENERATOR

Let's leave the Label Generator now. Highlight and select **E**xit to return to the Label Generator menu. Highlight and select **E**xit again to return to the R:BASE Main menu.

STEP 9: PRINT THE LABELS

Printing labels is very much like printing reports, except that labels have to be aligned more carefully in the printer. For this reason, R:BASE lets you print two rows of "test labels" with *x's* in every print position. This makes it easy to see if the labels are aligned before you begin printing your labels on the printer.

At the R:BASE Main menu, printing labels involves first choosing the labels you want to print.

1. Make sure the database that contains the label format you want is open.

2. Highlight Reports and select Labels.

3. Select the labels you want to print.

From the submenu that appears, you must next specify sorting and searching details.

- To sort the labels before they are printed, select Quick sort and specify the sorting criteria as you would when printing a report.

- To search for certain rows to include in the labels using straightforward search conditions, select Quick select. Follow the menus to specify the search criteria as you would when printing a report.

- To search for certain rows to include in the labels using more complicated search conditions, select Enter WHERE clause. Next, type in the conditions each row must satisfy in order to be included in the labels. Press ← when you are finished typing the conditions.

Next you must tell R:BASE where you want to send the label output.

If you don't specify where the output should go, it will be sent to the printer.

4. Select Print to and choose where to send the output—to the printer, a text file, or the screen.

5. Press F2 to start the label program.

If you are sending output to the printer, you will be asked

Print test label? Yes No

If you choose Yes, two rows of test labels will be printed with *x's* in every print position of each label. After test labels are printed, R:BASE will ask again whether you want your test labels printed. You will get as many chances as you need to align the labels.

6. When you are happy with the alignment of the labels in the printer, choose **No**. R:BASE will begin producing the label output.

You can use the LBLPRINT command to print labels from the R > prompt. This command is very similar to the PRINT command we have been using for reports, with a couple of differences:

- The name of the labels you want to produce follows the LBLPRINT command.

- If you want to check the alignment of the labels on the printer, type the word CHECK after the name of the labels and before the ORDER BY and WHERE clauses.

Of course, to send output to the printer (or a file), you can use the OUTPUT command.

Let's use the LBLPRINT command to try printing our labels on the printer. First, go to Command mode (highlight **E**xit on the Main menu and select **R**> prompt). Now, follow these steps:

1. Type **OUTPUT PRINTER** and press ↵.

2. Type **LBLPRINT Nameslbl CHECK** and press ↵.

3. When prompted to

    Print test label? Yes No

    choose **Y**es. You could now adjust the alignment of the labels in the printer.

4. When prompted to

    Print test label? Yes No

    choose **N**o.

5. Type **OUTPUT SCREEN** and press ⏎. The output on
    your printer should look like Figure 7.22.

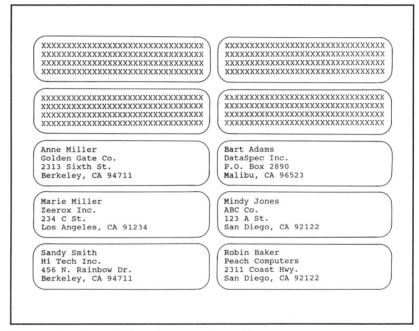

Figure 7.22: Printed labels from the Names file

MANAGING REPORTS AND LABELS

The Mail database now has two report formats, Director and
MLDetail, as well as one label format, Nameslbl. To see the names of
report formats associated with a database, enter the command LIST
REPORTS at the R > prompt. Use the command LIST LABELS
to see the names of all of the label formats associated with a database.
The LIST REPORTS and LIST LABELS commands are illus-
trated in Figure 7.23.

```
R>LIST REPORTS

   Report    Table / View         Report Description
   --------  -------------------  ------------------------------------------
   Director  Names                Mailing List Directory From Names Table
   MLDetail  Names                Mailing List Details
   Letter1   Names                Form letter for Names table

R>LIST LABELS

   Label     Table / View         Label Description
   --------  -------------------  ------------------------------------------
   Nameslbl  Names                Labels for the Names Table

R>_
```

Figure 7.23: Listing the Reports and Labels in the Mail database

On both the Report Generator menu (accessed by highlighting Reports and selecting Create/modify) and the Label Generator menu (accessed by highlighting Reports, selecting Labels, and selecting Create/modify), you have seen how to create and modify report and label formats. Additional options on these menus provide many capabilities; they are outlined below.

Delete	Deletes the report or label format you select. R:BASE will ask for confirmation before deleting the report or label format.
Rename	Changes the name of the report or label format you select. R:BASE prompts you for the new name for this report or label format.
Copy	Copies an existing report or label format in the database to another report or label format in the same database. After you have chosen the report or label format to copy, R:BASE prompts you to enter the name of the new report or label format; choose the table to supply the information; and change the description of the new report or label format, which defaults to the description of the old format.
List	Displays the table providing the information for the selected report or label format.

In this chapter, we've discussed many techniques used to design and create reports and labels. In later chapters, we'll discuss more advanced techniques for formatting reports, including using the advanced features of your printer and printing totals and subtotals. In the next chapter, we'll learn techniques for creating custom data-entry forms.

Chapter 8

Creating Custom Data-Entry Forms

IN THIS CHAPTER, WE'LL DISCUSS TECHNIQUES FOR creating forms for entering and editing table rows. The techniques used to create forms are similar to those that we used to create reports. If you are following along online, open the Mail database to prepare for the examples in this chapter.

CREATING CUSTOM FORMS

There are two primary reasons for creating custom forms: they generally look better than the standard displays, and you can add helpful advice to your screens that simplify the process of entering and editing data.

Let's look at an example. Figure 8.1 shows the standard display used for entering information on the edit screen. Figure 8.2, on the other hand, shows a custom form. Notice how the column names are spelled out and that the instructions for managing the highlighting and cursor appear at the bottom of the screen. Using the Form Generator, you can "draw" a facsimile of the form on the screen in much the same way that you used the Report Generator to draw a facsimile of a printed report in the last chapter.

Sort Edit Calculate Layout Query Manage views Print Exit			
L_Name	F_Name	Company	Address
Janda	Chrissie	UCLA Medical Centre	345 Westwood Blvd.
Miller	Anne	Golden Gate Co.	2313 Sixth St.
Adams	Bart	DataSpec Inc.	P.O. Box 2890
Miller	Marie	Zeerox Inc.	234 C St.
Jones	Mindy	ABC Co.	123 A St.
Smith	Sandy	Hi Tech Inc.	456 N. Rainbow Dr.
Baker	Robin	Peach Computers	2311 Coast Hwy.

Figure 8.1: The standard Edit screen

To create a simple form such as the one in Figure 8.2, follow these general steps:

1. Design the form.

2. Start the Form Generator.

Additional techniques for creating more complicated forms are discussed in Chapter 13.

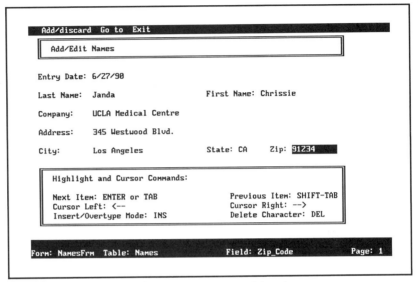

Figure 8.2: A custom form for entering and editing data

3. Enter the prompts and other explanatory text.

4. Place the data columns on the form.

5. Add boxes to highlight sections of the screen.

6. Save and test the form.

7. Leave the Form Generator.

As we discuss these steps, you will notice many similarities between creating a form and creating a report, which we discussed in the last chapter.

STEP 1: DESIGN THE FORM

Before you create a form, you should design it on paper. You want the form to be easy to use, pleasant to look at, and have fields located in a logical fashion. You may want the screen form to look like an existing paper form.

Figure 8.2 shows the form we will be creating. Although this form fits onto a single screen, you are not limited to that. R:BASE lets you create forms up to five screens long.

STEP 2: START THE FORM GENERATOR

Starting the Form Generator involves displaying the Form Generator menu, choosing the type of form to create, providing a name and description for the form, and providing additional information, such as the name of the table supplying the data. Let's examine these steps one at a time.

Displaying the Form Generator Menu There are two methods for displaying the Form Generator menu. From the R:BASE Main menu, you can highlight Forms and select Create/modify. Alternatively, from the R:BASE R> prompt you can type the command FORMS and press ◄───┘.

Let's start from the R:BASE Main menu. After you have highlighted Forms and selected Create/modify, you should see the Form Generator menu, shown in Figure 8.3. (If you have not yet opened the Mail database, you will be given an opportunity to do so before the menu is displayed.) As you can see, the Form Generator menu allows you to create new forms as well as modify, delete, rename, copy, and list existing forms.

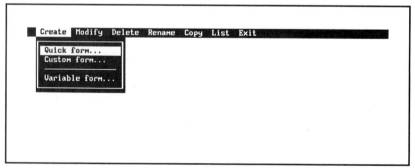

Figure 8.3: The Form Generator menu

Choosing the Type of Form Since you want to create a form, you will choose the Create option in the menu. Below Create, a pull-down menu provides three options: Quick form, Custom form, and Variable form.

- The Quick form option provides a "starter kit" of fields and column names arranged in a column in the center of the screen.

- The Custom form option allows you to create the form from scratch, starting without any fields on the screen.

- The Variable form option is used when you are writing programs to place information in variables.

In the case of our Mail database, the Custom form option is a better choice than the Quick form option, since our form is not very similar to the standard quick form. Highlight the **Custom** form option now and press ←⏎.

Providing a Form Name and Description   You are now asked to enter a new form name and description. For this example, type the name **NamesFrm** and press ←⏎. Then type in the description **Add/Edit Names** and press ←⏎.

Providing Additional Information   The next piece of information R:BASE needs is the name of the table that will receive the data from this form. Select the **N**ames table, and R:BASE will display the Form Generator screen. You use this screen to "draw" your form on the screen and place column names in much the same way you used the Report Generator screen to lay out reports.

STEP 3: ENTER THE PROMPTS AND OTHER TEXT

This screen looks very similar to the Report Generator screen, except there aren't as many menu items at the top and there are no header, detail, or footer sections at the left side. A position indicator in the bottom-right corner of the screen displays the page number and the row and column number. Our form only has one page, but it is possible to make forms with more than one page. You can move around the screen and enter text pretty much the same way you did with reports. For example, you can use the mouse to position the cursor and make menu selections. The keys used for creating forms are listed in Table 8.1. (Additional keys can be used when creating more complicated forms. We'll discuss them in Chapter 13.)

Table 8.1: Keys Used to Create and Edit Forms

KEY	PURPOSE
F1	Get help
Shift-F1	Get function key descriptions
F3	Display database information on available tables, columns, and variables
F6	Place a column or variable on the form
F9	Delete the current line, if the current line has no columns or variables
Shift-F9	Remove a column or variable from the form
F10	Insert a blank line above the cursor
↑	Move the cursor up one line
↓	Move the cursor down one line
→	Move the cursor to the right one character
←	Move the cursor to the left one character
Ctrl-→	Move the cursor to screen column number 80
Ctrl-←	Move the cursor to screen column number 1
Tab	Move the cursor 10 spaces to the right
Shift-Tab	Move the cursor 10 spaces to the left
Home	Move to the upper-left corner of the form
End	Move to the bottom-right corner of the form
↵	Move to the beginning of the next line
Ins	Toggle between Insert mode (the cursor is a block) and Overtype mode (the cursor is an underline)
Del	Delete the character at the cursor position

Let's begin by putting the title on the form. Move the cursor to row 2, column 6 (position indicator < 2, 6>), and type in the title

Add/Edit Names

Given your experience in drawing report formats in the last chapter, you should have no difficulty entering the prompts on this form. The starting locations for the various prompts and other text on the NamesFrm form are listed below. Position the cursor to the coordinates listed in the left column, and type in the text listed in the right column. Figure 8.4 shows how your screen should look after typing in all the prompts and other text.

LOCATION	*TEXT*
< 2, 6>	Add/Edit Names
< 5, 3>	Entry Date:
< 7, 3>	Last Name:
< 7,40>	First Name:
< 9, 3>	Company:
<11, 3>	Address:
<13, 3>	City:
<13,40>	State:
<13,54>	Zip:
<16, 6>	Highlight and Cursor Commands:
<18, 6>	Next Item: ENTER or TAB
<18,45>	Previous Item: SHIFT-TAB
<19, 6>	Cursor Left: <--
<19,45>	Cursor Right: -->
<20, 6>	Insert/Overtype Mode: INS
<20,45>	Delete Character: DEL

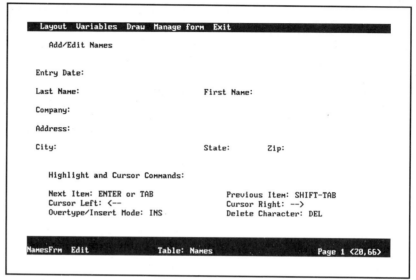

Figure 8.4: Text typed into the form

STEP 4: PLACE DATA COLUMNS ON THE FORM

After all the prompts and other text are on the screen, place the data columns on the screen with F6 or the Layout menu option. To do this, use the same techniques you used with the Report Generator screen.

To review, follow the steps below to place the Ent_Date field next to the "Entry Date" prompt in the form.

1. Move the cursor to row 5, column 15 ($<$ 5,15$>$).

2. Press **F6**.

3. Press ⏎ to bring up the menu for choosing columns and variables.

4. With **C**olumns highlighted, select **Ent_Date**.

5. Choose **N**o to defining an expression for Ent_Date.

6. Choose **N**o to customizing the field settings.

We will discuss how to customize the field settings later in this chapter in the section "Customizing the Features of Your Form."

7. Press **S** when prompted to "Move cursor to start location and press S." The field is now painted in inverse video and the cursor is sitting at position < 5,44 >.

8. Press **E** when prompted to "Move cursor to end and press E."

Of course, in place of steps 3 and 4 above, you could simply have typed Ent_Date and pressed ↩ at the "Enter Column or Variable Name" prompt. With the Ent_Date column defined, your screen should now have a long, highlighted block next to the Entry Date prompt.

Now let's review how to place a field using the Layout menu. We'll place the L_Name field beside the "Last Name" prompt.

1. Move the cursor to row 7, column 15 (< 7,15 >).

2. Highlight **Layout** and select **P**lace field.

Instead of typing in L_Name, you could press ↩ and choose L_Name from the Columns and Variables menu.

3. Type **L_Name** and press ↩ when asked to enter the column or variable name.

4. Choose **N**o to defining an expression for Ent_Date.

5. Choose **N**o to customizing the field settings.

6. Press **S** when prompted to "Move cursor to start location and press S."

Remember that pressing Ctrl-→ to move the cursor to the end of a field only works if the field is a table column with the TEXT data type.

7. Press **Ctrl-→** when prompted to "Move cursor to end and press W or E." This paints the field to the length of the L_Name field and moves the cursor to position < 7,29 >.

8. Press **E** to mark the end of the L_Name field.

The "Move cursor to end and press W or E" prompt you saw in step 7 above appears only when you're dealing with TEXT and NOTE columns. It tells you that you can create a multi-line field more than one line high. Suppose you wanted to create a multi-line field. You would follow these steps:

1. Press S to mark the start of the field, as in step 6 above. This indicates the top-left corner of the rectangle.

2. Indicate how many characters wide you would like the field to be by moving the cursor to the top-right corner of the rectangle and pressing W.

3. Move the cursor down how many lines you want the field to be and press E to mark the bottom-right corner of the rectangle.

Use the same techniques you used with the L_Name column to place the rest of the table columns on the form. Just answer "No" when R:BASE asks about defining expressions and about customizing field settings. The column names, start locations, and end locations to use on this form are listed below:

COLUMN NAME	START	END
F_Name	< 7,52>	< 7,66>
Company	< 9,15>	< 9,34>
Address	<11,15>	<11,39>
City	<13,15>	<13,29>
State	<13,47>	<13,48>
Zip_Code	<13,59>	<13,68>

After you're finished placing all of the column names, your screen should look like Figure 8.5.

STEP 5: ADD BOXES TO HIGHLIGHT SECTIONS OF THE SCREEN

For a fancier and easier-to-read display, you can add double- or single-line boxes. Let's try placing a double-line box around the title of the form.

1. Move the cursor to < 1, 3>.

If you wanted to make a single-line box, you would select Single lines under Draw on the menu.

2. Highlight **Draw** and select **Double** lines. Notice the words "Pen Up" in the lower-left corner of the screen. This indicates that you can move the cursor around without drawing anything on the screen.

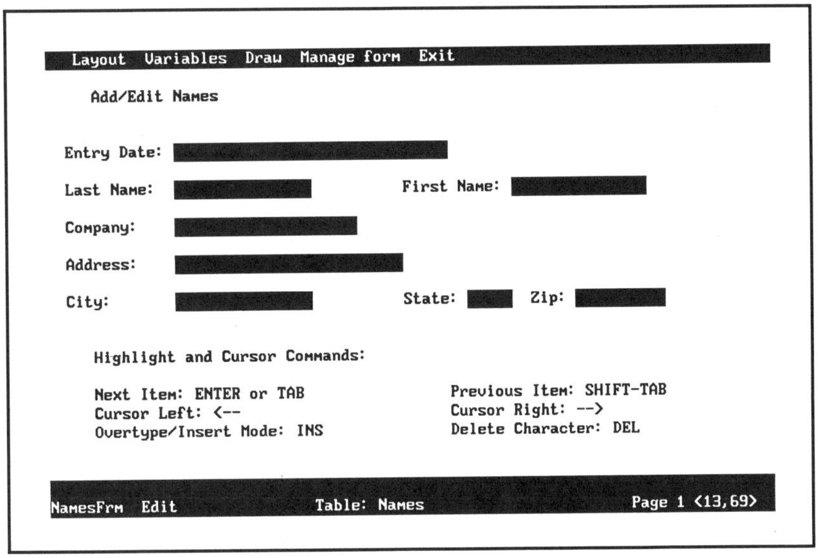

Figure 8.5: The table columns placed on the screen

3. Since we are at one corner of the box we want to draw, press **Ctrl-F6** to put the pen down and begin drawing. Now "Pen Down" appears in the lower-left corner of the screen.

4. Keep pressing → until the cursor is at < 1,70>. Now the cursor draws the double line as it moves.

5. Press ↓ twice to move the cursor to < 3,70>. When we changed direction, the top and right sides of the box were joined in a perfect right angle.

6. Keep pressing ← until the cursor is at < 3, 3>. Once again, the bottom-right corner of the box has a right angle.

7. Press ↑ twice to move the cursor to < 1, 3>, leaving a right angle at the bottom-left corner.

8. Press → to draw the right angle in the top-left corner.

9. Press **F2** to finish drawing.

If you overshoot the mark and make one of the lines too long, you can't just back up the cursor to erase the line you drew. To fix this kind of mistake, first press F2 to stop drawing. Then highlight Draw and select Erase. The Erase option erases either single or double lines as you move the cursor over the lines with the pen down. When you have erased your mistake, reposition the cursor to a point in the box before the mistake, highlight Draw, select Double lines, place the pen down and continue.

Using the same techniques you used with the first box, try drawing a double-line box around the instructions at the bottom of the screen. Put the top-left corner at <15, 3>, the top-right corner at <15,70>, the bottom-right corner at <21,70>, and the bottom-left corner at <21, 3>. Now your screen should have two double-line boxes, one around the form name and one around the highlight and cursor commands.

STEP 6: SAVE AND TEST THE FORM

Now that we have created the form, let's save the form and take it for a test drive. We can test this form in one of two modes, either by adding new data to the Names table or by editing existing data. Let's try using this form to add another row to the Names table.

The form is automatically saved when you test it.

1. Highlight **M**anage form and select **R**un.
2. Select **A**dd data.
3. Type **7/15/90** in the Entry Date field and press **Tab**.
4. Type **Ferguson** in the Last Name field and press **Tab**.
5. Type **Harold** in the First Name field and press **Tab**.
6. Type **PromoTech Sales** in the Company field and press **Tab**.
7. Type **4109 Crest St.** in the Address field and press **Tab**.
8. Type **Los Angeles** in the City field and press **Tab**.
9. Type **CA** in the State field and press **Tab**.
10. Type **91234** in the Zip field. At this point, your screen should look like Figure 8.6.

You can use the mouse to move the highlighter to a field or to highlight and select a menu option.

11. Highlight **A**dd/discard and select the **A**dd row option to add this row to the Names table. The fields are now empty, ready for you to add another row to the table.

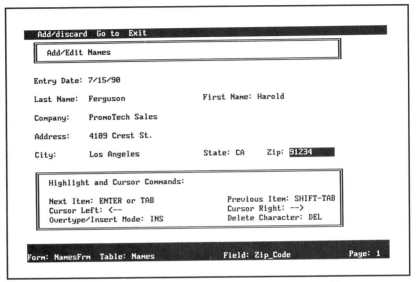

Figure 8.6: Testing the form by adding a row to the Names table

12. Select **Exit** on the menu to end the test and return to the Form Generator screen.

   In step 11, there were three other choices in the Add/discard pull-down menu: Add and duplicate row, Discard, and Add row and exit. The Add and duplicate row option allows you to not only add the row, but to leave the new values in the new row's fields. The Discard row option gives you a chance to start the row over without storing this row in the table. The Add row and exit option lets you add the row and then return to the Form Generator screen.

   Although you were only testing the form, you really did add Harold Ferguson to the Names table. You can remove this new row while testing your form using the Edit data option.

1. Highlight **Ma**nage form and select **R**un.

2. Select **Edit** data, and the first row of the Names table is displayed on our form.

3. Keep pressing **F8** until the row for Harold Ferguson appears on the screen.

4. Highlight **E**dit and select **D**elete row.

5. Choose **Y**es when asked if you want to delete this row.

6. Select **E**xit on the menu to return to the Form Generator screen.

Since our form has performed as expected, there are no changes to make before leaving the Form Generator screen.

STEP 7: LEAVE THE FORM GENERATOR

Just as with the Report Generator, you can save the form at any time by highlighting Manage form on the menu and selecting Save changes. When you select either Add data or Edit data to test the form, the form is saved automatically before the test begins.

To leave the Form Generator screen, select Exit on the menu. If you made changes to the form since the last time it was saved, you are given an opportunity to save the changes before leaving the Form Generator screen.

Remember, the form is saved each time you test it.

Select **E**xit now, and you will be returned to the Form Generator menu. Select **E**xit again to return to the R:BASE Main menu.

ADDING AND EDITING DATA WITH FORMS

You saw how to use the form to add and edit data when you were testing it in the Form Generator. As you might expect, you can start adding data to or editing data in the form either from the R:BASE Main menu or from the R> prompt.

WORKING WITH FORMS FROM THE MAIN MENU

Let's start from the R:BASE Main menu and add two people who work at the same company. Their company name and address information will be the same, so we can use the Add and duplicate row option under the Add/discard pull-down menu to save time.

1. Highlight **Forms** and select **NamesFrm**.

2. Select **Add** data.

3. Type **7/1/90** and press **Tab**.

4. Type **Teasdale** and press **Tab**.

5. Type **Trudy** and press **Tab**.

6. Type **Atomic Micros Inc.** and press **Tab**.

7. Type **321 Microwave St.** and press **Tab**.

8. Type **Lassiter** and press **Tab**.

9. Type **OH** and press **Tab**.

10. Type **12121**.

11. Highlight **Add/discard** and select the **Add and duplicate row** option.

12. Press **Tab** to move to the Last Name field.

13. Press **Shift-F9** to clear the field.

14. Type **Martin** and press **Tab**.

15. Press **Shift-F9** to clear the field.

16. Type **Mary**.

17. Highlight **Add/discard** and select the **Add row and exit** option.

After you entered the information for Trudy Teasdale, you may have noticed that the entry date changed from 7/1/90 to Jul 01, 1990. This will happen if you set the date format to MMM DD, YYYY, as we did in the last chapter.

You can also use the form to edit data when you are at the R:BASE Main menu. If you want, you can display only certain rows on the form and sort them in a particular order, just as you can when printing reports from the R:BASE Main menu. This involves highlighting Forms and selecting the name of the form you want to use. After that, select Edit data. When the submenu appears, specify the order you want the rows presented in and which rows to include.

- To sort the information, select Quick sort, select each column to sort on from most important to least important, whether you want an ascending or descending sort, and press F2.

- To search for certain rows to be edited using straightfor-ward search conditions, select Quick select, and for each column you want searched,

    a. Select the column,

    b. Select a comparison operator, and

    c. Type in a comparison value and press ←⏎.

To enter more conditions, select a logical connection such as AND, OR, AND NOT, or OR NOT, and repeat steps a to c above. To finish entering conditions, select (Done).

- To search for certain rows to be edited using more compli-cated search conditions, select Enter WHERE clause, type in the conditions you want a row to satisfy in order to be presented for editing, and press ←⏎ when you are finished typing the conditions.

Finally, press F2 when you are happy with the sort and search condi-tions and want to start editing.

Let's try changing Ms. Teasdale's first name from Trudy to Judy.

1. Highlight **Forms** and select **NamesFrm**.

2. Select **Edit** data.

3. Select **Q**uick select.

4. Select **L_**Name for the Column.

5. Select = EQUAL for the comparison Operator.

6. Type **Teasdale** and press ←⏎ for Value.

7. Select (Done) to leave the Quick Select screen.

8. Press **F2** to start the editing.

9. Move the highlighter to the First Name field.

10. Press **Shift-F9** to clear the field.

11. Type **Judy** and press ←⏎.

12. Highlight **E**dit and select **S**ave changes.

You will now hear a beep to tell you that, when R:BASE attempted to display the next row to be edited, it could not find any other rows.

13. Select **E**xit to return to the R:BASE Main menu.

After you've selected Edit data to begin making changes to a form, you could issue a sort command to bring up certain fields for editing. For example, we could use the following steps to examine all of the rows in which the last name starts with *M*. To do this, we'll sort the rows by last and first name.

1. Highlight **F**orms and select **N**amesFrm.

2. Select **E**dit data.

3. Select **Q**uick sort.

4. Select **L**_Name and then **A**scending.

5. Select **F**_Name and then **A**scending.

6. Press **F2** to finish specifying the sort.

7. Select **E**nter WHERE clause.

8. Type **L_Name LIKE 'M%'** and press ⏎.

9. Press **F2** to start editing. The record for Mary Martin is displayed.

10. Press **F8**. The record for Anne Miller is displayed.

11. Press **F8** again. The record for Marie Miller is displayed.

12. Select **E**xit to return to the R:BASE Main menu.

WORKING WITH FORMS FROM THE R > PROMPT

Of course, you can add or edit data in a form from the R > prompt as well. The ENTER command allows you to add data using a form. For example, to add data using NamesFrm you would type in the command

ENTER NamesFrm

If you edit a row and then select Exit without saving the changes you made, R:BASE will give you a chance to save your changes before returning you to the R:BASE Main menu.

To edit data using a form you can enter the EDIT USING command at the R > prompt. You have seen in earlier chapters that the EDIT ALL FROM Names command will display the Edit screen for the Names table. To edit data in the Names table using the NamesFrm form, you would enter the command

EDIT USING NamesFrm

Just as you saw for the EDIT command back in Chapters 4 and 5, you can use the ORDER BY clause to bring up the rows in sorted order and the WHERE clause to determine which rows are presented. To refresh your memory with an example, let's edit rows whose last names start with *M*. Enter the following command:

EDIT USING NamesFrm ORDER BY L_Name F_Name +
+ > WHERE L_Name LIKE 'M%'

You can also issue the EDIT USING command to add a new row that is very similar to an existing row. Suppose you want to add the name of someone who works at a company already listed in the table, such as ABC Co. To do this, you would begin by editing the existing data on the form. In our example, you would enter the command

EDIT USING NamesFrm WHERE Company = 'ABC Co.'

This displays the data in the first row that contains ABC Co. Next, you would change whatever is necessary for the new row—probably the Last and First Name and the Entry Date fields. After that, you would highlight Edit and select the Add row option to add the row to the table, and select Exit to return to the R > prompt.

EDITING EXISTING FORMS

To modify an existing form, first display the Form Generator menu, either by highlighting Forms on the R:BASE Main menu and selecting Create/modify, or by using the FORMS command at the R > prompt. Then highlight Modify on the Form Generator menu and select the name of the form you want to modify.

You can add, change or remove prompts and other text, lines, boxes, columns and variables on the form, just as you could when you first created the form.

Changing a location of a field on the form is a common task and involves the following steps:

1. Move the cursor onto the field.

2. Either press **F6** or highlight **Layout**, and select **P**lace field.

3. Choose **N**o when asked if you want to customize field settings.

4. Choose **Y**es when asked if you want to relocate the field position.

5. Move the cursor to the new location where you want the field to start.

6. Press **S** to start the field.

7. Move the cursor where you want the field to end.

8. Press **E** to end the field.

To delete a field from the form, move the cursor onto the field and then either press Shift-F9 or highlight Layout and select Clear field. Other ways of customizing forms are discussed in the following sections.

We'll discuss field settings later in this chapter in the section "Customizing Field Settings."

To establish the size of multi-line TEXT and NOTE fields that occupy more than one line, move the cursor to the top-right corner of the rectangle and press W. Then move the cursor to the bottom-right corner and press E.

CUSTOMIZING THE FEATURES OF YOUR FORM

You can customize several overall features of a form, such as its color and some of the pull-down menus. To do so, highlight **Layout** and select **F**orm settings. You'll see a screen, as in Figure 8.7, displaying all your options for customizing the overall form.

You can use the ↑ and ↓ keys to move the highlighter from question to question. Typing Y changes a No answer to Yes, and vice versa. Questions followed by a N/A are not applicable to the form being customized.

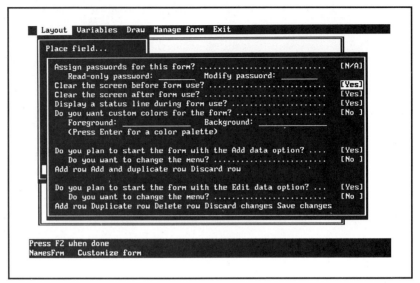

Figure 8.7: The Form Customizing menu

The first question on the form reads

Assign passwords for this form? . . . . [N/A]
        Read-only password: _____   Modify password: _____

On tables that use password protection, you can change this option to Yes, and then assign passwords for Read-only access and Modify access. If you assign a password for Read-only access, only users who know the password will be able to view data through this form. If you assign a Modify password, any user will be able to view data on the form, but only those who know the password will be able to change data on the form. We'll be discussing more about password protection in Chapter 9.

The second two questions on the screen are

Clear the screen before form use? . . . . [Yes]
Clear the screen after form use? . . . . [Yes]

Usually you'll want to leave these as Yes so that the form appears on a clear screen and erases itself from the screen when no longer in use.

The next question on the form,

> Display a status line during form use?. . . . . [Yes]

lets you decide whether to leave the status bar on the bottom of the screen while the form is in use [Yes] or to hide it while the form is in use [No].

The next section, shown below, refers to color monitors:

> Do you want custom colors for the form? . . . . [No]
> Foreground: _____ Background: _____
> (Press Enter for a color palette)

If you change this answer to Yes, you can then press ↵ twice for a palette of colors to select from. Select the colors for the form in the same fashion as you would using the SET COLOR command, and then press F2.

The next question

> Do you plan to start the form with the Add data option? . . . [Yes]

asks whether the form will be used with the Add data option or the ENTER command (for adding new rows to the table). Usually, you will want to leave this as a Yes answer.

If you do want to use the Add data option, you can change the pull-down menu under the Add/discard option, as the next question on the form indicates:

> Do you want to change the menu?. . . . . [No]
> Add row Add and duplicate row Discard row Add row and exit

If you select Yes, R:BASE will display a menu with the four possible choices. You have seen check-mark menus like this before, where you can select as many choices on the menu as you would like. To select (or unselect) a choice, place the cursor beside the choice and press ↵. A check mark (✓) will appear beside the choice. When you are finished making your choices, press F2.

The next question is

Do you plan to start the form with the Edit data option? ... [Yes]
Do you want to change the menu?................ [No]
Add row Duplicate row Delete row Discard changes Save changes

The question, like the previous one, allows you to determine whether the form can be used with the Edit data option or the EDIT USING command, and it allows you to modify the default pull-down menu under the Edit option.

When you've finished selecting the form characteristics, press the F2 key.

CUSTOMIZING TABLE SETTINGS

You can customize several settings for the table associated with the form. When you highlight Layout and select Table settings, the Table Settings menu appears, as shown in Figure 8.8. The first question asks

Do you want to add new rows to the table?............ [Yes]

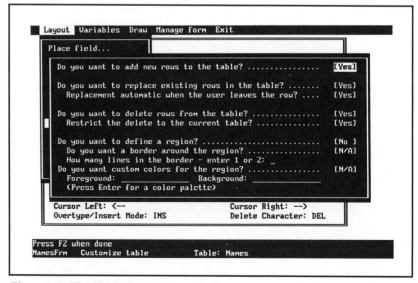

Figure 8.8: The Table Settings menu

Unless you do not ever want to add new rows to a table, this answer should be left as Yes. Similarly, the following three answers should be left as Yes unless the data on the table are never to be edited or deleted:

Do you want to replace existing rows in the table? . . . .   [Yes]
  Replacement automatic when the user leaves the row? .   [Yes]

Do you want to delete rows from the table?. . . . .   [Yes]

The remaining questions on the menu are for more advanced applications. We'll discuss them in the next few chapters.

CUSTOMIZING FIELD SETTINGS

The Form Generator gives you the opportunity to change the settings that affect one field without altering the other fields in the form or table. This is a valuable feature to have, as now and then you will want to alter a particular field to make it stand out. Important fields are often candidates for customization.

You have already been introduced to custom field settings. When you placed or moved a field on the screen by pressing the F6 key (or by highlighting Layout and selecting Place field), you were asked if you wanted to customize the field settings. Answering Yes to this question displays the Field Settings menu. Another way to display the Field Settings menu is to select the Field settings option in the pull-down menu under Layout.

Let's see how the Field Settings menu works by customizing the Ent_Date field. Move onto the Ent_Date field, press **F6**, and answer **Y**es when asked if you want to customize the field settings. The Field Settings menu for the Ent_Date field appears, as in Figure 8.9. This menu has two screens, and you can press PgDn or PgUp to move between them.

The first three questions asked are

Will new data be entered in the field? . . . .   [Yes]

Can the user change the data displayed in the field? . . . . .   [Yes]
  Restrict changes to the current table? . . . .   [Yes]

Figure 8.9: The first screen of the Field Settings menu

These questions should all be left with Yes answers, except in more advanced applications involving multiple tables. (Again, this is a topic we'll discuss in Chapter 13.)

Skip the fourth and fifth questions for now. The next set of questions lets you select colors for the single field:

The fourth and fifth questions, about default values, will be discussed in detail in the next section.

> Do you want custom colors for the field?. . . . . [No]
>   Foreground: _____ Background: _____
>   (Press Enter for a color palette)

Changing the answer to Yes and pressing ↵ twice will allow you to define colors for the individual field from the color palette.

The last question on this screen asks if you want this field to blink when it is displayed. If you wanted the contents of this field to blink, then you could change this answer to Yes. Having a field blink can be very distracting, so this feature should only be used when you need to draw attention to the contents of a field.

Move to the second screen of this menu by pressing **PgDn**. Your screen should look like Figure 8.10. The first question

> Do you want a help line displayed for this field? . . . . [No]

allows you to enter a help line at the bottom of the screen that will be displayed whenever the highlighter moves to a particular field. To enter a help line, change the answer to Yes, press ←—, and then type in the help line.

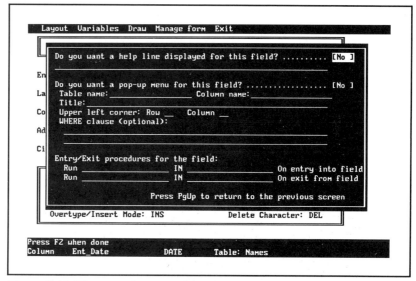

Figure 8.10: The second screen of the Field Settings menu

The second question should be left with a No answer and subsequent fields should be left blank. The second question is discussed in Chapter 17.

When you are finished defining the field settings, either press Esc if you do not want to make any changes or press F2 to keep the changes you have made. Then answer No when asked if you want to relocate the Ent_Date field.

DEFINING DEFAULT VALUES

Default values (also called *suggested responses*) are a valuable asset to forms, particularly in forms where information might otherwise have to be typed in repeatedly. For example, NamesFrm contains the column Ent_Date, which is the date that the row was entered into the database. On any given day, this is likely to be the same for every row entered into the database. Therefore, you could make the current date the *default value* for the field. When entering new rows into the database, the current date will automatically appear in the Ent-_Date field. You (or whoever is entering the data) can just press ◄┘ to accept the default date, or you can type in a new date.

Another example is the State column in the Names table. If 90 percent of the individuals in the table were from the state of California, you could make CA the default value for the field. That way, when entering data, you need only press ◄┘ to skip over the State field and use the "suggested" value, CA. If the state weren't CA, you could type a different state into the field.

To place a default value in a field, you simply customize the field setting and enter the value in response to the appropriate questions. Let's try adding a default of today's date in the Entry Date field:

1. Move onto the Ent_Date field and press **F6**.

2. Choose **Y**es when asked if you want to customize the field settings.

3. Move to the question that asks

    Do you want to display a default value in the field? . .   [No   ]

4. Change the answer to this question to **Y**es and press ◄┘.

5. You are now prompted to

    Enter default value or #DUP to use the previous row value

    Type **#DATE** (which stands for the current date).

6. Press **F2** to finish customizing the field settings.

7. Choose **N**o when asked if you want to relocate the field.

To add the default of CA for the State field, you would use the following steps:

1. Move onto the State field and press **F6**.

2. Choose **Y**es when asked if you want to customize the field settings.

3. Move to the question that asks

    Do you want to display a default value in the field? . .   [No   ]

4. Change the answer to this question to **Yes** and press ⏎.

5. You are now prompted to

   Enter default value or #DUP to use the previous row value

   Type **CA**.

6. Press **F2** to finish customizing the field settings.

7. Choose **No** when asked if you want to relocate the field.

The #DUP function is a special default value that repeats whatever was entered into the last row, in effect making it the default value. This function would be useful, or example, if you were entering data for individuals who happened to be grouped by states. You would enter TX (Texas) residents first, and TX would remain the default value for all the records until you typed in the next state on the form. Then the new state would be the default value, and so on.

When you are finished entering the default values for the fields, you can test our changes to make sure they came out right. Highlight Manage form, select Run, and select Add data. The form will appear with the default values already in their fields. By pressing ⏎ while the default value is highlighted, you accept the suggested value as the default. Optionally, you can type over the suggested value (or use Shift-F9 to erase it) to enter a different value into the column. When you have finished testing the default values on this screen, highlight and select **Exit** to return to the Form Generator screen.

CHANGING THE ORDER OF ENTRY FOR FIELDS

When you create a form, the order in which you place data columns determines the order in which R:BASE moves through them when you enter or edit data on the form. You can change the order in which R:BASE moves the highlighter through the prompts, however. To do this,

1. Highlight **Layout** and select **Change field order**. R:BASE displays a submenu showing the fields on the screen and their position when entering data.

2. Select the field that you want to move in the position list.

3. Type in the number of the new position you would like this field to have and press ←.

4. Press F2 when you are finished changing the order of the fields.

5. To test the new order, highlight **L**ayout and select **S**how field order.

6. Press ← repeatedly to see the order in which R:BASE will move the highlighter through the prompts.

7. Press **F2** when you are finished.

When you've determined the appropriate order for your form, leave the Form Generator screen in the usual way, by selecting **E**xit and then saving your changes if desired.

DELETING, RENAMING, COPYING AND LISTING FORMS

You have used the Create and Modify functions of the Form Generator menu. Just as for reports, you can also use this menu to delete, rename, copy, and list forms.

Another way to get a listing of the forms in your database is by entering the LIST FORMS command at the R> prompt.

In this chapter we've discussed the Form Generator and various techniques for creating and using forms. In the next chapter we'll look at ways in which you can add password protection for your data and alter the structure of your tables.

Chapter 9

Improving
Table Structure
and Protecting
Table Data

MURPHY'S LAW DICTATES THAT AFTER CAREFULLY planning a database structure and adding some data to it, you'll want to make some changes. For example, you might find that the assigned width of 20 characters is not enough for the Company column in the Names table. You might also decide that you want to add columns to the Names table for telephone numbers and customer numbers.

Once you've made the appropriate modifications to the basic structure of the table, you'll probably want to modify reports and forms accordingly. This chapter explains how to make these modifications.

Of course, you may not want everyone who uses your computer to be able to change the structure of your database or the information you have entered. We'll start this chapter by discussing how to protect your data with various types of passwords so that you can control who adds, changes, or examines the structure of your database and the data in it. If you are following along on-line, start R:BASE in the normal fashion so that you are at the R:BASE Main menu.

PROTECTING YOUR DATA WITH PASSWORDS

It's never too early to think about database security. If employee wages or salaries are part of your database in an employee table, you may not want everyone who uses the database to be able to see the payroll information. Perhaps you have a clients table which includes sensitive information, such as unlisted phone numbers meant for your eyes only. R:BASE provides you with a number of tools to establish varying levels of database security. Passwords are the most straightforward of these tools.

R:BASE allows you to set up two major types of password protection for your data: owner and user. The *owner password* affects the entire database and allows only those who know it to use all R:BASE commands. You can also set up one or more *user passwords* to restrict different users' access to specific data on a table-by-table basis. The owner password is the database's most important one. Once you've established an owner password, only individuals who know it will be able to make structural changes in the database. Furthermore, more

R:BASE 3.1 actually has two other versions of passwords left over from previous versions. You can have READ and MODIFY passwords for both tables and forms.

specific user passwords can only be set up once an owner password has already been established.

ESTABLISHING AN OWNER PASSWORD

You create owner and user passwords by way of the Access rights option on the menu used to modify databases. Let's try out this option and set up an owner password called MYMAIL for the Mail database.

We are using a simple password for this example, but you should make-up better, harder-to-guess passwords.

When you are setting up a password, you have be careful not to make any typing mistakes. If you make a typing mistake, you won't know your password and won't be able to access the database.

1. Highlight **D**atabases and select **MAIL** to connect to the Mail database.

2. Highlight **I**nfo and select **C**reate/modify.

3. Highlight **A**ccess rights and select **C**hange owner.

4. When prompted to enter the new owner password, type **MYMAIL** but don't press ◄── just yet. Verify that your screen looks the same as Figure 9.1 and that you have typed MYMAIL correctly. Then press ◄──.

5. Highlight and select **E**xit to return to the Main menu.

Figure 9.1: Setting up an owner password for the Mail database

Take a look at the menu options in the Access rights pull-down menu. You can use these menu items when you change the owner password. Of course, once you have set up an owner password, no one can modify the database structure (as you did in step 2 above) without entering the owner password first. This means that no one can change the owner password to a new value without first knowing what the owner password is now.

The same holds true if you want to set up, change, or remove the owner password at the R > prompt—you have to know the owner password first. Here you would use the RENAME command, as follows:

RENAME OWNER *oldpassword* TO *newpassword*

where *oldpassword* is the current owner password and *newpassword* is the name you want to change it to. Some of you may be wondering what to use for the old password when you don't have an owner password and you want to set one up. In this case, use the special word PUBLIC as the *oldpassword*. Similarly, if you want to remove an old password, you can use PUBLIC for the *newpassword*.

It doesn't matter whether you use uppercase letters (MYMAIL) or lowercase letters (mymail) or any combination (MyMail) when you type in a password. R:BASE does not treat uppercase letters different from lowercase letters in passwords.

Opening a Database with an Owner Password

Now you have set up an owner password for the Mail database, and R:BASE knows that whoever wants to access the database must enter the password to prove that he or she is authorized to do so. R:BASE will ask for the password the next time you try to open the database. Let's see this feature in action by trying the following steps with the R:BASE menus:

1. Highlight **E**xit and select **L**eave R:BASE to return to DOS.

2. Start R:BASE as usual, displaying the Main menu.

3. Highlight **D**atabases and select **M**AIL. R:BASE beeps and displays the message ''-ERROR- The current password will not allow access to any table.''

4. Press any key to remove the message.

5. Type **MYMAIL** and press ← when prompted to "Enter a new user identifier." The Mail database opens and appears in the bottom-left corner of the screen.

Of course, you can also use the CONNECT command at the R > prompt to open a database. R:BASE will ask you for the password when you enter the CONNECT command as well.

After you typed in MYMAIL in step 5 above, MYMAIL became the *current password*. Now when you access a table or open a database, R:BASE will see if the password MYMAIL gives you permission to do so. MYMAIL will remain the current password until you leave R:BASE or you change the current password. Later in this chapter, in the section "Testing Access Rights with User Passwords," you will learn how to tell R:BASE the current password without R:BASE beeping at you, and also how to change the current password.

When you create an owner password, R:BASE makes the owner password the current password, just as if you had entered the password when you connected to the database.

ESTABLISHING A USER PASSWORD

Now that you have created an owner password for the Mail database, you are ready to set up user passwords for the Names table. Typically, only the owner or manager of the database knows the owner password. Users, meanwhile, are given user passwords that allow them an appropriate type of access and the ability to perform certain types of actions on the table. You can set up user passwords to provide four types of access to a table: Select, Update, Insert, and Delete.

Select access	lets people who know the user password look at or print rows from the table.
Update access	lets people who know the user password change the column values in existing rows of the table.
Insert access	lets people who know the user password add rows to the table.
Delete access	lets people who know the password delete rows from the table.

R:BASE provides a lot of flexibility when it comes to creating user passwords and specifying what kind of access rights each password grants. You can create many user passwords for a table. A password can give the user a combination of access rights or only one. You can also create several user passwords that each grant the same access rights.

To illustrate how user passwords work, we'll create four user passwords for the Names table.

- ICHANGE1 will grant Select, Update, and Insert access. Users who know this password will have the right to update the information in all columns.

- ICHANGE2 will grant Select and Update access. Users given this password will have the right to update every column except Ent_Date.

- ILOOK1 and ILOOK2 will only grant Select access.

Notice that none of the user passwords will grant Delete access to the Names table. To delete a row from the names table, it will be necessary to enter the owner password. So only the database manager will be able to delete data from the Names table.

Establishing User Passwords from the R:BASE Menus

Starting from the R:BASE Main menu, follow the steps below to create the ICHANGE1 password. This one will grant Select, Update, and Insert access to the user.

1. Highlight **I**nfo and select **C**reate/modify.

2. Highlight **A**ccess rights and select **G**rant.

3. Select **SELECT**, **UPDATE**, and **INSERT** from the submenu. A check mark (✓) appears beside each of your choices.

4. Press **F2** to finish selecting access types.

5. Select **N**ames (the only choice in this list) as the table accessed with the passwords we are setting up.

6. The next submenu appears because you selected the Update access option. Whichever columns you select on this submenu can be updated by users who know the password you are creating. To select all columns, press **Shift-F6**. Then press **F2** to finish selecting columns.

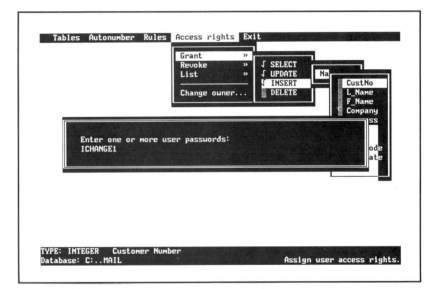

Be careful when typing user passwords as well as owner passwords.

7. Now you are prompted to "Enter one or more user passwords." The password you enter will give users Select, Update, and Insert access to the Names table. Type **ICHANGE1**, but before you press ←, make sure your screen looks like Figure 9.2.

Figure 9.2: Setting up a user password for the Names table

8. Now you are asked whether you want to "assign GRANT permission." Choose Yes if you want users who know the ICHANGE1 password to be able to create other passwords and in so doing grant Select, Update, or Insert access to others who possess the new, secondary passwords. Let's select **N**o for this example. You have now finished creating the password ICHANGE1.

Now let's create the password ICHANGE2 with Select and Update access. Possessors of this password will be able to change all columns *except* Ent_Date. For this password, let's include Grant permission. This way, anyone who knows this password can set up other passwords that grant the same permissions. Create this password now using these steps:

1. With the **A**ccess rights option still highlighted, select **G**rant.

2. Choose **SELECT** and **UPDATE**.

3. Press **F2** to finish selecting access types.

4. Select **N**ames.

5. Select every column on the next submenu *except* Ent_Date.

6. Press **F2** to finish selecting from this submenu.

7. Type **ICHANGE2**, confirm that you have typed the password correctly, and press ◄─┘.

8. Select **Y**es when asked about assigning Grant permission. You have now finished creating the password ICHANGE2.

An easy way to select all entries except Ent_Date is to first press Shift-F6, which selects all entries, and then select Ent_Date, which unselects it again.

Since the passwords ILOOK1 and ILOOK2 are the same in that both grant Select access only, you can create them at the same time.

1. With the **A**ccess rights option still highlighted, select **G**rant.

2. Choose **SELECT** and press **F2**.

3. Select **N**ames.

4. Type **ILOOK1,ILOOK2** and press ◄─┘.

5. Select **N**o to assigning Grant permission.

6. You have now finished creating the passwords ILOOK1 and ILOOK2. Highlight and select **E**xit now to return to the Main menu.

When you enter more than one password, separate them with a comma.

Establishing User Passwords with the GRANT Command

You can also use the GRANT command at the R> prompt to set up passwords. To prepare for an example using the GRANT command, enter Command mode by highlighting **E**xit and selecting **R>** prompt. Next, display the help screens for this command by typing

HELP GRANT. The second help screen, shown in Figure 9.3, shows the syntax diagram for the GRANT command.

Let's use the GRANT command to create another password called ICHANGE3. We'll give this password Select and Update access to the Names table, and users who possess it will be able to change only the Address, City, State, and Zip_Code columns. Type the following command at the R > prompt:

GRANT SELECT, UPDATE (Address, City, State, Zip_Code) +
+ > ON Names TO ICHANGE3

Then type **MENU** and press ← to return to the Main menu.

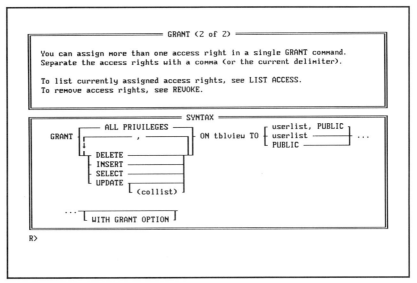

Figure 9.3: The syntax diagram for the GRANT command

LISTING USER PASSWORDS

You can list the passwords you've created for your tables from the R:BASE menus or by issuing the LIST ACCESS command at the R > prompt.

The R:BASE menu you used to create the user passwords has a List option. This option, in case you didn't guess already, lists user passwords. Let's see how it works.

1. Highlight **Info** and select **Create/modify**.

2. Highlight **Access rights** and select **List**.

3. Select **ALL**.

The user passwords we have been defining and the access rights for each password are now displayed on your screen, as shown in Figure 9.4. Notice the asterisks (*) beside SELECT and UPDATE in the Access column of the rows pertaining to ICHANGE2. They tell you that users who know the ICHANGE2 password have permission to create new passwords that grant Select and Update access to the Names table. If your screen does not match Figure 9.4, you can fix mistakes with the techniques discussed in the next section, which explains how to modify the access rights for a user password. When you are finished looking at the access rights, press any key to return to the menu.

When you listed user passwords above, you chose to see ALL user passwords for the Mail database. Alternatively, you could have chosen USER to list the details for only one user password. Or you could have chosen TABLE to see user passwords for only one table in the database.

If you want to find out what access rights the current user password has, use the LIST ACCESS command.

You can also issue the LIST ACCESS command to list passwords at the R> prompt. The password that you are currently using determines which passwords are displayed. For example, if you used the owner password to enter the database, then the owner password is the current password and LIST ACCESS will list all of the user passwords. On the other hand, if the current password is a user password, then only the access rights for that password will be listed. The information that LIST ACCESS provides for each password is the same as that shown above in Figure 9.4.

CHANGING ACCESS RIGHTS

People's responsibilities change, and you may have to change the access rights that their passwords allow them. And when someone leaves your department or company, you may want to change a password altogether to ensure that the person no longer has access to

```
User Password        Table                Access    Column
-------------------  -------------------  --------  -------------------
ICHANGE1             Names                SELECT
ICHANGE1             Names                UPDATE    CustNo
                                                    L_Name
                                                    F_Name
                                                    Company
                                                    Address
                                                    City
                                                    State
                                                    Zip_Code
                                                    Ent_Date
                                                    Phone
ICHANGE1             Names                INSERT
ICHANGE2             Names                *SELECT
ICHANGE2             Names                *UPDATE   CustNo
                                                    L_Name
                                                    F_Name
                                                    Company
                                                    Address
                                                    City
                                                    State
                                                    Zip_Code
                                                    Ent_Date
                                                    Phone
ICHANGE1             Names                INSERT
ICHANGE2             Names                *SELECT
ICHANGE2             Names                *UPDATE   CustNo
                                                    L_Name
                                                    F_Name
                                                    Company
                                                    Address
                                                    City
                                                    State
                                                    Zip_Code

                                                    Phone
ILOOK1               Names                SELECT
ILOOK2               Names                SELECT
ICHANGE3             Names                SELECT
ICHANGE3             Names                UPDATE    Address
                                                    City
                                                    State
                                                    Zip_Code

Press any key to continue
```

Figure 9.4: A list of access rights granted to user passwords assigned to the
Names table (this figure shows two screens)

the database. When you change the access rights assigned to a
password, you have the option of removing some of the access rights
or adding additional access rights as required. To change the
password itself, you first remove the old password by revoking all of
its access rights, and then you enter a new password.

Let's first try adding Insert access to the ILOOK2 password. This is done just as if you were adding the ILOOK2 password for the first time with Insert access, as follows:

1. With the **Access rights** option still highlighted, select **Grant**.

2. Select **Insert** and press **F2**.

3. Select **Names**.

4. Type **ILOOK2** and press ◄┘.

5. Select **No** to assigning Grant permission.

Try using the List option to list all of the access rights, and you will find that the password ILOOK2 has Insert access in addition to Select access.

Now let's change the password ILOOK2 to ICANSEE2 by first removing ILOOK2 and then adding ICANSEE2. To remove a password, we simply revoke all of the access rights it has been granted. Revoking access rights involves almost the same procedure as granting access rights, except that you start with the Revoke option on the menu.

1. With the **Access rights** option still highlighted, select **Revoke**.

2. Select **Select** and **Insert**, since both access rights are now defined for the password ILOOK2.

3. Press **F2**.

4. Select **Names**.

5. Type **ILOOK2** and press ◄┘. All of the access rights for password ILOOK2 (and hence the password itself) have been removed.

6. With the **Access rights** option still highlighted, select **Grant**.

7. Choose **Select** and **Insert**, to match the access rights which were defined for the password ILOOK2.

8. Press **F2**.

9. Select **Names**.

10. Type **ICANSEE2** and press ⏎.

11. Select **N**o to assigning Grant permission. The password ICANSEE2 has now been added with both Select and Insert access rights.

To verify that the password ICANSEE2 has replaced the password ILOOK2, activate the **L**ist option and select **A**ll. The password ILOOK2 does not appear, and the password ICANSEE2 shows up on the second page of the listing with SELECT and INSERT permissions. When you are finished looking at the listing, press any key to return to the menu.

You can also remove passwords or specific access rights by using the REVOKE command at the R > prompt. To prepare for some examples, highlight and select **E**xit to return to the Main menu. Next, highlight **E**xit and select **R** > prompt. The following command removes the UPDATE and INSERT access rights from the ICHANGE1 password:

REVOKE UPDATE, INSERT ON Names FROM ICHANGE1

You can also use the REVOKE command with the ALL option to remove all access rights for all tables from the ICHANGE2 password, like so:

REVOKE ALL FROM ICHANGE3

This is an easy way to remove a user password. To see the results of your efforts, type **LIST ACCESS** and press ⏎. Your screen should look like Figure 9.5.

TESTING ACCESS RIGHTS WITH USER PASSWORDS

Now that we've created some user passwords with various types of access, let's try some operations to see what we are allowed to do. We'll do a variety of tests using the Edit screen and Data Entry forms, starting from both the R > prompt and the R:BASE menus. To prepare for our examples, type **MENU** and press ⏎ to return to the R:BASE Main menu.

```
R>REVOKE UPDATE, INSERT ON Names FROM ICHANGE1
R>REVOKE ALL FROM ICHANGE3
R>LIST ACCESS
User Password        Table               Access     Column
------------------   ------------------  --------   ------------------
ICHANGE1             Names               SELECT
ICHANGE2             Names               *SELECT
ICHANGE2             Names               *UPDATE    CustNo
                                                    L_Name
                                                    F_Name
                                                    Company
                                                    Address
                                                    City
                                                    State
                                                    Zip_Code
                                                    Phone

ILOOK1               Names               SELECT
ICANSEE2             Names               SELECT
ICANSEE2             Names               INSERT
R>
```

Figure 9.5: Viewing access rights after removing access rights with the
REVOKE command

First, let's see what you are allowed to do with the user password
ICHANGE2. Start by setting the current user password to
ICHANGE2, as follows:

1. Highlight **Tools** and select **User password**.

2. Type **ICHANGE2** and press ⬅ when prompted to enter
    your password.

Because what you type is not displayed on the screen, you have to
type very carefully. If R:BASE beeps and displays the message

> **ERROR The current password will not allow access to any table**

then you probably typed the password incorrectly. Just press any key
to remove the message and repeat steps 1 and 2 above, being very
careful to type the password correctly this time. If R:BASE continues
to display the error message, enter the owner password MYMAIL,
list the user passwords, and compare your list with Figure 9.5. If
some of the passwords are incorrect, correct them and continue with
this exercise.

When you type in a
user password,
R:BASE does not display
what you type on the
screen. This prevents
someone looking over
your shoulder from see-
ing your password.

See "Listing User
Passwords" earlier
in this chapter to find out
how to get a listing of
user passwords. How to
make changes to pass-
words is described in
"Changing Access
Rights," the section in
this chapter previous
to this one.

The password ICHANGE2 gives Update access to every field in the Names table except Ent_Date. Let's test some operations with ICHANGE2 as the current password.

1. Highlight **I**nfo and select **N**ames to display the Edit screen for the Names table.

2. Press **F4** to go into Edit mode.

3. Type **A** to alter the last name. R:BASE allows the change.

4. Press **F5** to restore the field you just changed back to its original value.

5. Press **Tab** seven times to move the highlighter to the Ent_Date column.

A shortcut to move the Ent_Date column is to press ↓ and then Shift-Tab.

6. Type **10** to attempt to alter the date. When you try to leave this field, R:BASE beeps and displays a message telling you to press F5 to restore the field. Press any key to remove the message and **F5** to restore the field.

7. Press **F9** to attempt to delete a row. R:BASE beeps and displays a message telling you that you can't delete rows in this table. Press any key to remove the message.

8. Press **F10** to attempt to insert a row. R:BASE beeps and displays a message telling you that you aren't authorized for this kind of access to the table. Press any key to remove the message.

9. Highlight and select **E**xit to return to the Main menu.

As expected, the ICHANGE2 password with its Update access lets you change values in the table, but not add or delete rows. You can change, or update, only the columns you identified when you set up the ICHANGE2 password.

Of course, you can also use commands at the R > prompt to test what kind of access is provided by a password. Let's use R:BASE commands to enter the user password ICANSEE2 and try accessing some data.

1. Highlight **E**xit and select **R** > prompt to display the R > prompt.

If you type the command CON-NECT Mail IDENTI-FIED BY and do not type the password in your command, R:BASE will provide a box in the center of the screen for you to type in the password. This allows you to type in the password without having the password displayed on the screen.

2. Type **CONNECT Mail IDENTIFIED BY ICANSEE2** and press ← to set the user password to ICANSEE2.

To see what operations you are allowed to perform with this password, let's try using the NamesFrm form.

3. Type **EDIT USING NamesFrm** and press ←. The form is displayed with no highlighter on the screen, and the message "No editable data in this table" appears in the bottom-left corner of the screen.

4. Press **A** and nothing happens.

5. Press **F9** to attempt to delete a row. You'll hear a beep, but the screen won't change.

6. Press **F8** and the next row of the table is displayed.

7. Highlight and select **E**xit to return to the R > prompt.

8. Type **ENTER NamesFrm** and press ←.

9. Fill out the form with today's date in the Entry Date; Last Name **Jones**; First Name **Fred**; Company **HarryTech Co.**; Address **9216 John St.**; City **Los Angeles**; State **CA**; and Zip **91234**.

10. Highlight **A**dd/discard and select **A**dd row.

11. Highlight and select **E**xit to return to the R > prompt.

When you set up the password ICANSEE2, you included only SELECT and INSERT access to the Names table. The above tests confirmed that you can add a new row to the table with this password, but cannot change or delete existing rows.

When you began creating passwords earlier in this chapter, you entered the owner password as the current password. Doing so allowed you to create any password you wanted and give it any or all access rights. But suppose a user password was the current password. You could still create new passwords as long as your user password was assigned Grant permission when it was created. In order to grant a new password an access right, the current password has to have been assigned the access right and have been given Grant permission when it was created.

In a list of passwords, an asterisk (*) appears beside the name of every access right assigned Grant permission.

The current password is now ICANSEE2. This password was not assigned Grant permission for any access rights. If you try creating a password called TESTPW with the Update access right for the L_Name and F_Name columns using the command

GRANT UPDATE (L_Name, F_Name) ON Names TO TESTPW

R:BASE will tell you that you have no authority to grant the specified permissions. On the other hand, if the current password is ICHANGE2, you can use this GRANT commnd to create the password TESTPW. Why? Because ICHANGE2 had the Update access assigned with Grant permission when it was created.

PASSWORDS FOR FORMS

R:BASE provides an extra level of password protection when you are using forms: you can set up special passwords with specific access rights that require the user to know the password before he or she can access the form—passwords set up with the GRANT command or the Grant menu option will not be sufficient.

You can set up passwords for a form on the Form Settings menu, which is available when you are modifying the form. Starting at the R> prompt, try this procedure now with the following steps:

1. Type **CONNECT Mail IDENTIFIED BY MYMAIL** so that the current password is the owner password for the Mail database. This is necessary for you to modify a form.

2. Type **FORMS NamesFrm** and press ◀── to display the Form Generator screen for the NamesFrm form.

3. Highlight **L**ayout and select **F**orm settings to display the Form Settings menu.

4. Change the answer to the question "Assign passwords for this form?" to **Y**es and press ◀──.

5. Type **READPW** and press ◀── to create READPW as a read-only password for this form. When READPW is the current password, you will be able to display but not change information using this form.

The owner password must be the current one in order to use the FORMS command.

6. Type **MODIFYPW** and press ⟵ to create MODIFYPW as a modify password for this form. When MODIFYPW is the current password, you will be able to change as well as display information using this form. Your screen should now look like Figure 9.6.

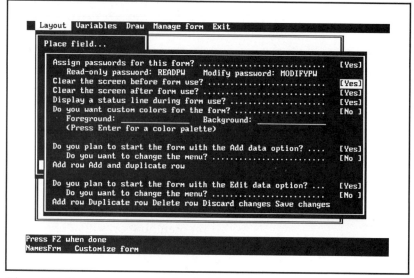

```
■ Layout  Variables  Draw  Manage form  Exit

  Place field...

   Assign passwords for this form? ..........................  [Yes]
        Read-only password: READPW    Modify password: MODIFYPW
   Clear the screen before form use? .........................  [Yes]
   Clear the screen after form use? ..........................  [Yes]
   Display a status line during form use? ....................  [Yes]
   Do you want custom colors for the form? ...................  [No ]
       Foreground: _____    Background: _____
       (Press Enter for a color palette)

   Do you plan to start the form with the Add data option? ....  [Yes]
       Do you want to change the menu? .......................  [No ]
   Add row Add and duplicate row

   Do you plan to start the form with the Edit data option? ...  [Yes]
       Do you want to change the menu? .......................  [No ]
   Add row Duplicate row Delete row Discard changes Save changes


Press F2 when done
NamesFrm   Customize form
```

Figure 9.6: Creating passwords for the NamesFrm form

7. Press **F2** to finish making changes to the Form Settings menu.

8. Highlight and select **E**xit to leave the Form Generator screen.

9. Reply **Y**es when asked if you want to save the changes.

10. Highlight and select **E**xit to return to the R > prompt.

Now that you have created passwords for NamesFrm, you will not be allowed to use this form unless the current password is either the owner password for the database (MYMAIL) or one of the form passwords (READPW or MODIFPW). As you would expect, the read-only password (READPW) will let you look at data but not add, change, or delete rows, and the modify password (MODIFPW) will let you do any of these operations.

TIPS FOR INVENTING PASSWORDS

As you have seen, a password is a combination of letters, numbers, and symbols that someone has to type in order to gain access to a database or a table. For a password to be effective, it must be known only to the people allowed to use the data in the computer.

People make several common mistakes when they are thinking up passwords. Sometimes they make the password very easy to remember so that they won't forget it. But if it's easy to remember—if you use your name, birthdate, or a short word like "cat" as a password—it may be easy to guess as well. Of course, some people overreact in the other direction, and they make up a totally random collection of characters (such as 3C9#X5U%AP6QDL2) that they must tape to the side of their computers in order to remember. Passwords shouldn't be so short that someone casually looking over your shoulder can easily figure them out when you are typing them in. Although an R:BASE password cannot be longer than eighteen characters, a password should be at least six characters long. And it should not be an easily recognized pattern, such as ABCABC.

With all these do's and don'ts, how can you think of a good password? One easy way is to borrow the first letter of each word in part of a poem, song, or phrase. For example, "Mary Had a Little Lamb." You might choose the first letters of

Mary had a little lamb,
Whose fleece was white as snow,

to come up with "mhallwfwwas." Of course, you can use whatever song or phrase you like. You should change your password periodically to minimize the risk of accidental discovery. Once you decide on a password, keep it written down in a safe place away from the computer so that you can refer to it if you have to. If you create an owner password for a database and later you can't remember it, you can't look in the database to find it. Which means you will not be able to modify the structure of the database and will only have access to the database through user passwords.

CHANGING THE STRUCTURE OF YOUR DATABASE

Now that you know how to control who has access to your database and can change its structure, let's look at some of the changes you might want to make to the structure of your database. If you've been following along, you will be connected to the Mail database and the owner password MYMAIL will be the current password. To prepare for the examples in the next section, return to the Main menu by typing **MENU** and pressing ←.

CHANGING COLUMN NAMES

Probably the simplest type of table modification involves changing a column's name. Let's say you've decided you'd like to call the last name column "Lastname" instead of L_Name. In Chapter 2, you learned how to change the structure of a table with the R:BASE menus by displaying the Table Definition screen. To review this process, you could change the name of this column from L_Name to Lastname, as follows:

R:BASE will not let you modify the Mail database unless the current password is the owner password.

1. Highlight **Info** and select **Create/modify.**

2. Highlight **Tables** and select **Modify.**

3. Select **Names.**

4. Press ← twice to accept the name of the table and the description.

5. Type **Lastname** and press ← to change the column name.

6. Press ← four times to accept the column description (Last Name), the data type (TEXT), the length (15), and whether to index on this column (No).

7. Press **F2** to save the new table structure and return to the R:BASE menu.

8. Highlight and select **Exit** to return to the R:BASE Main menu.

To see if the name of the column really changed, go to Command mode now by highlighting **E**xit, selecting **R** > prompt, and entering the LIST Names command. The name of the first column should be Lastname.

You can also change a column name from the R > prompt with the RENAME command. Earlier in this chapter, you saw how the command RENAME OWNER changes the owner password of a database. You can use RENAME COLUMN to change the name of a column. To do so, use the following syntax:

> RENAME COLUMN *column name 1* TO *column name 2* IN *table name*

The IN *table name* clause is optional. To restore the column containing last names to its original name, type the command

> RENAME COLUMN Lastname TO L_Name IN Names

(and press ◄─┘). This time, several messages appear on the screen telling you that R:BASE is changing the column name Lastname to L_Name in the Names table and also in forms and reports. However, the message also warns you that there are other places where you will have to change the old name to the new one, including VIEWS (discussed in Chapter 12), RULES, and expressions in forms, reports, and labels. You will learn more about the changes needed in these other places later in this chapter. Once again, you can issue the LIST Names command to verify that the column name was changed.

CHANGING COLUMN DEFINITIONS

Another simple form of table modification is changing the definition of a column. For example, let's change the width of the Company column from 20 to 25 characters. You have already seen how to use the R:BASE menus to modify the table structure. At the R > prompt, you could use the REDEFINE command with the following syntax:

> REDEFINE *column name* IN *table name* TO < *data type* > < *width* >

For our example, at the R > prompt enter the command

REDEFINE Company IN Names TO TEXT 25

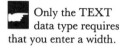 Only the TEXT data type requires that you enter a width.

The TEXT part of the command assigns the TEXT data type, and the 25 specifies the new width. That's all there is to it. If you enter the command SELECT ALL FROM Names, you'll notice that the column is, indeed, five characters wider. If you wanted to, you could change the reports and forms associated with the Names table to take advantage of the new width.

You can also use the REDEFINE command to change a column's data type—within reason. You can't, however, change an INTEGER column to TIME, because the two formats simply aren't compatible. R:BASE has no idea how to convert someting like 10:32:43 into an integer, or a value such as 500 into a time. You *can* change an INTEGER column to TEXT, or vice versa, although in the latter case you would lose any data that wasn't numeric. R:BASE would simply change any nonnumeric data to nulls.

SIDE EFFECTS OF CHANGING COLUMN NAMES AND DEFINITIONS

You've seen how easy it is to change column names and definitions, but you should also realize that doing so can be a risky proposition. For example, consider all that would have happened had we permanently changed the name of two of the column names, L_Name to Lastname and Ent_Date to Entrydat:

- The rule we set up requiring an entry date to be after the beginning of 1990—

  Ent_Date > = 01/01/90 OR Ent_Date IS NULL

  —would no longer work, since the Ent_Date field wouldn't exist.

- The Director report would not work properly, since it relies on the FullName variable, which joins L_Name and F_Name. But now L_Name wouldn't exist.

These and other results are referred to as *side effects,* which occur because R:BASE doesn't automatically change all references to a given column when you change its name or definition. If you make such a change in your table, you need to change these types of references yourself.

ADDING COLUMNS TO YOUR TABLE

The ALTER TABLE command is discussed later in this chapter in the section "Adding Columns with the ALTER TABLE Command."

There are two ways to add columns to your table using the Table Definition screen, or the ALTER TABLE command. (The Table Definition screen was introduced in Chapter 2 and reviewed earlier in this chapter in the section on changing column names.) On the table definition screen, you press F10 to insert a column and then enter all of the information it requires.

If you are in Command mode, a convenient way to display the R:BASE menus for changing the structure of your tables is with the RBDEFINE command. If you are not connected to a database, this command displays the Database Create/modify menu, where you create, modify, delete, rename, and copy databases. Since you are connected to the Mail database, entering the RBDEFINE command now will place you on the menu for changing tables in this database. You have used this menu before for creating and modifying table structures and names, as well as for creating rules and defining passwords and access rights. From this menu, we can access the Table Definition screen and add columns to the Names table.

Let's add a CustNo (customer number) column to the Names table. If you are not already at the R > prompt, highlight **Exit** and select **R >** prompt to display the R > prompt. Then follow these steps to add the CustNo column:

1. Type **RBDEFINE** and press ◄──┘.

2. Highlight **T**ables and select **M**odify.

3. Select **N**ames.

4. Press ◄──┘ twice to accept the name and description of the table.

5. Press **F10** to insert a new column to the left of the L_Name column. All other column names shift one space to the right.

6. Type **CustNo** and press ← for the column name.

7. Type **Customer Number** and press ← for the column description.

8. Select **INTEGER** for the data type.

9. Reply **No** to indexing. Figure 9.7 shows how the screen looks after adding the CustNo column into the Names table.

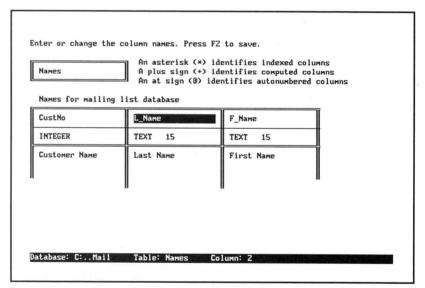

```
Enter or change the column names. Press F2 to save.

                          An asterisk (*) identifies indexed columns
  ┌────────────────────┐  A plus sign (+) identifies computed columns
  │ Names              │  An at sign (@) identifies autonumbered columns
  └────────────────────┘

  Names for mailing list database

  ┌───────────────┬───────────────┬───────────────┐
  │ CustNo        │ L_Name        │ F_Name        │
  ├───────────────┼───────────────┼───────────────┤
  │ INTEGER       │ TEXT    15    │ TEXT    15    │
  ├───────────────┼───────────────┼───────────────┤
  │ Customer Name │ Last Name     │ First Name    │
  └───────────────┴───────────────┴───────────────┘




 Database: C:..Mail     Table: Names     Column: 2
```

Figure 9.7: The CustNo column added to the Names table

Now suppose you also want to add a column for phone numbers. First, what data type should a phone number be? Granted, a phone number consists mostly of numbers, but of course it also consists of some nonnumeric characters, such as parentheses and a hyphen— for example, (818)555-1212. Therefore, since phone numbers are not truly numbers, they should be treated as Text data.

Let's add the Phone column to the Names table.

1. Press **End** to move the highlighter to an empty column to the right of the Ent_Date column.

2. Type **Phone** and press ⟵ for the column name.

3. Type **Phone Number** and press ⟵ for the column description.

4. Select **TEXT** for the data type.

5. A length of 13 characters should be adequate for storing North American phone numbers. Type **13** and press ⟵ for the length.

6. Reply **No** to indexing. Figure 9.8 shows the Names table with the new Phone column added.

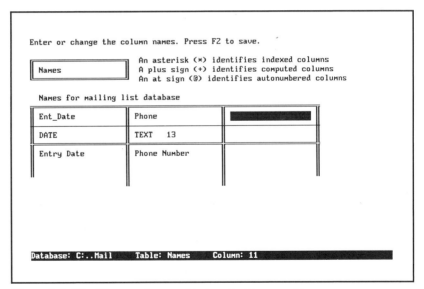

Figure 9.8: The Phone column added to the Names table

When you have finished making changes to the table structure, press **F2** to return to the R:BASE menu. Then highlight and select **Exit** to return to Command mode.

To fill in data for the new columns, enter the command

EDIT CustNo L_Name F_Name Phone FROM Names

The screen should look like Figure 9.9.

Notice that the new columns contain null characters (–0–), since there are no data in them. Go ahead and type the data shown in Figure 9.10 in these columns. Highlight and select Exit after you've filled in the new data.

Sort	Edit	Calculate	Layout	Query	Manage views	Print	Exit

CustNo	L_Name	F_Name	Phone
-0-	Miller	Anne	-0-
-0-	Adams	Bart	-0-
-0-	Miller	Marie	-0-
-0-	Jones	Mindy	-0-
-0-	Smith	Sandy	-0-
-0-	Baker	Robin	-0-
-0-	Jones	Fred	-0-

Figure 9.9: The Names table with new columns displayed on the Edit screen

Sort	Edit	Calculate	Layout	Query	Manage views	Print	Exit

CustNo	L_Name	F_Name	Phone
1001	Miller	Anne	(123)555-1234
1002	Adams	Bart	(234)555-1010
1003	Miller	Marie	(345)555-2222
1004	Jones	Mindy	(456)555-4567
1005	Smith	Sandy	(123)555-5678
1006	Baker	Robin	(234)555-9012
1007	Jones	Fred	(345)555-1111

Figure 9.10: The Names table with data entered in the new columns

As you will see later in this chapter, the CustNo field is very useful because it is unique for every row and it is easy to type. Let's delete the row with a Customer Number of 1007 using the DELETE ROWS command you saw in Chapter 5. Type the command

DELETE ROWS FROM Names WHERE CustNo = '1007'

R:BASE displays a message confirming that one row was deleted.

ADDING COLUMNS WITH THE ALTER TABLE COMMAND

The ALTER TABLE command, unlike the Table Definition screen, doesn't allow you to specify the location of new columns.

The benefit of using the Table Definition screen to add columns—which we used in the previous section—is that you can insert a new column in any position you choose in the database. Although the relative column positions are really irrelevant in a relational database, most of us like to have columns listed in a logical fashion. R:BASE's other method for adding columns is to use the ALTER TABLE command, which doesn't allow you to specify the position of the new column; the new column is added automatically to the end of the table. The syntax of the ALTER TABLE command is

> ALTER TABLE *table name* ADD *column name* <*data type*> +
> +> <*length*>

Length need only be specified for TEXT fields longer or shorter than the eight character default.

If you look at the help screens for these commands, you'll notice that R:BASE lets you add a column as an expression. When you add such a column, it's called a *computed column* and it's generally based on data in some other column. For example, if you had an Invoice table with a purchase date (PDate) column and wanted to add a due date (DDate) column, where the due date was to be 30 days after the purchase date, you could enter the following to create a computed DDate column:

> ALTER TABLE Invoice ADD DDate = (PDate + 30) DATE

MODIFYING REPORTS

The addition of the CustNo and Phone columns will not affect the Labels report we developed earlier, but the Director and MLDetail reports should be modified to display these new columns. (Alternatively, you could create two new reports to display these new data.) In this section, we'll revise the Director report so that it appears as shown in Figure 9.11.

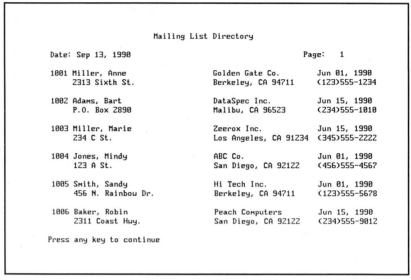

```
                    Mailing List Directory

Date: Sep 13, 1990                              Page:    1

1001 Miller, Anne            Golden Gate Co.      Jun 01, 1990
     2313 Sixth St.          Berkeley, CA 94711   (123)555-1234

1002 Adams, Bart             DataSpec Inc.        Jun 15, 1990
     P.O. Box 2890           Malibu, CA 96523     (234)555-1010

1003 Miller, Marie           Zeerox Inc.          Jun 15, 1990
     234 C St.               Los Angeles, CA 91234 (345)555-2222

1004 Jones, Mindy            ABC Co.              Jun 01, 1990
     123 A St.               San Diego, CA 92122  (456)555-4567

1005 Smith, Sandy            Hi Tech Inc.         Jun 01, 1990
     456 N. Rainbow Dr.      Berkeley, CA 94711   (123)555-5678

1006 Baker, Robin            Peach Computers      Jun 15, 1990
     2311 Coast Hwy.         San Diego, CA 92122  (234)555-9012

Press any key to continue
```

Figure 9.11: The modified Director report

Make sure you are in Command mode and then follow these steps to modify the Director report:

1. Type **REPORTS Director** to display the Report Generator screen for the Director report.

2. Move the cursor to row 5, column 1 (< 5: 7, 1 >).

3. To make room for the CustNo field, press **Ins** to enter Insert mode (the cursor is a block); press the **spacebar** five times to shift the FullName, Company and Date fields to the right; and then press **Ins** again to return to Overtype mode (the cursor becomes an underline). This gives you room to place the CustNo field to the left of the FullName field.

4. To place the CustNo field on the report, move the cursor back to column 1 (< 5: 7, 1 >); press **F6**; type **CustNo** and press ◄──┘; press **S** to start the field; press ← to make a space between the CustNo and FullName fields; press **E** to end the CustNo field; and reply **No** to adding a picture format.

Another way to move a field is to place the cursor on the field, press F6, and reply Yes when asked if you want to relocate the field.

You have now added the CustNo field. Let's realign the other fields so that the report looks neater.

5. To move the beginning of Address under the beginning of FullName, move to row 6, column 1 (< 6: 7, 1>); press **Ins** for Insert mode (the cursor is a block); press the **space-bar** twice; and press **Ins** for Overtype mode (the cursor is an underline).

Notice that the Ent_Date field now extends beyond the right side of the screen. Let's reduce the size of the row containing Ent_Date by reducing the size of the FullName column to 20 characters.

6. To shorten the FullName field, move the cursor to the beginning of FullName, row 5 column 7 (< 5: 7, 7>); press **F6**; reply **Y**es to relocating the field; press **S** to start the field; move the cursor to column 36 (< 5: 7, 36>); press **E** to end the field; and reply **N**o to adding a picture format. The cursor is now just to the right of the FullName field.

7. To align the Company field with the FullCSZ field below, press **Del** three times.

Since we want to place the Phone field beneath the Ent_Date field, we have to shorten the FullCSZ field.

8. To shorten the FullCSZ field, move the cursor to the beginning of FullCSZ, line 6 column 38 (< 6: 7, 38>); press **F6**; reply **Y**es to relocating the field; press **S** to start the field; move the cursor to column 59 (< 6: 7, 59>); press **E** to end the field; and reply **N**o to adding a picture format.

9. To add the Phone field, move to column 61 (6: 7, 61>); press **F6**; type **Phone** and press ◄─┘; press **S** to start the field; move the cursor to column 73 (6: 7, 73); press **E** to end the field; and reply **N**o to adding a picture format. You have now finished the changes. The modified Director report should now look like Figure 9.12.

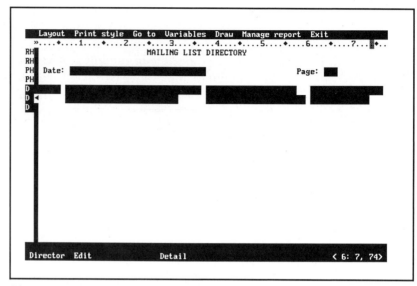

Figure 9.12: The Director report with CustNo and Phone added

10. To preview the report, highlight **M**anage report and select **P**review to screen. Figure 9.11 shows a preview of this report on the screen.

11. To return to the R > prompt, highlight and select **E**xit twice.

MODIFYING FORMS

Now that the Names table has two new columns, the NamesFrm form screen needs to be modified so that you can use it for entering and editing rows. We'll modify the basic appearance of the screen and add the CustNo and Phone columns so that the screen looks like Figure 9.13.

If you've been following along with the examples, you will be in Command mode. Try the following steps to add the two new fields to the NamesFrm form:

1. To display the Form Generator screen with NamesFrm, type **FORMS NamesFrm** and press ◄─┘. On the Form Generator screen, we have to move the Ent_Date field to the

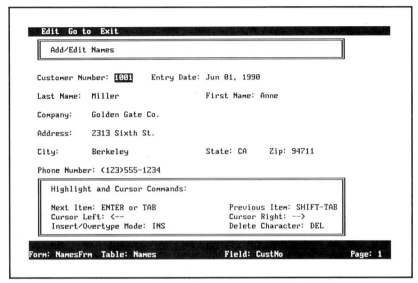

Figure 9.13: The modified NamesFrm screen in data-entry mode

right to make room for the CustNo field at the beginning of row 5.

2. To move the Ent_Date field to the right, move to row 5, column 3 ($<$ 5, 3$>$); press **Ins** for Insert mode (the cursor becomes a block); press the **spacebar** about 25 times to move the Ent_Date field to the right; press **Ins** for Overtype mode (the cursor becomes an underline). Now you have room for the CustNo field.

3. To place CustNo on the form, move to row 5, column 3 ($<$ 5, 3$>$); type the prompt **Customer Number:**; press the **spacebar** to move to column 20 ($<$ 5,20$>$); press **F6**; type **CustNo** and press ←; reply **No** to defining an expression; reply **No** to customizing field settings; press **S** to start the field; move the cursor back to column 23 ($<$ 5,23$>$), so that this field is just large enough for four-digit customer numbers; and press **E** to end the field.

If some of the prompt "Entry Date" was wiped out when defining the CustNo field, retype any missing letters. Now we want to put the phone number on a new line inserted just above the instructions in the box at the bottom of the screen.

4. To insert a blank line just above the box, move to row 15, column 3 (<15, 3>) and press **F10** to insert a blank line. Now we are ready to place the phone number on this line.

5. To place the phone number on the form, with the cursor at row 15, column 3 (<15, 3>), type the prompt **Phone Number:**; press the **spacebar** to move to column 17 (<15,17>); press **F6**; type **Phone** and press ←; reply **No** to defining an expression; reply **No** to customizing the field settings; press **S** to start the field; move the cursor to column 29 (<15,29>); and press **E** to end the field.

The new prompts and column names are now placed on the screen, as shown in Figure 9.14. However, you still have to ensure that the Customer Number field is the first to be highlighted when entering or editing data.

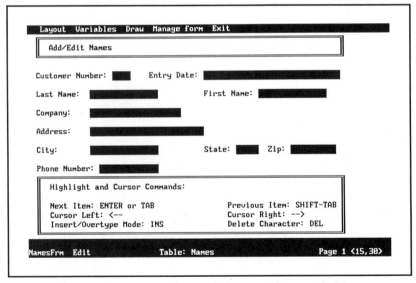

Figure 9.14: The customer number and phone on the modified form

If you don't reorder the fields, then the highlighting will move in an awkward fashion, starting with the Entry Date, and ending with the Zip, Customer Number, and finally the Phone Number.

6. To make sure the Customer Number is highlighted first, highlight **L**ayout; select **C**hange field order; select **9**. CustNo; type **1** and press ◄─┘; and press **F2** to finish making changes to the field order.

7. To test the form, highlight **M**anage form; select **R**un; and select **E**dit data.

Your screen should look like Figure 9.13. Pressing ◄─┘ should move the highlighter through the fields in order from the Customer Number to the Phone Number.

8. When you're finished testing the form, highlight and select **E**xit to return to the form generator screen.

9. To leave the Form Generator and return to the R> prompt, highlight and select **E**xit twice.

RENAMING AND DROPPING

R:BASE's RENAME and DROP commands are extremely useful general tools for modifying the structure of a table. Study their syntax diagrams in Figure 9.15.

The RENAME Command Revisited

Let's look at the RENAME command first. You've already seen earlier in the chapter that this command can be used to change the owner password and the name of a column. Then we discussed possible unwanted side effects of using RENAME. In Chapter 6, you saw how the RENAME command can also be used to change file names. This command can be used in other situations as well. You can use it to change the name of a table, form, report, or label. You can also change the name of a *view,* the pseudo-tables we'll be talking about in the next chapter.

In addition to using RENAME to change the owner password, you can use it to change the RPW and MPW passwords for a table. These are special passwords used with R:BASE companion products, such as the R:BASE Compiler and the Program Interface. We will discuss some R:BASE companion products in Chapter 18.

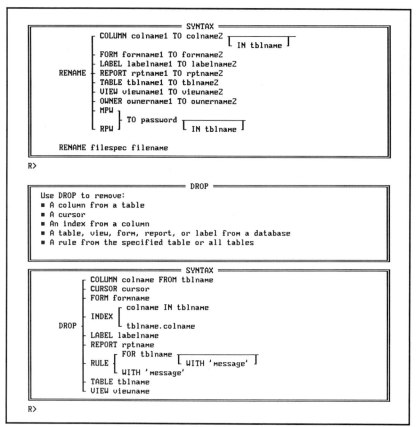

Figure 9.15: Syntax diagram for the RENAME and DROP commands

The DROP Command Revisited

The DROP command is also easy to use. You used the DROP command in Chapter 4 to drop a table that you had created when you were experimenting with the PROJECT command. With the DROP command, you can remove an individual column from a given table, remove a rule, report, label, or form from their respective tables, or remove a view, index, or cursor from the database. We'll be discussing indexes in the next section and cursors in Chapter 16.

USING INDEXES TO SPEED DATABASE OPERATIONS

You may remember that when you used the table definition screen to define—and later modify—the Mail database, you were asked with each column whether it was to serve as an index. We'll take a look at indexes now, and see how they can help make your database operations more efficient.

Indexes are often established to help speed up searches and sorts. You should consider establishing indexes for columns that you use often to look up data that is unique to each row. In the case of the Names table, CustNo is the best candidate for index column status, since each customer will have a unique customer number. If Names were a large table, having an index column for CustNo would significantly enhance performance. Assuming Mary Jones's customer number was 1044, for example, the command

    SELECT ALL FROM Names WHERE CustNo = '1044'

would work faster than

    SELECT ALL FROM Names WHERE L_Name = 'Jones' AND +
    + > F_Name = 'Mary'

You can establish a column as an index column in any one of several ways. When you are first defining a table, you can answer Yes to the question "Do you want this column to be an indexed column?" If you don't decide until later that you want a given column to be an index, you can either modify the table's structure on the Table Definition screen and redefine any column you wish as an index, or use the CREATE INDEX command from the R > prompt.

Let's say we want to make CustNo an index column. Assuming the Mail database is open, and you're at the R > prompt, enter the following command:

    CREATE INDEX ON Names CustNo

Nothing much seems to happen. However, if you type

    LIST Names

you'll see an asterisk (*) to the right of CustNo underneath the word Index. Other, more subtle changes have also taken place. Part of the Mail3.RBF file will now be used to keep a fast "lookup" table that R:BASE can use to locate data quickly from the Names table when the CustNo is supplied. You may notice a slight decrease in speed when you are adding data to or editing data in the Names table, because R:BASE must now change both the column and the index file to keep the database up-to-date.

Removing a column's index status is as easy as establishing it. The easiest way to do this is from the R> prompt, using the command

> DROP INDEX CustNo IN Names

Go ahead and drop the index. Indexes are generally inefficient in small tables; R:BASE's overhead in maintaining them simply isn't worth the minor increase in search and sort performance.

CHANGING RULES

Occasionally you'll set up a rule that doesn't work, and you'll want to delete it. As your database grows, you may even decide that using rule-checking slows things down too much, and that you value speedy data entry more than you do error-trapping. In either case, the easiest way to delete rules is to use the DROP command. If you look at the syntax for the DROP RULE command in Figure 9.15, you'll notice that you need to know a rule's message before you can delete it. One way of finding a particular rule message is to type

> LIST RULES

at the R> prompt, which will display the screen shown in Figure 9.16. This screen displays the details of the one rule you have defined for the Names table.

The first line of this display reminds you that rule-checking is on. Although active rule-checking is R:BASE's default, it can be turned off with the SET command. The next line displays the message associated with this rule. The third line lists the table that this rule applies

```
R>LIST RULES
(RULES    ) ON  Check data validation RULES
MESSAGE :  Entry Date cannot be before 1990
  TABLE :  Names    Row is added or changed if condition SUCCEEDS
  WHERE :  Ent_Date >= 01/01/90 OR Ent_Date IS NULL

R>
```

Figure 9.16: Reviewing your rules

to and indicates that the row will be accepted if the condition succeeds. The last row contains the condition that must (according to the third row) succeed in order for the row to be accepted.

To remove the rule you created in Chapter 2, type

DROP RULE WITH 'Entry Date cannot be before 1990'

and press ◄─┘.

To edit a rule, you need to use an option on the R:BASE Table Definition menu. From the R:BASE Main menu, you can reach the table definition menu by highlighting Info and selecting Create/modify. From the R > prompt, you can display the Table Definition menu by entering the RBDEFINE command when connected to the appropriate database. On the Table Definition menu, highlight Rules, select Modify, and then select the rule you wish to edit.

Let's finish our overview of techniques for changing database structure now. In this chapter, you've learned how to use passwords to protect your data from unauthorized access as well as several new commands and techniques for modifying the basic structure of a table in a database. You're proficient at managing data in a single-table database, and are now ready to work with a database that contains multiple tables.

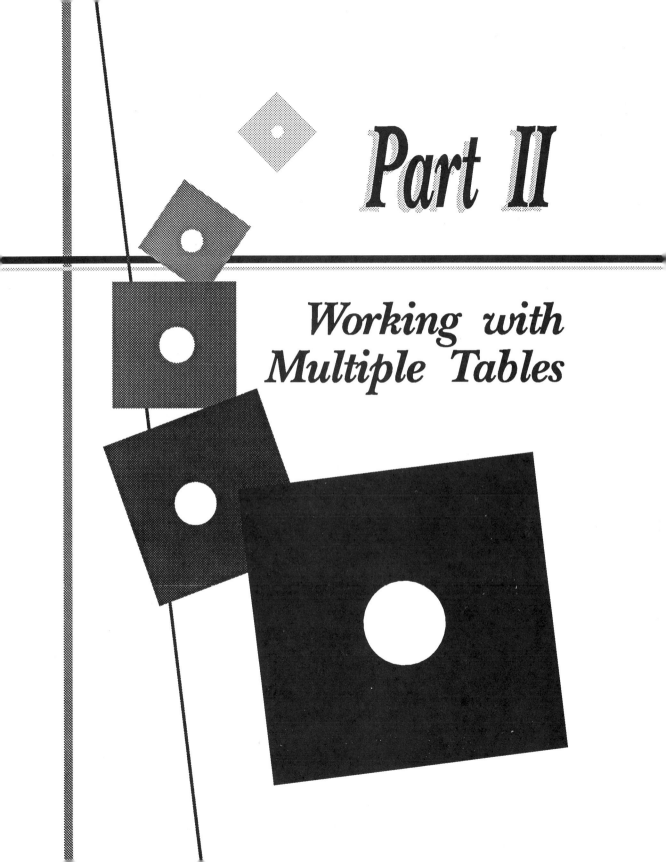

Part II

Working with Multiple Tables

Chapter 10

Increasing Your Database's Power with Multiple Tables

IN THIS CHAPTER, WE'LL ADD A NEW TABLE TO THE
Mail database and explore techniques for setting up a relationship
between two tables. We'll set up a form that serves two tables simultaneously. We'll also discuss techniques for defining various types of
rules to help catch errors before they are stored in a table. Finally, at
the end of the chapter, we'll take another look at designing databases.

DESIGNING RELATIONSHIPS INTO YOUR TABLES

Let's start expanding the Mail database so that it can serve as a sales-
register system. To do so, we need to add another table to record individual charge transactions. For each charge, we want to record the
amount of the charge, the date, and the items purchased.

Since it is likely that each customer will charge many purchases, it
makes no sense to record the name and address along with every charge
transaction. Instead, we need a *code* that relates numerous charge transactions to an individual in the Names table. We don't want to use individuals' last names as this code because they are not accurate enough.
For example, if we recorded a charge made by "Smith," we'd have
problems sending the bill to the correct individual if there were twenty
Smiths listed in the Names table. We could use both first and last names
to improve the accuracy, but even this would be risky.

A better approach is to use the unique *customer number* that we
assigned to each person in the Names table (we did this in the last
chapter). Then the table for charge transactions needs to record only
the customer number to set up a link that will eliminate any confusion in billing.

Dividing the data into two separate tables within a database is
known as recognizing a *one-to-many* relationship between the tables.
This relationship is so named because for every *one* row on one table,
there may be *many* related rows on another table. In this example, for
every one individual in the Names table, there may be many individual sales-transaction records stored in the Charges table.

ADDING A NEW TABLE TO YOUR DATABASE

Take a moment to look at the structure for the Charges table, described below.

NAME	DESCRIPTION	TYPE	LENGTH
CustNo	Customer Number	INTEGER	
ProdNo	Product Number	TEXT	8
Qty	Quantity Purchased	INTEGER	
U_Price	Unit Price (as sold)	CURRENCY	
Taxable	Is Item Taxable?	TEXT	1
Total	Calculated Total	CURRENCY	
P_Date	Date of Purchase	DATE	

The customer number (CustNo) will be the *index field* that relates data from the Charges table to individuals in the Names table. As in the Names table, its data type is INTEGER. The ProdNo column will store the product number of the item purchased. We could later add an Inventory table listing items in stock to our Mail database and use the ProdNo column to link the Charges table with items in the Inventory table. Each transaction would then reduce the quantity of the product shown to be in inventory. The ProdNo column is TEXT data with a length of eight characters. Using the TEXT data type will allow you to enter hyphenated numbers, such as A-111.

The Qty column is for recording the quantity of items purchased. The U_Price column is for the unit price of items purchased. Its data type is CURRENCY, which will cause numbers to be displayed with a leading dollar sign and two decimal places.

The Taxable column is a one-character TEXT field that will contain either a *Y* for taxable items or an *N* for nontaxable items. The Total column will contain the total of the row—either the quantity times the unit price for nontaxable items, or the quantity times the unit price plus 6 percent sales tax for taxable items. R:BASE will calculate the total automatically, so you don't need to fill in this column when you're entering data. The P_Date column will store the date of purchase.

Let's create the Charges table. Referring to the structure of the table, you can see that all the columns are straightforward except for Total. This column is not stored in the database, but is calculated. For this column, choose COMPUTED as the data type. R:BASE will ask that you

Enter expression value:

What R:BASE needs to know is how to compute the data in this column. If there were not a Taxable column in our table, we could determine the total by multiplying the Qty field times the U_Price field, and the expression could simply be (Qty*U_Price). But some of the items in the inventory are taxable, and for those items the total becomes ((Qty*Price)*1.06), assuming a 6 percent sales tax. We will have to find a way to tell R:BASE that if the item is not taxable, then the total for the row is indeed (Qty*U_Price).

We can use an R:BASE *function* to help solve this problem. First, we need to know how to determine whether an item is taxable, so let's make up a rule. If the Taxable column contains the letter *N*, the item is not taxable. If the Taxable column contains the letter *Y*, the item is taxable.

We'll discuss other functions in Chapter 11.

Given this knowledge, we can use the IFEQ function to calculate the total for the transaction. The IFEQ function uses this syntax:

IFEQ(this item, = this item, then this, else this)

The exact expression that you would enter on the screen is

(IFEQ(Taxable,'N',Qty*U_Price,(Qty*U_Price)*1.06))

In English, this expression means, "If the Taxable column equals 'N', calculate the quantity times the unit price; otherwise calculate the quantity times the unit price times the tax rate." IFEQ is just one of many functions that R:BASE offers.

Once you've entered the expression for Total, R:BASE presents you with a list of valid data types for this column. Notice that the list is smaller than usual, that it contains only valid choices, and that CURRENCY is highlighted as the default. R:BASE has looked at the Total expression and determined that certain data types—such as

DATE, TIME, and NOTE—are impossible for this column, and that CURRENCY is the most likely choice.

Now that you know how to define the Total field, you are ready to create the Charges table. Refer to the steps below if you need a reminder of how to create a new table.

1. Open the Mail database if necessary by highlighting **Data-bases** and selecting **MAIL**.

2. To display the Table Definition menu, highlight **Info** and select **Create/modify**; and highlight **Tables** and select **Create**.

3. To enter the table name, type **Charges** and press ←; to enter the table description, type **Charges** and press ← again.

4. To define the CustNo column, type **CustNo** and press ←; type **Customer Number** and press ←; and reply **Yes** to indexing.

When you are defining CustNo, R:BASE will automatically assign INTEGER as the data type, since this was the way the CustNo column name was defined in the Names table. If CustNo had been a TEXT field, the length would also have been supplied from the Names table. This ensures that both tables store customer numbers in the same type of column.

5. To define the ProdNo column, type **ProdNo** and press ←; type **Product Number** and press ←; select **TEXT**; type **8** and press ←; and reply **No** to indexing.

6. To define the Qty column, type **Qty** and press ←; type **Quantity Purchased** and press ←; Select **INTEGER**; and reply **No** to indexing.

7. To define the U_Price column, type **U_Price** and press ←; type **Unit Price (as sold)** and press ←; Select **CURRENCY**; and reply **No** to indexing.

8. To define the Taxable column, type **Taxable** and press ←; type **Is Item Taxable?** and press ←; Select **TEXT**; type **1** and press ←; and reply **No** to indexing.

9. To define the Total column, type **Total** and press ←; type **Calculated Total** and press ←; select **COMPUTED**; type **(IFEQ(Taxable,'N',Qty∗U_Price,(Qty∗U_Price)∗1.06))** and press ←; select **CURRENCY**; and reply **No** to indexing.

Pressing **End** moves the cursor directly to the COMPUTED data type, which is at the end of the list on the menu of data types.

10. To define the P_Date column, type **P_Date** and press ←; type **Date of Purchase** and press ←; select **Date**; and reply **No** to indexing.

11. Press **F2** to leave the Table Definition screen; and highlight and select **Exit** to return to the R:BASE Main menu.

A FORM FOR TWO TABLES

Now that you've added a second table to the Mail database, let's create a form for entering information into the new Charges table. Rather than just creating a simple form, however, we'll discuss some more advanced techniques that you can use when creating forms with multiple tables and computed columns.

You'll be creating the form displayed in Figure 10.1. After the practice you had creating forms in Chapter 7, laying out the prompts, text, and boxes in this form should be a piece of cake.

The prompts on this form are located as follows:

POSITION	PROMPT
< 2, 3>	Enter/Edit Transactions
< 5, 1>	Customer Number:
< 5,30>	Customer Name:
< 6,36>	Company:
< 8, 1>	Product Number:
< 8,29>	Taxable? (Y,N):
<10, 1>	Qty:
<10,19>	Unit Price:
<10,47>	Total:
<12, 1>	Date of Sale:
<15, 3>	Highlighter and Cursor Movement
<17, 5>	Next Item: ENTER or TAB
<17,40>	Previous Item: SHIFT-TAB
<18, 5>	Cursor Right: -->
<18,40>	Cursor Left: <--
<19, 5>	Insert/Overtype Mode: INS
<19,40>	Delete Character: DEL

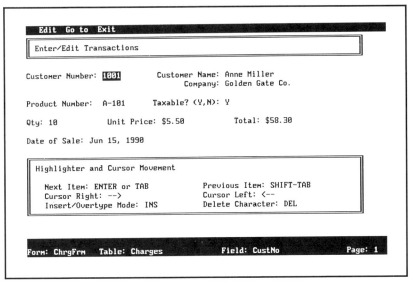

Figure 10.1: A form for entering data in the Charges table

Create the form and add the prompts and draw boxes in Figure 10.1 as well. Refer to the following steps if you get stuck:

1. Open the Mail database if necessary by highlighting **Data**bases and selecting **Mail**.

2. To display the Form Generator screen, highlight **F**orms and select **C**reate/modify; highlight **C**reate and select **C**ustom form; type **ChrgFrm** and press ◄━┛ for the form name; type **Enter/Edit Transactions** and press ◄━┛ for the form description; and select the **C**harges table.

3. To enter the prompts listed above, move the cursor to the position in the left column and type in the prompt listed in the right column. For example, to type in the first prompt listed, move the cursor to position < 2, 3 > and type **Enter/ Edit Transactions**. Continue entering the rest of the prompts in the list.

If you make one of the lines in the boxes too long, you can correct your mistake. Press F2 to stop drawing, highlight Draw, and select Erase. Next, put the pen down, erase the mistake, and press F2 to finish erasing. Then move the cursor to where you left off. Now highlight Draw and select Double lines, put the pen down, and continue drawing the box.

4. To draw the top box shown in Figure 10.1, move the cursor to < 1, 1 >; highlight **Draw** and select **Double** lines; press **Ctrl-F6** to put the pen down; move the cursor to < 1,75 >, then < 3,75 >, then < 3, 1 >, then < 1, 1 >, and finally < 1, 2 >; and press **F2** to finish drawing the box.

5. To draw the bottom box in Figure 10.1, move the cursor to <14, 1 >; highlight **Draw** and select **Double** lines; press **Ctrl-F6** to put the pen down; move the cursor to <14,75 >, then <20,75 >, then <20, 1 >, then <14, 1 >, and finally <14, 2 >; and press **F2** to finish drawing the box.

DEFINING VARIABLES FOR THE FORM

As in reports, you can include variables (or expressions) to place information on the form that is not readily available from the table in use. We can use form variables in several ways in this form. First, when entering or editing data in the Charges table, you will need to enter a customer number. To verify that you've entered the correct customer number, it would be helpful to display the associated person's name and company from the Names table on the form.

Second, even though R:BASE automatically calculates the total for the transaction on the database, this total will not automatically appear on the screen. Therefore, we'll create a variable to calculate and display the total directly on the form.

The first variable we will be using is Name1, which is defined as follows:

Name1 = F_Name IN Names WHERE CustNo = CustNo

The line above is a *lookup expression,* which states that the *lookup variable* Name1 will contain the contents of the F_Name column from the Names table where the customer number in the Names table matches the customer number entered onto the form. Hence, if you enter 1001 onto the ChrgFrm, the variable Name1 will store the corresponding customer's first name. Name1 is called a lookup variable because R:BASE must look up the appropriate customer number in the Names table to find the correct name.

The second variable we will be using is Name2, which is defined with this expression:

Name2 = L_Name IN Names WHERE CustNo = CustNo

As you may have guessed, Name2 will contain the last name (L_Name) of the appropriate customer on the Names table.

We need to create a third variable that contains both the first and last name with a space between them. We can call this third variable CName (Customer Name) and define it like so:

CName = Name1 & Name2

CName is the actual variable that will be located on the form.

The fourth variable, CCompany (Customer Company), will store the company of the appropriate person with this definition:

CCompany = Company IN Names WHERE CustNo = CustNo

Notice that this formula uses the same basic syntax as the other lookup expressions, as follows:

variable = column name IN *table* WHERE +
+ > *column name = column name*

The expression defining the fifth variable does not perform a lookup. Instead, it calculates the total sale using the same formula as the computed column, but it stores this result in a variable named ShowTot (Show Total). The expression defining this variable is

ShowTot = (IFEQ(Taxable,'N',Qty*U_Price,(Qty*U_Price)*1.06))

Defining variables on a form is very similar to defining variables for a report. However, when you define a lookup variable on a form, R:BASE asks if you want to customize the lookup settings. With customized lookup settings, you can tell R:BASE what to do if the lookup fails—in other words, if there is no matching row in the Names table. Later in this chapter, we will create a rule to ensure that the lookup succeeds when it looks for a matching CustNo in the Names table. For now, we will choose No when asked if we want to customize the lookup settings.

Let's define the form variables now. Refer to the following steps if you need to.

1. To define Name1, highlight **Variables** and select **Define**; type **Name1 = F_Name IN Names WHERE CustNo = CustNo** and press ←; and reply **No** to customizing lookup settings.

2. To define Name2, highlight **Variables** and select **Define**; type **Name2 = L_Name IN Names WHERE CustNo = CustNo** and press ←; and reply **No** to customizing lookup settings.

3. To define CName, highlight **Variables** and select **Define**; type **CName = Name1 & Name2** and press ←

4. To define CCompany, highlight **Variables** and select **Define**; type **CCompany = Company IN Names WHERE CustNo = CustNo** and press ←; and reply **No** to customizing lookup settings.

5. To define ShowTot, highlight **Variables** and select **Define**; type **ShowTot = (IFEQ(Taxable,'N',Qty*U_Price, (Qty*U_Price)*1.06))** and press ←.

6. Now that you have defined all five variables, highlight **Variables** and select **List**. Before you continue, make sure your variable definitions match those displayed in Figure 10.2.

If you find mistakes in any of the variables listed, highlight Variables and select Modify to edit, or Delete to delete, the definition of the incorrect variable.

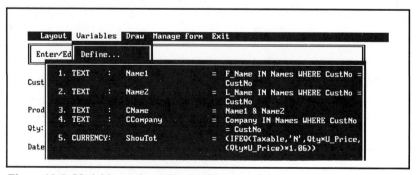

Figure 10.2: Variables defined for the ChrgFrm form

PLACING VARIABLES AND COLUMNS

You've already had experience placing column and variable names in reports and forms. Let's place the column and variable names for the charges form by using the start and end coordinates listed below. Place each column and variable name in the left column at the start and end locations listed in the two columns to the right. For now, select No when asked about defining expressions and customizing field settings. R:BASE will prompt you for this information as you locate the fields on the screen. When you are done, your screen should look like Figure 10.3.

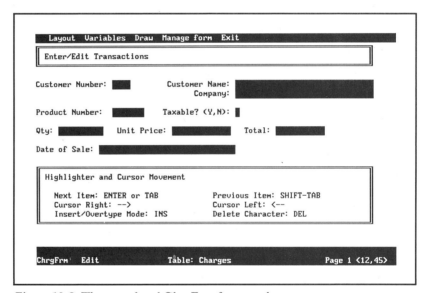

Figure 10.3: The completed ChrgFrm form on the screen

COLUMN/VARIABLE NAME	START	END
CustNo	< 5,18>	< 5,21>
CName	< 5,45>	< 5,75>
CCompany	< 6,45>	< 6,75>
ProdNo	< 8,18>	< 8,25>

CH. 10

COLUMN/VARIABLE NAME	START	END
Taxable	< 8,45>	< 8,45>
Qty	<10, 6>	<10,15>
U_Price	<10,31>	<10,43>
ShowTot	<10,54>	<10,64>
P_Date	<12,15>	<12,44>

Let's suppose that most of the items in the inventory are taxable. For added convenience, you could define a default value of *Y* in the Taxable field. To refresh your memory, here is the procedure for adding a default value:

1. To display the Field Settings menu for the Taxable field, move the cursor onto the Taxable field, press **F6**, and reply **Y**es when asked if you want to customize field settings.

2. To add the default value on this menu, press ↓ three times to move to the default value question; press **Y** and press ⬅ to move to the default value field; and type **Y** as the default value.

3. To return to the Form Generator screen, press **F2** to leave the Field Settings menu and reply **N**o to relocating the field.

You can make the current date the default in the P_Date column as well. Follow similar steps to those above, and type **#Date** as the default value for the P_Date field. When you are done, return to the Form Layout screen just as you did when you finished entering the Taxable default.

TESTING THE FORM

To test the form, highlight **M**anage form, select **R**un, and then select **A**dd data. The form appears on the screen with only the default *Y* in the Taxable? field and today's date in the Date of Sale field. Enter any valid customer number at this point and R:BASE will immediately display the customer's name and company on the form.

Try it by entering any number from 1001 to 1006, the customer numbers you entered in the last chapter. You can press ↑ and change the customer number at any time, and the name and company will change accordingly.

To complete the transaction, fill in a product number, a taxable status (*Y* for Yes, *N* for No), a quantity, and a unit price. The total for the transaction appears on the screen immediately, and the cursor moves to the Date of Sale field. You can press the ↑ key to move back to previous fields and make corrections. At the Date of Sale field, you can press ◄─┘ to accept the default date, or you can type in a new date and press ◄─┘. Take a look at Figure 10.1 again. This figure shows a complete transaction on the screen.

When you are done entering transactions, highlight and select **E**xit to return to the Form Layout screen. Then highlight and select **E**xit twice more to return to the R:BASE Main menu.

The ChrgFrm in its current state is useful, but it still has a few weaknesses. If you enter an invalid customer number (such as 9999), the form will accept your entry and store it on the Charges table without warning you that an error has occurred. Later, at billing time, nobody will be billed for the transaction because there is no customer number 9999. Also, if you accidentally enter an invalid Taxable code (such as A), the form will accept it and consider the transaction to be for a taxable item. We can ensure that errors such as these do not occur when entering transactions by defining rules for the form.

When you change any of the fields that are used to calculate the Total, the Total field changes automatically—because the total has changed.

You'll learn how to create true multi-table forms that allow you to enter data into more than one table at once in Chapter 13.

ENSURING ACCURATE DATA ENTRY WITH RULES

In Chapter 2, you created a rule to reject Entry Dates before 1990 in the Names table. In this section, you will learn how to create more complex rules to ensure that the data in your tables is accurate.

RULE TO REJECT INVALID CUSTOMER NUMBERS

Our first rule will state that any transaction entered into the Charges table must contain a customer number that exists in the Names table. Without this customer number, the transaction will be rejected and an error message will appear. R:BASE offers a menu choice that makes this rule easy to create. Follow these steps:

1. To display the R:BASE menu on which the Rules option appears, Highlight **I**nfo and select **C**reate/modify.

2. To create the rule, highlight **R**ules and select **C**reate; select **V**erify a value; select **C**harges as the Rule Table; select **C**ustNo as the Rule Column; select **N**ames as the Verification Table (your screen should now look like Figure 10.4); and select **C**ustNo as the Verification Column.

3. Select **L**ist to see a list of your rules, which should look like Figure 10.5.

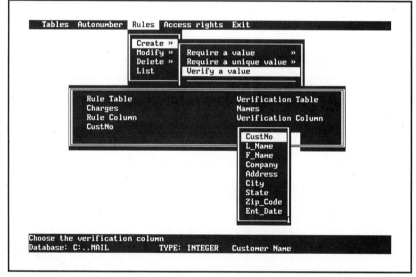

Figure 10.4: Adding a rule to verify that the customer number is in the Names table

The second rule is the one that you just entered. Notice that R:BASE will display the error message

Value for CustNo must exist in CustNo in Names

when the customer number is not found in the Names table. Let's make this message easier to understand and change it to "No such customer number!"

```
<RULES    > ON  Check data validation RULES
MESSAGE :  Entry Date cannot be before 1990
   TABLE :  Names     Row is added or changed if condition SUCCEEDS
   WHERE :  Ent_Date >= 01/01/90 OR Ent_Date IS NULL

MESSAGE :  Value for CustNo must exist in CustNo in Names
   TABLE :  Charges    Row is added or changed if condition SUCCEEDS
   WHERE :  CustNo IN ( SELECT CustNo FROM Names )

Press any key to continue
```

Figure 10.5: The list of rules

4. Press any key to return to the R:BASE menu.

5. To change the message for the customer number rule, select **Modify**; select **Charges**—Value for CustNo must exist in; select **Succeeds**; select **Charges**; press ◄─┘ to keep the same WHERE condition; press **Shift-F9** to erase the message; type **No such customer number!** and press ◄─┘ to enter the new error message.

6. Select **List** again to examine the rule, and you will see the new message displayed for your rule.

7. Press any key to finish looking at the rules.

When you made your choices on the menus and defined the rule, you guided R:BASE to create the following WHERE condition:

CustNo IN (SELECT CustNo FROM Names)

This condition contains a *sub-select,* a SELECT within a SELECT. In this WHERE condition, the sub-select "SELECT CustNo FROM Names" can be thought of as producing a list of all the customer numbers in the Names table. The WHERE condition will succeed if the customer number from the Charges table is in the list of customer numbers from the Names table produced by the sub-select condition.

Before testing this rule, let's define a few more rules.

In the submenu you use to select which rule to modify, R:BASE lists both the name of the table and the first part of the error message.

When you are modifying a rule, you may want to keep some of the selections you have in the existing rule. Press ◄─┘ for each choice you want to keep—R:BASE will bypass it and proceed to the next choice.

RULE TO REJECT
DUPLICATE CUSTOMER NUMBERS

We created the CustNo column in both the Names and the Charges tables in order to tell which customer each charge transaction refers to. For this to work, every customer in the Names table has to have a unique customer number. For example, suppose two people in the Names table have the customer number 1001. Any transaction referring to customer number 1001 in the Charges table is going to create problems, because R:BASE won't know which customer number 1001 to give the bill for the charges.

There are two methods we could use to ensure that every customer in the Names table has a unique customer number. The first method is to make the CustNo column an *autonumber column* so that the computer would generate sequential customer numbers automatically. To define an autonumber column, simply highlight Autonumber on the same menu with the Rules pull-down menu, select the table, select the column, and enter an initial value and an increment. In our example, we could enter an initial value of 1001 and an increment of 1 to instruct R:BASE to generate customer numbers 1001, 1002, 1003, and so on. R:BASE would remember the last customer number used. When a new customer is entered, R:BASE would automatically supply a customer number that is one larger than the last one used.

The second method of ensuring that every customer number in the Names table is unique is to define a rule that rejects any attempt to add a duplicate customer number to the Names table. This method allows you to enter any customer number you want, as long as it has not been used before for another customer.

To create this rule, you can use another of the standard choices on the pull-down menu under the Rule menu option. Once again, let's customize the error message so that it says "Duplicate customer number!" when a duplicate is entered. Beginning from the Rules pull-down menu, let's define such a rule now.

From the Main menu, you reach the menu that displays the Rules pull-down menu by highlighting Info and selecting Create/modify.

1. With **R**ules highlighted, select **C**reate; select **R**equire a unique value; select the **N**ames table; and select the **C**ustNo column.

2. Select **L**ist to see a list of your rules.

You should see three rules, the last one being the rule you just entered. For this rule, R:BASE will display the error message

Value for CustNo must be unique

if the customer number has already been assigned in the Names table. Let's change this message to "Duplicate customer number!"

3. Press any key to return to the R:BASE menu.

4. To change the message for this rule, select **Modify**; select **Names**—Value for CustNo must be unique; select **Succeeds**; select **Names**; press ⏎ to keep the same WHERE condition; press **Shift-F9** to erase the message; type **Duplicate customer number!** and press ⏎ to enter the new error message.

5. Select **List** again to examine the rule. You will see the revised message displayed on your list of rules.

6. Press any key to return to the R:BASE menu.

Once again, the WHERE condition R:BASE constructed for this rule includes a sub-select:

CustNo IS NOT NULL AND CustNo NOT IN (SELECT CustNo FROM Names)

In plain English, this rule says that the condition will succeed if the customer number has been filled in and the customer number is not in a list of the customer numbers from the Names table.

RULE TO FORCE THE UNIT PRICE TO BE FILLED IN

To determine how much to charge the customer, both the Quantity and Unit Price field have to be filled in. If the Unit Price is empty, R:BASE leaves the Total field empty as well. To guard against this, you can define a rule that rejects the row unless the Unit Price field is filled in. Once again, there is a choice on the pull-down menu under Rules that makes it easy to create such a rule. Beginning from the Rules pull-down menu (which you can reach by highlighting Info and selecting Create/modify):

1. Highlight **R**ules and select **C**reate; select **R**equire a value; select the **C**harges table; and select the **U**_Price column.

2. Select **L**ist to see a list of your rules.

The last rule is the one that you just entered. For this rule, R:BASE will display the error message

Value for U_Price cannot be null

when the unit price is not filled in. Let's change this message to "Unit price required!"

3. Press any key to return to the Rules pull-down menu.

4. To change the message for this rule, select **M**odify; select Charges—Value for U_Price cannot be null; select **S**ucceeds; select Charges; press ◄── to keep the same WHERE condition; press **Shift-F9** to erase the message; type **Unit price required!** and press ◄── to enter the new error message.

5. Select **L**ist to examine the revised message displayed for your rule.

6. Press any key to return to the R:BASE menu.

RULE TO REJECT INVALID TAXABLE CODES

Suppose we create a rule that displays the error message "Taxable must be Y on N!" if the Taxable column in the Charges table does not contain a *Y* or an *N*. This rule is not like any of the rules we have created so far. It is not making sure that a value exists in another table (like our Customer Number rule), or making sure that a value is unique (like our duplicate Customer Number rule), or checking to be sure that a value has been entered (like our Unit Price rule). For this rule, we can't use any of the standard rule types; instead, we'll create a custom rule.

From the Rules pull-down menu (reached from the Main menu by highlighting Info and selecting Create/modify), let's define a rule that rejects invalid taxable codes.

1. With **R**ules highlighted, select **C**reate; select **C**ustom rule; select **S**ucceeds; select **C**harges; type **Taxable = 'Y' OR Taxable = 'N'** and press ⬅ for the WHERE condition; and type **Taxable must by Y or N!** and press ⬅ for the Message.

2. Select **L**ist to see a list of your rules. They should look like the ones in Figure 10.6.

```
<RULES      > ON  Check data validation RULES
MESSAGE :   Entry Date cannot be before 1990
   TABLE :  Names    Row is added or changed if condition SUCCEEDS
   WHERE :  Ent_Date >= 01/01/90 OR Ent_Date IS NULL

MESSAGE :   No such customer number!
   TABLE :  Charges   Row is added or changed if condition SUCCEEDS
   WHERE :  CustNo IN ( SELECT CustNo FROM Names )

MESSAGE :   Duplicate customer number!
   TABLE :  Charges    Row is added or changed if condition SUCCEEDS
   WHERE :  CustNo IS NOT NULL AND CustNo NOT IN ( SELECT CustNo FROM Charges )

MESSAGE :   Unit price required!
   TABLE :  Charges    Row is added or changed if condition SUCCEEDS
   WHERE :  U_Price IS NOT NULL

MESSAGE :   Taxable must be Y or N!
   TABLE :  Charges    Row is added or changed if condition SUCCEEDS
   WHERE :  Taxable = 'Y' OR Taxable = 'N'

Press any key to continue
```

Figure 10.6: List of rules for the Charges table

Before you test the rules you have defined, make sure you have entered all of the rules correctly. If you find any discrepancies, modify the rules to correct your mistakes. Press any key when you are finished looking at the list.

TESTING THE RULES

To test the rules for the Charges table, let's enter some data. Follow these steps to conduct your test:

1. Return to the R:BASE Main menu by highlighting and selecting **Exit**.

2. Display the ChrgFrm form for adding data by highlighting **Forms**, selecting **ChrgFrm**, and selecting **Add data**.

Now let's test the rule that the customer number has to exist in the Names table.

3. Type **5555** for the customer number; highlight **Add/discard**; and select **Add row**. R:BASE beeps and displays your error message, "No such customer number!"

4. Press any key to remove the message. The cursor moves to the Customer Number field and waits for you to enter a valid customer number.

Now we'll test the rule that the Unit Price has to be filled in.

5. Type **1001** and press ←┘ for the Customer Number; type **A-123** and press ←┘ for the Product Number; highlight **Add/discard**; and select **Add row**. In addition to beeping, R:BASE displays your message, "Unit price required!"

6. Press any key to remove the message. The cursor moves to the Unit Price field. Again, the program is waiting for you to enter a valid unit price.

7. Type **5.50** for the unit price.

We'll test the rule that the Taxable field has to be either *Y* or *N*.

8. Press ↑ twice to move to the Taxable field; type **X** for the Taxable field; highlight **Add/Discard** and select **Add row**. Once again, R:BASE beeps and the error message is displayed.

9. Press any key to remove the message and move the cursor back to the Taxable field.

10. Type **Y** for the Taxable field and press ←⏎.

Now, let's test to make sure that a completely correct record is accepted.

11. Type **10** for the Qty and press ←⏎; press ←⏎ to skip to the Unit Price field; type **Jun 15, 1990** for the Date of Sale; and highlight **Add/discard** and select **Add row**. This time the record is accepted and another empty screen is displayed.

12. Now that we've tested all the rules for the Charges table, highlight and select **Exit** to return to the R:BASE Main menu.

Now let's test the rule that the customer number in the Names table has to be unique.

1. To display the NamesFrm form for adding data, highlight **Forms** and select **NamesFrm**; and select **Add data**.

2. To enter another row with a customer number already in use, type **1001** for Customer Number and press ←⏎; type **Jul 15, 1990** and press ←⏎ for the Entry Date; type **Ferguson** for Last Name and press ←⏎; type **Harold** for First Name and press ←⏎; type **PromoTech Sales** for Company and press ←⏎; type **4109 Crest St.** for Address and press ←⏎; type **Los Angeles** for City and press ←⏎; press ←⏎ to accept the default State; type **91234** for Zip and press ←⏎; type **(213)555-1248** for Phone; and highlight **Add/discard** and select **Add row**.

R:BASE beeps and displays the message "Duplicate customer number!"

3. Press any key to remove the message.

4. To correct the problem, type **1007** for the Customer Number, highlight **Add/discard**, and select **Add row**. The row is now successfully added to the Names table.

5. Highlight and select **Exit** to return to the R:BASE Main menu.

These rules also apply when you are editing data with the forms you've defined as well as when you are editing data directly on the Edit screen. If you like, experiment with these rules when editing data or using the Edit screen.

SPEEDING UP DATA ENTRY WITH AUTOSKIP

R:BASE includes the Autoskip feature, which can help speed data entry. With the Autoskip feature off, you need to press ◄┘ after filling in a highlighted field on the screen. With the Autoskip feature on, the highlighting automatically moves to the next field on the screen when the highlighted field is filled.

Turn Autoskip on by highlighting **T**ools and selecting **S**ettings; and highlighting **S**ettings and selecting **A**utoskip. Notice that the current setting of OFF is shown under Current. Select **ON** under the Set to prompt, and highlight and select **E**xit to return to the Main menu.

From the R> prompt, you can set Autoskip on with the command SET AUTOSKIP ON and turn it off with the command SET AUTOSKIP OFF. The SHOW command displays the current status of Autoskip.

Leave Autoskip on to see how it works.

ADDING DATA TO THE CHARGES TABLE

To add data to the Charges table, you can use the ChrgFrm form you created. When you were testing the error messages earlier in this chapter, you displayed the ChrgFrm form for adding data by highlighting Forms and selecting ChrgFrm.

For a change, let's bring up the ChrgFrm form from Command mode. Highlight **E**xit, select R> prompt, and type the command

    ENTER ChrgFrm

Then enter the following data into the Charges table. We'll use these new data in the next chapter.

Remember that Autoskip is on. You will not have to press ↵ or Tab when you finish entering the CustNo or when you press Y or N in the Taxable fields.

When you add the rows to the Charges table, you may find it more convenient to use the Add and duplicate row option. This way, the Date of Sale from the previous row remains the default for the current one.

CUSTNO	PRODNO	TAXABLE	QTY	U_PRICE	P_DATE
1001	A-111	Y	12	10.00	Jun 15, 1990
1001	B-222	Y	5	12.50	Jun 15, 1990
1001	C-434	Y	2	100.00	Jun 15, 1990
1004	A-111	Y	5	10.00	Jun 15, 1990
1004	Z-128	N	10	12.80	Jun 15, 1990
1007	A-111	Y	10	10.00	Jun 15, 1990
1007	Z-128	N	10	12.80	Jun 15, 1990
1002	B-222	Y	12	12.50	Jul 30, 1990
1002	A-111	Y	10	10.00	Jul 30, 1990

After you've entered the new data, highlight and select **Exit** to return to the R > prompt. To verify your entries, enter the command

SELECT ALL FROM Charges

at the R > prompt. If you need to make changes, you can enter either of these commands:

EDIT ALL FROM Charges
EDIT USING ChrgFrm

MANAGING MULTI-TABLE DATABASES

Although life may seem more complicated when you first start working with a multi-table database, there are some powerful tools that will make your work much easier. One of these is the *view*. You've seen views alluded to in syntax diagrams; now it's time to learn about them.

WHAT'S IN A VIEW?

Views are *pseudo-tables* that have columns taken from up to five different related tables. As such, they share many characteristics of tables, but are not tables by definition. Although a view is displayed like a table and can be manipulated with many of the commands you use for tables, it is not a table.

In Chapter 5, when you were using the Query screen to select columns and rows to display on the Edit screen, you were really constructing a view that included only one table. To include columns from more than one table in a view, you use the Add tables option. This option can be found in the pull-down menu under Query on the Query screen.

You can also display the Query screen directly from the R:BASE Main menu by highlighting Views and selecting Create/modify. A slightly more flexible but much more complicated way to create views is to use the CREATE VIEW command at the R> prompt.

A prerequisite for constructing multi-table views is to include the linking (or common) columns as you move from table to table. Furthermore, if you're constructing a view from tables that have different passwords, you'll have to have access to all tables or identify yourself as the owner first.

All view definitions are stored in the SYSVIEWS table. This way, a view's actual data is not stored in a table of its own, taking up valuable disk space. However, storing all view definitions in one table means that R:BASE assembles views "on the fly," which may result in somewhat slower performance. Views are most often used with the SELECT, COMPUTE, CROSSTAB, and TALLY commands, and as the basis for reports. By basing a report on a view, you can

Views are discussed in more detail in Chapter 12.

avoid defining elaborate lookup expressions. For example, if we wanted to create an invoice report for the Mail database with a combination of data from the Names and Charges tables, it would be easiest to do if we set up a view that contained all of the necessary columns.

Views inherit user passwords from their parent tables. If the current password is not the database owner password, you must have all access rights or SELECT permission on a table in order to include the table in a view. View passwords, like user passwords, can be changed with the GRANT and REVOKE commands at the R> prompt and the Grant and Revoke options under Access rights on the R:BASE menu (reached from the Main menu by highlighting Info and selecting Create/modify). Judicious selection of columns to be included in a view combined with use of the WHERE clause allows you to protect any field from casual inspection. If a personnel table contained sensitive information about employees' bonuses that only the personnel director was supposed to see, a personnel view could be created using all but the bonus column from the personnel table. The single-table personnel view could be viewed and edited, much like a "real" table.

Views have their limitations, however. You can't EDIT multi-table views. You can't add or delete rows to a view, which means you can't base a form on a view. You can't redefine columns that are in a view without deleting the view (with the REMOVE VIEW command). Worse yet, any changes you make in a table that has columns used in a view may corrupt the view.

DATABASE DESIGN REVISITED

Now that you've seen some of the techniques for using multi-table databases, many of you will want to set up one of your own. If you're not ready to do so, you may want to skip the rest of this chapter for now. In this section, we will give you a *pragmatic* approach to database design. But before we talk about good database design, let's look at some poorly designed databases to see what their effects can be.

PROBLEMS RESULTING FROM POOR DATABASE DESIGN

If you try to use a poorly designed database, you may encounter any of the following problems:

- Your system simply won't work properly.

- Data is inaccurate or unreliable.

- Data is unstable.

- Performance is slow.

- Data-entry personnel are made to enter redundant data.

Imagine what would have happened to the Mail database if we had tried to include information about both customers and their charges in one table, with one row for each transaction. If we store information about the customer's name, address, city, state, ZIP code, and so forth with each charge transaction, then there will be a great deal of redundant data. This consequence of poor database design is called, reasonably enough, *data redundancy.*

For example, even though there are only three unique customers (Smith, Miller, and Jones) in the database in Figure 10.7, the table uses a lot of disk space because of all the redundant data in the L_Name, F_Name, and Address fields. Also, if a data-entry operator needs to type in the name and address of each customer repeatedly, he or she will certainly be wasting a lot of time. Finally, if one of the customers moves and changes their address, it is not going to be easy to change the address in the table, since the change will have to be made several times. However, failing to change all references to the old address would lead to conflicting data. This consequence of poor database design is called *data inconsistency* and results in loss of the database's integrity.

You might then consider modifying the table's design so that it has several fields for charges. But doing so creates another set of problems. For example, look at an alternative table design in Figure 10.8.

This design is also a poor one, for several reasons. First, it limits the number of transactions a particular customer can be assigned (120 in this example). Second, this design makes it virtually impossible to answer questions such as, "How many charge transactions

```
L_Name    F_Name    Address          Product     Qty    U_Price

Smith     Adam      123 A St.        A-111       10       1.22
Smith     Adam      123 A St.        B-222        5      12.34
Smith     Adam      123 A St.        C-444        1      45.67
Miller    Mandy     234 Oak St.      A-111        5       1.22
Miller    Mandy     234 Oak St.      C-444       10      45.67
Jones     Jake      P.O. Box 123     A-111        8       1.22
Jones     Jake      P.O. Box 123     B-222       15      12.34
Jones     Jake      P.O. Box 123     C-444        5      45.67
```

Figure 10.7: A database table containing data redundancy

```
 # Name                Type      Index Expression
 1 LName               TEXT    12
           Last Name
 2 FrsName             TEXT    10
           First Name
 3 Company             TEXT    15
 4 Address             TEXT    15
 5 City                TEXT    15
 6 State               TEXT     5
 7 Zip_Code            TEXT    10
 8 Phone               TEXT    13
 9 Trans1              CURRENCY
           Transaction #1
10 Trans2              CURRENCY
           Transaction #2
11 Trans3              CURRENCY
           Transaction #3
12 Trans4              CURRENCY
           Transaction #4
...
...
...
123 Trans120           CURRENCY
           Transaction #128
```

Figure 10.8: A revised, but also poor, table design

this month involved part number A-123?'' Third, there's a tremendous amount of wasted space associated with storing so many currency fields for each customer. Most customers won't have anywhere near 120 transactions per month.

It turns out that the best way to handle transactions relationally is to use at least two tables: a master table with the relatively permanent data and a transaction table that is linked to the master table. We'll talk about linking tables in a moment.

A PRAGMATIST'S GUIDE TO DATABASE DESIGN

Databases and the applications associated with them exist to provide accurate and timely information, which can then be used to answer questions. A good way to start designing a database is to make a list of the types of questions the database might be expected to answer.

STEP 1: FIND OUT WHAT INFORMATION WILL BE NEEDED

To find out what the information requirements of an organization are, you need to talk to people. If a friend wants you to set up a database for his company that sells used books, get to know how information flows within this company. There's a pretty obvious need for supplier, inventory, and sales data, but he may also want to keep track of advertising and seasonal market changes.

When you interview people about their information needs, ask to see current forms and reports. Don't hesitate to prompt them; you may see areas they have either forgotten or may not have even considered. Informal brainstorming sessions often work well. It's far better to find out at the beginning that, for example, sales need to be tracked by time of day.

STEP 2: GROUP THE DATA

If this sounds like deciding what tables you need, you're right! By looking at the data requirements, it's usually pretty easy to spot categories such as inventory, suppliers, sales, customers, employees, expenses, and so on. Each table should have its own subject.

Probably the most important step here is to limit the scope of the database. Make sure everyone involved realizes the trade-off between development time and the sophistication of the application. Frequently, you'll only need to answer part of an organization's data requirements; just be sure that everyone agrees on what is expected. We'll assume that for now your friend is only interested in tracking his sales.

STEP 3: DETERMINE THE RELATIONSHIPS AMONG THE TABLES

This can be a difficult step for beginners. Basically, there are three types of relationships between database tables: one-to-one, one-to-many, and many-to-many. One-to-one relationships don't occur that frequently between different objects; when they do, you can often collapse the tables into a single one. For example, you might conceive of a database with one table for names and another for social security numbers. These tables have a one-to-one relationship: for every name, there is a single, matching social security number. It really doesn't make sense to keep the data in two separate tables.

One-to-many and many-to-many relationships are far more common. Good relational database design requires that you break many-to-many relationships into one-to-many relationships, so it's important to be able to distinguish them. In a one-to-many relationship, for each row in the first table, there are (or could be) many corresponding rows in the second table. The relationship between Names and Charges in the Mail database is a one-to-many relationship.

In a many-to-many relationship, for each row in the first table, there are (or could be) many corresponding rows in the second table. However, for each row in the second table, there are (or could be) many corresponding rows in the first table as well. Tables containing parents and children would have a many-to-many relationship.

Your friend seems to need to keep track of customers and sales. The question is, what sort of relationship exists between the two? We find that most people find it easiest to visualize pairs of lists. In our example, one list would contain all the customers; the other all the sales. Then, imagine drawing lines from one list to the other. For each customer, could there be more than one line going to the sales list? Sure. What about the other way? No, of course not. So customer-to-sales is a one-to-many relationship.

Even when you have a far more complicated data model, this method still works. You simply plot it out for each pair of tables. Some tables won't have any direct relationship between them. Suppliers and sales, for example, wouldn't normally be directly related.

STEP 4: DECIDE ON THE COLUMNS FOR EACH TABLE

Deciding on the columns for each table is usually a pretty easy task, since you're just listing the important facts about each object. You might initially come up with something like the following:

SALES	CUSTOMER
Invoice#	CustNo
P_Date	L_Name
ProdNo	F_Name
Qty	Address
U_Price	City
Taxable	State
Total	Zip_Code
	Phone

It might not be until you arrive at this step that you recognize a problem with your design. What if customers purchase several items at a time? One solution would be to have separate invoices for each item, but this probably wouldn't be desirable. You might, then, decide to include a third table with invoice details, and thus reorganize the Sales table as follows:

INVDET	SALES	CUSTOMER
ProdNo	Invoice#	CustNo
Qty	P_Date	L_Name
U_Price	InvTotal	F_Name
Taxable		Address
		City
		State
		Zip
		Phone

Many people start thinking about data types and lengths at this point, too. Probably the most common error at this stage is to go wild and include data that really isn't needed. Keep in mind that the overhead associated with carrying unneeded data is heavy: more data entry, more disk space, and slower performance.

STEP 5: ASSIGN INDEXES

Index columns, you may remember from the last chapter, uniquely identify a row. If you know the key fact (or group of facts) about an entity in your table, you should be able to retrieve the data about the entity quickly and efficiently. If you have a Customer table in your database, indexed on CustNo, you can expect R:BASE to find no more than one customer's record when you type

SELECT ALL FROM Customer WHERE CustNo = '1004'

Remember, an index speeds up access to a table when you know a value from the index column.

There ought to be a law stating that all well-designed tables shall have indexes and that no entries in the table will be allowed without the index column entry. Unfortunately, R:BASE doesn't enforce such laws; the burden is on you to establish indexes and set up rules that make sure that data entered into index fields is unique.

As you assign indexed columns, the list of attributes associated with each table may change. This is normal. For example, you may need to add a column to a table to serve as its index column. This adds an attribute (column) to that table's definition.

What indexes might you use for the book sales database? The answers seem to be fairly obvious for the Sales and Customer tables: Invoice# and CustNo are good indexes, since each customer and each invoice will bear unique numbers. However, what index should the Invdet table use? ProdNo won't do, because a given product type will be sold more than once. Perhaps Invoice# should be added to the Invdet table. However, Invoice# alone isn't a good index for the Invdet table either, because some invoices will have many items on them. You may want to index both Invoice# and ProdNo. Alternatively, you could add a column for the invoice item number. Either method will require modifying the original design of the Invdet table.

STEP 6: ESTABLISH LINKS BETWEEN RELATED TABLES

Establishing links between related tables may seem hard at first, but it becomes intuitive with practice. So if you find this step tough, lean on our pragmatic rules at first.

When you establish links between related tables, you're providing the "glue" that makes the database relational. Links are columns that appear in more than one table. At first, it will go against your grain to add columns to tables, because it's contrary to the notion of minimizing redundancy. However, you will soon learn to accept the fact that links are necessary.

So what are the ground rules for selecting links? We can summarize them as follows:

- Links should also be indexes, so that data is linked unambiguously.

- To link tables with a one-to-many relationship, put the index from the "one" side of the relationship into the table from the "many" side of the relationship. This will create a situation where you effectively have two indexes in the "many" table. The link index, however, is referred to as a *foreign* index.

- To link tables that have a many-to-many relationship, create a new table that contains the indexes from each side of the relationship. This new table may or may not correspond to any physical entity. It may simply be a product of good relational design.

Before we can use the above rules, we need to know about the relationships that exist among the tables. Since we've added a new table, we need to reevaluate the relationships. Customer to Sales is still a one-to-many relationship. Sales to Invdet is also a one-to-many relationship, since any given invoice can contain several items. Finally, Customer and Invdet have a one-to-many relationship, but it is indirect, since Sales will link customers and their transactions.

The second rule above reminds us that the index from the Customer table needs to be in the Sales table and that the index from the Sales table needs to be in the Invdet table. The design might be modified as follows:

INVDET	*SALES*	*CUSTOMER*
Invoice# (index)	Invoice# (index)	CustNo (index)
ProdNo (index)	CustNo	L_Name
Qty	P_Date	F_Name
U_Price	InvTotal	Address
Taxable		City
		State
		Zip
		Phone

A common mistake is to create separate tables for separate items of information (which is a step in the right direction), but to forget to provide a common column that links them. If you hadn't put the CustNo column in the Sales table, you wouldn't be able to answer the question "Who bought *Gone with the Wind* on Invoice 321?"

STEP 7: SET UP THE DATABASE

At this stage, you still shouldn't have done any hands-on data entry. Only after having designed the database on paper, and worked out the indexes and links, should you actually use R:BASE to set it up. And bear in mind that even after having gone through the design steps listed above, changes may still need to be made in your database design. The beauty of relational databases such as R:BASE is that it's easy to make changes.

COMMON ERRORS IN DATABASE DESIGN

What are some common errors in database design? Based on our experience, here is a list of a few:

- Having many-to-many relationships without a link table.

- Setting up tables without indexes (or without good indexes).

- Not having rules set up to ensure entry of index values.

- Putting the link column for one-to-many relationships in the wrong table.

- Having tables that contain more than one emphasis, such as an orders table with supplier information alongside purchase order details.

- Not taking advantage of calculated fields.

- Having too many common columns relating a pair of tables.

However, if you employ this step-by-step approach to database design, you should be able to avoid these errors.

In this chapter, we've added a new table and form to the Mail database. We've also created some rules to minimize the likelihood of erroneous data being entered into the database. Finally, we've looked at seven steps that lead to good database design. In the next chapter, you'll learn some new techniques for handling calculations using R:BASE's variables and SuperMath functions.

Chapter 11

*Performing
Complex Calculations
with Variables and
Functions*

NOW THAT YOU'VE GRADUATED FROM THE R:BASE novice stage, it's time learn to create and manage R:BASE *variables*, which are also referred to as *global variables*. The adjective refers to the fact that data in variables can be passed from one database to another, and hence are accessible, or "global," to all databases. Unlike information stored in databases and tables, variables are stored in the computer's random access memory (RAM), and they are normally used as temporary, or "scratch pad," data.

A variable is a character or word that holds a value that is subject to change. This definition is identical to the use of variables in basic mathematics. For example, if we state that X equals 10 and Y equals 15, then X plus Y equals 25, and Y minus X equals 5.

In this chapter, we'll explore techniques for creating and using R:BASE variables. We'll discuss the practical applications of variables in the following chapters.

CREATING VARIABLES

In R:BASE, you use the SET VARIABLE command (abbreviated to SET VAR or SET V) to store and manipulate variables. The SHOW VARIABLES command (abbreviated SHOW VAR or SHO V) displays the current value of all the variables. You can also use the SHOW VARIABLES command to display a single variable. You enter these commands at the R> prompt; it does not matter whether a database is open at the time.

Here are some examples that you may want to try. First, from the R> prompt, enter the command

SHOW VARIABLES

As you saw in Chapter 7, the #DATE and #TIME variables hold the current date and time. You'll be using the #PI variable to calculate the area of a circle later in this chapter in the section "Manipulating Variables." We will discuss the SQLCODE variable in Chapter 16, when we begin programming.

You'll see four variables, #DATE, #TIME, #PI, and SQLCODE displayed on the screen, as below:

VARIABLE	= VALUE	TYPE
#DATE	= Oct 30, 1990	DATE
#TIME	= 12:20:45	TIME
#PI	= 3.14159265358979	DOUBLE
SQLCODE	= 0	INTEGER

These variables are always available in R:BASE and are sometimes referred to as *system variables*.

Let's try creating and displaying some variables with the following commands:

1. Type **SET VARIABLE X = 10** and press ◄─┘; type **SET VARIABLE Y = 15** and press ◄─┘; and type **SHOW VARIABLES** and press ◄─┘. You'll see these two new variables added to the table of existing variables, as below:

VARIABLE	= VALUE	TYPE
X	= 10	INTEGER
Y	= 15	INTEGER

> The new variables have the INTEGER data type. R:BASE assigned this data type because the values being stored, 10 and 15, are whole numbers.

2. To create and display two TEXT variables, type **SET VARIABLE A = 'Hello'** and press ◄─┘; type **SET VARIABLE B = 'There'** and press ◄─┘; and type **SHOW VARIABLES** and press ◄─┘. The new A and B variables are added to the list, as below:

VARIABLE	= VALUE	TYPE
A	= Hello	TEXT
B	= There	TEXT

> R:BASE assigned the TEXT data type to these new variables, again because it made an assumption based on the values being stored, letters in this case.

3. To create and display other types of variables, type **SET VARIABLE Today = 9/25/90** and press ◄─┘; type **SET VARIABLE Now = 12:30:00** and press ◄─┘; type **SET VARIABLE Salary = 12345.67** and press ◄─┘; type **SET VARIABLE DecNumb = 1.1** and press ◄─┘; and type **SHOW VARIABLES** and press ◄─┘. You'll see that R:BASE made valid assumptions about the data types of each variable, as shown below:

VARIABLE	= VALUE	TYPE
Today	= 09/25/90	DATE
Now	= 12:30:00	TIME
Salary	= 12345.67	DOUBLE
DecNumb	= 1.1	DOUBLE

> The value displayed for Today will be Sep 25, 1990 if you set the DATE format to MMM DD, 19YY.

Note that each variable name (A, B, Today, Now, and so on) is purely arbitrary. You can use whatever variable names you like as long as you follow several rules when choosing variable names. A variable name

- must start with a letter;

- can include only letters, numbers, and a number sign (#), a dollar sign ($), an underscore (_), or a percent sign (%);

- can't be longer than 18 characters;

- can't be a *reserved word*—a word already used for a feature of R:BASE, such as a command.

R:BASE uses all 18 characters to distinguish variable names. So CORPORATE_TAX and CORPORATE _SHARES would be two different variable names.

See the Reserved Words topic in the "Command Dictionary" section of the R:BASE *Reference Manual* for a list of reserved words.

The number of variables that you can create is limited only by the amount of computer memory available. You should be able to use at least 40 variables, and the maximum is about 1000 variables. Before taking a look at ways to manipulate variables, let's talk about R:BASE's arithmetic operators.

R:BASE'S ARITHMETIC OPERATORS

When you used the asterisk operator (*) in previous chapters to represent multiplication, you were using one of R:BASE's predefined arithmetic operators. Of course, R:BASE also provides operators for addition, subtraction, division, and percentages. These are shown in Table 11.1 in their order of *precedence*. Precedence refers to the order in which the calculations take place. For example, the formula $10 + 5 * 2$ results in 20, because the multiplication take precedence over (occurs before) the addition. You can use parentheses to change the order of precedence. For example, the formula $(10 + 5) * 2$ results in 30, because the operation inside the parentheses takes precedence.

R:BASE also offers many *functions* for performing advanced trigonometric and financial calculations that we'll talk about later in this chapter. Remember for now that parentheses and functions have higher precedence than any of the arithmetic operators.

Table 11.1: R:BASE's Arithmetic Operators

OPERATOR	FUNCTION	EXAMPLE
−, +	Unary minus or plus	− 10 means negative 10
**	Exponentiation	3**2 = 9 (3 squared); 27**(1/3) = 3
*, /	Multiplication, Division	3 * 5 = 15; 100/10 = 10
%	Percentage	50 % 100 = 50
+, −	Addition, Subtraction	2 + 2 = 4; 10 − 5 = 5
+, &	Concatenation, Concatenation (with space)	'ABC' + 'DEF' = 'ABCDEF'; 'ABC' & 'DEF' = 'ABC DEF'

MANIPULATING VARIABLES

We've already discussed the R:BASE operators that you can use for addition, subtraction, and other operations. You can use all of these operators to create and manipulate variables. For example, to find the cube root of 27, you would enter the command below:

    SET VAR Cube = (27**(1/3))

The two asterisks (**) represent the exponent sign, and the parentheses around the fraction (1/3) ensure that the division will take place before the exponentiation. When you enter the SHOW VARIABLES command at the R> prompt, you'll see the answer 3, stored in the variable named Cube.

The expression above contains only *constants*; that is, 27 is a constant and (1/3) is a constant because they are numbers. Similarly, the expression below contains two constants, the text string 'So' and the text string 'Long':

    SET VARIABLE ByeBye = ('So' & 'Long')

When you set a variable equal to an expression, you must enclose the expression in parentheses in order to be sure that R:BASE will evaluate the expression correctly and efficiently.

Sometimes the numbers or strings which make up a constant are referred to as *literals*, because the value is exactly what appears in the command.

After you've entered this command at the R > prompt, the variable ByeBye will contain the text 'So Long'. (Use SHOW VARIABLES to see the results.)

Expressions can contain variables as well as constants. When using variable names in expressions, however, you should always precede the variable name with a period, in order to avoid confusing variables and constants. For example, recall that you created a variable named A, which contains the word 'Hello'. You also created a variable named B, which contains the word 'There'. To use these two variable names in an expression, precede each variable name with a period (or dot), as follows:

SET VAR Howdy = (.A & .B)

If you enter the SHOW VARIABLES command after entering this command, you'll see that the variable Howdy now contains the TEXT string

Hello There

You can use the predefined (or *system*) variables in expressions such as #DATE, #TIME, and #PI. For example, you may recall from geometry that the area of a circle can be found using the formula pi (π) times the radius squared. Assuming that you know the radius is 5, the expression below can calculate the area of the circle and store the result in a variable named Area:

SET VAR Area = (.#PI * 5 ** 2)

The SHOW VARIABLES command displays the following result:

Area = 78.5398163397447 DOUBLE

You can manipulate dates in expressions just as you can manipulate text and numbers. For example, recall that we created a variable named Today a short time ago, and we assigned 9/25/90 to the date. To find out what the date will be 90 days past the Today variable, you could enter the command

SET VARIABLE Ninety = (.Today + 90)

When you use a variable on the right side of an equal sign, you can precede the variable with a dot. This is not required, but it helps R:BASE evaluate your expression slightly faster.

Note that the variable #PI is preceded with a dot.

and then enter the command

SHOW VARIABLE Ninety

You'll see the date 90 days beyond Today, as below:

12/24/91

When you mix data types, the results can be confusing. For example, suppose you add the X variable (which is an INTEGER data type) to the DecNumb variable (which is a DOUBLE number data type), as in

SET VARIABLE Mix = (.X + .DecNumb)

In this case, when you enter the command

SHOW VARIABLES

you'll see the new variable Mix is the DOUBLE data type, as below:

Mix = 11.1 DOUBLE

Generally, when you mix an INTEGER data type with a DOUBLE or CURRENCY data type amount, the result will be the data type with the most decimal places. However, you can control the data type of a variable before defining a variable or performing a calculation, through a process known as *explicit data typing*.

EXPLICIT DATA TYPING

You can define a variable's type by using the SET VARIABLE command without the = option, followed by a data type. For example, the command

SET VARIABLE JJ CURRENCY

creates an "empty" variable named JJ with the CURRENCY data type. The command

SET VARIABLE Later DATE

creates an empty variable named Later with the DATE data type. The data types for variables are the same as those used for columns: CURRENCY, DATE, DOUBLE, INTEGER, NOTE, NUMERIC, REAL, TEXT, and TIME. In addition, you can use an alternate name for some of the data types: CHARACTER for TEXT, DECIMAL for NUMERIC, FLOAT for DOUBLE, and SMALLINT for INTEGER. We'll see the value of explicit data typing in Chapter 16 and 17 when we develop command files.

PASSING TABLE DATA TO VARIABLES

Variables can also be assigned values directly from a table in a database using a lookup expression. To do so, you need to open the appropriate database first. Then you use a version of the SET VARIABLE command with the following syntax:

Although you can use parentheses within the WHERE condition, you may not enclose the lookup expression *column name* IN *table name* WHERE *condition* in parentheses.

```
SET VARIABLE variable name = column name IN table name +
+ > WHERE condition
```

Let's try an example using the Names table in the Mail database:

1. Type **CONNECT MAIL IDENTIFIED BY MYMAIL** and press ◄─┘ to open the MAIL database.

2. Type **SET VARIABLE Name1 = F_Name IN Names WHERE CustNo = '1003'** and press ◄─┘ to put the first name of customer number 1003 into the Name1 variable.

3. Type **SET VARIABLE Name2 = L_Name IN Names WHERE CustNo = '1003'** and press ◄─┘ to put the last name of customer number 1003 into the Name2 variable.

4. Type **SET VARIABLE FullName = (.Name1 & .Name2)** and press ◄─┘ to create the variable FullName containing the first and last name separated by a space.

5. Type **SHOW VARIABLES** and press ◄─┘. You'll see, among the existing variables, the new Name1, Name2, and Full

Name variables, as below:

VARIABLE	= *VALUE*	*TYPE*
Name1	= Marie	TEXT
Name2	= Miller	TEXT
FullName	= Marie Miller	TEXT

THE COMPUTE COMMAND REVISITED

Variables can also be used to store the results of computations performed on a table using the general syntax for the COMPUTE command which is

COMPUTE *variable name* AS <*calculation*> <*column name*> +
+ > FROM *table name* WHERE *conditions*

The WHERE clause is optional. Although you used this powerful command in Chapter 6, you never stored the results.

Suppose, for example, that you want to compute the sum of the Total column in the Charges table and store the result in a variable named GrandTot. Enter the following command:

COMPUTE GrandTot AS SUM Total FROM Charges

When you enter the command

SHOW VARIABLE GrandTot

you'll see the total, $1,143.75.

To compute the average unit price from the Charges table and store the results in a variable named AvgPrice, enter the command

COMPUTE AvgPrice AS AVG U_Price FROM Charges

To see the results, enter the command

SHOW VARIABLE AvgPrice

R:BASE will display the average unit price of $19.61.

You can count the number of rows in a table and store this number in a variable using the ROWS option with the COMPUTE command, as below:

COMPUTE RowCount AS ROWS FROM Names

You can then enter the command

SHOW VARIABLE RowCount

to see that there are nine rows in the table.

The optional WHERE clause allows you to create COMPUTE commands that are more specific. For example, to compute the total sales from the Charges table for product number A-111 and store this value in a variable named ATot, enter the command

COMPUTE ATot AS SUM Qty FROM Charges WHERE +
+ > ProdNo = 'A-111'

Entering the command

SHOW VARIABLE ATot

shows the result, 37.

You can verify this calculation by entering the command

SELECT ALL FROM Charges WHERE ProdNo = 'A-111'

which displays all product number A-111 transactions from the Charges table, as shown in Figure 11.1.

To determine the largest single transaction amount for product number A-111, enter the command

COMPUTE HiSale AS MAXIMUM Total FROM Charges +
+ > WHERE ProdNo = 'A-111'

To determine the lowest sale for product number A-111, enter this command:

COMPUTE LowSale AS MINIMUM Total FROM Charges +
+ > WHERE ProdNo = 'A-111'

```
R>SELECT ALL FROM Charges WHERE ProdNo = 'A-111'
  CustNo     ProdNo   Qty         U_Price       Taxable  Total
  ---------- -------- --------- ---------------- -------- ---------------
      1001 A-111          12       $10.00 Y               $127.20
      1004 A-111           5       $10.00 Y                $53.00
      1006 A-111          10       $10.00 Y               $106.00
      1002 A-111          10       $10.00 Y               $106.00
R>
```

Figure 11.1: Product number A-111 transactions in the Charges table

To count the number of rows in a table that meet a specific criterion, use the COMPUTE command with the COUNT option rather than with the ROWS option. For example, the command

> COMPUTE RowCount AS COUNT ProdNo FROM Charges +
> + > WHERE ProdNo = 'A-111'

counts the number of rows from the Charges table that have A-111 in the ProdNo column and then stores the result in a variable named RowCount.

If you now enter the command

SHOW VARIABLES

you'll see, among the other variables we've created in this chapter, those listed below:

VARIABLE	= *VALUE*	*TYPE*
GrandTot	= $1,143.75	CURRENCY
AvgPrice	= $19.61	CURRENCY
ATot	= 37	INTEGER
HiSale	= $127.20	CURRENCY
LowSale	= $53.00	CURRENCY
RowCount	= 4	INTEGER

Note that the data types for the variables have been assigned the same data types as the columns that were computed. Again, R:BASE has made reasonable assumptions about the data types based on the type of data being computed.

CLEARING VARIABLES

When you exit R:BASE, all variables (except #DATE, #TIME, #PI, and SQLCODE) are immediately erased, and they cannot be recalled other than to re-create them using the SET VARIABLE command. Prior to exiting, however, the variables are available in memory even as you open and close databases.

You can also eliminate variables using the CLEAR VARIABLES command. For example, the command

```
CLEAR VARIABLES Salary
```

erases the Salary variable. You can clear all variables (except #DATE, #TIME, and SQLCODE) using the command

```
CLEAR ALL VARIABLES
```

You can even clear all variables except for the Salary and TotalPaid variables with the command

```
CLEAR ALL VARIABLES EXCEPT Salary, TotalPaid
```

MACRO SUBSTITUTIONS

You can also make variables a part of R:BASE commands using a technique often called *macro substitution*. An example will best demonstrate this technique. First, assume you create a TEXT variable named ColNames using the SET VARIABLE command as below:

```
SET VARIABLE ColNames = 'CustNo L_Name F_Name +
+ > Company'
```

Assuming that the Mail database is open, you could then use the ColNames variable as part of a command, as long as you precede the variable name with an ampersand (&) character. For example, entering the command

> SELECT &ColNames FROM Names

displays the CustNo, L_Name, F_Name, and Company columns from the Names table, because R:BASE automatically substitutes the text stored in the variable ColNames into the command. In other words, R:BASE changes the command to

> SELECT CustNo L_Name F_Name Company FROM Names

by substituting the contents of ColNames variable before executing the command. (The substitution takes place "behind the scenes," so you see only the final result and not the actual substitution.)

Macro substitution is an advanced, though often useful, technique used primarily in programming with the R:BASE programming language.

EXPRESSION LIMITATIONS

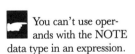 You can't use operands with the NOTE data type in an expression.

An expression in a SET VARIABLES command can be up to 160 characters long. Any expression can contain up to 50 operators and operands. *Operands* are the data that the operators act upon. For example, the expression below contains three operators: two multiplication signs (*) and one minus sign (–). The expression also contains four operands (.A, .X, .Y, and .Z):

> .A * (.X – .Y) * .Z

You can't use operands with the Note data type in an expression.

THE POWER OF
FUNCTIONS (SUPERMATH)

Most pocket calculators that you can purchase for more than 99 cents have at least a few function keys on them. The function keys are included to perform calculations that extend beyond simple arithmetic, such as square roots and logarithms.

R:BASE also offers a set of *functions* collectively referred to as SuperMath. In fact, R:BASE offers about 70 functions that you can use to perform sophisticated calculations with variables. These functions can also be used to define expressions for computed columns in a database and for variables in reports and forms. (In Chapter 10, you already saw how to use the IFEQ function when you calculated a total sale based on the status of the Taxable column in the Charges table.)

Functions can also be used in command lines, including ORDER BY and WHERE clauses. Furthermore, functions can be used freely within the R:BASE programming language. When you use a SET VARIABLE statement to set a variable equal to a function, you have to enclose the function in parentheses, just as you would an expression.

Almost all functions require at least one *argument*, which is the information that the function operates on. For example, the SQRT function calculates the square root of a number and requires one argument. In the expression

We'll discuss how to use functions in R:BASE programs in Chapter 16.

SET VARIABLE Root = (SQRT(9))

the number 9 is the argument to the function. The result of the calculation is stored in the variable named Root.

The argument can be another variable. For example, the expression below stores the number 9 in a variable named StartNum:

SET VARIABLE StartNum = 9

The next command calculates the square root of the value stored in the StartNum variable and replaces the prior value of Root:

Just like expressions, R:BASE functions have to be enclosed in parentheses.

SET VARIABLE Root = (SQRT(.StartNum))

In some cases, the arguments to a function can also be a column name.

When using functions, you must be careful to use the correct data type in the argument. For example, the command

SET VARIABLE Root = (SQRT("Smith"))

makes no sense, because you cannot possibly calculate the square root of a person's last name. If you try, R:BASE will respond with an error message.

Function arguments can also be expressions in themselves. For example, the command

SET VARIABLE Root = (SQRT(80 + 20))

stores the square root of 100 in the variable named Root. (One exception to this rule is TEXT functions, which do not allow expressions in TEXT string arguments.)

Functions other than TEXT (or string) functions may be nested within an expression, as long as there is an equal number of opening and closing parentheses in the expression. For example, the ABS function converts a negative number to a positive number, but leaves a positive number as positive. The square root function accepts only positive numbers. Therefore, you could use the ABS function inside the SQRT function to ensure that the argument to the SQRT function is positive.

In the example below, the negative number – 49 is stored in a variable named NegNumb:

SET VARIABLE NegNumb = – 49

In the next expression, the square root of the absolute value of NegNumb is stored in the variable named Root. Notice that the parentheses are *balanced* (there are three opening parentheses and three closing parentheses):

SET VARIABLE Root = (SQRT(ABS(NegNumb)))

Since the ABS function is nested inside the SQRT function, R:BASE first calculates the absolute value of the NegNumb variable, and then calculates the square root of that result. The resulting number, 7, is stored in the variable named Root.

The remainder of this chapter lists the R:BASE functions categorized by the types of calculations they perform. Each function is shown with the correct placement and data types of the argument(s) that the function operates on. The types of arguments include the following:

Arg	An argument of any data type
Number	A real, double-precision, or integer number
Real	Either a real or double-precision number
Date	The DATE data type
Time	The TIME data type
Integer	The INTEGER data type
Text	The TEXT data type
Angle	An angle measurement expressed in radians
List	A list of column names, variables, constants, or expressions

A few other examples of arguments are also included in the summary that follows. These are explained in more detail when they are used.

An example of each function is also included. To verify that the function performs as expected, or to experiment with new values, use the SET VARIABLE and SHOW VARIABLES commands at the R> prompt on your own computer. For instance, the example shown in the SQRT function is

SQRT(81) is 9

To try this, enter the command

SET VARIABLE Test = (SQRT(81))

(Of course, Test is just a sample variable name; you can use any variable name you like.) To see the result, enter the command

SHOW VARIABLE Test

or enter the command

SHOW VARIABLES

and you'll see that the variable named Test does indeed contain the number 9.

The examples all assume that the variable name used has not already been assigned a data type, either through explicit data typing or through previous use. If you use the same variable name repeatedly, your results may be inconsistent with the examples given. To rectify any discrepancies caused by existing data types, use the CLEAR ALL VARIABLES or CLEAR VARIABLES *variable list* command before entering the SET VARIABLE command.

Several additional examples of using R:BASE functions are included at the end of this chapter.

ARITHMETIC AND MATHEMATICAL FUNCTIONS

The arithmetic and mathematical functions that follow perform common calculations on numbers and are used in both scientific and business applications.

ABS(*Number*)

Absolute Value—Converts a negative number to a positive number, or leaves a positive number as positive. Examples: (ABS(– 2)) equals 2, as does ABS(2).

DIM(*Number,Number*)

Positive Difference—Subtracts the second *Number* from the first. The result is either a positive number or zero. Examples: (DIM(12,10)) is 2. DIM(10,12) is 0.

EXP(*Number*)

Inverse of Logarithm—Raises the constant *e* (2.71828) to the power of *Number*. Example: (EXP(1)) is 2.71828.

LAVG(*Number*)

Average—Computes the average of the numbers in *List*. Example: (LAVG(9,3,4,5,11,16)) is 8.

LMAX(*List*)

Highest Value—Finds the largest number in the specified *List* of values. Example: (LMAX(2, – 3,87, – 99,16)) is 87.

LMIN(*List*)

> **Lowest Value**—Finds the smallest number in the specified *List* of values. Example: (LMIN(2, – 3,87, – 99,16) is – 99.

LOG(*Number*)

> **Natural Logarithm**—Computes the logarithm base *e* of *Number*, where *Number* is positive. Example: (LOG(2.71828)) equals 1.

LOG10(*Number*)

> **Logarithm Base 10**—Returns the logarithm base 10 of *Number*, where *Number* is positive. Example: (LOG10(100)) is 2.

MOD(*Number,Number*)

> **Modulus**—Returns the remainder after dividing the first *Number* by the second *Number*. Examples: (MOD(6,4)) is 2. (MOD(10,5)) is 0, because 10 is evenly divisible by 5.

SIGN(*Number,Number*)

> **Sign Transfer**—Transfers the sign of the second *Number* to the first *Number*. Example: (SIGN(12, – 7)) is – 12.

SQRT(*Number*)

> **Square Root**—Returns the square root of *Number*, where *Number* is positive. Example: (SQRT(81)) is 9.

TRIGONOMETRIC FUNCTIONS

The trigonometric functions are used primarily in scientific and engineering applications. If your work generally does not require the use of these functions, you can probably skip these. Note that all trigonometric angle measurements are in radians, not degrees. Also, R:BASE will typically display the results of trigonometric functions with 14 decimal places of accuracy, although we'll show only five decimal places in these examples.

ACOS(*Number*)

> **Arccosine**—Computes the arccosine of *Number*, where *Number* is a value in the range – 1 to 1. The result is an angle, in radians, between zero and pi. Example: (ACOS(– 0.5)) is 2.09440.

ASIN(*Number*)

Arcsine—Computes the arcsine of *Number*, where *Number* is in the range −1 to 1. The result is an angle expressed in radians. Example: (ASIN(−0.75)) is −0.84806.

ATAN(*Number*)

Arctangent—Computes the arctangent of *Number*, with the result being an angle expressed in radians. Example: (ATAN(1)) returns 0.78540.

ATAN2(*Angle,Angle*)

Arctangent of Coordinate Angle—Computes the arctangent of *Angle,Angle*, where *Angle,Angle* is a coordinate angle expressed in radians. Example: (ATAN2(1,1)) returns 0.78540.

COS(*Angle*)

Cosine—Computes the cosine of *Angle*, where *Angle* is expressed in radians. Example: (COS(0.78)) is 0.71091.

COSH(*Angle*)

Hyperbolic Cosine—Computes the hyperbolic cosine of *Angle*. Example: (COSH(1.047)) results in 1.60004.

SIN(*Angle*)

Sine—Computes the sine of *Angle*, where *Angle* is expressed in radians. Example: (SIN(0.78)) returns 0.70328. *Angle* can also be expressed as a fraction of the #PI function. Example: (SIN(.#PI/2)) returns 1.

SINH(*Angle*)

Hyperbolic Sine—Computes the hyperbolic sine of *Angle*. Example: (SINH(1.047)) returns 1.24905.

TAN(*Angle*)

Tangent—Computes the tangent of *Angle*, expressed in radians. Example: (TAN(0.78)) is 0.98926.

TANH(*Angle*)

Hyperbolic Tangent—Computes the hyperbolic tangent of *Angle*. Example: (TANH(0.785)) returns 0.65557.

CONVERSION FUNCTIONS

The conversion functions modify the data types of variables and are generally used only in programming. The R:BASE data types are described in Chapter 2 of this book.

AINT(*Real*)

Truncates Real Number—Truncates the decimal portion of a real (or double-precision) number, returning only the integer portion in the DOUBLE data type. Example: (AINT(1.8888)) returns 1., where 1. is a double-precision number.

ANINT(*Real*)

Rounds Real Number—Rounds the *Real* number to a double-precision value. Example: (ANINT(1.888)) results in 2., where 2. is a double-precision number.

CHAR(*Integer*)

Character for ASCII Code—Returns the character associated with the *Integer* code. This function can be used to store printer control codes. Examples: (CHAR(27)) codes the ''Escape'' character that often initiates a series of printer-control codes. Can be used after the OUTPUT PRINTER command in conjunction with WRITE to send printer control codes directly to your printer.

CTXT(*Number*)

Converts Number to Text String—Converts *Number* to a text string. Example: (CTXT(1.2345)) returns '1.2345' as the TEXT data type.

FLOAT(*Integer*)

Converts Integer to Real Number—Converts an integer to the DOUBLE data type. Example: (FLOAT(9)) returns 9 as a double-precision number.

ICHAR(*Text*)

ASCII code for Character—Returns the ASCII code for a character of *Text*. Example: (ICHAR('A')) returns 65 as an integer (the ASCII code for the uppercase letter A).

INT(*Real*)

> **Converts Real to Integer Number**—Converts a *Real* number to the Integer data type by truncating the decimal portion of the number. Example: (INT(9.999)) returns 9, where 9 is an integer.

NINT(*Real*)

> **Rounds Real to Integer Number**—Converts a *Real* number to an integer by rounding the decimal portion to the nearest whole number. Example: (NINT(9.999)) returns 10 as an integer.

STRING-MANIPULATION FUNCTIONS

The string-manipulation functions operate on TEXT data. They allow you to manipulate (and change) uppercase and lowercase letters, pad text with blank spaces, trim blank spaces from the text, and move sections of text. Many of these functions are used for "tricky" programming techniques. Even though they seem uninteresting or meaningless to beginners and nonprogrammers, they are worth skimming over because you may find them useful occasionally. When you use them, be sure to enclose the entire string function in parentheses, as in this example:

> SELECT ALL FROM Names WHERE (SGET(L_Name,1,1)) + + >
> CONTAINS 'M'

Here are the string-manipulation functions:

CTR(*Text,Width*)

> **Centers Text**—Centers *Text* within the specified *Width*. Example: (CTR('Best',10)) produces ' Best '.

ICAP1(*Text*)

> **Uppercase First Letter Only**—Converts *Text* to a text string with a capital letter as the first character of the first word only. Example: (ICAP1('this Is It')) produces 'This is it'.

ICAP2(*Text*)

Uppercase All First Letters—Converts *Text* to a text string with a capital letter as the first character of each word. Examples: (ICAP2('ADAM P. JONES, JR.')) produces 'Adam P. Jones, Jr.'. (ICAP2('this is a test')) produces 'This Is A Test'.

LJS(*Text,Width*)

Left-Justifies Text—Left-justifies *Text* within the specified *Width*. Example: (LJS('Best',10)) produces 'Best   '.

LUC(*Text*)

Converts Lowercase to Uppercase—Converts all lowercase letters in *Text* to uppercase. Example: (LUC('Give me a break')) returns 'GIVE ME A BREAK'.

RJS(*Text,Width*)

Right-Justifies Text—Right-justifies *Text* within the specified *Width*. Example: (RJS('Best',10)) produces '   Best'.

SFIL(*Text,Number*)

Fill Character String—Creates a text variable consisting of *Text* characters, *Number* characters long. Example: (SFIL('-',80)) creates a text variable consisting of 80 hyphens.

SGET(*Text,Number,Location*)

Get from Text—Selects *Number* characters from a *Text* string starting at *Location*. Example: (SGET('CatDogFish',3,4)) results in *Dog*, because *Dog* is three letters long, and it begins at the fourth character in the 'CatDogFish' character string.

SLEN(*Text*)

Length of String—Returns the length of a **Text** string. Example: (SLEN('Snowball')) returns 8.

SLOC(*Text,Smaller*)

Location of Text—Searches the *Text* string for the *Smaller* string and returns the location of the start of the smaller string within the larger string. If the smaller string is not found inside the larger string, the result is zero. Example: (SLOC('CatDogFish','Dog')) returns 4, because the word DOG starts at the fourth character in 'CatDogFish'. (SLOC('CatDogFish','MooMoo')) returns 0, because there is no 'MooMoo' inside 'CatDogFish'.

SMOVE(*Text,Position 1,Number,String,Position 2*)

Moves Text into String—Moves the characters in *Text*, starting at numeric *Position 1*, for a length of *Number* characters into *String*, starting at numeric *Position 2*. Example: (SMOVE ('ddogg',2,3,'ABCDE',2)) returns 'AdogE'.

SPUT(*Text,String,Location*)

Puts Text into String—Moves a *String* of characters in *Text* starting at *Location*. Example: (SPUT('ABCDE','mm',3)) returns 'ABmmE'.

SSUB(*Text,Integer*)

Get Member from List—In the list of strings in *Text*, selects the member at position *Integer*. Example: (SSUB('Dog,Cat, Hamster',2)) returns 'Cat'.

STRIM(*Text*)

Trailing blanks are blanks at the end of a string.

Trims Trailing Blanks—Removes any trailing blank spaces from the *Text* variable. Example: If a variable named Sentence contains the characters 'This is a test' (notice the *trailing blanks* in front of the closing quotation mark), then (STRIM(Sentence)) produces 'This is a test' with the trailing blanks removed.

ULC(*Text*)

Converts Uppercase to Lowercase—Converts all uppercase letters in *Text* to lowercase. Example: (ULC('Hi There')) returns 'hi there'.

DATE AND TIME FUNCTIONS

The Date and Time functions operate on data stored as the DATE or TIME data type. These functions can convert TEXT data to

DATE and TIME data and can isolate portions of dates and times. Date and Time functions can be particularly useful in WHERE clauses. For example, the TDWK function isolates the day of the week as text. Therefore, the command

SELECT ALL FROM Charges WHERE (TDWK(P_Date)) = +
+ > 'Friday'

displays the seven rows from the Charges table in which the date falls on a Friday.

Note that when operating on dates that are not already stored in columns or variables defined as DATE data, the *Date* argument in the function must be enclosed in single quotation marks as shown in the examples below:

IDAY(*Date*)

Day of the Month—Returns the day of the month (1-31) of *Date* as an integer. Example: (IDAY('12/31/90')) produces 31.

IDWK(*Date*)

Integer Day of the Week—Returns the day of the week (1-7) of *Date* as an integer, where Monday is 1. Example: (IDWK('12/29/1990')) produces 6 (Saturday).

IHR(*Time*)

Integer Hour—Isolates the hour from *Time* data as an integer. Example: (IHR(11:59:00)) produces 11.

IMIN(*Time*)

Integer Minute—Isolates the minute from *Time* data as an integer. Example: (IHR(11:59:00)) produces 59.

IMON(*Date*)

Integer Month—Returns the month (1-12) of *Date* as an integer, where January is 1. Example: (IMON('12/31/1990')) produces 12.

ISEC(*Time*)

Integer Second—Isolates the second from *Time* data as an integer. Example: (IHR(11:59:22)) produces 22.

IYR(*Date*)

Integer Year—Returns the year of *Date* as an integer. Example: (IYR('12/31/90')) returns 90.

JDATE(*Date*)

Julian Date—Converts *Date* to a Julian date in the range of 1 (for 01/01/1900) to 99365 (for 12/31/1999). Example: (JDATE('1/1/1900')) produces 1.

RDATE(*Mon,Day,Year*)

Converts to Date Data Type—Where *Mon* is an integer from 1 to 12, *Day* is an integer from 1 to 31, and *Year* is an integer representing a year, creates a variable of the DATE data type. Example: (RDATE(12,31,1990)) creates a DATE data type containing the date 12/31/90.

RTIME(*Hrs,Min,Sec*)

Converts to Time Data Type—Where *Hrs* is an integer from 1 to 24, *Min* is an integer from 1 to 60, and *Sec* is an integer representing seconds, creates a variable of the TIME data type. Example: (RTIME(12,59,30)) creates a TIME data type containing the time 12:59:30.

TDWK(*Date*)

Text Day of the Week—Returns the day of the week of *Date* as text. Example: (TDWK('12/29/1990')) produces 'Saturday.'

TMON(*Date*)

Text Month—Returns the month of *Date* as text. Example: (TMON('12/31/1990')) produces 'December.'

FINANCIAL FUNCTIONS

The financial functions perform numerous calculations that can be used in a variety of business settings. The main trick to using the financial functions is making certain that you do not confuse yearly and month data. For example, to find the *monthly* payment for a $150,000 loan, given a term of 20 *years*, and a 9.37 percent *annual* interest rate, you must first convert the years to months (multiplying by 12) and the convert the annual interest rate to a monthly interest rate (by dividing by 12). You can do so within the function argument. The formula below calculates the *monthly* payment ($1,385.49) on the loan described above:

SET VARIABLE MonPay TO (PMT1(.0937/12,20∗12,150000))

Note that the interest rate (the first argument) is divided by 12 and the term (second argument) is multiplied by 12.

When calculating values in which interest is compounded daily, you can divide the annual interest rate by 365 and multiply the term by 365. The examples below will demonstrate these conversions:

FV1(*Pmt,Int,Per*)

> **Future Value of Payments**—Computes the future value of a series of regular equal payments of the amount specified in *Pmt* and the per-period interest rate specified by *Int* for the number of periods given in *Per*. Example: If you deposit $250 monthly into an account that pays 8 percent annual interest, how much money will be in the account after ten years? The expression (FV1(250,.08/12,10∗12)) returns the answer $45,736.51.

FV2(*Dep,Int,Per*)

> **Future Value of Deposit**—Computes the future value of a single deposit in the amount specified in *Int* for the number of periods given in *Per*. Example: Suppose you deposit $10,000 in an account that pays 8 percent interest (compounded monthly) for ten years. How much money will be in the account after ten years? The answer is given by the expression (FV2(10000,.08/12,10∗12)), which computes the result $22,196.40.

PMT1(*Int,Per,Prin*)

> **Payment on Loan**—Calculates the payment required to pay off a loan with the principal specified in *Prin* at the per-period interest rate given in *Int* for the number of payment periods specified in *Per*. Example: You wish to borrow $5000 dollars for

three years at 2.9 percent interest to buy a car. What will the monthly payment on the loan be? The answer is given by the expression (PMT1(.029/12,3*12,5000)), which displays the monthly payment of $145.19.

PMT2(*Int,Per,Fv*)

Payments to Reach Future Value—Calculates the regular payment required to accumulate the future value given in *Fv* at the per-period interest rate given in *Int* for the number of periods given in *Per*. Example: You want to accumulate $10,000 in ten years in an account that pays 7 percent interest compounded monthly. How much must you pay each month to reach your goal? The answer is given by the expression (PMT2(.07/12,10*12,10000)), which returns $57.78.

PV1(*Pmt,Int,Per*)

Present Value of Cash Flow—Computes the present value of a series of equal payments of the amount specified in *Pmt* at the periodic interest rate specified in *Int* for the number of periods specified in *Per*. Example: You purchase an annuity into which you pay $200 a month, at an annual interest rate of 10 percent, for ten years. What is the present value of the annuity? The answer is given by the expression (PV1(200,.10/12,10*12)), which returns $15,134.23.

PV2(*Fv,Int,Per*)

Present Value—Computes the present value based on the future value given in *Fv* at the periodic interest rate specified in *Int* for the number of periods specified in *Per*. Example: You want to have $10,000 in a savings account at the end of ten years. The interest rate, compounded daily, is 8 percent. How much money must you invest now to ensure $10,000 in the future? The answer is given with the expression (PV2(10000,.08/365,10*365)), which returns $4,493.68.

RATE1(*Fv,Pv,Per*)

Required Interest Rate—Calculates the interest rate required for the sum of money given in *Pv* to reach the future value given in *Fv* in the term given in *Per*. Example: You have $5000 to invest for ten years. What interest rate will you need to double your money within that time? The answer given with the expression (RATE1(10000,5000,12*10)) is the monthly interest rate (about 0.0058) or when multiplied by 12, 0.0695, or a little under 7 percent annual interest rate.

RATE2(*Fv,Pmt,Per*)

Required Interest Rate—Calculates the interest rate required for a series of regular payments given in *Pmt* to reach the future value given in *Fv* in the number of payment periods given in *Per*. Example: You wish to deposit $250 per month into an account for five years. What interest rate is required to accrue $20,000 at the end of the five years? The expression (RATE2(20000,250,5*12)) returns the answer, 0.00936 monthly interest, or about 11 percent annual interest.

RATE3(*Pv,Pmt,Per*)

Required Interest Rate—Calculates the periodic interest rate required for an annuity with the value given in *Pv* to return a series of future cash flows given in *Pmt* for the number of periods given in *Per*. Example: You want to purchase a $100,000 annuity that will pay $1500 monthly for a period of ten years. What interest rate is required to reach your goal? The answer is given in the expression (RATE3(100000,1500,10*12)), which yields 0.01093 monthly interest, or about 12 percent annual interest.

TERM1(*Pv,Int,Fv*)

Required Term—Computes the term required for the present value specified in *Pv* to reach the future value given in *Fv* given the periodic interest rate in *Int*. Example: You want to invest $5000 in an account that pays 10 percent annual interest. How long will it take to double your money? The expression (TERM1(5000,.10/12,10000)) gives the answer 84 months (or 7 years).

TERM2(*Pmt,Int,Fv*)

> **Required Term**—Calculates the number of compounding periods for a number of equal payments given in *Pmt* at the periodic interest rate given in *Int* to reach the future value given in *Fv*. Example: You want to deposit $250 a month at 10 percent annual interest. How long will it take until you accumulate $10,000? The expression (TERM2 (250,.10/12,10000)) gives the answer, 35 months.

TERM3(*Pmt,Int,Pv*)

> **Computed Term**—Calculates the number of periods that an annuity will last, given the payment you wish to receive in each term (*Pmt*), the periodic interest rate for the annuity (*Int*), and the present value of the annuity (*Pv*). Example: You wish to purchase a $20,000 annuity that pays 8 percent annual interest. How long will the annuity last (before reaching 0) if you receive $250 monthly payments from the annuity? The expression (TERM3(250,.08/12,20000)) gives the answer, 115 months (or about $9^1/_2$ years).

LOGICAL FUNCTIONS

The logical functions make decisions based on two alternatives. We've seen an example of the IFEQ function in Chapter 10, with the expression

(IFEQ(Taxable,'N',Qty*U_Price,(Qty*U_Price)*1.06))

This expression calculated the total of a transaction, excluding tax if the column names Taxable contained an 'N'. Otherwise, the total is calculated as the quantity times the unit price times 1.06 (to add 6 percent sales tax).

In the logical functions, the data types of the first two arguments must be the same. As well, the data types of the last two arguments must be the same. For example, the following expression is not allowed:

(IFEQ(L_Name,12:30:33,'Yes','No'))

because L_Name is not a TIME column. Also, the following expression

(IFEQ(L_Name,'Miller',7.4,'No'))

is not allowed because 7.4 is a REAL number and 'No' has the TEXT data type.

Here are the logical functions:

IFEQ(*Arg1,Arg2,Yes,No*)

If Equal—Returns the value, or result of the expression, given in the argument *Yes*, if *Arg1* equals *Arg2*. If *Arg1* does not equal *Arg2*, then the value or result of the expression specified in the argument *No* is returned. Examples: (IFEQ(10,10,0,100)) returns 0, because 10 is equal to 10. The expression (IFEQ(10,9,0,100)) returns 100, because 10 is not equal to 9.

IFGT(*Arg1,Arg2,Yes,No*)

If Greater Than—Returns the value, or result of the expression, given in the argument *Yes*, if *Arg1* is greater than *Arg2*. If *Arg1* is not greater than *Arg2*, then the value or result of the expression specified in the argument *No* is returned. Examples: (IFGT(99,50,0,100)) returns 0, because 99 is greater than 50. The expression (IFGT(2,99,0,100)) returns 100, because 2 is not greater than 99.

IFLT(*Arg1,Arg2,Yes,No*)

If Less Than—Returns the value, or result of the expression, given in the argument *Yes*, if *Arg1* is less than *Arg2*. If *Arg1* is not less than *Arg2*, then the value or result of the expression specified in the argument *No* is returned. Examples: (IFLT(– 1,0,0,100)) returns 0, because – 1 is less than 0. The expression (IFLT(10,9,0,100)) returns 100, because 10 is not less than 9.

EXPERIMENTS WITH FUNCTIONS

The easiest way to experiment with functions is to try a few in conjunction with the SELECT command. For example, if the Mail database is open and the R> prompt is on the screen, you can enter the command

```
SELECT Company = 14 LUC(Company) = 14 +
+ > ULC(Company) = 14 ICAP1(Company) = 14 +
+ > ICAP2(Company) = 14 FROM Names
```

to view the Company column from the Names table in its current state, and after treatment with the LUC, ULC, ICAP1, and ICAP2 functions. (For a good fit on the screen, the width is set to 14 characters in each column.) The Company column from each record will be displayed, although the listing below shows only a single row:

ABC Co.   ABC CO.   abc co.   Abc co.   Abc Co.

The commands below set the date format to MM/DD/YY, and then display the P_Date column, the day of the week (TDWK), the month (TMON), and the Julian date (JDATE) of the date from the Charges table:

```
SET DATE 'MM/DD/YY'
SELECT P_Date TDWK(P_Date) TMON(P_Date) JDATE(P_Date) +
+ > FROM Charges
```

A portion of the display is shown below:

P_Date	TDWK (P_Date)	TMON (P_Date)	JDATE (P_D)
09/25/90	Tuesday	September	90268
06/15/90	Friday	June	90166

FUNCTIONS IN COMPUTED COLUMNS

You can use functions in computed columns. For example, Figure 11.2 shows the listing for a table named Loans that consists of the columns named Princ, APR, Years, MoPmt, and TotBack.

MoPmt is a computed field with the expression:

```
(PMT1(((APR/100)/12),(Years*12),Princ))
```

```
R>LIST Loans

    Table: Loans
    Read Password: No
    Modify Password: No

    Loans table

    Column definitions
    # Name                Type          Index Expression
    1 Princ               CURRENCY
                Principal Amount
    2 APR                 REAL
                Annual Interest Rate
    3 Years               INTEGER
                Term of the Loan
    4 MoPmt               CURRENCY      (PMT1(((APR/100)/12)
                                        ,(Years*12),Princ))
                Monthly Payment
    5 TotBack             CURRENCY      ((12*Years)*MoPmt)
                Total Loan Payback

    Current number of rows:       0

R>
```

Figure 11.2: The table listing for the Loans Table

The first argument inside the PMT1 function, ((APR/100)/12), divides the annual interest rate by 100 (so that when the APR is entered as 9.375, it is correctly converted to the decimal 0.09375), and then divides the annual interest rate by 12 for the monthly interest rate. The second argument, (Years*12), multiplies the years in the loan by 12 to calculate the months. The third argument is the principal of the loan. Hence, for each row entered into the table, R:BASE automatically calculates the monthly payment.

The TotBack column is also a computed column, and it calculates the entire payback on the loan using the expression

(12 * Years) * MoPmt

This expression calculates the term of the loan in months (the number of years times 12) times the monthly payment, which is already calculated in the MoPmt column.

Each time you enter or edit data on the Loans table, R:BASE will automatically calculate the payment on the loan and the total payback on the loan.

FUNCTIONS IN FORMS

If you want to create a form that allows you to enter data into the Loans table and also display the monthly payment and total payback immediately, you can use the Form Generator to create the form.

Each time you enter or edit data on the Loans table, R:BASE will automatically calculate the payment on the loan and the total payback on the loan. However, computed fields are not evaluated until you are adding, or saving the changes to, a row in the table. In order to display these values on the form as you are entering data and making changes, you have to display the contents of variables with the same calculations as the columns in the Loans table. You can define the variable VMoPmt with the expression as the computed column MoPmt, and the variable VTotBack with the expression

$$((12*Years)*VMoPmt)$$

and place these variables on the form.

Let's create the form shown in Figure 11.3 for entering data into the Loans table.

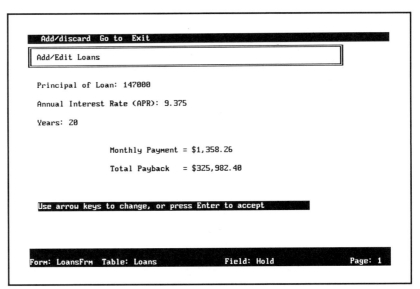

Figure 11.3: A form for entering data into the Loans table

CH. 11

See Chapter 8 if you need to refresh your memory about how to perform some of these steps.

1. On the Form Generator menu, **C**reate a **C**ustom form with the name **LoansFrm** and the description **Add/Edit Loans**. Make sure you use the **L**oans table for the form.

2. Under the **V**ariables menu choice, **D**efine the variables listed below:

   VMoPymt = (PMT1(((APR/100)/12),(Years*12),Princ))
   VTotBack = ((12*Years)*VMoPmt)
   Hold = 'Use arrow keys to change, or press Enter to accept'

3. Place the text on the screen and draw the box at the top of the form as shown in Figure 11.3. Note that the message "Use arrow keys to change, or press Enter to accept" is displayed using the Hold variable. This message is not text.

4. To add the data columns and variables to the form, place Princ beside "Principal of Loan:"; place APR beside "Annual Interest Rate (APR):"; place Years beside "Years:"; place MoPymt beside "Monthly Payment ="; place TotBack beside "Total Payback"; and place Hold where the message "Use arrow keys to change, or press Enter to accept" appears.

5. Customize the field settings for the Hold variable so that the answers to the first two questions

   Will new data be entered in the field?
   Can the user change the data displayed in the field?

   are changed to Yes. Make sure that the length of the Hold variable on the screen is long enough to hold the message it contains.

6. To test the form, use the **M**anage form option to **R**un the form, **A**dding data.

Figure 11.3 shows the LoansFrm form in use. The principal, interest, and term have already been typed onto the screen, and the monthly payment and total payback were calculated automatically. The highlight is currently on the Hold variable, waiting for the next keystroke. When you are finished testing the form, leave the Form Generator.

FUNCTIONS IN REPORTS

Functions can be used in reports in the same fashion that they are used in forms. For example, suppose the Loans table consisted of only the Princ, APR, and Years columns, without computed columns for the monthly payment and total payback.

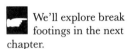
We'll explore break footings in the next chapter.

You could easily create a report using the Report Generator to calculate and display the payment and payback. Once on the Report Layout screen, you could define the VMoPmt and VTotBack variables as you did for the LoansFrm form. When locating column and variable names on the report format, include the VMoPmt and VTotBack variables in the detail lines of the report. You can even use functions in break footings to group data.

USING FUNCTIONS WITH THE UPDATE COMMAND

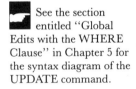
See the section entitled "Global Edits with the WHERE Clause" in Chapter 5 for the syntax diagram of the UPDATE command.

You can use functions with the UPDATE command to modify existing data in a database. For example, suppose you had initially entered all the names in the Names table with the Caps Lock key on. All of the last names would be in uppercase, but you could convert those names to initial capital letters using the ICAP1 function in the UPDATE command, as follows:

> UPDATE Names SET L_Name = (ICAP1(L_Name)) WHERE +
> + > L_Name IS NOT NULL

Let's see how to use the UPDATE command to modify data. The UPDATE command makes permanent changes to a table immediately and should be used with care. In our example, we will use the PROJECT command to make a copy of the table first, and then experiment with the copied table. With the Mail database open and the R > prompt displayed,

1. Type **PROJECT Temp FROM Names USING ALL** and press ↵ to make a copy of the Names table.

2. Type **UPDATE Temp SET L_Name = (LUC(L_Name)) WHERE L_Name IS NOT NULL** and press ↵ to change all last names to uppercase.

3. Type **SELECT L_Name FROM Temp** and press ← to see that the last names are all uppercase.

4. Type **UPDATE Temp SET L_Name = (ICAP1(L_Name)) WHERE L_Name IS NOT NULL** and press ← to change the last names back to initial capitals.

5. Type **SELECT L_Name FROM Temp** and press ← to see that the last names have only initial capitals.

6. Type **DROP TABLE Temp** and press ← to remove the Temp table.

As an alternative to changing the data in the column, you can always use the appropriate function in a report expression and place the variable on the report format instead of the original column. If you defined

    RptLName = (LUC(L_Name))

as a report variable, you could place it at those points where you wanted last names to be printed completely in uppercase. All last names would appear in uppercase on the report, but would remain unchanged in the Names table.

Now that you have a basic knowledge of R:BASE variables and functions, we can move to the next step in building complex applications: creating command files.

Chapter 12

Refining Your Reports

R:BASE 3.1 IS THE SIXTH VERSION OF THE R:BASE database-management system for microcomputers. Like its predecessors, R:BASE 4000, R:BASE 5000, R:BASE System V, R:BASE for DOS, and R:BASE 3.0, version 3.1 is a powerful, flexible tool for storing, organizing, analyzing, and retrieving information on a microcomputer. The new R:BASE, though, offers significant improvements over its predecessors.

DEVELOPING A COMPLEX REPORT

We'll start by developing a report named "Sales." This report will show charge transactions, a subtotal for each individual, and a grand total. Take a look at Figure 12.1 to see how your report will look when it's done. This report groups together rows in the Charges table for each customer in the Mail database.

```
                          Charge Transactions
      Date: 10/15/90                                     Page:   1
      Customer
             Prod #      Qty      Unit
                                  Price        Total     Date
      Anne Miller: Golden Gate Co.
          A-123         10        $5.50        $58.30    09/25/90
          A-111         12       $10.00       $127.20    06/15/90
          B-222          5       $12.50        $66.25    06/15/90
          C-434          2      $100.00       $212.00    06/15/90
                                            ----------
      Subtotal:                               $463.75
      Bart Adams: DataSpec Inc.
          B-222         12       $12.50       $159.00    06/30/90
          A-111         10       $10.00       $106.00    06/30/90
                                            ----------
      Subtotal:                               $265.00
      Mindy Jones: ABC Co.
          A-111          5       $10.00        $53.00    06/15/90
          A-128         10       $12.80       $128.00    06/15/90
                                            ----------
      Subtotal:                               $181.00
      Robin Baker: Peach Computers
          A-111         10       $10.00       $106.00    06/15/90
          Z-128         10       $12.80       $128.00    06/15/90
                                            ----------
      Subtotal:                               $234.00
                                            ----------
      Grand Total:                          $1,143.75
```

Figure 12.1: The completed Sales report

Before we begin making the report, let's look at some of the terminology involved. The term *break*, or *breakpoint*, refers to the point where one grouping of rows stops and the next grouping begins. In this report we are grouping together the charges for each customer, so a breakpoint indicates where the data for one customer stops and the data for the next one starts. We will group the rows in the Charges column by the customer number column, so the customer number column will be the *break column*. (Even though the customer number does not appear in the report, it can be used as the break column because it is in the Charges table.) A *break header* can be placed at the beginning of a grouping of records. In this report, a break header appears just above the charges for each person and contains the customer name and company. A *break footer* can be placed at the end of a grouping of records. The total charges for each person appear in the break footer—a subtotal in the case of our report.

We will follow the same basic steps we followed in Chapter 7 to create this report, except this time we will have to consider the report breaks as we plan the variables we need.

STEP 1: DESIGN THE REPORT

Begin by designing your report. Consider carefully how you want the columns laid out. As we mentioned earlier, we will group together the changes for each person in the break column. Figure 12.2 shows the design of the Sales report. To review the sections that appear in this report:

Page header	Displayed once at the top of each page in the report
Break header	Displayed at the top of each subtotal break
Detail Lines	Displayed, once for each row, in a subtotal section
Break footer	Displayed at the bottom of each subtotal break
Report footer	Displayed once at the end of the entire report

Although we haven't included them in this report, a report can also contain a report header, which is only printed on the first page of the report, and a page footer, which is printed once at the bottom of each page.

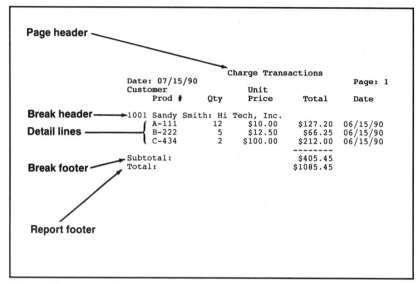

Figure 12.2: A rough draft of the Sales report

STEP 2:
PLAN THE REPORT VARIABLES AND BREAKS

Let's group together the charges for each person by using the CustNo column as the break column. We'll need variables that determine both the subtotal for each person's charges and the grand total, which will appear at the end of the report. We can define these variables as follows:

SubTotal   Sum of the Total column for each individual

Grandtot   Sum of the Total column in all rows

In this example, most of the data will be from the Charges table, but we'll need to get the name and company for each individual from the Names table. We can define the necessary variables as follows:

Name1   First name from the Names table

Name2   Last name from the Names table

CompName   Company from the Names table

NameCo   First name, last name, a colon, and the company name

STEP 3: START THE REPORT GENERATOR

Now it's time to start the Report Generator and create a custom report. Call it "Sales," and when R:BASE asks for the report description, enter the words "Charge Transactions." Refer to the following steps if you get stuck:

For a review of how to use the Report Generator, see "Creating Customized Reports" in Chapter 7.

1. To display the Report Generator menu, highlight **R**eports and select **C**reate/modify.

2. Under **C**reate, select **C**ustom report.

3. Beside the Report Name prompt, type **Sales** and press ←.

4. Below the Report Description prompt, type **Charge Transactions** and press ←.

5. Select **C**harges as the table supplying the data.

STEP 4: DEFINE THE VARIABLES

The GrandTot and SubTotal variables are defined using the SUM OF operator. Since the GrandTot variable is the sum of the Total column for all charges displayed on the report, the GrandTot variable can be defined as

> GrandTot = SUM OF Total

Don't worry if it seems odd that the GrandTot and SubTotal variables have the same expression. You will tell R:BASE to set the Sub-Total variable to zero after each customer when you define the break in step 5 below.

To get each customer's SubTotal variable, you want the sum of the Total column rows for each individual customer. To define this SubTotal variable, you usc a similar expression to that for GrandTot, namely

> SubTotal = SUM OF Total

When you define the break that determines how the information for each customer is grouped, you can instruct R:BASE to reset Sub-Total to zero after each customer.

See Chapter 10 for a thorough explanation of how to use lookup variables.

All the information you need for this report is contained in the Charges table, except for each person's name and company, which is only available in the Names table. To get this information from the Names table, you can use lookup variables. To review, you can define a lookup variable to obtain a value from the Names table with the following expression:

variable = column in Names table IN Names WHERE +
+ > <*column in Names table*> = <*column in Charges table*>

To define the variable Name1 and obtain the first name of the customer, use the following expression:

Name1 = F_Name IN Names WHERE CustNo = CustNo

Similarly, you can obtain the customer's last name and company with the following variables:

Name2 = L_Name IN Names WHERE CustNo = CustNo
CompName = Company IN Names WHERE CustNo = CustNo

Finally, you can store the name and company combined in a variable called NameCo with the definition

NameCo = Name1 & Name2 + ':' & CompName

As you may remember from Chapter 7, you can use the following steps to define these variables:

1. To define GrandTot, highlight **Variables**; select **Create**; type **GrandTot = SUM OF Total**; and press ◄┘.

2. To define SubTotal, highlight **Variables**; select **Create**; type **SubTotal = SUM OF Total**; and press ◄┘.

3. To define Name1, highlight **Variables**; select **Create**; type **Name1 = F_Name IN Names WHERE CustNo = CustNo**; and press ◄┘.

4. To define Name2, highlight **Variables**; select **Create**; type **Name2 = L_Name IN Names WHERE CustNo = CustNo**; and press ◄┘.

5. To define CompName, highlight **Variables**; select **Create**; type **CompName = Company IN Names WHERE CustNo = CustNo**; and press ◄┘.

6. To define NameCo, highlight **Variables**; select **Create**; type
NameCo = Name1 & Name2 + ':' & CompName; and
press ←.

STEP 5: DEFINE THE REPORT BREAKS

The general procedure for defining a break on a column or variable is to first display the Breakpoint table by highlighting Layout and selecting Create breakpoints. Next, for each break you want to create,

- under Break Column, enter the name of the break column or variable;

- under Variable Reset, enter Yes if you want to create subtotals and choose any variables that you would like to reset to zero before the break header is printed; and

- under FORM FEEDS Before Header, enter Yes if you want to start the Break Header on a new page.

When you are finished defining breaks, press F2.
For our Sales report, let's define a break that will group the data by customer.

1. Highlight **Layout** and select **Create** breakpoints.

2. Type **CustNo** under Break Column.

3. Press → and press **Y** to choose Yes under Variable Reset.

4. Select **SubTotal** and press **F2** to tell R:BASE to reset the SubTotal variable to zero after each customer. Your screen should now look like Figure 12.3.

5. Press **F2** to finish defining breaks.

STEP 6: ENTER THE REPORT TEXT

With the experience you gained laying out the reports in Chapter 7, you should have little difficulty entering most of the text for the

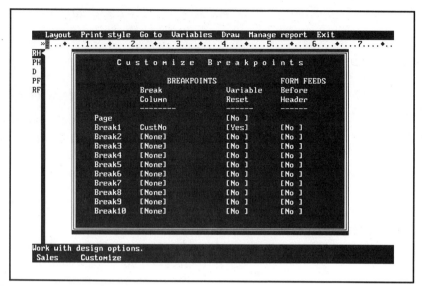

Figure 12.3: Defining the break on the CustNo column

report whose design is shown in Figure 12.2. However, there is no section on the screen corresponding to the break header or break footer. As you will see in the steps below, you can create a break header. You do this with the Goto menu function, which can take you to the break header just before you place information into it. Follow these steps to enter the report text into the Sales report:

1. To remove the report header, move the cursor to the first row and press **F9**. The cursor should be in the page header section, identified by PH at the left side of the screen.

2. To create six additional page header lines, press **F10** six times.

3. To enter the page header, move to position < 1:10, 30>; type **Charge Transactions**; move to < 3:10, 5>; type **Date:**; move to < 3:10, 61>; type **Page:**; move to < 5:10, 5>; type **Customer**; move to < 5:10, 33>; type **Unit**; move to < 6:10, 10>; type **Prod #**; move to < 6:10, 23>; type **Qty**; move to < 6:10, 33>; type **Price**; move to < 6:10, 48>; type **Total**; move to < 6:10, 61>; and type **Date**.

After you create a break footer, you have to add lines or enter information into it right away. If you forget to do so and you move the cursor out of a break footer, the break footer will disappear.

Now let's create a break footer for the subtotal of charges for each person.

4. Highlight **G**oto; select **B**reak footer; and select Level 1. The cursor moves to the break footer line, labelled F1 at the left side of the screen.

5. To add three additional break footer lines, press **F10** three times.

6. To enter the break footer text, move to < 9:14, 44>; type ten hyphens (-); move to <11:14, 5>; and type **Subtotal:**.

7. To remove the page footer, move to <13:14, 1> and press **F9**. The cursor is now in the report footer section, identified by RF at the left side of the screen.

8. To add two additional report footer lines, press **F10** twice.

9. To enter the report footer text, move to <13:15, 44>; type ten hyphens (-); move to <15:15, 5>; and type **Grand Total:**.

STEP 7: PLACE COLUMNS AND VARIABLES ON THE REPORT

Placing the data columns and variables on the report should be a straightforward procedure. Be careful, though, to create the break header section before you place the NameCo variable in it. Refer to the following steps if necessary:

1. To place the date and page number in the page header, move to < 3:15, 11>; press **F6**; type **#DATE** and press ←; press **S**; press **E**; reply **N**o when asked if you want a picture format; move to < 3:15, 67>; press **F6**; type **#PAGE** and press ←; press **S**; move back to < 3:15, 69>; press **E**; and reply **N**o when asked if you want a picture format.

Just as with a break footer, you have to add lines or enter information into a break header right after you create it. If you move the cursor out of a break header that consists of only one empty line, it will disappear.

2. To create the break header section, highlight **G**oto; select **B**reak header; and select Level 1. The cursor should now be in the break header, identified by the H1 at the left side of the screen.

3. Add an additional line to the break header by pressing **F10**.

4. Place the NameCo variable in the break header, as follows: move to < 8:17, 5>; press **F6**; type **NameCo** and press ⏎; press **S**; move to < 8:17, 65> (allowing 61 characters for the first name, last name and company); press **E**; and reply **No** when asked if you want a picture format.

5. Move to the Detail section (<10:17, 1>) and add an additional detail line by pressing **F10**.

6. Place the columns and variables on the first detail line, line 10. Reply **No** when asked if you want to add a picture format.

COLUMN *OR* VARIABLE	START COLUMN	END COLUMN
ProdNo	10	17
Qty	22	25
U_Price	30	38
Total	44	53
P_Date	59	66

7. Place the SubTotal variable in the break footer on line 14, starting at location 44 and ending at location 53. As before, reply **No** to adding a picture format.

8. Place the GrandTot variable in the report footer on line 18, starting at location 44 and ending at location 53. As before, reply **No** to adding a picture format. Your report format should now be complete, as shown in Figure 12.4.

STEP 8: SAVE AND TEST THE REPORT

To save the report and test it on the screen, highlight **M**anage report and select **P**review to screen. The preview will cover more than one screen—the beginning part will roll off the top. Still, your report will resemble Figure 12.1. Notice that the report is automatically sorted on the breakpoint column, CustNo. This is a handy feature of breakpoints. Press a key to return to the Report Generator screen.

If you set your date format wider than 8 characters, R:Base will print asterisks (*) under the Date column. Later in this chapter, in the section called "Controlling the Appearance of Data with Picture Formats," you'll find out how to add a picture format to the Date column and ensure that the dates are displayed in the MM/DD/YY format.

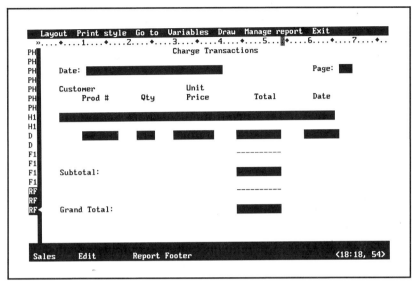

Figure 12.4: The format for the Sales report

STEP 9: LEAVE THE REPORT GENERATOR

To leave the Report Generator and return to the R:BASE Main menu, highlight and select Exit twice. Of course, if you have made any changes since the last time you saved the report, R:BASE will give you an opportunity to save your changes before you leave the Report Generator screen.

STEP 10: PRINT THE REPORT

See Chapter 7 for detailed information on printing a report—from the Main menu and from the R> prompt.

To print the report from the R:BASE Main menu, highlight **R**eports, select **S**ales, and then select any sorting, searching, or print destination options you would like.

Of course, you can also use the PRINT command to produce report output. Use the ORDER BY and WHERE clauses to sort and filter the report, and the OUTPUT command to direct the report to the printer or a file.

ADDING NESTED SUBTOTALS

In the sample Sales report, we used only a single breakpoint column: Customer Number. R:BASE will let you define up to ten breakpoints for a single report. For example, you could create a report format that presents subtotals for each customer, and within each customer, subtotals by product code. Our sample Charges table is too small to demonstrate this, but the hypothetical report in Figure 12.5 shows how such a format might appear. Notice that a subtotal appears for each customer. Furthermore, a subtotal for each product purchased appears within each customer listing.

```
Date: 10/15/90                                           Page:    1

Customer                      Unit
        Prod #       Qty      Price        Total       Date
1001 Anne Miller: Golden Gate Co.

        A-111         12      $10.00       $127.20     06/15/90
        A-111          8      $10.00        $84.80     07/15/90
                                          ----------
Subtotal for product A-111                 $212.00

        A-123         10       $5.50        $58.30     09/25/90
                                          ----------
Subtotal for product A-123                  $58.30


                                          ----------
Total for customer 1001                    $270.30
                                          ==========


1006 Robin Baker: Peach Computers

        A-111          6      $10.00        $63.60     06/15/90
        A-111         10      $10.00       $106.00     07/01/90
                                          ----------
Subtotal for product A-111                 $169.60

        Z-128         10      $12.80       $128.00     06/15/90
        Z-128         10      $12.80       $128.00     08/15/90
                                          ----------
Subtotal for product Z-128                 $256.00


                                          ----------
Total for customer 1006                    $425.60
                                          ==========


                                          ----------
Grand total of all customers:              $695.90
```

Figure 12.5: A report with two subtotal breakpoints

To create such a report, you would need to define two subtotaling variables using the Define option under Variables on the Report Generator screen. You'd probably still want a GrandTot variable for the grand total, as below:

SubTot1   SUM OF Total

SubTot2   SUM OF Total

GrandTot   SUM OF Total

Using the Create breakpoints option under Layout on the menu, you would want CustNo to be the Break1 column and ProdNo to be the Break2 column. Each of these columns must reset the appropriate subtotaling variable. In this example, Break1 is based on the CustNo column and resets the SubTot1 variable. Break2 is based on the ProdNo column and resets the SubTot2 variable. Figure 12.6 shows the Create breakpoints menu with two breakpoints defined.

When you lay out the report format, the Report Generator screen gives you the opportunity to define two break headers (H1 and H2) and two break footers (F1 and F2). These multiple break headers and

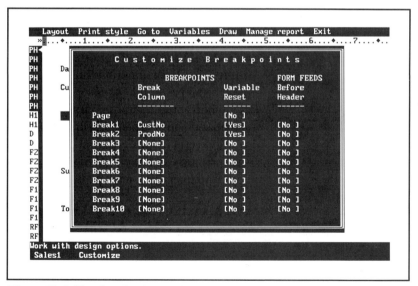

Figure 12.6: Two breakpoints defined for a report

footers should surround the detail lines and be nested within one another, as shown below:

RH	Report Header
PH	Page Header
H1	Break Header 1 (Customer Number)
H2	Break Header 2 (Produce Code)
D	Detail Lines
F2	Break Footer 2 (with SubTot2 variable to show subtotal by product)
F1	Break Footer 1 (with SubTot1 variable to show subtotal by customer)
PF	Page Footer
RF	Report Footer (including the GrandTot variable, if any)

Figure 12.7 shows the report format that was used to print the sample report in Figure 12.5. This report did not need all of the sections mentioned in the list above. However, the sections that are in the report are placed in the same order as they appear on the list: page header, break header 1, detail lines, break footer 2, break footer 1, and report footer. The variable in report footer 2 is SubTot2, and the variable in report footer 1 is SubTot1.

The same basic structure can be used with any number of headers. For example, suppose you wanted a report with five subtotal levels. You would need to define five subtotaling variables and each one would need to be reset at each breakpoint.

When laying out the report format, you'd still want to nest the various break headers and footers within one another, as follows:

RH	Report Header
PH	Page Header
H1	Break Header 1
H2	Break Header 2
H3	Break Header 3

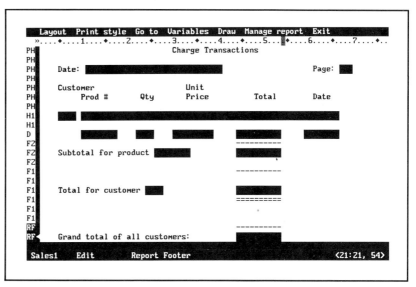

Figure 12.7: The report layout for a report with two breakpoints

H4	Break Header 4
H5	Break Header 5
D	Detail Lines
F5	Break Footer 5 (and subtotaling variable)
F4	Break Footer 4 (and subtotaling variable)
F3	Break Footer 3 (and subtotaling variable)
F2	Break Footer 2 (and subtotaling variable)
F1	Break Footer 1 (and subtotaling variable)
PF	Page Footer
RF	Report Footer (and grand total variable if any)

Any section in the report, be it a header, a detail line, or a break header or footer, can consist of any number of lines and any number of variables or table columns. If you wish to display a cumulative total along with (or in place of) a subtotal, don't reset the variable. In other words, leave the Variable Reset column of the Define breakpoints menu at the default [No] setting for the appropriate breakpoint and variable.

A breakpoint doesn't have to have a subtotal variable associated with it. For example, you might want to put breakpoints for State and City in a report format for the Names table. Doing so will display the names grouped by state and grouped by city within each state. The grouping, in this case, is only for organization and therefore you need not define subtotal variables.

ENHANCING REPORTS WITH BOXES AND LINES

As with the Form Generator, you can draw boxes and lines on reports with the Draw option on the top menu. The lines and boxes will appear on your screen, but whether they appear on your printed report depends on your particular printer. Your best bet is to draw a simple box on a report format with the Draw menu option and preview the report to the printer with the Manage report option on the menu.

If the box does not appear properly on the printed report, you can erase it with the Erase option in the Draw pull-down menu. Even if the custom boxes don't work with your report, you can still use hyphens and the underscore character on your keyboard to draw underlines. These will show up on any printer's output.

USING PRINT STYLES FOR PROFESSIONAL-LOOKING REPORTS

See Appendix A for information on how to set up R:BASE to work with your printer.

Most printers come with special printer features, such as compressed or expanded print. Some printers even allow you to change type sizes and fonts. If your printer has these features, you can use them in reports, provided R:BASE has been configured for your printer.

To see which printer R:BASE is set up for on your computer, type **SHOW PRINTER** at the R > prompt and press ←. For example, if R:BASE is set up for use on an Epson printer, it will respond

The current printer is: EPSON1

Once R:BASE knows what type of printer you are using, you can use the special features of your printer in reports. The general procedure for doing so is to go to the Report Generator screen and

Boldface type is heavier than ordinary, roman type. For example, the headings in this book are printed in boldface, and so is this word: **hello!**

- Place an indicator in the report where you want the printer to begin using a special feature. For example, to print a word in boldface type, you would place the bold print style indicator, *#Bold*, over the top of the first letter of the word.

- With the beginning indicator in place, place the *_off* indicator where you want the printer to stop using the special feature. Getting back to the bold example, you would place the ending bold print style indicator, *#Bold_off*, after the last letter in the word you want boldfaced.

An indicator will appear on the report format as a highlighted diamond.

Let's see what print styles are available on your computer. First bring up the Sales report you created earlier in this chapter. Highlight **R**eports, select **C**reate/modify, highlight **M**odify, and select Sales. Now highlight **P**rint styles. The pull-down menu that appears shows a list of the print styles available to your particular computer. Although print styles vary from printer to printer, here are some common ones:

#Underline	<u>This is underlined text.</u>
#Bold	**This is bold text.**
#Italics	*This is italicized text.*

Of course, to turn off these print styles you would enter #Underline_off, #Bold_off, and #Italics_off, respectively. Most dot-matrix printers have a #Letter_quality print style. Instead of entering #Letter_quality_off to turn off this print style, you usually enter the #Draft_print style command, which turns on draft quality printing.

If no pull-down menu appears when you highlight Print style, that means you have no print styles available. If this is the case, perhaps your copy of R:BASE was not configured properly for your printer. Or, your particular model of printer may not be one for which

R:BASE has print styles. See Appendix A for more information on how to tell R:BASE what kind of printer you have.

If you do have #Underline in your list of print styles, you can underline the words "Charge Transactions" on the first line of the page header of the Sales report in boldface. Here's how:

1. With **P**rint style highlighted, select #Underline.

2. Move to the first character of the word "Charge" in the first line, at position < 1:18, 30>.

3. Press **S** to indicate where the underlining should start.

4. Move one position to the right of the last character in the word "Transactions," at position < 1:18, 49>.

5. Highlight **P**rint style and select #Underline_off.

6. Press **S** to indicate where the underlining should stop.

7. Highlight **M**anage report and select the **P**review to printer option to test this report on your printer.

Although the dia-mond indicating the position of the #Under-line print style covers the *C* in "Charge," the *C* will appear underlined when the report is printed.

In our example, you placed the #Underline diamond on top of the *C* in "Charge." You might be tempted to place the #Underline dia-mond just to the left of the *C*, but then you would underline the space to the left of the *C*. With some print styles, such as #Bold, you could avoid hiding the *C* by placing the #Bold diamond to the left of the *C*. Why? Because when you boldface an empty space, it is still a space.

You can remove a print style in the same way that you remove a data column or variable from the report format. Just move the cursor onto the diamond and press Shift-F9.

CONTROLLING THE APPEARANCE OF DATA WITH PICTURE FORMATS

Each time you placed a data column or variable on the report for-mat from the Report Generator screen, R:BASE asked whether you wanted to add a picture format. A *picture format* allows you to specify how field data should appear in a printed report. You can use picture formats to tell R:BASE to

- right-justify, left-justify, or center the data in a field;
- print negative numbers with a minus sign (–) on the right, parentheses around the number, or the letters *DB* (debit) on the right;
- print positive numbers with the letters *CR* (credit) on the right;
- print data using uppercase or lowercase letters;
- print numbers with leading zeroes or asterisks (*); or
- print date or time data in a specific format.

You use special picture format symbols to specify how you want data to appear in a field. The symbols in Table 12.1, which are placed at the beginning of a picture format and enclosed by brackets ([ ]), are used for justifying text and for number formatting. To use more than one of these symbols, you place all the ones you want to use inside one set of brackets and separate them by commas. The symbols in Table 12.2 are for printing letters in upper- or lowercase and for handling leading zeros and other leading characters. You place one of these symbols in each character position that you want formatted a specific way. Notice that some symbols only work with text fields and others only work with numeric fields. To specify date and time formats, you use the standard formats you learned about in Chapter 6.

Left-justified data or text is printed in a field or on a page beginning on the left side or margin. *Right-justified* data or text is printed in a field or on a page so that it runs squarely against the right side or margin. The text in this book, for example, is both left- and right-justified. Text in margin notes like this one, however, is left-justified only.

You specify a picture format for a date or time field to be sure that the date or time output is the same regardless of how you set the date with the DATE OUTPUT FORMAT or the time with the TIME OUTPUT FORMAT on the Settings menu.

Table 12.1: Picture Format Symbols Placed at the Beginning of the Picture Format

SYMBOL	RESULT
[<]	Left-justifies data in the field
[>]	Right-justifies data in the field
[^]	Centers data in the field
[CR]	Prints the letters *CR* (credit) after all positive numbers

Table 12.1: Picture Format Symbols Placed at the Beginning of the Picture Format (continued)

SYMBOL	RESULT
[DB]	Prints the letters *DB* (debit) after all negative numbers
[( )]	Encloses all negative numbers in parentheses
[-]	Prints a minus sign after all negative numbers

Table 12.2: Picture Format Symbols Placed at Each Character Position

SYMBOL	RESULT
–	Prints all letters in uppercase, and leaves blanks in place of all characters that are not letters, such as digits and punctuation marks (for TEXT fields only)
|	Prints letters in lowercase, and leaves blanks in place of all characters that are not letters, such as digits and punctuation marks (for TEXT fields only)
%	Prints all letters in uppercase, but leaves other characters—such as digits and punctuation marks—unchanged (for TEXT fields only)
?	Prints all letters in lowercase, but leaves other characters—such as digits and punctuation marks—unchanged (for TEXT fields only)
9	Prints a digit in this position, or a leading blank if the number is not big enough to fill the position (for NUMERIC fields only)
0	Prints a digit in this position, or a leading zero if the number is not big enough to fill the position (for NUMERIC fields only)
*	Prints the digit in this position, or a leading asterisk if the number is not big enough to fill the position (for NUMERIC fields only)

You can also place text in the picture format—it will be printed just as it appears there, combined with the field being printed. When you are printing a text field, the characters of the data field will appear wherever there is a blank space in the format. For a numeric field, the digits and punctuation will appear in the places specified by the special symbols.

The picture format feature may seem complicated, but once you get used to the symbols it's a breeze. Some examples of picture formats are shown below. Study them closely to familiarize yourself with how the symbols are used.

PICTURE FORMAT	*MEANING*
[<]	Left-justify the data in this field.
[DB,CR]	Print the letters *CR* (credit) after a positive number or the letters *DB* (debit) after a negative number.
[^]00000	Print a number with leading zeros so that five digits are shown, and center the number in the field.
***,**0.00	Print a number with leading asterisks and a comma if the number is greater than 999.99 (this format is common for check writing).
[^]Title:	Print the word "Title:" followed by the data, and center it in the field.
[>]WWW+, MMM+ DD, YYYY	Print a date as Friday, October 12, 1990, and right-justify it in the field.
999,999.00000	Print a number with five decimal places (the decimal point of the data will line up with the decimal point in the picture format).

You can also use picture formats to specify what to print in a field that is empty or null. For example, if you were printing a mailing list, you could have R:BASE print "Please provide address" in the address field if it was empty.

As you can see, picture formats are a very powerful way to control the appearance of the data in your reports. Let's try out some simple examples on the Sales report to see the advantages of picture formats. It's easy to add a picture format to a field that is already on a report. The general procedure is to

1. Move the cursor onto the field whose picture format you want to change. The Picture Format menu appears.

2. Highlight **Layout** and select **Format** field. R:BASE will display a box for entering a picture and a null format.

   - Under the "Enter a picture format" prompt, type the picture format symbols, numbers or letters you want, and press ⏎.

   - Under the "Enter the NULL format" prompt, type the information you want printed if the field is null, and press ⏎.

Let's add picture formats to the Sales report that display the day of the week in the page header, show the first letter of the product number as a lowercase letter, and set the date format of the Date column to MM/DD/YY. We'll add this picture format to the Date column to ensure that the date is always eight characters long, regardless of the setting of the DATE OUTPUT format on the Settings menu. With the Report Generator screen displayed for the Sales report, follow these steps:

1. Place the cursor on the #DATE field in the page header at location < 3:18, 11 >.

2. Highlight **Layout** and select **Format** field.

3. Type **WWW+ MMM DD, YYYY** and press ⏎ to enter the picture format. Your screen should look like Figure 12.8.

4. Press ⏎ to leave the NULL format empty.

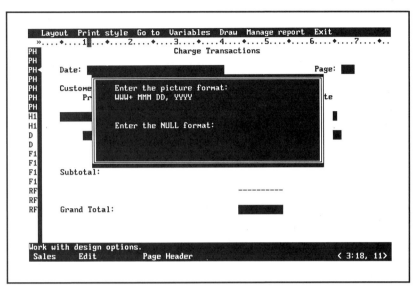

Figure 12.8: Adding a picture format

5. Place the cursor on the ProdNo field in the Detail section, at location <10:18, 10>.

6. Highlight **L**ayout and select **F**ormat field.

7. Type **?** and press ⏎ for the picture format.

8. Press ⏎ to leave the NULL format empty.

9. Place the cursor on the Date field in the Detail section, at location <10:18, 59>.

10. Highlight **L**ayout and select **F**ormat field.

11. Type **MM/DD/YY** and press ⏎ to enter the picture format.

12. Press ⏎ to leave the NULL format empty.

13. Highlight **M**anage report and select **P**review to printer to test the report.

When you are finished experimenting with picture formats on this report, leave the Report Generator and return to the R:BASE Main menu by highlighting and selecting **E**xit twice.

CREATING A REPORT BASED ON A VIEW

Earlier in this chapter you created a Sales report that contained information from two tables: Charges and Names. Why did we have the report on the Charges table rather than the Names table? This sort of question is often hard to answer and merits some discussion.

Since the Sales report is designed to print details about charges, the Charges table provides the most logical *base*, or *driver* table. You can see this clearly if you visualize the data in the Names table: there's only one row for each customer. Now visualize data in the Charges table: most customers have more than one row, since they have made multiple purchases. We want a report that summarizes information about charges by customer, so we used the Charges table. The information located in the Detail section of the report can then correspond to individual rows in the driver table.

The drawback to using the Charges table as a driver table is that we have to define three lookup variables (Name1, Name2, and Comp-Name) to get data from the Names table. An alternative approach would be to define a view that contains all the necessary data in one "table."

Recall from Chapter 10 that a view can contain columns from up to five different tables. The Sales report needs only the following columns:

FROM NAMES	*FROM CHARGES*
CustNo	CustNo
L_Name	ProdNo
F_Name	Qty
Company	U_Price
	Total
	P_Date

Sometimes you'll make lists like these only to discover that your lists don't contain common columns. If, for example, we didn't want to print customer numbers, we wouldn't have included CustNo on our lists. However, when you establish a view, you must include the common, or link, column in your view, even if you don't plan to use that data.

Let's define a view for an alternative Sales report by using the Views option on the R:BASE Main menu, as follows:

1. Highlight **Views** and select **Create/modify**. The screen displayed is similar to the Query screen you see when you are working from the Edit screen.

2. With **Query** highlighted, select **Add** tables.

3. Select **Charges**.

4. Press **Shift-F6** to select all columns.

5. Highlight **Query**, select **Add** tables, and select **Names**.

6. Select the CustNo, L_Name, F_Name, and Company fields by moving to each of these columns and pressing **F6** when the highlighter is in each column.

7. Highlight **Query** and select the **Save** query as a view option.

8. Type **Saleview** and press ⏎ when asked for the name of the view.

9. Highlight and select **Exit** to return to the R:BASE Main menu.

Now see if you can define a report called "Salesrpt" based on the Saleview view. Define the SubTotal and GrandTot variables, as you did for the original Sales report. But do not define variables for Name1 or Name2, since that data is directly available through the view. Define NameCo as

NameCo = F_Name & L_Name + ':' & Company

Then, use the Create breakpoints option under Layout to set up CustNo as the break column for Break1, as you did before. Change the Variable Reset to Yes, and select SubTotal as the variable to reset, as before. Continue by typing in the text and placing the columns and variables. Then save and test the new report.

Using a view as the driver table for a report can be a real timesaver when the alternative is defining a lot of lookup variables.

MORE TIPS AND TECHNIQUES FOR REPORTS

Although you can use the mouse when you are placing and sizing fields on the report format, it is not very convenient for several reasons. When you mark the end of a NOTE or TEXT field with the mouse, you can only make the field one line high. Also, the cursor position indicator in the lower-right corner of the screen does not tell you where the mouse is, which means you have to guess at the size of field you are making. For these reasons, it is usually more convenient to use the keyboard to place fields on the report format.

DEFAULT WIDTHS

As you place your fields, you may not understand what the process is behind the default size of the highlighted block (the block which is displayed when you press S to start a field). The table below summarizes what is occurring:

DATA TYPE	ALIGNMENT	DEFAULT LENGTH
DATE	Left	30
TIME	Left	20
CURRENCY	Right	26
TEXT	Left	2
INTEGER	Right	10
REAL	Right	8
DOUBLE	Right	22
NOTE	Left	2
NUMERIC	Right	17

Keep in mind as well that variables of all data types are placed with a default length of 2. Of course, you can adjust the default size of any data column or variable with the arrow keys. This is particularly easy if you want to expand a TEXT data column to its maximum length —just press Ctrl-→.

DECIMAL POINT ALIGNMENT

You can control decimal point alignment for any type of numeric field by using a picture format. Of course, it's your responsibility to make sure the defined field is wide enough to handle the data that will be printed. As you have seen before, if the field is too small to print the data, R:BASE will display asterisks (*) in the field.

Placing Decimal Points on the Report Format

Another way to control decimal place alignment for REAL and DOUBLE data types is to place, on the report format, a decimal point right where you want it inside the highlighted block for the field. With this technique, R:BASE prints something other than asterisks when there isn't enough room to display a number. If R:BASE has to, it will move the decimal place from the location you chose in order to display the entire number. So R:BASE will print the number, but the decimal point will not line up with others in the column.

Similarly, if there is enough room for the digits to the left of the decimal point but not enough room for the digits to the right, R:BASE will round the decimal digits. But suppose there isn't room for the digits to the left of the decimal point either. R:BASE will display a rounded number using *scientific notation*, sometimes called *E notation*. A number in scientific notation consists of a number followed by the letter E followed by a scaling factor. To convert a number from scientific notation to a decimal number, multiply the number to the left of the letter E by 10 to the power of the number to the right of the letter E. For example, the number 1.234567E3 is really 1.234567×1000, or 1234.567. If the number 1234.567 was displayed in a field of width 7, then R:BASE would round this number to 1.23E3. (R:BASE leaves a blank space at the beginning of the number.) As you can see, the numbers R:BASE displays in scientific notation give you an approximation of the actual number, so you cannot rely on these numbers to be accurate.

PLACING MULTI-LINE TEXT AND NOTE FIELDS

Although none of the databases you have created so far have any NOTE fields, you may want to set up reports that contain both TEXT and NOTE data. Placing TEXT and NOTE fields on a report format is a bit more complicated than placing other fields. As you saw when you placed TEXT fields, you can press W instead of E to indicate the length of the field. This activates the wrap-around feature and prints long fields like paragraphs. You can establish a right margin, so to speak, by typing a W rather than an E. If you type W, R:BASE will prompt you to

Move cursor down and press T, or press Esc

If you only want to devote three lines to the long field, for example, you would move your cursor down two lines from the W and type a T (for Truncate). This would tell R:BASE to print three lines worth of data from the field and to break at a space. Something like "and th" would not be printed; the line would end with "and." If you press Esc without moving the cursor, R:BASE will use as many lines as necessary to print the entire field.

Figure 12.9, for example, displays a report layout for a vocabulary database. Its only table, Vocab, has two columns: Word and Defn. Defn is defined as a NOTE field to accommodate widely varying definition lengths. In the report, the W tells R:BASE to wrap the definition onto the next line. Part of the VocabRep report is shown in Figure 12.10.

Finally, the Report Generator gives you the option of indenting or outdenting any wrapped fields. After you have pressed T to truncate the field or Esc to let the field have as many lines as required, you will be asked

Move to indent and press I, or press Esc

If you want indenting, type I to the *right* of the beginning of the highlighted block representing the field. If you want outdenting, type it to the *left*. If you don't want either, you can press Esc.

This completes our look at wrap-around in reports.

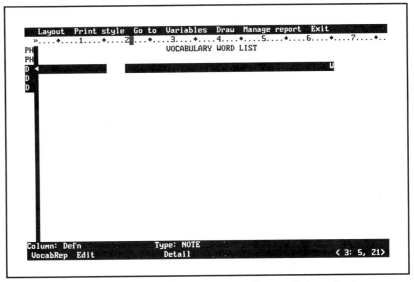

Figure 12.9: The report layout for a report on the vocabulary database

```
                        VOCABULARY WORD LIST

        abat-jour        A device, as a skylight or reflector, for diverting
                         light into a building

        abulia           Abnormal lack of ability to act or to make
                         decisions

        accoutrement     An article of equipment or dress, especially when
                         used as an accessory

        acerbate         To excite impatience, anger, or displeasure in;
                         exasperate

        ad hoc           For this (special purpose) only; with respect to
                         this (subject or thing)

        adagio           A love-duet sequence in ballet; a duet or trio
                         emphasizing difficult feat

        adduce           To offer as example, reason, or proof in discussion
                         or analysis

        adiabatic        Occurring without gain or loss of heat e.g. the
                         power and compression strokes of a gasoline engine

        adjuration       A solemn oath; an earnest urging or advising

        adumbration      A sketchy representation or outline; a vague
                         foreshadowing; intimation

        adventitious     Associated with something by chance, extrinsic
```

Figure 12.10: Sample report from the vocabulary database

Chapter 19 explains how to merge form letters with R:BASE and Microsoft Word, and R:BASE and WordPerfect.

GENERATING FORM LETTERS

Form letters are just reports that are mostly text with a few data fields used here and there. As such, you can create form letters that are only one page in length with the R:BASE Reports Generator. You need only the detail section—no headers or footers are required.

If you wanted to send a form letter to everyone in the Names table, you would type in the return address, date, and body of the letter as text on the report format. The inside address and the salutation could come from the Names table, with variables defined to combine the first and last name into a full name and the city, state, and ZIP code into one line for the address. In order to make sure that every letter is printed on a new page, you would define a breakpoint on the CustNo column with [Yes] under the FORM FEEDS Before Header column.

CREATING A REPORT WITHOUT DETAIL LINES

Although most reports will have at least one line marked D for Detail, it's not necessary to have them. It's quite possible to set up a summary report that prints only subtotal variables associated with break footers.

R:BASE has a powerful Report Generator, and you've learned a good deal about its advanced features in this chapter. You're probably feeling overwhelmed, but remember, the more you practice, the easier it becomes. The techniques we've used in this chapter illustrate the variety of formats you can use for reports; now we'll turn to some advanced formats and techniques available for forms.

Chapter 13

Refining Your Data-Entry Forms

ONE OF THE MOST POWERFUL FEATURES OF R:BASE is its ability to display data from multiple tables on a single form and to allow data to be entered into and edited on many tables simultaneously. Now that you've learned a bit about database design, you know that tables often contain columns whose only purpose is to link them to other tables. If you've been bothered by the prospect of entering redundant data associated with common columns into many tables, worry no more. You only have to enter data for common columns once when you use multi-table data-entry forms. Another advantage of multi-table forms is that you can usually design screens that look like existing paper forms. If data-entry personnel will be transcribing data from paper forms into R:BASE, this will make life easier.

In Chapter 10, we introduced you to some of the more advanced features of the Form Generator when you created the ChrgFrm form. You may want to look at it to refresh your memory. It is based on the Charges table and includes a number of lookup variables and an automatic date-entry feature. If the Mail database is open and you type

ENTER ChrgFrm

at the R> prompt, R:BASE will display the form on the screen. If you enter an actual customer number next to the Customer number prompt, R:BASE will automatically display that person's name and company.

In this chapter, we're going to explore multi-table forms, which allow you to enter data into or edit data from two or more tables. The ChrgFrm form, by comparison, was only designed to let you enter new data into the Charges table. But before we proceed, let's take a moment to discuss a general approach to designing and creating a complex form.

THE PRAGMATIST'S GUIDE TO FORM DESIGN AND IMPLEMENTATION

O.K., so you're ready to create a form. What now? Start the Form Generator? No! As we suggested in Chapter 8, before you do any hands-on programming with R:BASE, you should do some hands-on work with your paper and pencil.

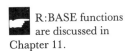
R:BASE functions
are discussed in
Chapter 11.

Common sense dictates that you should plan your form. You want it to be easy-to-use and have fields located in a logical fashion. You may also want the screen form to look like an existing paper form. A well-designed data form will minimize the number of keystrokes the data-entry person will have to make, and also make it easy for that person to correct mistakes.

You should also think about your form's general characteristics. Is the form going to be used for data entry, editing data display, or some combination of activities? What tables are involved? R:BASE will let you create a form that serves up to five tables. Will part of the form display background (or lookup) information? Will you want to enter several rows of data into one form, as in the case of multi-item invoices? R:BASE lets you define *regions* where many rows of data can be entered at once; we'll explore such regions later in the chapter. Do you want the data to be all upper- or all lowercase? You may want to use some of R:BASE's functions to ensure that data is entered into your tables in a consistent fashion.

Next, you should make a preliminary sketch of the form. Remember that R:BASE lets you use up to five screens for your form, so you don't need to pack all the necessary data onto one screen.

After you've sketched the form, you're ready to start setting it up. The next steps should be done in order, one table at a time. Generally, it's best to set up your expressions before entering text and prompts onto the form, because you may encounter problems with the expressions that force you to rethink your form's basic design.

In Chapter 10 you created the ChrgFrm form and defined variables that "looked up" data from other tables for display on the form. Your Name1, Name2, and CName variables are referred to as *standard lookups* because they access data from the Names table.

R:BASE also lets you define what's referred to as a *master lookup* or *same-table lookup*. Master lookups are used to look up data in the current table—not another table. For example, we'll create a form that lets you enter data both into the Names and Charges tables. When a new customer makes a transaction, you'll want to enter basic customer information (for the Names table) *and* details about the charge (for the Charges table). However, if a customer is already on record in the Names table, you don't want to have to enter his or her data again. You'll establish a master lookup expression, so that when you type in an existing customer's number, all the current data about that customer will be displayed automatically.

The next step is to place the columns and variables. Once you've finished placing columns and variables, you'll want to fine-tune your form by customizing table and field characteristics. After doing that, you'll move on to the next table. Ready to try out some of these techniques?

CREATING A MULTI-TABLE FORM

Rather than create an entirely new form to demonstrate this capability, we'll modify a copy of the NamesFrm form you created earlier. We'll call the new form "Both." To make the copy and to prepare to modify the Both form, make sure the Mail database is open and follow these steps at the R:BASE Main menu:

1. Highlight **F**orms and select **C**reate/modify.

2. Highlight **C**opy and select **N**amesFrm.

3. Type **Both** and press ⏎ when asked for the new form name. Now there are two identical forms in the Mail database, one named NamesFrm and one named Both.

4. Highlight **M**odify and select **B**oth.

CREATING A REGION

Let's place a region on the Both form for displaying data from the Charges table near the bottom of the screen. A region, you recall, is an area on a form that can display data from a group of rows. The region for Both will allow you to enter multiple charges for a given customer on one screen. And by defining a region you'll be able to scroll through *all* of a given customer's charges.

First, to make room for the region, we will clear out the box near the bottom of the form that describes highlight and cursor commands. To do this, move the cursor to the box at <16, 1> and press **F9** seven times. The bottom of the screen is now empty, giving you room to create the region.

Notice that the words *Table: Names* appear in the middle of the status bar at the bottom of the screen. This indicates that the form is currently "attached to" the Names table. To create a region on the form for the Charges table, you need to attach the form to the Charges table. After that, you'll customize the table settings for the Charges table to describe the region. Follow these steps to create the region for the Charges table:

Instead of highlighting Layout and selecting Add table to attach the form, you could simply press Shift-F8.

1. To attach the form to the Charges table, highlight **Layout**, select **Add table**, and select **Charges**.

2. Reply **Yes** when asked if you want to customize the table settings.

3. On the Table Settings menu, move the cursor to the question "Do you want to define a region?" and change the answer to Yes by pressing **Y** and then ◄─┘. The form will reappear along with the prompt "Move the cursor to locate a corner of the region—press Enter."

4. With the cursor at <16, 1>, press ◄─┘. Now the screen prompts you to "Move the cursor to paint the region's area—press Enter when done."

5. Move the cursor to <22,80>, painting the area where you want the region to appear. The screen should now look like Figure 13.1.

6. Press ◄─┘. The message at the bottom of the screen now says "Region created. Press any key to continue."

7. Press ◄─┘. The Table Settings menu reappears.

The remaining questions on the Table Settings menus refer to the appearance of the region on the form. The first question

Do you want a border around the region?

controls whether or not there will be a border around the region. A border will make the region stand out on the form. The choice is yours, but generally the form will look better with the border, so Yes, the default, is the preferred answer. The second question

How many lines in the border — enter 1 or 2:

```
┌─────────────────────────────────────────────────────────────┐
│                                                               │
│     ┌─────────────────────────────────────────────────┐      │
│     │Layout  Variables  Draw  Manage form  Exit         │      │
│     │ ┌───────────────────────────────────────────────┐│      │
│     │ │ Add/Edit Names                                 ││      │
│     │ └───────────────────────────────────────────────┘│      │
│     │                                                   │      │
│     │ Customer Number: ▇▇▇   Entry Date: ▇▇▇▇▇▇▇▇▇▇▇▇▇  │      │
│     │                                                   │      │
│     │ Last Name: ▇▇▇▇▇▇▇▇      First Name: ▇▇▇▇▇▇▇▇     │      │
│     │                                                   │      │
│     │ Company: ▇▇▇▇▇▇▇▇▇▇▇                               │      │
│     │                                                   │      │
│     │ Address: ▇▇▇▇▇▇▇▇▇▇▇▇                              │      │
│     │                                                   │      │
│     │ City: ▇▇▇▇▇▇▇▇▇      State: ▇▇   Zip: ▇▇▇▇▇        │      │
│     │                                                   │      │
│     │ Phone Number: ▇▇▇▇▇▇▇                              │      │
│     └─────────────────────────────────────────────────┘      │
│                                                               │
│                                                               │
│     Move the cursor to paint the region's area - press Enter when done│
│     Both       Define region      Table: Charges        Expand  Page 1 <22,80>│
│                                                               │
└─────────────────────────────────────────────────────────────┘
```

Figure 13.1: A region area highlighted on the form

lets you determine whether the border is displayed with a single line
or double line. For this example, 2 is preferred because a double
line will match the existing box near the top of the screen. (Again,
however, this is purely an aesthetic decision.) Notice that R:BASE
defaults to double-line borders.

If you have a color monitor, you can also define colors for the
region by answering the final questions on the Table Settings menu.
When you are finished, press **F2** to return to the Form Generator
screen.

PLACING TEXT AND PROMPTS IN THE REGION

Now you can place text and column names from the Charges table
inside the region. The procedure for doing so is the same as for any
form. For typing in text, position the cursor with the arrow keys and
type in the text. For this example, place the cursor at each of the start
locations in the left column below, and then type in the text listed in

the right column:

START LOCATION	TEXT
<17, 2>	Cust #
<17,10>	Prod #
<17,19>	Taxable
<17,28>	Qty
<17,35>	Unit Price
<17,52>	Total
<17,62>	Date of Sale

You can place column names with the F6 key and arrow keys. When placing columns, you can generally reply No when asked if you want to define an expression for the column or customize the field settings. However, you might want to put the default value of Y in the Taxable column and the default of #DATE in the P_Date column, as we've done before.

Using the F6 key and arrow keys, place the column names listed below at the start and end locations listed to the right of each column name:

COLUMN NAME	START	END
CustNo	<18, 2>	<18, 5>
ProdNo	<18,10>	<18,17>
Taxable	<18,22>	<18,22>
Qty	<18,27>	<18,30>
U_Price	<18,33>	<18,43>
Total	<18,46>	<18,56>
P_Date	<18,59>	<18,74>

When you are finished, your screen should look like Figure 13.2. Don't worry that the data headings don't line up with the highlighted areas below. Later in this chapter you will learn how to make changes to, or adjust, a form.

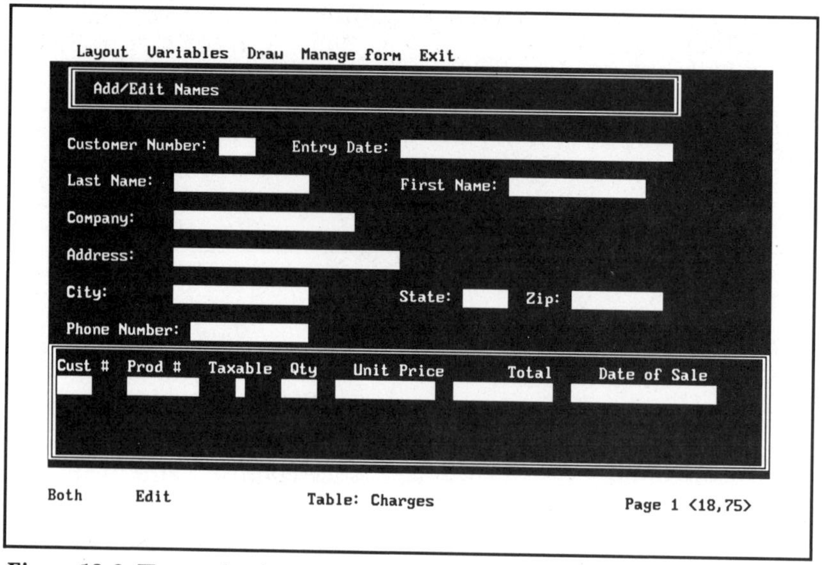

Figure 13.2: Text and column names placed in the region

Since there may be many rows in the Charges table associated with a single row in the Names table, you'll want to duplicate the column placements in the region. That way, when a particular customer is displayed on the screen, you'll be able to scroll through and edit any of the transactions.

COPYING TIERS IN A REGION

Your form's region currently has one tier. A *tier* is the area, which can include text as well as column and variable fields, associated with a single row. However, we've made the region large enough to accommodate several tiers. The process for doing so involves the following steps:

1. Press **Shift-F10**. R:BASE prompts you to "Move the cursor to locate a corner of the area to be duplicated—press Enter."

2. Move the cursor to <18, 2>, the left end of the area to copy.

3. Press ←┘. You are prompted to "Move the cursor to paint the area to be duplicated—press Enter."

4. Press → to move the cursor to <18,79>, the right end of the area to copy.

5. Press ←┘.

Automatically, the entire region will be filled with the highlighted blocks for the column fields, as in Figure 13.3. At this point you've finished creating the screen portion of the new form named Both. Before testing it, however, we can add another feature called a *master lookup*.

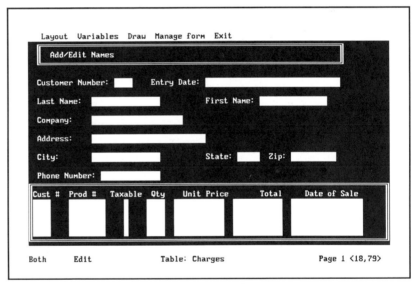

Figure 13.3: Tiers copied in the Charges region

DEFINING A MASTER LOOKUP EXPRESSION

A master lookup expression is used in forms that serve multiple tables to display the data from a particular row in one of the tables. Generally, the expression takes the form

column = *column* IN *table* WHERE *id* = *id*

The *column* portion is the name of any column in the named *table*. The *id* portion is the name of the matching column in the table. In this example, you can define a master lookup for the Names table as follows:

> The status bar is located along the bottom of the screen.

1. To make Names the active table, highlight **Layout**; select **Select table**; and select **Names**. Note the change in the status bar.

2. To define the master lookup expression, highlight **Variables**; select **Define**; type **L_Name = L_Name IN Names WHERE CustNo = CustNo** and press ◄─┘; and reply **No** to customizing lookup settings.

When you use the form later, you will enter a customer number in the first field. R:BASE will use your master lookup expression to match the customer number entered onto the form to customer numbers in the Names and Charges tables. L_Name in this case is simply an arbitrary column; you could have used F_Name, Company, Address, or any of the others. The purpose of the expression is to attempt to find out if the customer number entered onto the form already exists. If it does, *all* the remaining fields in the Names portion of the form will automatically display that customer's data.

We'll see the effects of this master lookup expression in a moment, and this might shed more light on this expression. For the time being, we're finished creating the form and we're ready to test it.

TESTING THE MULTI-TABLE FORM

You can test the form with either the Add data or the Edit data options. To test the new form with the Edit data option, highlight **Manage form**, select **Run**, and select **Edit data**.

You'll notice right away that the form displays both the first row in the Names table and all the charges associated with that name, as in Figure 13.4.

You can press F8 or F7 to scroll through the names in the Names table and watch how the form displays data. To move the cursor back and forth between the data for the Names table and the data for the Charges table, press Shift-F8. If you would rather use menu selections to move around the form, you can use the Next row, Previous

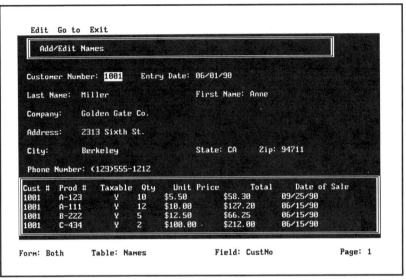

```
        Edit  Go to  Exit
    ┌─────────────────────────────────────────────────────────────────┐
    │   Add/Edit Names                                                  │
    └─────────────────────────────────────────────────────────────────┘

    Customer Number: ▐1001▌    Entry Date: 06/01/90

    Last Name:  Miller                    First Name: Anne

    Company:    Golden Gate Co.

    Address:    2313 Sixth St.

    City:       Berkeley             State: CA    Zip: 94711

    Phone Number: (123)555-1212
  ┌───────────────────────────────────────────────────────────────────┐
  │Cust #  Prod #   Taxable  Qty   Unit Price     Total     Date of Sale│
  │1001    A-123      Y      10    $5.50         $58.30      09/25/90    │
  │1001    A-111      Y      12    $10.00        $127.20     06/15/90    │
  │1001    B-222      Y       5    $12.50        $66.25      06/15/90    │
  │1001    C-434      Y       2    $100.00 ·     $212.00     06/15/90    │
  └───────────────────────────────────────────────────────────────────┘

    Form: Both      Table: Names           Field: CustNo       Page: 1
```

Figure 13.4: Data displayed from both the Names and Charges table

row, and Next section options in the Goto pull-down menu. These options are equivalent in function to F8, F7, and Shift-F8.

Of course, you can change any data on the form you wish. When you are finished editing, highlight and select **Exit** to return to the Form Generator screen.

To test if you can enter new data in the form, highlight **Manage** form, select **Run**, and select **Add** data. The form appears with no data in it (except for the default date and state), ready to accept new data.

Here is where the master lookup expression comes in. Normally when you enter data into a database, R:BASE accepts any entry you type in, or it checks the rules (if any) to see if a violation took place. But with the master lookup expression defined, R:BASE will simply display existing data if you enter an existing customer number. For example, if you enter customer number 1003 onto the form and press ←┘, the screen will display all existing data for customer number 1003.

If, for your next data entry, you enter a new customer number (such as 9999) and press ←┘, the following message is displayed on the screen:

Could not find a matching row. Do you want to add a new row?

R:BASE is telling you that the customer number you entered does not exist yet in the Names table, and it gives you two options. If you choose Yes, a row for the new customer number will be created on the Names table, and you can fill in the rest of the data (including data on the Charges table) for this new customer. If you choose No, R:BASE will reject the new customer number and let you enter another one.

As usual, highlight and select **Exit** when you are finished entering new data.

With some experience entering and editing data through a form that serves multiple tables, you'll soon find this method convenient for managing several tables.

MAKING CHANGES IN THE FORM

Rarely will your first attempt at setting up a form be perfect. Some of you may have noticed that the data from the Charges table in the region doesn't line up very well with the headings (see Figure 13.4). R:BASE displays the data starting at the beginning of the highlighted block on the Form Generator screen that you used to establish boundaries for a field.

To change the form so that the alignment looks better, you'll have to move the Qty, U_Price, Total, and P_Date fields to the right. You can do this with the following steps:

1. To begin modifying the Both form, highlight **Forms**, select **Create/modify**, highlight **Modify**, and select **Both**.

2. To make the Charges table the active one, highlight **Layout**, select **Select table**, and select **Charges**.

3. Move the cursor to the beginning of the Qty field, position <18,27>.

4. To remove the duplicate tiers in the region for the Charges table, press **Shift-F10** and choose **Yes** when asked if you want to remove duplicate rows from the region.

5. To move the Qty field one position to the right, press **F6**; choose **No** when asked if you want to customize field settings; choose **Yes** when asked if you want to relocate the field position; press →; press **S**; press ←; and press **E**.

You must remove the duplicate tiers before you can move any field in the Charges region.

6. To move the U_Price, Total, and P_Date fields to the right, let's use a shortcut: with the cursor at position <18,32>, press **Ins** to go to Insert mode (the cursor is a block); press the **spacebar** three times; move to <18,48>; press the **spacebar** twice; and press **Ins** to go back to Overtype mode (the cursor is an underline).

7. To duplicate the tiers again, press **Shift-F10**; move to <18, 2>; press ←; move to <18,79>; and press ←.

8. To observe the fruits of your effort, test the form with the Edit data option by highlighting **M**anage form, selecting **R**un, and selecting **E**dit data. Your screen should look like Figure 13.5.

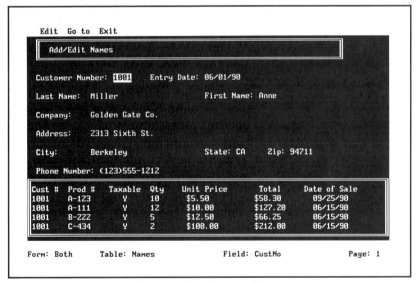

Figure 13.5: The data reformatted for better alignment

9. Highlight and select **E**xit to return to the Form Generator screen.

ACTIVATING MULTI-TABLE FORMS

As you would expect, you can activate this form either from the R:BASE Main menu or from the R> prompt. From the R:BASE

Main menu, you would highlight Forms, select Both, and select Add data or Edit data. If you selected Edit data, you would then specify sorting criteria and searching conditions for the Names rows that R:BASE presents with the form. At the R > prompt, you would use the command

>   EDIT USING Both

to edit existing data and the command

>   ENTER Both

to enter new data. Of course, with the EDIT USING Both command, you could use the WHERE and ORDER BY clauses to tell R:BASE how to search for and sort Names rows.

TIPS AND TECHNIQUES FOR MULTI-TABLE FORMS

Before concluding this chapter, there are a few more tips and techniques that you should know about forms and regions. Three common problems associated with multi-table forms are changing the size of a region, preventing changes to index columns that link related tables, and reordering field and table names.

CHANGING A REGION'S SIZE

You can change the size, location, or appearance of a region with the Form Generator. When the appropriate form is on the screen, you can insert lines above or beneath a region by pressing the F10 key (assuming that there is room on the form to insert new lines). You can also delete lines above or beneath the region by pressing F9. (The F9 key only deletes lines that do not have column names or variables placed. If necessary, press Shift-F9 to delete columns and variable names, and then press F9 to delete the line.)

To change the size of a region, first make sure that the table the region serves is the active table and that duplicate tiers have been removed. When the name of the table associated with the region appears in the status bar, press Ctrl-F4. The cursor will move to the upper-left corner of the region, and the entire region will be highlighted. You can then move between the upper-left corner and the lower-right corner of the region by pressing the Home and End keys. To alter the size of a region, adjust the size of the highlighted area with the arrow keys.

After you've made your changes to the column locations and text inside the tier, you can press the Shift-F10 key again to copy the tier.

PREVENTING CHANGES
TO THE CUSTOMER NUMBER

When using the form with multiple tables to add data with the ENTER command, the user can enter any customer number. If the customer number exists, the data are displayed on the screen. At this point, the user could change the customer number, but the results of doing so could cause problems, because the corresponding existing charges on the Charges table would not automatically be updated to reflect the new customer number.

You can prevent changes to the CustNo column with the following technique. Starting at the Form Generator menu,

Remember that you can display the Form Generator menu from the R:BASE Main menu by highlighting Forms and selecting Create/modify, or from the R > prompt with the FORMS command.

1. Modify the Both form by highlighting **M**odify and selecting **B**oth.

2. If necessary, make the Names table the active table by highlighting **L**ayout, selecting **S**elect table, and selecting **N**ames.

3. Move the cursor onto the CustNo field (for example, position < 5,20 >).

4. Press **F6**.

5. Choose **Y**es when R:BASE asks if you want to customize field settings.

6. On the Field Settings menu, change the answer to the question ''Can the user change the data displayed in the field?'' to **N**o.

7. Press **F2** to return to the Form Generator screen.

8. Reply **N**o when asked if you want to relocate the field position.

9. To test this change, highlight **M**anage form; select **R**un; and select **A**dd data. Notice that the highlighter does not move back to the Customer number field. Thus, this field cannot be changed.

10. Leave this form and return to the R:BASE Main menu by highlighting and selecting **E**xit three times.

REORDERING FIELD AND TABLE NAMES

See "Changing the Order of Entry for Fields" in Chapter 8 for a discussion of how to change the field order in a data-entry from.

If you noticed that your cursor was jumping around erratically in your form, remember that you can change the field order in the Form Generator. Just make sure that the table that has the field order problem is the active table and then use the Change field order option in the Layout pull-down menu.

If in the future you create a form that serves more than two tables, you may want to change the order in which the Shift-F8 key cycles through the tables in the form. To do so, use the Change table order option in the Layout pull-down menu in much the same way that you would use the Change field order option to change the order of fields.

In this chapter, you've seen how easy it is to create sophisticated forms that let the user enter data into several tables from one form. You've also learned how the Form Generator provides several levels of customization, which allow you to specify default values for fields and have existing data displayed for the user's convenience. In the next chapter we'll look at some *relational* commands for combining and summarizing multiple tables.

Chapter 14

Combining and
Copying Tables

R:BASE OFFERS SIX COMMANDS FOR COMBINING AND copying tables in a database: PROJECT, INSERT, UNION, INTERSECT, SUBTRACT, and JOIN. Like all commands, these can be entered directly at the R> prompt. Alternatively, you can highlight Tools and select Relational tools on the R:BASE Main menu to access these functions.

Before trying the sample operations in this chapter, make sure that the Mail database is open and the R> prompt is on the screen. Keep in mind that your results may differ if your Names or Charges table contains data other than those used in the sample operations.

COPYING TABLES WITH THE PROJECT COMMAND

The PROJECT command makes a copy of all or part of a table, creating a new table in the process. It is useful for making backup copies of tables, creating summary tables, and reordering columns and rows in a table. The basic syntax for the project command is

> PROJECT *new table name* FROM *existing table name* USING +
> +> *column names* ORDER BY *column names* WHERE +
> +> *conditions list*

The ORDER BY and WHERE clauses are optional with this command, and you can add an asterisk (*) after USING to represent all columns. A simple example of the PROJECT command is:

> PROJECT Table3 FROM Table1 USING *

This command would create a table called Table3 exactly the same as Table1, except that Table3 would not contain either the table description or any of the column descriptions in Table1.

Let's suppose that you want to create a list of names, telephone numbers, and entry dates for everyone in the Names table whose entry dates are between June 1 and June 15, 1990. Furthermore, you want to store the list in order by telephone number. To create a new

▶ The section called "Making a Backup Copy of a Table" later in this chapter tells you how to use the R:BASE menus to make an exact copy of a database, complete with table and column descriptions.

table named "PhoneLst" for these data, enter the command

```
PROJECT PhoneLst FROM Names USING Phone +
+> L_Name F_Name Ent_Date ORDER BY Phone WHERE +
+> Ent_Date BETWEEN '5/31/90' AND '6/15/90'
```

R:BASE will respond with the message "Successful project operation, 6 rows generated." To see the contents of the PhoneLst table, enter the command

```
SELECT ALL FROM PhoneLst
```

R:BASE displays the new PhoneLst table, as below:

PHONE	L_NAME	F_NAME	ENT_DATE
(123)555-1234	Miller	Anne	06/01/90
(123)555-9012	Smith	Sandy	06/01/90
(234)555-1010	Adams	Bart	06/15/90
(345)555-2222	Miller	Marie	06/15/90
(456)555-0123	Baker	Robin	06/15/90
(456)555-4567	Jones	Mindy	06/01/90

REARRANGING COLUMNS WITH THE PROJECT COMMAND

Let's take a look at how you can use the PROJECT command to rearrange columns in a table. Suppose you wanted to rearrange the columns in the Names table so that Ent_Date is the column farthest left and CustNo is the column farthest right. You would proceed with the following steps:

1. Enter the command

```
PROJECT Temp FROM Names USING Ent_Date L_Name +
+> F_Name Company Address City State +
+> Zip_Code Phone CustNo
```

If the Temp table already existed when you issued the PROJECT command, R:BASE would tell you that you cannot create another table with a duplicate name.

to copy the Names table to a temporary table (named "Temp" in this example) and specify all the column names in the order that you want them. When you leave out the ORDER BY and WHERE clauses, you retain the original sort order and ensure that all the rows from the Names table are copied to the Temp table.

2. Type **LIST Temp** and press ←┘ to look at the Temp table and ensure that the PROJECT command was correctly executed.

3. Type **DROP TABLE Temp** and press ←┘ to remove the Temp table.

4. Choose **Yes** when R:BASE asks if you are sure you want to remove the Temp table.

Suppose you wanted the Names table to keep this new column arrangement. You would skip steps 3 and 4 above, delete the Names table with the DROP TABLE Names command, and rename the Temp table "Names" with the RENAME TABLE Temp TO Names command. However, since the PROJECT command does not copy the column or table descriptions to the new table, you would lose the column and table descriptions if you followed this method and gave the Names table the new column arrangement.

REARRANGING ROWS WITH THE PROJECT COMMAND

Although the ORDER BY clause allows you to arrange rows in any order that you wish, you might want to use a quicker and more permanent method when you're working with a large table. If this is the case, you can use the PROJECT command to rearrange all the rows in a table.

For example, suppose you regularly send letters in ZIP-code order to the individuals listed in the Names table. Though you shouldn't try it on-line now, you could use the PROJECT command with the following technique:

1. Type **PROJECT Temp FROM Names USING * ORDER BY Zip_Code ASC** to create a copy of the Names table sorted in ascending order by ZIP code.

2. Type **REMOVE TABLE Names** to remove the Names table.

3. Type **RENAME TABLE Temp TO Names** to change the name of the Temp table to Names.

Now issue the SELECT command without an ORDER BY clause, and the rows in the Names table are displayed in ZIP-code order.

MAKING A BACKUP COPY OF A TABLE

To make a backup copy of a table within the same database, you could issue the PROJECT command with the USING * option. For example, the following command makes a backup copy of the Charges table called "Chrgsbak":

PROJECT Chrgsbak FROM Charges USING *

The Chrgsbak table will contain all of the data in the Charges table and will have the same columns defined, except that the Chrgsbak table will not have any table or column descriptions. To make an exact copy of the Charges table, including all table and column descriptions, you could use the R:BASE menus. Let's try making a backup of the Charges table using the R:BASE menus.

1. Type **RBDEFINE** and press ⏎.

2. With **T**ables highlighted, select **C**opy.

3. Select **C**harges.

4. Type **Chrgsbak** and press ⏎ when prompted to "Enter the name for this table."

5. Highlight and select **E**xit to return to the R> prompt.

ADDING ROWS WITH INSERT

The INSERT command adds rows to the bottom of a table, obtaining the data either from values supplied in the INSERT command or from another table. The INSERT command for adding the data in one table to another table has the following syntax:

INSERT INTO *receiving table (receiving columns)* +
+> SELECT *sending columns* FROM *sending table* +
+> WHERE *conditions*

Rows from the *sending table* are added to the bottom of the *receiving table*. Each column listed in the *receiving columns* will be filled in with data from columns in the corresponding positions in the list of *sending columns*. If you are providing a value for each column in the receiving table, you can leave out the receiving column list (as well as the parentheses). If you are sending each column in the sending table, you can use ALL for the sending column list. The *conditions* in the WHERE clause determine which rows in the sending table are added to the receiving table. If you leave out the WHERE clause, all rows in the sending table will be added to the receiving table. Figure 14.1 shows an example of the INSERT command.

The INSERT command is often used for managing *transaction* tables and *history* tables, particularly in inventory and accounting systems. For example, the Charges table in the Mail database could grow indefinitely throughout the course of the year. However, most businesses bill monthly, so there is no need to keep all the transactions of the year on the Charges table. Instead, after the customers have been billed at the end of the month, you could move all of that month's transactions to a history table for later reference, emptying the Charges table to make room for the following month's transactions.

Let's try moving the Charge table transactions for June, 1990 over to the History table, as you would do at the end of June. Figure 14.2 shows the current contents of the Charges table. You could follow these steps to move the June Charges transactions to a table called "History":

1. Enter the command

   PROJECT History FROM Charges USING * WHERE
   COUNT = 0

   to create a table named History for storing transactions and give it the same structure as the Charges table. This command

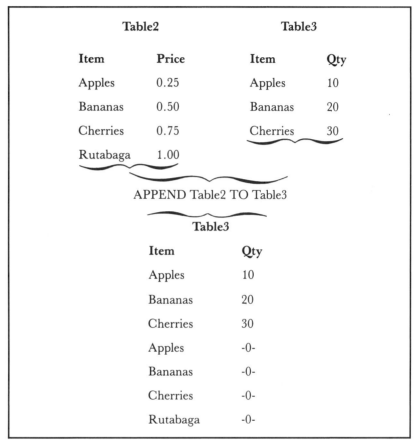

Figure 14.1: An example of the INSERT command

```
R>SELECT #1=5 #2 #3=4 #4=8 #5=3 #6=8 #7 FROM Charges
 CustN ProdNo   Qty  U_Price Tax Total    P_Date
 ----- -------- ---- -------- --- -------- --------
  1001 A-123     10    $5.50 Y   $58.30 09/25/90
  1001 A-111     12   $10.00 Y  $127.20 06/15/90
  1001 B-222      5   $12.50 Y   $66.25 06/15/90
  1001 C-434      2  $100.00 Y  $212.00 06/15/90
  1004 A-111      5   $10.00 Y   $53.00 06/15/90
  1004 A-128     10   $12.80 N  $128.00 06/15/90
  1006 A-111     10   $10.00 Y  $106.00 06/15/90
  1006 Z-128     10   $12.80 N  $128.00 06/15/90
  1002 B-222     12   $12.50 Y  $159.00 06/30/90
  1002 A-111     10   $10.00 Y  $106.00 06/30/90
  1003 A-111      5   $10.00 Y   $53.00 10/14/90
 R>
```

Figure 14.2: The current contents of the Charges table

copies the *structure* of the Charges table without any of the data. R:BASE responds with the message

Successful project operation, 0 rows generated

2. Enter the command

When you insert data into a table with computed columns, do not supply any values for the computed columns.

> INSERT INTO History SELECT CustNo ProdNo Qty U_Price +
> +> Taxable P_Date FROM Charges WHERE +
> +> P_Date > = '6/1/90' AND P_Date < = '6/30/90'

Notice that a value was supplied for every column in History except the Total column, which is a computed column. R:BASE responds with the message

Successful INSERT operation, 9 rows generated

3. Type the command

> DELETE FROM Charges WHERE P_Date > = '6/1/90' +
> +> AND P_Date < = '6/30/90'

R:BASE replies

9 row(s) have been deleted from Charges

Figure 14.3 shows the results of using the SELECT command to view the contents of the Charges and History tables. All of the transactions from the month of June, 1990 have been removed from the Charges table and added to the History table.

From now on, when the end of each month rolls around, you can repeat steps 2 and 3 above, substituting the appropriate WHERE clause. For example, at the end of July, you would include the following INSERT clause in step 2:

> INSERT INTO History SELECT CustNo ProdNo Qty U_Price +
> +> Taxable P_Date FROM Charges WHERE +
> +> P_Date > = '7/1/90' AND P_Date < = '7/31/90'

and the following DELETE clause in step 3:

> DELETE FROM Charges WHERE P_Date > = '7/1/90' +
> +> AND P_Date < = '7/31/90'

```
R>SELECT #1=5 #2 #3=4 #4=8 #5=3 #6=8 #7 FROM Charges
CustN ProdNo   Qty  U_Price  Tax Total     P_Date
----- -------- ---- -------- --- -------- --------
 1001 A-123      10   $5.50  Y    $58.30 09/25/90
 1003 A-111       5  $10.00  Y    $53.00 10/14/90
R>SELECT #1=5 #2 #3=4 #4=8 #5=3 #6=8 #7 FROM History
CustN ProdNo   Qty  U_Price  Tax Total     P_Date
----- -------- ---- -------- --- -------- --------
 1001 A-111      12  $10.00  Y   $127.20 06/15/90
 1001 B-222       5  $12.50  Y    $66.25 06/15/90
 1001 C-434       2 $100.00  Y   $212.00 06/15/90
 1004 A-111       5  $10.00  Y    $53.00 06/15/90
 1004 A-128      10  $12.80  N   $128.00 06/15/90
 1006 A-111      10  $10.00  Y   $106.00 06/15/90
 1006 Z-128      10  $12.80  N   $128.00 06/15/90
 1002 B-222      12  $12.50  Y   $159.00 06/30/90
 1002 A-111      10  $10.00  Y   $106.00 06/30/90
R>
```

Figure 14.3: Contents of the Charges and History tables after moving June transactions

This would leave the Charges table clear for adding new transactions for August, and the History table would have a record of all June and July transactions.

If you've followed along on-line through these exercises, you can get more practice with the INSERT and DELETE commands by restoring all of the original transactions back to the Charges table.

1. Enter the command

   INSERT INTO History SELECT CustNo ProdNo Qty +
   +> U_Price Taxable P_Date FROM Charges

   to move all remaining transactions from the Charges table to the History table.

2. Type **DELETE ROWS FROM Charges** and press ←.

3. Press ← when R:BASE asks you to "Press Enter to continue DELETE, Esc to stop." All of the transactions are now removed from the Charges table.

Another way to restore the Charges table would be to remove the Charges table with the DROP TABLE command and then to use the R:BASE menus to copy the backup Chrgsbak table to the Charges table. See the section "Making a Backup Copy of a Table" earlier in this chapter for details on copying a table.

4. Enter the command

    INSERT INTO Charges SELECT CustNo ProdNo Qty +
    +> U_Price Taxable P_Date FROM History

    to move all of the transactions from the History table back
    into the Charges table. All of the transactions that were in
    the Charges table before you started these exercises should
    now be back in the Charges table.

COMBINING TWO TABLES WITH THE UNION COMMAND

To join two tables with the UNION command, the tables must share at least one column in common.

The UNION command allows you to combine all or part of two
existing tables into a new third table. To issue this command, however,
the two tables must have at least one common column. Common
columns are those that have identical names, data types, and widths. An
example of the UNION command is shown in Figure 14.4.

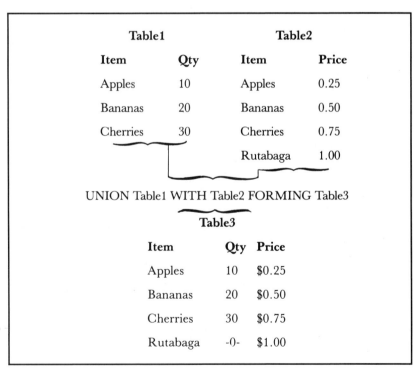

Figure 14.4: An example of the UNION command

The basic syntax for the UNION command is

UNION *table1* **WITH** *table2* **FORMING** *table3* **USING** *columns*

The UNION command combines common columns into a single column on the new table. By specifying certain column names in the USING portion, you tell R:BASE to include the named columns in the order that you specified in the new table. If you leave off the USING portion of the command, the new table will include all the columns from the original two tables, with the columns from *table1* coming before the columns from *table2*.

Suppose that you want a listing of the product numbers, customer numbers, names, quantities, and unit prices from the Charges and Names tables. You could proceed with the following steps to obtain this listing:

1. Enter the command

   UNION Charges WITH Names FORMING Temp USING +
   +> ProdNo CustNo L_Name F_Name Qty U_Price

   to create a new table named "Temp" with the appropriate information. R:BASE responds with the message "Successful union operation, 16 rows generated."

2. Enter the command

   SELECT ProdNo = 6 CustNo = 5 L_Name = 10 +
   +> F_Name = 7 Qty = 4 U_Price = 8 FROM Temp

   R:BASE displays the contents of the Temp table, as shown in Figure 14.5. This is the listing you wanted.

3. Type **DROP TABLE Temp** and press ⏎ to remove the Temp table, now that we have seen our listing.

The UNION command will create the Temp table. If the Temp table already exists, R:BASE will display an error message.

Notice that several rows have a null character (-0-) in the ProdNo, Qty, and U_Price columns. These null characters indicate that those individuals were not listed in the Charges table (because they didn't make any purchases). When one table has rows that do not match the second table, the UNION command will copy those rows to the new table and add null characters to the columns in nonmatching rows.

```
R>SELECT ProdNo=6 CustNo=5 L_Name=10 F_Name=7 Qty=4 U_Price=8 FROM Temp
  ProdNo CustN L_Name      F_Name  Qty  U_Price
  ------  ----- ----------  ------- ---- --------
  A-123   1001  Miller      Anne      10    $5.50
  A-111   1001  Miller      Anne      12   $10.00
  B-222   1001  Miller      Anne       5   $12.50
  C-434   1001  Miller      Anne       2  $100.00
  A-111   1004  Jones       Mindy      5   $10.00
  A-128   1004  Jones       Mindy     10   $12.80
  A-111   1006  Baker       Robin     10   $10.00
  Z-128   1006  Baker       Robin     10   $12.80
  B-222   1002  Adams       Bart      12   $12.50
  A-111   1002  Adams       Bart      10   $10.00
  A-111   1003  Miller      Marie      5   $10.00
  -0-     1005  Smith       Sandy    -0-  -0-
  -0-     1008  Teasdale    Trudy    -0-  -0-
  -0-     1009  Martin      Mary     -0-  -0-
  -0-     1010  Ferguson    Harold   -0-  -0-
  -0-     1007  Ferguson    Harold   -0-  -0-
R>
```

Figure 14.5: The results of the UNION command

Now let's try creating a different listing with all customer numbers and company names, followed by a list of items purchased. See if you can create this listing, using the following steps as a guide:

1. Enter the command

   UNION Charges WITH Names FORMING Temp USING +
   +> CustNo Company ProdNo Qty U_Price

   to create the Temp table with the appropriate information. R:BASE responds "Successful union operation, 16 rows generated."

2. Type **SELECT ALL FROM Temp** and press ◄┘ to produce the listing you wanted, which is shown in Figure 14.6.

3. Type **DROP TABLE Temp** and press ◄┘ to remove the Temp table, now that we have seen our listing.

Again, notice how the UNION command handled nonmatching rows. Since the Charges table showed no transactions for customers 1005, 1007, 1008, 1009, and 1010, these rows were displayed in the Temp table with null values in the ProdNo, Qty, and U_Price

```
R>SELECT ALL FROM Temp
CustNo     Company                          ProdNo    Qty         U_Price
---------- -------------------------------- --------- ----------- ----------------
      1001 Golden Gate Co.                   A-123               10          $5.50
      1001 Golden Gate Co.                   A-111               12         $10.00
      1001 Golden Gate Co.                   B-222                5         $12.50
      1001 Golden Gate Co.                   C-434                2        $100.00
      1004 ABC Co.                           A-111                5         $10.00
      1004 ABC Co.                           A-128               10         $12.80
      1006 Peach Computers                   A-111               10         $10.00
      1006 Peach Computers                   Z-128               10         $12.80
      1002 DataSpec Inc.                     B-222               12         $12.50
      1002 DataSpec Inc.                     A-111               10         $10.00
      1003 Zeerox Inc.                       A-111                5         $10.00
      1005 Hi Tech Inc.                      -0-        -0-         -0-
      1008 Atomic Micros Inc.                -0-        -0-         -0-
      1009 Atomic Micros Inc.                -0-        -0-         -0-
      1010 PromoTech Sales                   -0-        -0-         -0-
      1007 PromoTech Sales                   -0-        -0-         -0-
R>
```

Figure 14.6: The results of the second UNION command

columns. As you'll see, the INTERSECT command handles this situation differently.

COMBINING TABLES WITH THE INTERSECT COMMAND

The INTERSECT command is similar to the UNION command, except that it does not generate rows with null values. When you combined the Charges and Names tables with the UNION command, rows from the Names table that were not listed in the Charges table appeared in the Temp table with null values. With the INTERSECT command, nonmatching rows are not added to the new table.

Like the UNION command, the INTERSECT command requires the two tables to have at least one common column (with identical names, data types, and widths). An example of the INTERSECT command is shown in Figure 14.7. The general syntax for the INTERSECT command is identical to the syntax for the UNION command:

INTERSECT *table1* WITH *table2* FORMING *table3* USING +
+> *columns*

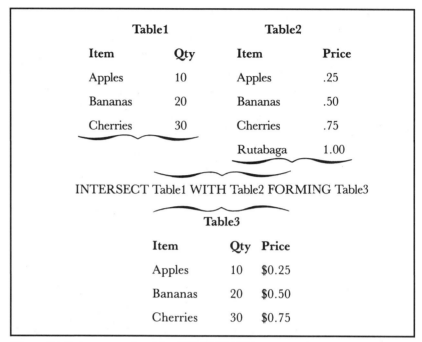

Figure 14.7: An example of the INTERSECT command

Suppose you wanted a listing of charges, with product numbers, customer numbers, customer names, quantities, and prices. You could produce this listing as follows:

1. Enter the command

    **INTERSECT Charges WITH Names FORMING Temp +
    +> USING ProdNo CustNo L_Name F_Name Qty U_Price**

    to create the Temp table with the desired information. R:BASE responds with the message

    Successful intersect operation, 11 rows generated

2. Enter the command

    **SELECT ProdNo CustNo L_Name = 10 F_Name = 10 +
    +> Qty = 4 U_Price = 8 FROM Temp**

    to see the contents of the Temp table, as shown in Figure 14.8.

```
R>SELECT ProdNo CustNo L_Name=10 F_Name=10 Qty=4 U_Price=8 FROM Temp
  ProdNo    CustNo     L_Name      F_Name    Qty  U_Price
  --------  ---------  ----------  ---------- ---- ---------
  A-123        1001 Miller     Anne        10    $5.50
  A-111        1001 Miller     Anne        12   $10.00
  B-222        1001 Miller     Anne         5   $12.50
  C-434        1001 Miller     Anne         2  $100.00
  B-222        1002 Adams      Bart        12   $12.50
  A-111        1002 Adams      Bart        10   $10.00
  A-111        1003 Miller     Marie        5   $10.00
  A-111        1004 Jones      Mindy        5   $10.00
  A-128        1004 Jones      Mindy       10   $12.80
  A-111        1006 Baker      Robin       10   $10.00
  Z-128        1006 Baker      Robin       10   $12.80
R>
```

Figure 14.8: The results of the INTERSECT command

3. Type **DROP TABLE Temp** and press ⏎ to remove the Temp table, now that we have seen our listing.

As Figure 14.9 shows, only the customers that appear in both the Names and Charges tables are included in the new table.

For our next example, let's create a listing with customer numbers and company names, followed by product numbers, quantities, and unit prices. In order to see only customers with charges, we will use the INTERSECT command.

1. Enter the command

   INTERSECT Charges WITH Names FORMING Temp +
   +> USING CustNo Company ProdNo Qty U_Price

   to create the Temp table with the desired information. R:BASE responds with "Successful intersect operation, 11 rows generated."

2. Enter the command **SELECT ALL FROM Temp** and press ⏎ to see the desired listing.

3. Type **DROP TABLE Temp** and press ⏎ to remove the Temp table.

Once again, only the customers listed in both the Names and Charges tables made it to the Temp table.

We've seen how the UNION command transferred all the rows from both the Names and Charges table to the new table, including those that did not have common customer numbers. The result was that we could see the purchases made by various customers, as well as the customers who made no purchases. The INTERSECT command, however, copied only those rows that had common values in both the Names and Charges tables; we thus saw a listing of purchases made by various customers, without seeing the customers who didn't make purchases.

Suppose you wanted to see a listing of customers who didn't make any purchases (the opposite of what the INTERSECT command provided). In this case, you could use the SUBTRACT command.

VIEWING DIFFERENCES WITH THE SUBTRACT COMMAND

The SUBTRACT command forms a new table of rows that do not match on two existing tables. An example of the SUBTRACT command is shown in Figure 14.9. The general syntax for the command is

SUBTRACT *small table* FROM *large table* FORMING +
+> *new table* USING *columns*

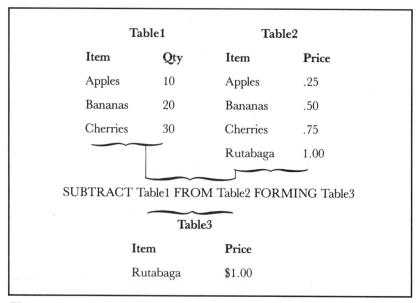

Figure 14.9: An example of the SUBTRACT command

If you leave out the optional USING *columns* part of the command, the new table will have the same columns as the large table.

The *small table* is not necessarily physically smaller than the *large table*, but instead it might be a subset of the other table. For example, even if the Charges table contained 1000 rows, it would be the smaller table in this example because it might not contain every customer number. The Names table is the *large table* because it does contain every customer number.

To find out which customers in the Names table did not make purchases (that is, the ones that do not appear in the Charges table), use the SUBTRACT command.

1. Type **SUBTRACT Charges FROM Names FORMING Temp** and press ← to place the rows in the Temp table that are in Names but not Charges. R:BASE responds with the message "Successful subtract operation, 5 rows generated."

2. Type **SELECT ALL FROM Temp** and press ← to see the five customers who are not included in the Charges file, as shown in Figure 14.10.

```
R>SELECT CustNo=6 L_Name=8 F_Name=8 Company=20 Address=20 FROM Temp
CustNo L_Name    F_Name   Company               Address
------ --------- -------- --------------------- --------------------
  1005 Smith     Sandy    Hi Tech Inc.          456 N. Rainbow Dr.
  1008 Teasdale  Trudy    Atomic Micros Inc.    321 Microwave St.
  1009 Martin    Mary     Atomic Micros Inc.    321 Microwave St.
  1010 Ferguson  Harold   PromoTech Sales       4109 Crest St.
  1007 Ferguson  Harold   PromoTech Sales       4109 Crest St.
R>
```

Figure 14.10: The results of the SUBTRACT command (the customers not included in the Charges file)

3. Type **DROP TABLE Temp** and press ← to remove the Temp table.

If you do attempt to subtract a large table from a smaller one, you'll end up with no rows on the new table, as below. Notice the message "0 rows generated."

    SUBTRACT Names FROM Charges FORMING Temp
    Successful subtract operation, 0 rows generated

COMBINING AND COMPARING TABLES WITH THE JOIN COMMAND

The JOIN command works in much the same way as the UNION command, except for two important differences:

- You can compare column data from two tables using any of the various operators, such as equal, not equal, greater than, and less than.

- The columns used for comparing the two tables may have different names; however, the two columns must be of the same data type and length.

The general syntax of the JOIN command is

JOIN *table1* USING *column name* WITH *table2* USING +
+> *column name* FORMING *table3* WHERE *operator*

If you do not specify the WHERE *operator* portion, the operator is assumed to be equal (=).

You may use any of the following operators with the WHERE clause:

OPERATOR	MEANING
=	Equal
< >	Not equal
>	Greater than
> =	Greater than or equal to
<	Less than
< =	Less than or equal to

Figure 14.11 gives an example of the JOIN command used with the Equal (=) operator. Since the Names and Charges tables both have a column named CustNo, we'll demonstrate this command with a hypothetical database.

Suppose that you have a database with two tables, one named Sales and the other named Commiss. The Sales table contains salespersons'

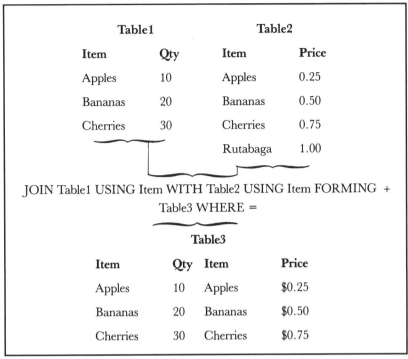

Figure 14.11: An example of the JOIN command with the Equal (=) operator

names and sales amounts, as below:

NAME	*SALE*
Andrews	$12,500.00
Baker	$17,000.00
Carlson	$10,000.00
Edwards	$5,000.00
Davis	$45,000.00

The Commiss table contains commission rates and cutoff values, starting with a base rate of 15 percent for any sale that's at least $10,000, and adding another 2 percent of the total for larger sales, as below:

SALESAMT	C_RATE
$10,000.00	0.15
$15,000.00	0.02
$20,000.00	0.02
$25,000.00	0.02

We want to use the JOIN command to combine the Sales table with the Commiss table. We'll use the Sale and SalesAmt columns for comparison and form a new table named "Rates." For the comparison, we'll use the greater than or equal to operator ($>=$). To do this, issue the command

> JOIN Sales USING Sale WITH Commiss USING SalesAmt +
> +> FORMING Rates WHERE >=

The resulting Rates table is listed below:

NAME	SALE	SALESAMT	C_RATE
Andrews	$12,500.00	$10,000.00	0.15
Baker	$17,000.00	$10,000.00	0.15
Baker	$17,000.00	$15,000.00	0.02
Carlson	$10,000.00	$10,000.00	0.15
Davis	$45,000.00	$10,000.00	0.15
Davis	$45,000.00	$15,000.00	0.02
Davis	$45,000.00	$20,000.00	0.02
Davis	$45,000.00	$25,000.00	0.02

Notice that Mr. Anderson receives a 15 percent commission for his $12,500 sale; Mr. Baker receives 15 percent, plus another 2 percent, for his $17,000 sale; and Mr. Davis receives 15 percent, plus another 6 percent (2 percent three times) for his $45,000 sale. Displaying this table without the SalesAmt column, but instead displaying the total commission, makes the table clearer. For proof, see Figure 14.12.

```
R>SELECT Name Sale C_Rate (Sale × C_Rate) FROM Rates
Name      Sale            C_Rate   (Sale × C_Rate)
--------- --------------- -------- ----------------
Andrews     $12,500.00     0.15       $1,875.00
Baker       $17,000.00     0.15       $2,550.00
Baker       $17,000.00     0.02         $340.00
Carlson     $10,000.00     0.15       $1,500.00
Davis       $45,000.00     0.15       $6,750.00
Davis       $45,000.00     0.02         $900.00
Davis       $45,000.00     0.02         $900.00
Davis       $45,000.00     0.02         $900.00
R>
```

Figure 14.12: Rows from the Rates table, including a computed column

Notice that the JOIN command creates a row for each comparison that satisfies the WHERE operator. Davis is listed four times because his $45,000 sale is greater than or equal to all of the SalesAmt figures in the Commiss table. However, Edward's $5000 sale was not included in the Rates table, because it was not greater than or equal to any of the SalesAmt cutoff values in the Commiss table.

Finally, note that you could also use the SUBTRACT command to determine lackluster sales performance. By subtracting the Rates table from the Sales table, using the command

SUBTRACT Rates FROM Sales FORMING Temp

you can isolate those salespeople who do not appear on the Rates table in a new table named Temp. Edwards is the only entry in the Temp table, since he hasn't made a sale big enough to merit a commission.

CONSTRUCTING VIEWS

We've already talked about views in general terms in Chapters 10 and 12, but because of their usefulness, we should spend a bit more time going over them in depth now. A view, you will remember, is a pseudo-table that does not contain data of its own but displays data from up to five related tables. The tables in a view must have at least one key column (with the same column name, width, and data type) in common. Once you have created a view, you can view data through it as you would any other table. For example, you can use the view with the SELECT command and the ORDER BY and WHERE clauses. Or, you can use the view as a table for creating report formats in the Report Generator.

There are limitations on views, however. Since a view only displays data from existing tables, you cannot enter data directly into it. Nor can you edit data through the view except in the special case of single-table views. For that matter, you cannot create forms for a view at all. Instead, you'll want to enter and edit data through the actual tables from which the view gets its data. Nonetheless, a view is a convenient and dynamic tool for viewing data from multiple tables quickly and easily.

For this exercise, we'll create a view that displays the customer number, product number, quantity, tax status, unit price, transaction total, and date of sale from the Charges table, along with the appropriate last name, first name, and company from the Names table. We will use the customer number to *link* the two tables, so that the view only adds information from the Names table to the corresponding row in the Charges table. To further demonstrate the power of views, we'll limit the view to customers in the state of California (although R:BASE does not require that you place such limits on views). We'll name the view "CaTrans" (for California Transactions).

DEFINING A MULTI-TABLE VIEW

Let's define this view starting from the Query screen as you did back in Chapter 12 when you created the Saleview view. In Chapter 5, you defined a query on the Query screen and then pressed F2 to see the data selected by the query on the Edit screen. Once the query displays the data you want in your view, you can save the query as a view. Follow these steps now to construct the CaTrans view:

1. To display the Edit screen for the Charges table, type **EDIT ALL FROM Charges** and press ←⏎.

2. To display the Query screen, press **Ctrl-F3**. Note that all of the columns in the Charges table are included in the Query—you can tell because the check mark (✔) is beside each column name.

3. Add the Names table to the Query screen by highlighting **Q**uery, selecting **A**dd tables, and selecting **Names**.

4. To add the L_Name, F_Name, Company, and State columns in the Names table to the query, move the highlighter to the L_Name column and press **F6**; move to the F_Name column and press **F6**; move to the Company column and press **F6**; and move to the State column and press **F6**. Note the check mark beside each of the column names you chose.

5. Now enter the condition that the State has to be California (CA). With the highlighter in the State column, press ◄─┘; select = EQUAL; type **CA**; and press ◄─┘.

6. To set up the customer number columns as link columns, press **Shift-F7** to move up to the Charges table; with the highlighter in the CustNo column, highlight **Q**uery; select **L**ink tables; select = EQUAL; press **Shift-F8** to move down to the Names table; move to the CustNo column; and press ◄─┘. R:BASE has marked the CustNo column for the Charges table with " = <link1>" and the CustNo column for the Names table with "<link1>". Your screen should now look like Figure 14.13.

Notice that you are not allowed to change any data using this Edit screen, since the Query includes more than one table.

7. See whether this query displays the information you want by pressing **F2** to display the Edit screen. By moving around the table, you can see that this query displays the columns you want and includes only charges for customers from California.

8. To create the view that corresponds to this query, press **Ctrl-F3** to return to the Query screen; highlight **Q**uery; select the **S**ave this query as a view option; type CaTrans; and press ◄─┘.

9. To return to the R> prompt, highlight and select **E**xit.

DISPLAYING DATA WITH A VIEW

You can display the data in the CaTrans view with a SELECT command by using the name of the view (that is, CaTrans) in place of

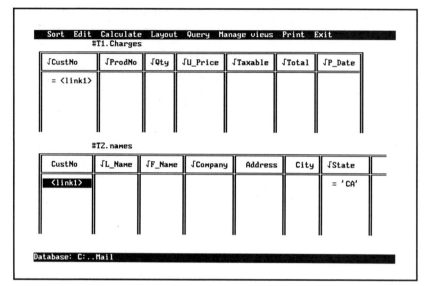

Figure 14.13: Defining the CaTrans view on the Query screen

a particular table name. For example, suppose you want to see all the transactions for California residents, with name, company, and state for each transaction, sorted into ascending product number order and descending total order. The command below will show the information you want.

```
SELECT ProdNo = 6 Qty = 4 U_Price = 8 Total = 8  +
+> CustNo = 6 L_Name = 7 F_Name = 7 Company = 16 State  +
+> FROM CaTrans ORDER BY ProdNo Qty DESC
```

The results of this SELECT command are shown in Figure 14.14.

As you saw in Chapter 12, you can also use a view as the basis for a report. When you start the Report Generator, select CaTrans as the name of the table supplying data for the report.

VIEWS COMPARED WITH INTERSECT TABLES

Some of you may have wondered about the relationship between a view and tables created with the INTERSECT or UNION commands. At the beginning of the chapter you saw the difference

```
R>SELECT ProdNo=6 Qty=4 U_Price=8 Total=8 +
+>CustNo=6 L_Name=7 F_Name=7 Company=16 State +
+>FROM CaTrans ORDER BY ProdNo Qty DESC
 ProdNo Qty  U_Price  Total    CustNo L_Name F_Name Company            State
 ------ ---  -------  -------  ------ ------ ------ -----------------  -----
 A-111  12   $10.00   $127.20   1001 Miller  Anne   Golden Gate Co.    CA
 A-111  10   $10.00   $106.00   1002 Adams   Bart   DataSpec Inc.      CA
 A-111  10   $10.00   $106.00   1006 Baker   Robin  Peach Computers    CA
 A-111   5   $10.00    $53.00   1003 Miller  Marie  Zeerox Inc.        CA
 A-111   5   $10.00    $53.00   1004 Jones   Mindy  ABC Co.            CA
 A-123  10    $5.50    $58.30   1001 Miller  Anne   Golden Gate Co.    CA
 A-128  10   $12.80   $128.00   1004 Jones   Mindy  ABC Co.            CA
 B-222  12   $12.50   $159.00   1002 Adams   Bart   DataSpec Inc.      CA
 B-222   5   $12.50    $66.25   1001 Miller  Anne   Golden Gate Co.    CA
 C-434   2  $100.00   $212.00   1001 Miller  Anne   Golden Gate Co.    CA
 Z-128  10   $12.80   $128.00   1006 Baker   Robin  Peach Computers    CA
R>
```

Figure 14.14: A display from the CaTrans view

You can see a comprehensive help screen for CREATE VIEW by typing HELP CREATE and pressing ↵ at the R> prompt. Next, select VIEW from the CREATE help screen.

You cannot use the CREATE VIEW command to update an existing view. To modify a view with CREATE VIEW, you would first DROP the existing view and then enter a new CREATE VIEW command that incorporated the desired updates.

between the INTERSECT and UNION commands when you created a new table with the ProdNo, CustNo, L_Name, F_Name, Qty, and U_Price columns. The UNION command was more comprehensive, yielding a new table that included all rows from both tables. On the other hand, the new table created with INTERSECT only included rows if there was matching data from both of the parent tables. How does a view work?

To make the comparison, let's create a view that parallels these tables. You can do that either with the Query screen or directly from the R> prompt with the CREATE VIEW command. A simplified syntax for the CREATE VIEW command is the following:

CREATE VIEW *view name* AS SELECT *column list* FROM +
+> *table list* WHERE *conditions*

To create a view called Newview, enter the command

CREATE VIEW Newview AS SELECT ProdNo, #T1.CustNo, +
+> L_Name, F_Name, Qty, U_Price FROM Charges #T1, +
+> Names #T2 WHERE (#T1.CustNo = #T2.CustNo)

The #T1 and #T2 in this command are called *correlation names.* You use them to tell R:BASE which table you are referring to when more than one table has the same column name. The phrase "FROM Charges #T1, Names #T2" sets up #T1 as the correlation name for the Charges table and #T2 as the correlation name for the Names table. Then #T1.CustNo refers to the CustNo column in the Charges table and #T2.CustNo is the CustNo column in the Names table.

To see the rows in Newview, enter the command

```
SELECT ProdNo CustNo L_Name = 10 F_Name = 10 +
+> Qty = 4 U_Price = 8 FROM Newview
```

By comparing the rows with those in Figure 14.9, you'll see they're the same.

Although the view you created seems to yield the same result as an INTERSECT command, there is one important difference. When you create a new table with INTERSECT, you are in effect taking a snapshot of the two parent table's contents at a given moment. If you make additions to either of the parent tables, you'll have to enter another INTERSECT command if you need to have the new data in a single table. A view, however, is dynamic. Any changes in the parent tables are automatically recognized by the view.

You may want to remove the view Newview by typing

```
DROP VIEW Newview
```

CREATING A FORM LETTER REPORT WITH A VIEW

Let's assume that your friend in the book business wants to follow up on a new product line he's been marketing. His company wants to write each of its California customers a personal letter to see how they like the products they've purchased. This is a job for the Report Generator. However, before jumping into the report, you need to choose the table or view upon which to base the report. We need the following information: client name, address, city, state, ZIP code, and the types of products purchased by that client. The CaTrans view has everything we need except the address, city, and ZIP code. Why not just modify it? No problem. We can use the Query screen to modify our view.

MODIFYING A VIEW

To add the extra columns to your view, use the following steps beginning at the R > prompt:

1. Display the Query screen directly by typing **QUERY** and pressing ⏎.

2. To begin modifying the CaTrans view, highlight **M**anage views; select **M**odify; select **C**aTrans; and reply **Y**es when asked if you want to retrieve the new query.

3. Now add the address, city, and ZIP code. Press **Shift-F8** to move to the Names table; move to the Address column and press **F6**; move to the City column and press **F6**; and move to the Zip_Code column and press **F6**.

4. To save the changes and return to the R > prompt, highlight and select **E**xit; choose **Y**es to saving this query as a view; press ⏎ to confirm CaTrans as the view to save; and reply **Y**es to overwriting the CaTrans view.

Now you're ready to create the form letter report.

MERGING A FORM LETTER WITH R:BASE

As we mentioned in Chapter 12, you can create form letters with the Report Generator. To do this, you type the body of the letter as text in the report and supply the *variable information*—the information that changes from one letter to the next, such as the inside address and salutation—as columns or variables. In the next exercise, we will create a form letter called "CaLetter." It will be based on the CaTrans view which we defined in the previous section. Figure 14.15 shows the sample letter.

```
                                              Oct 19, 1990
Anne Miller
Golden Gate Co.
2313 Sixth St.
Berkeley
CA 94711

Dear Anne Miller:

Our records indicate that you have purchased the following products
from us:

          A-123
          A-111
          B-222
          C-434

We want to know how you like them.  Please take a moment to fill
out the enclosed questionnaire and mail it in the postage-paid
envelope we've included.

Our aim is to provide you with the best products at the lowest
prices.  Ensuring your satisfaction is our goal.

Sincerely,



Bob Smith, President
ABC Company
```

Figure 14.15: A sample letter from the CaLetter report

The CaTrans view has multiple rows for customers who've ordered more than one item, but we don't want to send customers multiple copies of the letter. What can we do? One solution is to make CustNo the first breakpoint and to locate most of the letter on the H1 and F1 lines. Then we can locate ProdNo on a single Detail line. The report will then print a single letter for each customer, but list all the items they've charged.

In this report, we will need two variables:

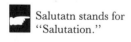
Salutatn stands for "Salutation."

FullName = (F_Name & L_Name)
Salutatn = (.FullName + ':')

You are now ready to create the CaLetter report. The following steps outline the procedure involved, starting at the R > prompt:

See Chapter 12 if you need to review some of the techniques involved in creating a report.

1. To display the Report Generator screen for the CaLetter report, type **REPORTS** and press ←⎯; select **C**ustom report; enter **CaLetter** for the report name and **California**

Form Letter for the report description; and select **Ca** Trans as the driving table.

2. Define the following two variables:

   FullName = (F_Name & L_Name)
   Salutatn = (.FullName + ':')

3. Remove the report header, page header, page footer, and report footer lines.

4. Create a breakpoint on CustNo, entering **Y**es in the FORM FEEDS before header column.

5. Create the break header. To the initial break header line, add twelve more lines to expand the H1 section to thirteen lines.

6. Create the break footer. To the initial break footer line, add thirteen more lines to expand the F1 section to fourteen lines.

7. Type the text below onto the screen.

START	*TEXT*
< 9:28, 10>	**Dear**
<11:28, 10>	**Our records indicate that you have purchased the following products**
<12:28, 10>	**from us:**
<16:28, 10>	**We want to know how you like them. Please take a moment to fill**
<17:28, 10>	**out the enclosed questionnaire and mail it in the postage-paid**
<18:28, 10>	**envelope we've included.**
<20:28, 10>	**Our aim is to provide you with the best products at the lowest**
<21:28, 10>	**prices. Ensuring your satisfaction is our goal.**
<23:28, 10>	**Sincerely,**
<27:28, 10>	**Bob Smith, President**
<28:28, 10>	**ABC Company**

8. Place the following columns and variables in the positions indicated:

COLUMN OR VARIABLE	START	END
#DATE	< 1:28, 55 >	< 1:28, 66 >
FullName	< 3:28, 10 >	< 3:28, 40 >
Company	< 4:28, 10 >	< 4:28, 34 >
Address	< 5:28, 10 >	< 5:28, 34 >
City	< 6:28, 10 >	< 6:28, 24 >
State	< 7:28, 10 >	< 7:28, 11 >
Zip_Code	< 7:28, 13 >	< 7:28, 22 >
Salutatn	< 9:28, 15 >	< 9:28, 45 >
ProdNo	<14:28, 20 >	<14:28, 27 >

9. Add a picture format to the #DATE field so that dates are printed in MMM DD, YYYY format.

10. Press **Home** to move to the top-left corner of the report, and compare your screen with Figure 14.16. Make any changes you think are necessary to make your screen look like the figure.

11. Save and test your report by previewing it to the screen. Compare your output with Figure 14.15. If changes are required, preview after the changes until you are satisfied with the report.

12. Leave the Report Generator and return to the R > prompt.

If you want, you can try printing the form letter from the R > prompt with the PRINT CaLetter command.

DATABASE MAINTENANCE TIPS

Those of you who have done the exercises in this chapter may have noticed that your Mail2.RBF file has grown considerably. That's

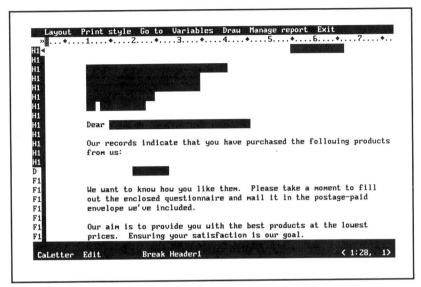

Figure 14.16: The definition of the form letter report

because when you remove a table from a database, R:BASE doesn't automatically free the disk space that was used by the data. For that matter, it doesn't free the disk space used by rows that have subsequently been deleted from a table, either. R:BASE provides two different commands that squeeze unused disk space from your database, but before you use either of them, you should back up your database.

BACKING UP AND RESTORING A DATABASE

In Chapter 6 you learned to use the COPY and BACKUP commands to back up your database, either from within R:BASE or directly from the operating system. To decide which command to use, you should look at the size of your database files and compare them with the capacity of your floppy disks. (Generally, it's not a good idea to back up a database onto the same hard disk it's already on, because this wouldn't help if your hard disk ''crashed.'') If none of your database files is larger than the capacity of a floppy disk, it's easiest simply to back up your database onto floppies with the COPY command.

But if your database is too large for floppies, you'll have to use either R:BASE's or DOS's BACKUP command. We recommend R:BASE's, because it's optimized to back up R:BASE databases. To back up your open database, prepare a stack of formatted floppy disks, put one of them into your floppy drive, and type

```
SET NULL –0–
OUTPUT filespec
BACKUP ALL
OUTPUT SCREEN
```

The SET NULL -0-
command ensures
that R:BASE handles
null values properly when
you perform a backup or
a restore. In Chapter 17,
you'll set NULL to a
different value when
printing a report. If you
or someone else forgot to
set NULL back to -0-,
the backup would not
handle null values
correctly.

where *filespec* is the name of the backup file, such as A:Names.BAK. If your database is large, you'll be prompted to insert additional disks. Be sure to number your disks as Backup disk #1, Backup disk #2, and so on. Don't be surprised if the backed up version of your database takes up less space than you expected—the database files are compressed during the BACKUP procedure.

If you need to use the backed up version of your database, erase the existing version of the database from your hard disk, put Backup disk #1 in your floppy drive, and from the R > prompt type

```
SET NULL –0–
RESTORE filespec
```

where *filespec* is the name of your backup file. For example, a backup file name could be A:Names.BAK. As before, R:BASE will prompt you to change disks if necessary.

RECOVERING UNUSED DISK SPACE

To recover unused disk space that results from DELETE and DROP commands, you can choose between two R:BASE commands, PACK and RELOAD. The easiest, PACK, is also the riskiest, because PACK acts on the actual database files you specify. For example, if you have one copy of the Mail database on your hard disk, and you want to squeeze unused disk space out of it, you could type

```
CONNECT Mail
PACK
```

R:BASE will remind you to backup your database before you pack it. The program will also ask you to confirm if you want to continue with the PACK command.

Generally, R:BASE will simply pack the database and give you a new version of the Mail database that takes up less space. However, if an error or machine malfunction occurs during the PACK, you could end up with an unusable version of Mail. Without a backup copy of Mail, you'd be out of luck. The virtues of the PACK command are that it is fast and it will execute even if you don't have much free space on your hard disk.

The second method is to use R:BASE's RELOAD command. Since RELOAD makes an entirely new copy of the database, you need to have sufficient hard disk space to accommodate the new copy of the database. The RELOAD command differs from the PACK command in another way, too. RELOAD not only removes unused disk space from your database files, it also optimizes them; and in so doing it places all rows from a given table in a single area on your hard disk. If you wanted to RELOAD your Mail database, you could type

CONNECT Mail
RELOAD Mailbak

and have R:BASE create a database called Mailbak in the default directory. Before erasing the Mail files, however, you should CON-NECT Mailbak, and use the LIST and SELECT commands to be sure the Mailbak database is intact. Then, after erasing the Mail files, you could use the RENAME command to change the names of the Mailbak1.RBF file to Mail1.RBF, Mailbak2.RBF to Mail2.RBF, and Mailbak3.RBF to Mail3.RBF.

In this chapter, we've looked at R:BASE's six relational commands: PROJECT, INSERT, UNION, INTERSECT, SUB-TRACT, and JOIN. We've also looked at some new techniques for views, printing form letters, and backing up files. With the next chapter, we'll start developing all the techniques you've learned so far into a unified application.

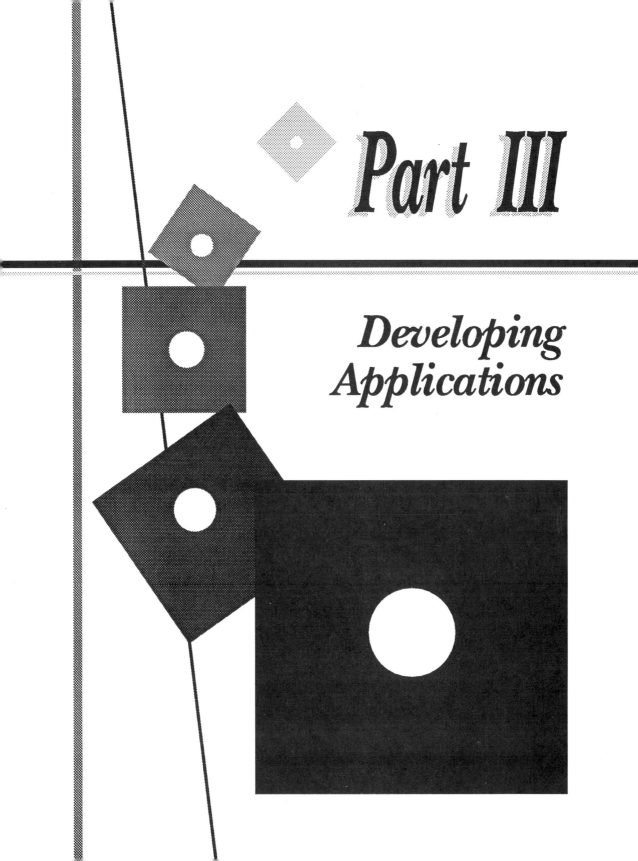

Part III

Developing Applications

Chapter 15

Creating Your own Custom-Made Applications

IN THIS CHAPTER, WE'LL LEARN TECHNIQUES FOR organizing all the tables, forms, and reports in a database into a unified *application*. While R:BASE is a general database-management system, an application is a system of menus that manages all aspects of a specific database for a particular task. For example, an application may manage a mailing, accounts receivable, general ledger, or inventory system.

The real advantage of an application is that it allows even a novice user to manage a database by using a series of menus, rather than by typing commands. As you'll learn in this chapter, R:BASE applications are easy to develop since R:BASE contains an Application Generator (called Applications EXPRESS) that is similar to the Form Generator and Report Generator. In fact, you can create applications more quickly and efficiently with R:BASE than you can with most database-management systems.

The best way to understand how applications work is to develop and use one. In this chapter, we'll develop a sample application called "MailSys" using the familiar Mail database.

DESIGNING AN APPLICATION

Try to create menu structures that other users can understand intuitively.

Once you've designed and developed the tables, forms, and reports that you want to use in a database, designing the application simply involves defining a *hierarchical structure* of menus. Figure 15.1 shows the menu structure that we'll use to manage the Names and Charges tables in the Mail database. Notice how the options are arranged logically, with general topics at the top of the hierarchy and particular topics at the bottom. When you design your application, try to put yourself in the place of the person who will use it. Try to create a menu structure that the novice user can understand intuitively.

The Main menu in the figure presents three options: 1, Manage Customer List (meaning the Names table); 2, Manage Charges List (meaning the Charges table); and 3, Exit (meaning that you want to leave the MailSys application). If the user selects menu option 1, SubMenu 1 is displayed on the screen. From this menu, the user can select from several options to add new data to the Names table, edit the table, print any of three different reports, or return to the Main

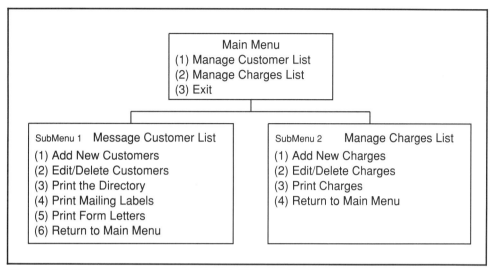

Figure 15.1: The menu structure for the MailSys application

Menu. Similarly, if the user selects option 2, a submenu for managing the Charges table is displayed on the screen.

You can design your menu system in any way that you wish. For example, you could include an option on the Main menu for printing reports, and group all the various report options under a separate menu. Also, you can create sub-submenus below submenus. Finally, and perhaps most importantly, you can always change your mind and redesign your application at any time. You can add new menus, change menu items, and even insert new options into existing menus. This is important because application development is usually an iterative process, and perfecting an application usually involves making many enhancements and refinements.

Once you have decided what menu items you will need, the next step is to decide which type of menu you want. You can choose from pull-down, pop-up, vertical or horizontal menus.

> **Pull-down menus**—offer choices along a bar at the top of the screen, with submenus underneath the menu options, like the R:BASE Main menu. The submenu choices associated with a menu option are displayed when the option is highlighted.

You can have three levels of menus: the main menu; submenus, which are displayed when options on the main menu are selected; and sub-submenus, which are displayed when an option on a submenu is selected.

Titles are not displayed on pull-down menus. A pull-down menu can offer as many as six options on the menu bar across the top, with each option being as long as 12 characters. The pull-down submenus can have up to nineteen options, each option being as long as 27 characters.

Pop-up menus—appear in a box that covers part of the screen; you are allowed one choice per line in the box. On the R:BASE Main menu and submenus, choices followed by a double arrow (») display pop-up menus. Pop-up menus include a title and can display up to nineteen options, each as long as 60 characters. The title is displayed in the status lines at the bottom of the screen.

Vertical menus—offer numbered choices arranged one per line. Vertical menus can include a title at the top and up to nine choices, each as long as 60 characters. The Prompt By Example (PBE) Main menu is an example of a vertical menu.

Horizontal menus—offer options arranged in rows across the screen. Most of the PBE menus other than the Main menu are horizontal menus. These menus can include a title at the top and up to twelve options, each option as long as 10 characters.

The best choice for our menu would be a vertical menu. This way, we can place a title at the top and we'll have adequate space for a description of each option on the menu.

DEVELOPING AN APPLICATION

Once you've sketched the menu choices for your application and chosen which type of menu to use, you are ready to start building the application. When you develop an application, you start the process as follows:

1. Highlight Create and select New application from the Applications EXPRESS menu. If you are not connected to a database, R:BASE will ask you to choose the database

that contains the reports, forms, etc. that will make up your application.

2. Enter the application name.

Now you are ready to define the top level menu. R:BASE will guide you through the general steps, which are summarized below.

Specifying the menu colors is optional. If you don't specify the menu colors, the menu will be displayed in the same colors as the R:BASE menus.

1. Enter general information such as the menu name, menu type, menu colors, and—if it's appropriate for the type of menu you chose—the location and size of the menu on the screen.

2. If the type of menu you chose can have a title, enter the title.

3. Enter the description for each menu option.

4. Choose whether you want the user to be able to press Esc to exit the menu.

5. Enter a help screen for the menu if you want.

6. Define an action for R:BASE to perform when each menu option is chosen. Depending on the type of action, this might mean specifying sorting and searching criteria; or, if the action is a submenu, entering the type, colors, and title for the submenu as well as the descriptions for each submenu option.

In step 4 above, you would chose whether or not you want the user to be able to press Esc to exit the menu. We recommend that you allow the Esc key to be used to exit a menu. Although each of your menus will probably include an exit option, there is certainly no harm in being able to press Esc to exit the menu as well. Besides, if a menu is full and there isn't room for an Exit option, letting the user press Esc to exit the menu solves the space problem.

In step 6 above, to help you define which action to perform when each menu option is chosen, R:BASE offers you a menu of actions to choose from. The action choices are summarized in Table 15.1 (you'll learn more about them later in this chapter).

Table 15.1: Actions that You Can Assign to Customized Menu Options

ACTION	EQUIVALENT R:BASE COMMAND	MEANING
Load	ENTER USING	Enter new data into a table
Edit	EDIT USING	Edit and delete data using a predefined form
Delete	DELETE	Globally delete rows from a table
Modify	EDIT	Edit and delete rows using an Edit screen
Select	SELECT	Look up specific information in a table
Print Reports	PRINT	Print a report
Print Labels	LBLPRINT	Print labels
Menu		Build a submenu for this menu option
Custom		Develop a custom action for this menu option
Macro		Use a predefined custom action
Template		Access a custom procedure
Password		Initiate a password
Exit		Exit this menu

Once you've finished defining the top level menu, you will begin defining the lower level menus. For each submenu accessed with an option on the top level menu, R:BASE once again guides you through the definition process, as follows:

1. Choose whether you want the user to be able to press Esc to exit the submenu.

2. Enter a help screen for the submenu if you want to.

3. Define an action for R:BASE to perform when each submenu option is chosen. As you did for the top level menu, you will specify sorting and searching details where appropriate. If the option you are defining is a sub-submenu of this submenu, you will enter the menu type, colors, title, and option descriptions for the sub-submenu.

When you have finished defining all of the menus in your application, you have a few final details to specify.

1. If you choose to, change the default settings for screen colors, status messages, and error messages for your application. You may also choose to have R:BASE beep when errors occur.

2. Indicate whether you want this application to be run automatically when you start R:BASE.

You can tell R:BASE to perform more than one action when a menu option is chosen. For our purposes, though, we will define only one action for each option on the MailSys application menus. Some of the more advanced actions in Table 15.1, such as Custom, Macro, Template, and Password, will be more meaningful to you after we discuss the R:BASE programming language in the next chapter. For now, however, the other options are sufficient for developing the MailSys application.

See Figure 15.1 for a list of the menu options we'll need for the MailSys application.

Determining which action to assign to each menu option in the MailSys application is easy enough. A glance at Table 15.1 tells you that the Load action fits our application's Add New Customers options, that the Edit action does well for the Edit/Delete Customers option, that the Print Reports action matches Print Charges on the application, that the Print Labels action fits the Prints Mailing Labels options, and that the Exit action will do the job for the Return to the Main Menu option.

The Edit/Delete Customers and Edit/Delete Charges as well as the various Print options on the MailSys menus can be specified with sorting and searching criteria. For example, we could sort customers by last and first name when editing or deleting customers or printing a directory, and by ZIP code when printing mailing labels or form letters. And it might be useful to enter search conditions so that only customers with a particular last name will be presented in the Edit/Delete Customers option. R:BASE allows us to define these search conditions so that the person selecting the Edit/Delete Customers menu item can enter the last name of customers to be edited. For menu items involving editing/ deleting and printing charges, we could sort the charges by customer number.

CREATING A SAMPLE APPLICATION

Let's develop our MailSys application now. Starting from the R:BASE Main menu,

If you make a mistake in Applications EXPRESS, pressing Esc will often give you a chance to correct it before continuing. You can start over at the Applications EXPRESS menu without saving an application by pressing Ctrl-Break or Ctrl-C.

1. Connect to the Mail database if necessary, and enter the owner password MYMAIL.

2. Display the Applications EXPRESS menu from the R:BASE Main menu by highlighting **A**pplications and selecting **C**reate/modify.

From the R> prompt, you could display the Applications EXPRESS menu by typing **EXPRESS** and pressing ←.

3. With **C**reate highlighted, select **N**ew application; and type **MailSys** and press ← for the name of this application.

Defining the Main Menu

You are now ready to start defining the MailSys Main Menu. Remember, the first two options on the Main Menu bring up submenus. When you define the actions for those two Main Menu options, you will have to choose a menu type and enter the text of the submenus. To start defining the Main Menu,

If the Mail database is not open, you are given an opportunity to open it and enter the owner password. If the current password is not the owner password, you are asked to enter the owner password.

4. Press ← to confirm **Main** as the name of the Main menu; select **V**ertical; reply **N**o to customizing menu colors, and type **Main Menu** and press ← for the menu title.

5. To enter the description of each menu option, type **Manage Customer List** and press ←; type **Manage Charges List** and press ←; and type **Exit**. Compare your screen to Figure 15.2. Press **F2** now that you've finished entering the text on the Main Menu.

6. Choose **Yes** when asked if you want to be able to press Esc to exit this menu, and choose **No** to creating a help screen.

See Table 15.1 for a description of the action choices you can assign to menu options.

R:BASE displays a menu of action choices you can assign to menu options, as shown in Figure 15.3. Notice that (1) is highlighted in the menu at the top of the screen. This indicates you are defining menu actions for the (1) Manage Customer List option on the Main Menu. To define the action for the (1) Manage Customer List option,

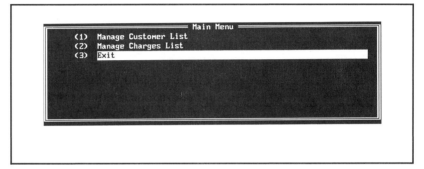

Figure 15.2: The Main Menu of the MailSys application

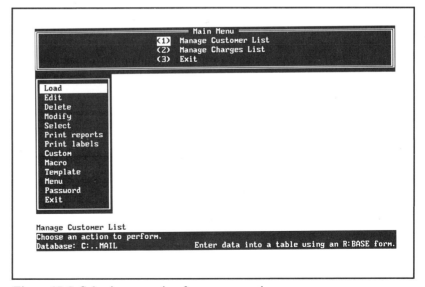

Figure 15.3: Selecting an action for a menu option

7. Select **Menu** from the pop-up menu on the left; type **Sub-Menu1** and press ← for the name of the submenu; choose **Vertical** as the submenu type; choose **No** to customizing colors for the submenu; type **Manage Customer List** as the submenu title. To enter the descriptions of the options on this submenu, type **Add New Customers** and press ←; type **Edit/Delete Customers** and press ←; type **Print the Directory** and press ←; type **Print Mailing Labels** and press ←; type **Print Form Letters** and press ←; type **Return to Main Menu**; and press **F2**. Reply **No** when asked if you want to define another action for the (1) Manage Customer List option on the Main Menu.

Notice that the (2) is highlighted. This tells you that you are defining menu actions for the (2) Manage Charges List option on the Main Menu. To define the action for the (2) Manage Charges List option,

8. Select **Menu** from the pop-up menu on the left; type **Sub-Menu2** and press ← for the name of the submenu; choose **Vertical** as the type of the submenu; choose **No** to customizing colors for the submenu; type **Manage Charges List** as the submenu title. To enter the descriptions of the options on this submenu, type **Add New Charges** and press ←; type **Edit/Delete Charges** and press ←; type **Print Charges** and press ←; type **Return to Main Menu**; and press **F2**. Reply **No** when asked if you want to define another action for the (2) Manage Charges List option on the Main Menu.

9. To define the action for the (3) Exit option, select **Exit** from the pop-up menu on the left.

Defining the Submenus

Now the MailSys Main Menu is completely specified. Applications EXPRESS asks you to finish defining the first submenu, Manage Customer List.

10. For the Manage Customer List submenu, choose **Yes** to allow users to press the Esc key to exit the menu; and reply **No** to creating a help screen.

11. To define the action for the (1) Add New Customers option on the Manage Customer List submenu, select **Load**; select **Names**; select **Namesfrm**; reply **No** to editing the form; and reply **No** to defining another action for this menu option.

Instead of choosing Namesfrm as the form to use for adding new customers, you could choose (New) and define a new form using the Form Generator.

12. To define the action for the (2) Edit/Delete Customers option on the Manage Customer List submenu, select **Edit**; select **Names**; select **Namesfrm**; and reply **No** to editing the form. To specify the sort criteria for the rows presented for editing, select **L_Name**, **Ascending**, **F_Name**, and **Ascending**; and press **F2**. To specify search conditions which determine which rows are presented for editing, select **L_Name** and = **EQUAL**; reply **Yes** to the user entering a comparison value; press **F2**; type **Enter last name of customer to edit:** and press ◄─┘ for the prompt message, and select (Done). Finally, reply **No** to defining another action for this menu option.

13. To define the action for the (3) Print the Directory option on the Manage Customer List submenu, select **Print reports**; select **Names**; select **Director**; and reply **No** to editing the report. To specify sort criteria, select **L_Name**, **Ascending**, **F_Name**, and **Ascending**; and press **F2**. Press **F2** to skip the choice of search criteria. Reply **No** to defining another action for this menu option.

14. To define the action for the (4) Print Mailing Labels option on the Manage Customer List submenu, select **Print labels**; select **Names**; select **Nameslbl**; and reply **No** to editing the label. To specify sort criteria, select **Zip_Code** and **Ascending**; and press **F2**. Press **F2** to skip the choice of search criteria. Reply **No** to defining another action for this menu option.

15. To define the action for the (5) Print Form Letters option on the Manage Customer List submenu, select **Print**

reports; select **Ca**Trans; select **Ca**Letter; and reply **N**o to editing the report. To specify sort criteria, select **Z**ip_Code and **A**scending; and press **F2**. Press **F2** to skip the choice of search criteria. Reply **N**o to defining another action for this menu option.

16. To define the action for the (6) Return to Main Menu option on the Manage Customer List submenu, select **E**xit.

With the Manage Customer List submenu completed, Applications EXPRESS asks you to finish defining the Manage Charges List submenu.

17. For the Manage Charges List submenu, choose **Y**es to allow users to press the Esc key to exit the menu; reply **N**o to creating a help screen.

18. To define the action for the (1) Add New Charges option on the Manage Charges List submenu, select **L**oad; select **C**harges; select **C**hrgfrm; reply **N**o to editing the form; and reply **N**o to defining another action for this menu option.

19. To define the action for the (2) Edit/Delete Charges option on the Manage Charges List submenu, select **M**odify; select **C**harges; and press **Shift-F6** to select all columns to be displayed on the Edit screen and press **F2**. To specify the sort criteria, select **C**ustNo and **A**scending; and press **F2**. Press **F2** to skip the choice of search criteria. Reply **N**o to defining another action for this menu option.

20. To define the action for the (3) Print Charges option on the Manage Charges List submenu, select **P**rint reports; select **C**harges; select **S**ales; and reply **N**o to editing the report. To specify the sort criteria, select **C**ustNo and **A**scending; and press **F2**. Press **F2** to skip the choice of search criteria. Reply **N**o to defining another action for this menu option.

21. To define the action for the (4) Return to Main Menu option on the Manage Charges List submenu, select **E**xit.

So far, you have defined all of the menus in this application, and specified what action to take for each option on each menu. You now have only a few more details to specify and you will be done!

22. Reply **N**o to changing the default settings.

R:BASE now writes a long *program* based on the information you have provided for the MailSys application—that is, R:BASE creates three files that store the details about the MailSys application:

- MailSys.API stores the choices you made with Applications EXPRESS as you created the application. MailSys.API is not stored in ASCII, which means you can't use the TYPE command to display the information it stores. R:BASE will use this file when you modify your application with Applications EXPRESS.

- MailSys.APX is the program that Applications EXPRESS creates. MailSys.APX, like MailSys.API, is not stored in ASCII. You will see how to run the MailSys.APX file to execute your application in the next section in this chapter.

- MailSys.APP is an ASCII version of the program in MailSys.APX. After you have some experience with programming in Chapter 16, you will be able to look at the MailSys.APP file and figure out how Applications EXPRESS constructed your application.

23. Reply **N**o to creating a startup file for your new application.

If you replied Yes and created a startup file, the MailSys application would automatically start running whenever you start R:BASE. Instead of the R:BASE Main menu, you would see the Main Menu of the MailSys application. When you exit from the MailSys application, you would leave R:BASE and return to DOS. However, you did not request a startup file, you will see the R:BASE Main menu the next time you start R:BASE.

24. Highlight and select **E**xit to return to the R:BASE Main menu.

RUNNING AN APPLICATION

There are two ways to run applications: from the Main menu, and the R > prompt. For example, to run the MailSys application from the R:BASE Main menu, you highlight Applications and select MailSys. To run it from the R > prompt, you type RUN MailSys IN MailSys.APX and press ←. Since we are at the R:BASE Main menu, let's start the application by highlighting Applications and selecting MailSys. The Main Menu for the MailSys application appears on the screen (see Figure 15.2). Let's take our system for a test drive and see how easy it is to use.

1. Select option **1**, Manage Customer List, to manage the Names table. The submenu we created will appear, as shown in Figure 15.4.

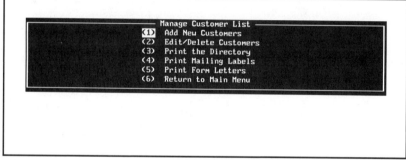

Figure 15.4: The submenu for managing the Names table

2. Select option **1** to add new customers. You'll see the custom NamesFrm screen for adding rows.

3. Highlight and select **Exit** when you want to finish adding to the Names table and return to the submenu.

4. Select option **2** to edit a list of customers.

5. When you see the "Enter last name of customer to edit" prompt, type **Miller** and press ←. You'll see the data for Anne Miller, ready for editing, as shown in Figure 15.5.

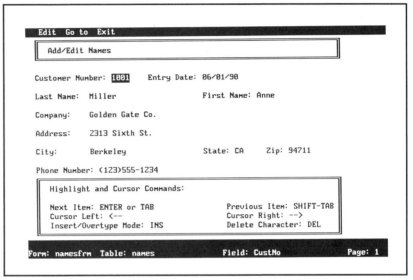

Figure 15.5: Data for Anne Miller ready to be edited

6. Press **F8** and you'll see that you can also edit the data for Marie Miller.

7. Highlight and select **E**xit to return to the submenu.

8. Select option **3** to print the directory. R:BASE allows you to choose Screen, Printer, or Both.

9. Select **S**creen. After the report is produced, you will be returned to the submenu.

10. Select option **4** to print mailing labels and select the Screen, Printer, or Both option.

11. Select option **5** to print form letters and select Screen, Printer, or Both again.

12. When you are finished testing the options on the Manage Customers List menu, select option **6** to return to the Main menu.

13. Select option **2** to see the submenu for managing the Charges table, as shown in Figure 15.6.

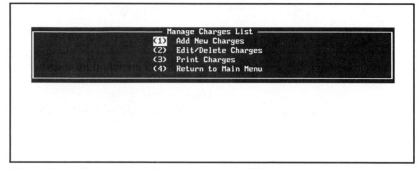

Figure 15.6: The submenu for managing the Charges table

The reason the Edit screen appears when you choose the Edit/Delete Charges option is you defined this option with the Modify action rather than the Edit action.

14. Select option **2**, and the data from the Charges table appears on the Edit screen, ready for editing.

15. After you are finished editing, highlight and select **Exit** to return to the submenu.

16. Test out the add and print options, if you so choose.

17. Press **Esc** to return to the MailSys Main Menu.

18. Press **Esc** to leave the MailSys application and return to the R:BASE Main menu.

You may want to experiment with the MailSys application for a while. Chances are, you'll come up with some ideas for changes and improvements. We'll discuss techniques for modifying an application in the next section.

MODIFYING APPLICATIONS FOR YOUR NEEDS

Display the Application EXPRESS menu by highlighting Applications and selecting Create/modify on the R:BASE Main menu, or by issuing the EXPRESS command at the R> prompt.

To modify an existing application, display the Applications EXPRESS menu. From this menu, not only can you create new applications, but you can also modify, delete, rename, or copy existing applications.

If you want to modify an application, highlight Modify and select the name of the application you wish to modify. You will be presented with the Applications EXPRESS Modify menu, which has the following options:

Layout	lets you add, change or delete menus. You can change a menu titles, text, colors, actions, exit methods, and help screens.
Settings	lets you suppress or display status and error messages, change the screen colors, suppress or enable the sound of the bell (beep) when an error occurs, and change the database on which your application is based.
Manage application	lets you run the application to save and test it, discard changes made since the last time the application was saved, or save changes made to the application.
Exit	lets you leave the Applications EXPRESS Modify menu and return to the Applications EXPRESS menu.

Let's discuss how to use each of these options to change, or modify, your applications.

CHANGING THE APPLICATION LAYOUT

After you highlight Layout, you are presented with three options:

- Modify menu lets you add or change menus.
- Change menu colors lets you change the colors of a menu.
- Delete a menu lets you remove a menu from your application.

After you've chosen one of the three options under Layout, you will choose the menu name you wish to modify, change the colors of, or delete. Modifying a menu requires many steps. In fact, you can change almost every aspect of a menu. In the next section, we will walk through this process.

MODIFYING A MENU

If you make a mistake as you are modifying an application, you can start over again by pressing Ctrl-Break. This returns you to the Applications EXPRESS Modify menu without saving the changes, if any, you made to the application.

Notice that Sub-Menu1 and Sub-Menu2 are indented on the selection menu. R:BASE does this so you can see the hierarchy of the menus.

The Modify a menu option leads you through a series of questions and selection screens, and so provides you with opportunities to modify various menu details. Let's see how the process works by modifying the Manage Customer List submenu. We'll make some minor changes and briefly describe the options available along the way.

To begin modifying SubMenu1, the Manage Customer List submenu, highlight **Layout**, select **Modify** menu, and select **SubMenu1**. Now SubMenu1 is displayed on your screen, with the highlighter on the menu title. Type in any changes you want to the title and press ←. Now the highlighter moves down to the first menu option. From here you have the choice of making several changes:

- To change the text in a menu option, move the highlighter to the option and type in the new text.

- To add a new menu item, press the End key. The highlighter will move to the bottom of the menu. Now type in the text for the new menu option.

- To insert a menu item between existing options, move the highlighter to the option that you want the new item to appear before, and press the F10 key. All the menu options below the highlighter will move down one row. Now type in the text for the new menu option.

- To delete a menu option, move the highlighter to the appropriate option and press F9.

When you finish making changes to the menu text, press the **F2** key. R:BASE will display the following prompt:

Do you want to change Esc or Help action?

Select Yes if you want to change the Esc key option for exiting the menus or if you wish to add or modify the help screens. If you are following along on-line, select **Yes**, and we'll add a help screen.

The advantage of being able to press Esc to exit a menu is that it saves menu space. You don't have to include an Exit option in your menu—Esc will do the job for you.

Changing the Escape Action

When you select Yes to the changing the Esc prompt, R:BASE first asks

Do you want Esc to exit this menu?

Select **Y**es to retain the Esc key method of exiting. You can select No to disable the Esc key if you wish, but generally it is a good idea to keep the Esc key as a way to exit from menus.

Adding a Custom Help Screen

Each help screen must be assigned a unique name.

After you answer the changing the Esc prompt, R:BASE displays the message

Do you want to create a help screen for this menu?

Since we're going to add a help screen to the MailSys application, select the **Y**es option. R:BASE asks that you enter a name for the new help message. As usual, the name cannot be longer than eight characters and cannot contain any spaces or punctuation marks. For this example, enter the name **SubHelp1**.

Remember that you can press Shift-F1 to display the function keys available for typing in the help screen.

You'll see a blank screen for entering the help screen text. Type in the help screen text just as you did when entering text on custom forms and reports. Figure 15.7 shows a help screen, which you can type in now if you are following along on-line. Press **F2** after you've filled in the help screen text. Later, when you run the application, you can press the Help key (F1) to view the help screen you just entered.

Even though Applications EXPRESS refers to a help screen, each "screen" can consist of up to 515 lines. R:BASE inserts a break every 20 lines of text to give the user a chance to read the screen. Try to design your help screens so there is a natural break every 20 lines. Also, help screens are most effective if they are short—only one or two 20-line screens.

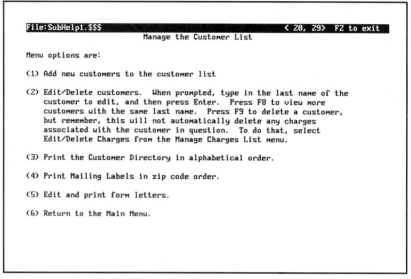

```
File:SubHelp1.$$$                                      < 20, 29>  F2 to exit
                            Manage the Customer List

Menu options are:

(1) Add new customers to the customer list

(2) Edit/Delete customers.  When prompted, type in the last name of the
    customer to edit, and then press Enter.  Press F8 to view more
    customers with the same last name.  Press F9 to delete a customer,
    but remember, this will not automatically delete any charges
    associated with the customer in question.  To do that, select
    Edit/Delete Charges from the Manage Charges List menu.

(3) Print the Customer Directory in alphabetical order.

(4) Print Mailing Labels in zip code order.

(5) Edit and print form letters.

(6) Return to the Main Menu.
```

Figure 15.7: A help screen for the MailSys application

CHANGING MENU ACTIONS

See Table 15.1 for an explanation of the actions you can assign.

Next, you'll be given the opportunity to change the actions that you originally assigned to the menu options in your application. The screen asks

Do you want to change the actions assigned to this menu?

If you answer No, you'll be given an opportunity to change another menu or to return to the Application EXPRESS Main menu. If you answer Yes, the screen will ask

Do you want to review all the options?

Answering Yes takes you step-by-step through each of the menu options and the actions assigned to them. If you answer No, the screen will display the current application menu (SubMenu1 in our example) and display the prompt

Choose a menu option to change

at the bottom of the screen.

You can move the highlighter to any option on your custom menu and press ◄─┘ to change the action associated with that menu option. Once you have selected a menu option, the screen asks

Do you want to insert an action before the current action?

You can insert another action above this action (which means that the newly inserted action will take place first) by selecting Yes in response to the question on the screen. If you select No, a prompt will appear at the bottom of the screen asking what you want to do with the current action:

Choose what you want to do with this action

You can select among three choices on a pop-up menu: Keep, Replace, or Delete.

- Keep leaves the menu action as it stands.
- Replace allows you to enter a new action in place of the currently defined action.
- Delete removes the currently defined action (but not the associated menu option from the menu itself).

Once you've opted to Keep, Replace, or Delete the current action (and defined a new action in the case of Replace), the screen asks

Do you want another action for the current menu option?

If you answer Yes to this question, you'll be given the opportunity to add another action, which will take place immediately after the existing actions. If you answer No, you'll see the question

Do you want to change the actions for another option?

If you answer Yes, you'll see all the options for the current application menu (still SubMenu1 in this example), and you can select the same option or another menu option to change. Doing so will repeat the process just described for the newly selected menu option. If you answer No to the question about changing the menu actions for another option, you will be returned to the Applications EXPRESS Modify menu.

At this point, you have an opportunity to test the changes you have made to your application. Highlight Manage application and select Run. After the revised application is saved to disk and the programs are generated based on the revised application, the Main Menu of your application is displayed.

Select option 1 from the Main Menu to manage the customer list. When the submenu appears, press F1 to view the custom help screen (similar to Figure 15.7). Press any key after you're finished viewing the help screen.

CHANGING THE MENU COLORS

To change the colors on a menu, highlight Layout, select Change menu colors, and then select the menu you wish to change the colors for. The appropriate color selection menu will be displayed, depending on you monitor. If you have a color monitor, you will be presented with a color palette from which you can choose foreground and background colors. If you have a monochrome monitor, you can choose foreground and background colors from a menu of color names in case you want to prepare an application to be used on a computer with a color monitor. In either case, you have a choice of eight background colors and sixteen foreground colors.

DELETING A MENU

To delete a menu, highlight Layout on the Applications EX-PRESS Modify menu, select Delete a menu, and then select the menu you want to delete. You will be asked to confirm before the menu is deleted. Since you can't delete the main menu of an application, this menu won't be included in the list of menus you can delete.

CHANGING THE APPLICATION SETTINGS

On the Applications EXPRESS Modify menu, one of the options on the menu at the top is Settings. Highlighting Settings displays the following options in the pull-down menu: Status messages, Error messages, Screen colors, Bell, and Select different database.

The Status messages option lets you display various R:BASE messages, such as "Database exists" or "5 row(s) have been deleted from Charges," as appropriate. If you select this option, the screen will ask

Do you want to display R:BASE status messages?

If you have made a mistake in developing the application and the system is not working properly, you can change this option to Yes and your application will display status messages. However, once you get your application working properly, you should select the default No option since these messages are distracting.

The Error messages option displays the message

Do you want to display R:BASE error messages?

When you enter a command at the R > prompt or make selections from R:BASE menus, R:BASE normally displays messages on the screen when an error occurs. If you select Yes for this option, your application will display these messages. If you select No, your application will not display these R:BASE error messages. Although error messages are not generated as often as status messages, they can still be annoying and may not be very informative to the user of your application. Choose Yes if you are trying to find a problem in your application, and No once you get the application working properly.

The Screen colors option allows you to select foreground and background colors for the application. If you have a color monitor, you can choose the colors from a color palette. If you have a monochrome monitor, you will be presented with two menus listing the names of your color choices, the first menu for background colors and the second menu for foreground choices.

Selecting the Bell option displays the question

Do you want your application to beep at errors?

Selecting Yes will ensure than any errors that occur while your application is in use will be accompanied by an audible beep. Selecting No, the default, suppresses this beep. R:BASE beeps for lots of reasons that require no action on the part of the user, so selecting No is probably a good idea.

The last option in this submenu, Select different database, allows you to move this application to a different database. This option displays a menu of available databases, from which you can choose a new database for your application. R:BASE then asks you to confirm your choice by asking if you are sure you want to change to this database. If you reply Yes, R:BASE remembers the name of the new database where you want this application. The next time you save this application, R:BASE will save your application to the new database.

MANAGING THE APPLICATION

See Chapter 7 for information on the Manage reports option on the Report Generator menu. The Manage forms option on the Form Generator menu is discussed in Chapter 8.

The Manage applications option on the Applications EXPRESS Modify menu gives you similar choices to the Manage reports option on the Report Generator screen and the Manage forms option on Form Generator screen.

- Run allows you to save and test your application.

- Discard changes allows you to leave the Application EXPRESS Modify menu without saving the changes you have made to this application.

- Save changes allows you to save the changes you have made to this application without leaving the Applications EXPRESS Modify menu.

You can leave the Applications EXPRESS Modify menu by highlighting and selecting Exit. Before you leave the Applications EXPRESS Modify menu, you will be given an opportunity to save your changes if you have made any since the last time you saved the application. A quirk of Applications EXPRESS is that if you highlight and select Exit, and then choose to save your changes, R:BASE saves your application and then returns to the Applications EXPRESS Modify menu. To leave this menu, you would have to highlight and select Exit again, since R:BASE will only leave the Applications EXPRESS Modify menu when there are no changes to save.

DELETING, RENAMING,
AND COPYING APPLICATIONS

Deleting, renaming, or copying an application is easy to do. Simply highlight the appropriate option on the Applications EXPRESS menu and select the name of the application you wish to delete, rename, or copy. If you are deleting, you will be asked to confirm whether you really want to delete the application. If you are renaming or copying an application, you will be asked to enter a new application name.

An alternate method of deleting an application is to delete the three files with extensions .APP, .APX, and .API. For example, to remove the entire MailSys application, you would enter the following commands separately at the R > prompt or the DOS prompt (don't do so now, however, unless you want to rebuild the entire application):

```
ERASE MailSys.API
ERASE MailSys.APX
ERASE MailSys.APP
```

To return to the R:BASE Main menu from the Applications EXPRESS menu, highlight and select Exit.

In this chapter, we've developed our first application. In the remaining chapters, we'll discuss techniques for building more complex applications.

Chapter 16

Automating Your Applications with Macros and Programs

Throughout this chapter, we'll use the terms *command file* and *program* interchangeably.

THE APPLICATIONS EXPRESS FEATURE PROVIDES A quick and easy way to develop applications, but there are limits to its flexibility. As an enhancement, you can write your own R:BASE programs to use in conjunction with those generated by the Applications EXPRESS feature, or even use your programs as entirely separate tools.

An R:BASE program is called a *command file* because it is a file stored on disk (like a table or database) that contains a series of commands to be carried out. This means that you can store an entire group of commands in a file and process them all with a single command, rather than typing in each command individually at the R> prompt.

For example, suppose you regularly print the Director and Sales reports from the Mail database. Each time you do so, you have to type in the following six commands individually at the R> prompt:

```
CONNECT MAIL
OUTPUT PRINTER WITH SCREEN
PRINT Director SORTED BY L_Name F_Name
NEWPAGE
PRINT Sales ORDER BY CustNo
OUTPUT SCREEN
```

You could instead create a command file that contained all these commands in order and have R:BASE automatically perform all six tasks using a single RUN command.

But there is much more to creating and using command files than simply storing commands. Command files allow you to perform tasks that are otherwise not possible within R:BASE. In this chapter, we'll discuss some of the basic constructs used in creating command files.

RECORDING KEYSTROKES

Before we get into the nitty-gritty of creating and running command files, we'll discuss a technique whereby you can create simple *script* files by recording keystrokes as you type them. Script files, which you create through recorded keystrokes, are not as powerful as the command files we'll develop later in the chapter. Nonetheless, recording and playing

Although some of you might think of script files as *macros,* R:BASE uses the term macro to refer to command files.

back keystrokes saves you from having to type in all the commands necessary to perform a task that you perform often.

Let's try creating a script file called "Labels." This file will print the Nameslbl labels, sorted by ZIP code. To prepare for this example, display the R> prompt by highlighting **E**xit and selecting **R>** prompt. Then follow these steps:

1. Press **Ctrl-F1** to display the Script/Key menu.

2. Select **R**ecord a script.

3. Type **Labels.SC** and press ◄— when R:BASE asks you for the name of the file to record the script to.

4. Type each of the commands below, pressing ◄— after each one.

    ```
    CLS
    CONNECT MAIL IDENTIFIED BY MYMAIL
    OUTPUT SCREEN
    LBLPRINT Nameslbl
    DISCONNECT
    ```

5. Press **Ctrl-F2** to stop recording keystrokes.

6. Press any key to acknowledge the message informing you that the script recording has ended.

Anytime you want to play back the recorded keystrokes, just do the following:

When you play back a script, you must do so under the same conditions and be at the same R:BASE prompt as when you recorded the script originally. Otherwise, the keystrokes in the script will not make sense. In our example, we have to start from the R> prompt.

1. Press **Ctrl-F1** to display the Script/Key menu.

2. Select **P**lay back a script.

3. Type **Labels.SC** and press ◄— when R:BASE asks you for the name of the script file to play back.

The commands you recorded are played back on the screen, and R:BASE executes each one as it is played back.

You can also activate a script file from the R> prompt by issuing the PLAYBACK command. For example, entering the command

    PLAYBACK Labels.SC

You'll be using the RBEDIT text editor extensively in this chapter, beginning with the section "Creating Command Files with RBEDIT." CodeLock is discussed in Chapter 18 and Gateway in Chapter 19.

would produce the same results we got from the Script/Key menu.

One of the nice things about script files is that they can be recorded at the R> prompt, in Applications EXPRESS, at R:BASE menus, in the Form Generator, in the Report Generator, or in the modules RBEDIT, CodeLock, and Gateway. Script files are stored in your default directory (\RBFILES\LEARN in our examples), not as part of any particular database's definition. That means that you could theoretically create a general-purpose script file and use it while working with any database. You can delete script files with the ERASE command either from R:BASE or from DOS.

To view the Labels.SC file, you can enter the command

TYPE Labels.SC

at the R> prompt; it will contain all the commands you typed in. You can also edit script files with RBEDIT, R:BASE's editor that you'll be using later in this chapter.

Although simple script files act much like command files, you cannot include programming commands such as WHILE, IF, FILLIN, and others that we'll discuss in this chapter in a script file.

DEFINING YOUR OWN KEY MAPS

You cannot define a key map for function keys F11 or F12.

R:BASE also lets you define single-command actions called *key maps*. You activate a key map by pressing the Alt key along with one of the first ten function keys (F1 through F10) or one of the ten number keys (0 through 9).

You can set up a key map from the R> prompt or any R:BASE module by using the Script/Key menu that you used above to record script files. Since most of us use the SELECT ALL FROM command frequently, let's set up a key map that makes pressing Alt-F10 a shortcut for typing SELECT ALL FROM. Follow these steps:

1. Press **Ctrl-F1** to display the Script/Key menu.

2. Select the **D**efine a key map option to display the Key Map Definition screen.

3. Press **Alt-F10** as the key combination you are defining in response to the "Key map" prompt. R:BASE displays [Alt][F10] beside the prompt to represent this key combination.

4. Under the "Key map, use Ctrl-F2 to quit" prompt, type **SELECT ALL FROM** and press the **spacebar**. Your screen should look like Figure 16.1

If you make a typing mistake while entering a key map definition, you can't press the backspace or Esc keys to correct your mistake. Simply press Ctrl-F2 to leave the Key Map Definition screen and then repeat this procedure from step 1, being careful to type the commands correctly.

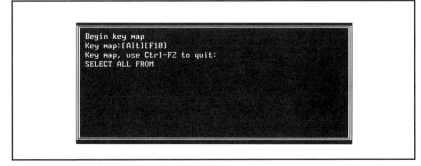

```
Begin key map
Key map:[Alt][F10]
Key map, use Ctrl-F2 to quit:
SELECT ALL FROM
```

Figure 16.1: Defining a key map

5. Press **Ctrl-F2** to finish defining the key map.

You may have noticed another option on the Script/Key menu called Display key maps. Press **Ctrl-F1** now to display the Script/Key menu, and select **D**isplay key maps. You will see the definition of the Alt-F10 key combination. Now press any key to return to the R> prompt.

To test your key map, make sure the Mail database is open and press **Alt-F10**. SELECT ALL FROM should appear as though you had typed it yourself. To complete this example, type **Names** and press ↵ to see the Names table displayed on your screen.

Remember that you can access the Settings menu by typing SET and pressing ↵ at the R > prompt or by highlighting Tools and selecting Settings on the R:BASE Main menu.

You can remove the definition from a key by following the same steps you would when defining a key map. However, when the "Key map, use Ctrl-F2 to quit" prompt appears, press Ctrl-F2 without entering a key action.

You can also display the Key Map Definition screen from the Settings menu. Highlight Configuration and select the Define function keys option. Once the Key Map Definition screen is displayed, you would reply to the "Key map" and "Key map, use Ctrl-F2 to quit" prompts and press Ctrl-F2 to finish your definition as you did above.

Unless you save them, the key maps you define will only remain active during the current session and will be lost when you leave R:BASE. To save the key maps you have defined, use the Settings menu as follows:

When you save the key maps, you also save all of the current settings that you can change on the Settings menu.

1. Highlight **C**onfiguration and select the **S**ave settings to option.

2. Press ⏎ to accept the default configuration file name of RBASE.CFG under the "Save current settings to file" prompt.

3. Choose **Y**es when asked if you want to overwrite the configuration file.

The key maps you have saved will be available the next time you start R:BASE from DOS.

Key maps can save you lots of typing, since you can activate them by pressing one combination of keys. However, the total length of all your key map definitions cannot be more than 512 characters.

CREATING COMMAND FILES WITH RBEDIT

You can create command files, or write programs, using the R:BASE RBEDIT editor. (You can also use external word processors such as Word or WordPerfect as long as you save the program in an unformatted ASCII file.) Access RBEDIT from the R:BASE Main menu by highlighting Tools and selecting Editor, or by typing the RBEDIT command at the R > prompt.

Let's try a simple exercise to practice creating and running command files. Display the R > prompt now and follow these steps:

1. Type **RBEDIT** and press ⏎ to display the RBEDIT initial menu. This menu has three options.

   • New file allows you to create a new command file.

- Old file allows you to modify an existing command file.

- Exit returns you to the R > prompt.

2. Select **N**ew file.

Press Shift-F1 to see a list of function key descriptions.

You'll see a blank screen with a status line at the top for composing your command file. If you are editing an existing file, the file name will be displayed on the left side of the status line. Near the right side of the status line you'll recognize the familiar position indicator showing the row and column of the cursor. At the right end of the status line is the "F2 to exit" prompt, a reminder to press F2 when you are finished entering your command file. Table 16.1 lists keys you can use while creating and editing command files.

Table 16.1: Keys Used with RBEDIT

KEY	FUNCTION
↵	Finish the current line and move down one line
↓	Move down one line
→	Move right one character
←	Move left one character
Tab	Move right to the next tab stop (tab stops are every ten characters)
Shift-Tab	Move left to the next tab stop (tab stops are every ten characters)
Ctrl-→	Move to the end of the line
Ctrl-←	Move to the beginning of the line
Home	Display the first page of text
End	Display the last line of text
PgUp	Move up one page
PgDn	Move down one page
F9	Delete the current line
F10	Insert a line above the current line

Table 16.1: Keys Used with RBEDIT (continued)

KEY	FUNCTION
Ins	Toggle between Insert mode (the cursor is a block) and Overtype mode (the cursor is an underline)
Del	Delete a character
F5	Clear marked block
F6	Mark the beginning and end of a block
Ctrl-F6	Enter and exit Repeat mode
Ctrl-F7	Copy marked block
Ctrl-F8	Move marked block
Ctrl-F9	Delete marked block
F7	Search for and replace text
Shift-F7	Specify text to search for and replace
F8	Search for text
Shift-F8	Specify text to search for

Remember, you can use the arrow keys to move the cursor and correct errors. Press Ins and Del to insert or delete characters, and F9 and F10 to delete and insert lines if you need to while making corrections.

3. Type in the command file (or program) shown in Figure 16.2. Make sure you press ← after typing each line.

4. Press **F2** when you've finished typing in the entire command file. You now see a pop-up menu with four options:

   - Edit again lets you continue editing the file.

   - Save file saves your changes on disk.

   - Next file gives you an opportunity to save your changes and then return to the RBEDIT initial menu, where you can choose Old file, New file, or Exit.

   - Exit lets you save your changes and leave RBEDIT.

5. Select **Exit**.

6. Reply **Yes** when asked if you want to save your changes.

7. Type **Sample1.CMD** and press ← under the "Name of file to save" prompt. You are now back at the R> prompt.

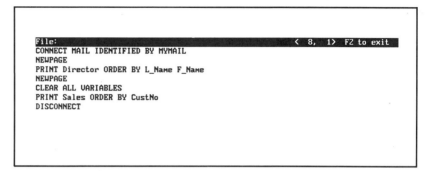

Figure 16.2: A sample command file typed in with RBEDIT

RUNNING A COMMAND FILE

Once you've saved the command file, use the RUN command with the name of the file to run the program. In this example, type

    RUN Sample1.CMD

and press ⏎. You'll see the message "Database exists" briefly as the program opens the Mail database. Then the screen will clear, and after a brief pause you'll see the Director report displayed in alphabetical order by last and first names. After that the screen will clear again (because of the NEWPAGE command), and you'll see the Sales report printed in order by customer number. When the command file is finished, you'll see the message

    Switching input back to keyboard

which means that R:BASE will be expecting the next command to come from the keyboard, rather than from the command file.

EDITING A COMMAND FILE

To edit an existing command file, use the RBEDIT editor. Let's add a couple of commands to clear the screen and to print mailing labels.

1. Type **RBEDIT Sample1.CMD** and press ⏎, a shortcut to begin editing the Sample1.CMD command file. Notice that Sample1.CMD appears on the left side of the status line next to the name of the file being edited.

2. Move the cursor to the beginning of the last line in the command file, just under the D in DISCONNECT.

3. Press **F10** twice to insert two blank lines, so that the command file looks like Figure 16.3.

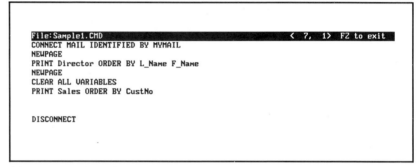

```
File:Sample1.CMD                                      < 7,  1> F2 to exit
CONNECT MAIL IDENTIFIED BY MYMAIL
NEWPAGE
PRINT Director ORDER BY L_Name F_Name
NEWPAGE
CLEAR ALL VARIABLES
PRINT Sales ORDER BY CustNo


DISCONNECT
```

Figure 16.3: Blank lines added to the Sample1.CMD command file

4. To add the new lines, type **NEWPAGE** and press ⏎; and type **LBLPRINT Nameslbl ORDER BY Zip_Code** and press ⏎. Your screen should now look like Figure 16.4.

```
File:Sample1.CMD                                      < 9,  1> F2 to exit
CONNECT MAIL IDENTIFIED BY MYMAIL
NEWPAGE
PRINT Director ORDER BY L_Name F_Name
NEWPAGE
CLEAR ALL VARIABLES
PRINT Sales ORDER BY CustNo
NEWPAGE
LBLPRINT Nameslbl ORDER BY Zip_Code
DISCONNECT
```

Figure 16.4: The edited Sample1.CMD command file

5. Let's save the changes and return to the R> prompt. Press **F2**, select **E**xit, reply **Y**es to saving the changes, and press ⏎ to confirm the file name Sample1.CMD.

To run the modified command file, once again enter the command

RUN Sample1.CMD

You'll see the Director, Sales, and Labels reports printed on the screen, and then you'll see the message

Switching input back to keyboard

This means that you are once again back to the normal R:BASE Command mode.

As you can see, creating a command file is as easy as calling up the RBEDIT editor, typing in the commands that you want to process, saving the command file, and then running it with the RUN command. With RBEDIT, you can create command files with about 750 command lines (depending on available memory).

With the addition of input/output, looping, decision making, and a few other tricks of the trade, you can build command files that go far beyond a simple list of commands and perform more sophisticated tasks. We'll discuss these techniques in the remainder of this chapter.

INPUT/OUTPUT COMMANDS

The input/output commands allow you to display messages, pause for a response, and assign values to variables from within a command file. The three primary input/output commands for R:BASE are WRITE, PAUSE, and FILLIN.

DISPLAYING MESSAGES
WITH THE WRITE COMMAND

The WRITE command uses the basic syntax

WRITE *'message'* AT *<row>* *<column>*

The AT portion is optional. Most screens contain 24 rows and 80 columns, the upper-left corner is row 1, column 1, and the lower-right corner is row 24, column 80.

Let's try using the WRITE command in a simple command file.

1. To create the command file in the editor, type **RBEDIT IO1.CMD** and press ←.

2. Type in the lines

   ```
   NEWPAGE
   WRITE 'This is the first message...'
   ```

3. To save the file, press **F2**; select **Exit**; reply **Yes** to saving the changes; and press ← to confirm the file name IO1.CMD.

4. Type **RUN IO1.CMD** and press ← to run the command file.

The command file will clear the screen and display the message

```
This is the first message . . .
```

before returning to the R> prompt.

Let's try another example that uses the optional AT clause with the WRITE command to specify the exact row and column position for displaying information on the screen.

1. Type **RBEDIT IO2.CMD** and press ←.

2. Type in the lines

   ```
   CLS
   WRITE 'This is the middle' AT 12,31
   ```

3. To save the file, press **F2**; select **Exit**; reply **Yes** to saving the changes; and press ← to confirm the file name IO2.CMD.

4. Type **RUN IO2.CMD** and press ← to run the command file.

This time the message is placed in the middle of the screen, at row 12, column 31.

COMBINING TEXT AND NUMBERS

Sometimes you may want to display a message from within a command file that contains both text and numeric data, such as the following message:

You just won $100,000.00!

Normally, you cannot directly combine text and numeric data in a variable for display. However, by using the CTXT function to convert the numeric data to text data, you can indeed combine the two types of data. Here is an example:

1. Type **RBEDIT IO3.CMD** and press ←┘.

2. Enter the following lines into this command file:

```
CLEAR ALL VARIABLES
SET VARIABLE Prize CURRENCY
SET VARIABLE Prize = 100000.00
SET VARIABLE Msg = ('You just won' & CTXT(.Prize) + '!')
WRITE .Msg AT 20,1
```

3. Save the file and leave RBEDIT as you did in step 3 above.

4. Type **RUN IO3.CMD** and press ←┘ to run the command file.

You'll see the message "You just won $100,000.00!" appear at row 20, column 1 on the screen, and then the R > prompt will reappear. Let's discuss why.

The first line in the command file, CLEAR ALL VARIABLES, simply erases any existing variables. Then the SET VARIABLE Prize CURRENCY command creates an empty variable nameed Prize, which is predefined as the CURRENCY data type. The next line, SET VARIABLE Prize = 100000.00, stores the number $100,000.00 in the variable named Prize. The next line

```
SET VARIABLE Msg = ('You just won' & CTXT(.Prize) + '!')
```

concatenates, or joins, the text version of the numeric Prize variable to the text string "You just won", and then concatenates the character "!" to the end of the variable.

Normally, these items could not be strung together because the Prize variable is numeric and the characters in quotation marks are text. However, the CTXT function converts the Prize variable to TEXT data within the SET VARIABLE command, so R:BASE accepts the concatenation.

The last line in the command file

WRITE .Msg AT 20,1

displays the entire Msg variable at row 20, column 1 on the screen.

Another example of using the CTXT function would be the following:

SET VARIABLE Today = ('Today is' & (CTXT(.#DATE)))

In this case, the CTXT function changes the DATE data to TEXT data prior to concatenation. The CTXT function can also be used to change time data to TEXT for concatenation.

☞ When you display the contents of a variable with the WRITE command, you *must* precede the variable name with a dot.

☞ The CTXT function uses the date output format when converting dates to TEXT and the time output format when converting times to TEXT.

TEMPORARILY STOPPING COMMAND EXECUTION WITH THE PAUSE COMMAND

The PAUSE command makes R:BASE temporarily stop processing the commands in a command file until the user presses a key. The PAUSE command is usually used in conjunction with a message displayed with the WRITE command. This example will illustrate the process:

1. Type **RBEDIT IO4.CMD** and press ↵.

2. Enter the following lines into this command file:

   ```
   NEWPAGE
   WRITE 'Press any key to continue' AT 12,30
   PAUSE
   WRITE 'Thank you' AT 23,5
   ```

3. Save the file and leave RBEDIT.

4. Type **RUN IO4.CMD** and press ↵ to run the command file.

The screen will clear, and you will see the "Press any key to continue" message. After you press a key, R:BASE will continue processing the command, and you'll see the message "Thank you" near the bottom of the screen.

WRITING INTERACTIVE PROGRAMS WITH THE FILLIN COMMAND

The FILLIN command pauses program execution and waits for some data to be entered by the user. Whatever the user types on the screen is stored in a variable. Generally, it is a good idea to define the data type for the variable explicitly before using the FILLIN command.

The general syntax for the FILLIN command is

FILLIN *variable name* USING *'message'* AT *<row>* *<column>*

To try this command, use RBEDIT to create a command file named IO5.CMD that contains these lines:

```
NEWPAGE
SET VARIABLE YourName TEXT
FILLIN YourName USING 'Enter your name: ' AT 12,5
NEWPAGE
SET VARIABLE Reply = ('Hello' & .YourName)
WRITE .Reply AT 12,30
```

A space is placed at the end of the 'Enter your name: ' prompt so that there will be a space between the prompt and the cursor when the user is asked for input.

Note that the command file first clears the screen (NEWPAGE) and creates an empty variable called YourName with the TEXT data type. The FILLIN command displays the message "Enter your Name:" at row 12, column 5 and waits for a value to be entered from the keyboard. Then the command file clears the screen and creates a variable named Reply that consists of the word "Hello," followed by the YourName variable. The last line of the program displays the Reply variable at row 12, column 30.

When you run the command file, it will first ask for your name. Type in your name and press ←⏎. You'll then see the message "Hello," followed by your name, as below:

```
Hello Joe
```

ADDING COMMENTS TO COMMAND FILES

You can add comments to your programs (command files). These comments are never displayed and do not affect the program in any way. Generally, the purpose of these comments is to write helpful notes to yourself within a program. If you ever need to go back and modify a program many weeks or months later, the comments can help you translate the commands into English.

Comments in R:BASE that fit on one line can start with two hyphens. The following line is a one line comment:

    --This is a program comment.

Comments can also begin with an asterisk and an opening parenthesis and end with a closing parenthesis. This type of comment can be one line or more than one line long, if desired. For example, the following comment takes two lines.

    *(This is a very long comment that you may
    decide to place on two lines.)

With this type of comment, you must remember to add the closing parenthesis; otherwise R:BASE might think that the entire program is a comment and ignore all commands. When that happens, you'll be returned to Command mode with the +> prompt showing. To correct the problem, type in a closing parenthesis next to the +> prompt and press ←┘. Then use RBEDIT to find the faulty comment and rectify it.

To make comments more visible in a program, programmers often add extra asterisks or hyphens, as in the two examples below:

    (* * * * * * * * * Program to display menus)
    ------------------------------ Update the master file

Figure 16.5 shows the IO5.CMD command file with some programmer comments added. Note that the first two comments provide the name of the command file, as well as a brief description of what the program does. Additional comments describe individual

```
*(*************************** IO5.CMD)
*(------------ Test the FILLIN command)
---- Clear the screen and initialize YourName variable
NEWPAGE
SET VARIABLE YourName TEXT
---- Ask for user's name, and store in YourName variable
FILLIN YourName USING 'Enter your name: ' AT 12,5
NEWPAGE
---- Create variable named Reply, and display it
SET VARIABLE Reply = 'Hello' & .YourName
WRITE .Reply AT 12,30
```

Figure 16.5: The command file with comments

routines within the command file. We'll use comments throughout the remaining sample programs in this book to help clarify various commands and routines.

PROGRAM LOOPS WITH WHILE AND ENDWHILE

One of the most common techniques used in programming is the *loop*. A loop allows a command file to repeat a single command, or several commands, as long as some condition exists. The WHILE and ENDWHILE commands are a convenient way to create a loop in your program. The general syntax for the WHILE and ENDWHILE commands is

> WHILE *condition* THEN
>   *do this command*
>   *and this command*
> ENDWHILE

Keep in mind that every WHILE command in a program *must* have an ENDWHILE command associated with it. Programmers typically indent instructions that are typed between WHILE and ENDWHILE commands to highlight these WHILE/ENDWHILE pairs and make it easy to identify the commands that are going to be executed over and over within the loop. Figure 16.6 shows a sample program with a WHILE loop in it.

```
*(******************************** Loop1.CMD)
*(----------- Program to test the WHILE loop)
NEWPAGE
---- Create variable named Counter
SET VARIABLE Counter = 1
---- Repeat loop 10 times
WHILE Counter <= 10 THEN
     ---- Create a prompt and display it
     SET VARIABLE Progress = ('Loop Number =' & CTXT(.Counter))
     WRITE .Progress
     ---- Increment Counter variable by 1
     SET VARIABLE Counter = (.Counter + 1)
ENDWHILE  --  Bottom of WHILE loop
```

Figure 16.6: A sample program with a WHILE loop

Let's look at the logic of the program, line by line. The first two lines are simply programmer comments. The NEWPAGE command on the third line then clears the screen. Next, the program creates a variable named Counter and assigns it the value 1, with the following lines:

```
---- Create variable named Counter
SET VARIABLE Counter = 1
```

The next line starts a loop that will repeat all commands between the WHILE and ENDWHILE commands, as long as the Counter variable is less than or equal to 10:

```
---- Repeat loop 10 times
WHILE Counter < = 10 THEN
```

Within the WHILE loop, these lines create a variable named Progress, which contains the text "Loop Number" and the current value of the Counter variable converted to text. The WRITE command then displays the message

```
---- Create a prompt and display it
SET VARIABLE Progress = ('Loop Number =' & CTXT(.Counter))
WRITE .Progress
```

Next, the program increments the Counter variable by one. It does this by adding 1 to its current value:

```
---- Increment Counter variable by 1
SET VARIABLE Counter = (.Counter + 1)
```

The line below marks the end of the WHILE loop:

```
ENDWHILE -- Bottom of WHILE loop
```

Remember that you can type SHOW VARIABLES from the R > prompt to see the contents of your variables. This may help locate a problem if your program isn't working as you expected.

You can use RBEDIT to create the command file. When you run the program, you'll see the following on the screen:

```
Loop Number = 1
Loop Number = 2
Loop Number = 3
Loop Number = 4
Loop Number = 5
Loop Number = 6
Loop Number = 7
Loop Number = 8
Loop Number = 9
Loop Number = 10
  Switching input back to keyboard
```

Notice that the WRITE command within the WHILE loop repeated ten times, and each time through, the Counter variable was incremented by one.

You can use variables to determine how many times the WHILE loop should repeat. For example, the command file Loop2.CMD in Figure 16.7, when run, displays the prompt "How high shall I count?" and waits for a response. After you enter a number, the WHILE loop will repeat the appropriate number of times. For example, if you enter a 5, you'll see the following on the screen:

```
Loop Number = 1
Loop Number = 2
Loop Number = 3
Loop Number = 4
Loop Number = 5
  Switching input back to keyboard
```

```
*(****************************** Loop2.CMD)
*(------------ Program to test the WHILE loop)
-------------- Create Counter and Done variable
SET VARIABLE Counter = 1
SET VARIABLE Done INTEGER
-------------- Ask how high to count
NEWPAGE
FILLIN Done USING 'How high shall I count?: ' AT 9,5
NEWPAGE
-------------- Repeat loop until Counter > Done
WHILE Counter <= .Done THEN
        -------- Create a prompt and display it
        SET VARIABLE Progress = ('Loop Number =' & CTXT(.Counter))
        WRITE .Progress
        -------- Increment Counter variable by 1
        SET VARIABLE Counter = (.Counter + 1)
ENDWHILE  ---  Bottom of WHILE loop
```

Figure 16.7: A program to test the WHILE command with a variable

Notice in the program that the commands

    SET VARIABLE Done INTEGER
    FILLIN Done USING 'How high shall I count?: ' AT 9,5

create a variable named Done. The FILLIN command displays the prompt "How high shall I count?:" and waits for a response from the user. The user's response is then stored in the Done variable. The WHILE loop repeats as long as the Counter variable is less than or equal to the Done variable, as follows:

    WHILE Counter < = .Done THEN

PROCESSING TABLE ROWS WITH CURSORS

You can use a *cursor* to make a WHILE loop step through a table a single row at a time. Once the cursor points to a row in a table, you can set variables to column values in that row and you can change the values of columns in that row. Cursors are very helpful when you want to provide special processing for the rows in a table. For example, in a payroll system, the calculation of the gross pay amount, the various deductions, and the net amount of the paycheck must take many factors into account. Using a cursor, a program could step through each

The cursor discussed in this section is used in R:BASE commands that process an individual row in a table. Don't confuse this type of cursor with the cursor that appears on your screen. Whenever the word CURSOR appears in an R:BASE command, the cursor being referred to is the kind used in commands that process a row in a table.

row in the employee table. For each employee, the program could obtain the salary, benefits, deductions, and any other data affecting pay, perform the necessary calculations, and store the results of the calculations in the row for that employee. After this program was finished calculating and storing the pay details for each employee, a report program could print paychecks and stubs.

The first step in using the cursor feature of R:BASE is to *declare the cursor.* That means specifying the name you will use for the cursor, the table you will be processing, as well as the columns and rows you will be examining from the table. Next you must *open the cursor.* In this step, R:BASE prepares to access the rows and columns of the tables you specified when you declared the cursor, and sets the cursor just before the first row to be examined. After that you have to *fetch the data* from the specified columns in the next row accessed with this cursor. This step is done repeatedly until the data from all the rows have been examined. Finally, you must *drop the cursor.* All of the memory used to specify the cursor and access the data will be freed up.

Let's illustrate the use of a cursor to obtain data from each row in a table with a very simple example. Suppose you wanted to display the last and first name of each customer in the Names table in sorted order, with only one space separating the last and first names and without showing any headings. The first step in our example is to declare the cursor.

DECLARING THE CURSOR

The basic syntax for the DECLARE CURSOR command is

```
DECLARE cursor name CURSOR FOR SELECT columns +
+ > FROM table WHERE conditions ORDER BY sort columns
```

The SELECT portion of the DECLARE CURSOR command is just like the familiar SELECT command, with the WHERE and ORDER BY clauses optional. The following DECLARE CURSOR command will prepare to access the last and first names in sorted order in all rows in the Names table:

```
DECLARE Cursor1 CURSOR FOR SELECT L_Name F_Name +
+ > FROM Names ORDER BY L_Name F_Name
```

OPENING THE CURSOR

The next step is to open the cursor, preparing to access the data specified in the DECLARE CURSOR command. The format for the OPEN command is

OPEN *cursor name*

For our example, OPEN Cursor1, will be the OPEN command.

FETCHING THE DATA

We will use the FETCH command to get the data we want from each row in the table. The FETCH command has the following syntax:

FETCH *cursor name* INTO *variable/indicator list*

where the *variable/indicator list* is a list of variables into which the data should be placed and indicators to identify null values in the data. Each entry in the *variable/indicator list* has the format

variable name INDICATOR *indicator name*

The INDICATOR *indicator name* part is optional in each entry of the *variable/indicator list*. R:BASE sets the *indicator* variable to -1 if the data fetched into *variable name* is null or 0 if it is not null. If R:BASE fetches a null value for a variable without an indicator, a message is displayed on the screen alerting the operator that a null value has been found. It is a good idea to include indicators in your FETCH commands to eliminate these messages and also to test to see if a null value has been fetched.

Each time the FETCH command is executed, R:BASE moves to the next row to be accessed with the specified cursor. The FETCH command then places the values from the columns named in the DECLARE CURSOR command into the variables named in the FETCH command.

For our example, the following FETCH command will obtain the last and first name from each row on the Names table

FETCH Cursor1 INTO Name1 INDICATOR Ind1, Name2 INDICATOR Ind2

When we are fetching the data, we will step through each row in the table with a WHILE loop. But how will we know when we have processed all the rows in the table? R:BASE provides several ways to determine when the end of a table has been reached. The most straightforward method is to test the *SQLCODE* variable. When an SQL command is executed, R:BASE automatically sets the SQLCODE variable to a value that shows the status of the SQL command. When an SQL command is successful, SQLCODE is set to 0. If an SQL command is not successful because no more data is available, SQLCODE is set to 100. If an SQL command has a serious error, such as a CONNECT command trying to connect to a database that doesn't exist, SQLCODE will be set to a negative number that identifies the problem. In our example, we can terminate the loop when SQLCODE is set to 100, which indicates that the FETCH command couldn't find any more data.

SQL commands include most of the commands that you use to access databases and tables, such as CONNECT, DISCONNECT, SELECT, DECLARE CURSOR, OPEN CURSOR, FETCH, and DROP CURSOR.

DROPPING THE CURSOR

When we have finished processing all rows in the table, we have to use the DROP CURSOR command to free the memory used by the cursor. The format of this command is straightforward:

DROP CURSOR *cursor name*

When you disconnect from a database or connect to a new one, R:BASE automatically drops any cursors you defined for tables in the database.

In our example, we will simply use the command

DROP CURSOR Cursor1

Listing the Names of Customers in the Names Table

Figure 16.8 shows the program that produces the listing of customers from the Names table. If you type in the command file and run it, the screen will show all the last and first names of customers in

Chapter 17 has more examples of how to use cursors to process tables.

the Names table, sorted alphabetically, and at the bottom you will
see the message

End-of-data encountered
Switching input back to keyboard

```
*(******************************** Loop3.CMD)
*(------------ Test WHILE loop through a table)
---- Connect to the MAIL database
CONNECT MAIL
---- Declare the Cursor to access the first and last name
---- in all rows of the Name table
DECLARE Cursor1 CURSOR FOR SELECT L_Name F_Name FROM Names +
    ORDER BY L_Name F_Name
---- Open the Cursor, preparing to access the first row
OPEN Cursor1
---- Clear the screen to prepare for the listing
NEWPAGE
---- Fetch data from the first row
FETCH Cursor1 INTO Name1 INDICATOR Ind1, Name2 INDICATOR Ind2
---- Repeat loop until no more data found by FETCH command
WHILE SQLCODE <> 100 THEN
        ---- Combine first and last names
        SET VARIABLE FullName = (.Name1 & .Name2)
        ---- Display the name
        WRITE .FullName
        ---- Fetch data from the next row
        FETCH Cursor1 INTO Name1 INDICATOR Ind1, Name2 INDICATOR Ind2
ENDWHILE   ---   Bottom of WHILE loop
---- Drop the cursor to free up the memory the cursor was using
DROP CURSOR Cursor1
---- End of program
QUIT
```

Figure 16.8: A sample program using a cursor and a WHILE loop to process
records in a table

DECISION MAKING WITH IF

Another commonly used programming technique is *decision making*
using the IF, THEN, ELSE, and ENDIF commands. The general
syntax for the IF command is:

```
IF conditions THEN
     Do this command
     and this command
ELSE
     Do this command
     and this command
ENDIF
```

The ELSE portion is optional, so the IF command might also use the following simpler syntax:

IF *conditions* THEN
    Do this command
    and this command
ENDIF

With either syntax, each IF command in a command file *must* have an ENDIF command associated with it. There can be any number of commands between the IF and ENDIF commands. The *conditions* portion can have up to ten expressions joined with the AND and OR operators.

Figure 16.9 shows a simple program that makes a decision whether or not to display information on the printer, based upon the user's response to the question

Send message to the printer? (Y/N)

In this program, the FILLIN command displays the prompt, then waits for the user to enter an answer. The answer is stored in a variable named YesNo. The commands

---- Decide whether to use printer or just screen
IF .YesNo = 'Y' THEN
    OUTPUT PRINTER WITH SCREEN

```
*(******************************* IF1.CMD)
*(----------- Program to test the IF command)
NEWPAGE
---- Create variable to hold answer
SET VARIABLE YesNo TEXT
---- Display prompt and get answer
FILLIN YesNo USING 'Send message to the printer? (Y/N) ' +
    AT 12,2
---- Decide whether to use printer or just screen
IF .YesNo = 'Y' THEN
    OUTPUT PRINTER WITH SCREEN
ELSE
    OUTPUT SCREEN
ENDIF
---- Display message
WRITE 'Here is the message'
OUTPUT SCREEN    -- back to normal screen display
```

Figure 16.9: A sample program to test the IF command

```
        ELSE
              OUTPUT SCREEN
        ENDIF
```

will channel output to the printer and screen if the YesNo variable contains the letter Y. If this variable contains an N, output will be sent to the screen only.

DECISION MAKING WITH SWITCH

R:BASE provides a facility similar to the IF command that tests an expression for many values using the SWITCH, CASE, BREAK, DEFAULT, and ENDSW commands. The general syntax of the SWITCH command is

```
        SWITCH (comparison value)
              CASE value 1
                    Do this command
                    and this command
                    BREAK
              CASE value 2
                    Do this command
                    and this command
                    BREAK

              . . .
              CASE value n
                    Do this command
                    and this command
                    BREAK
              DEFAULT
                    Do this command
                    and this command
        ENDSW
```

In the SWITCH command, the *comparison value* is an INTEGER or TEXT value that will be compared with each value in the CASE commands. The values in each CASE command must have the same data type as the comparison value in the SWITCH command. When a CASE command is found with a value equal to the comparison value, then the commands following that CASE command are executed until the BREAK command. The BREAK command instructs R:BASE to continue executing commands after the ENDSW command. The commands following the DEFAULT command are executed if none of the CASE values is equal to the comparison value. The DEFAULT command is optional. If the DEFAULT command is not included and none of the CASE values is equal to the comparison value, R:BASE continues execution with the command following the ENDSW command. As you might expect, each SWITCH command *must* have an ENDSW command associated with it.

There can be as many CASE commands as you want between a SWITCH and ENDSW command pair. Also, there can be as many commands following each CASE command or the DEFAULT command as are required.

Figure 16.10 shows a program similar to our previous example, except this program will not send the message unless either Y or N is entered. The program starts by clearing all variables and then creating a TEXT variable named YesNo. When any variable is created, it has a null value. This means that the first time the WHILE command is executed, the YesNo variable has a null value, the WHILE

```
*(***************************** SWITCH1.CMD)
*(--------- Program to test the SWITCH command)
---- Create variable to hold answer
CLEAR ALL VARIABLES
SET VARIABLE YesNo TEXT
---- Loop until a valid answer is entered
NEWPAGE
WHILE (.YesNo IS NULL) THEN
      ---- Display prompt and get answer
      FILLIN YesNo USING 'Send message to the printer? (Y/N) ' +
           AT 12,2
      ---- Decide whether to use printer or just screen
      SWITCH (.YesNo)
           CASE 'Y'    -- Printer
                OUTPUT PRINTER WITH SCREEN
                BREAK
           CASE 'N'    -- Screen
                OUTPUT SCREEN
                BREAK
           DEFAULT     -- Error  --  Get another answer
                SET VARIABLE YesNo = '-0-'
                NEWPAGE
                WRITE 'Please answer Y or N' AT 11,2
      ENDSW
ENDWHILE
---- Display message
WRITE 'Here is the message'
OUTPUT SCREEN    -- Back to normal screen display
```

Figure 16.10: A sample program using the SWITCH command

condition will be true, and the commands inside the WHILE loop will be executed. Inside the WHILE loop, the FILLIN command displays a prompt asking whether the message should be sent to the printer, and places the response in the YesNo variable. Depending on whether the YesNo variable contains a Y or N, the SWITCH command directs the output to the printer (and screen) or just the screen.

If the user makes a typing mistake and enters a letter other than Y or N, the YesNo variable will not be equal to any of the values in the CASE commands and the commands following the DEFAULT command are executed. The SET VARIABLE command sets YesNo to null (-0-) and the WRITE command displays an error message. After the ENDSW command, the ENDWHILE command is reached and R:BASE tests the WHILE condition. Since YesNo is null, the WHILE loop is executed again and the user gets another chance to answer the question.

When the user enters a Y or N, YesNo will not be null when the ENDWHILE command is reached. This means that the WHILE condition will not be true and the commands following the ENDWHILE command will be executed. After the WHILE loop, the WRITE command displays the message on the selected device and the output is reset to the screen.

BRANCHING WITH GOTO

You use the GOTO and LABEL commands to pass over a group of commands in a command file and branch to another group of commands. The basic syntax for the GOTO command is

GOTO *label name*

The syntax for the LABEL command is

LABEL *label name*

The *label name* may be up to eight characters long. Figure 16.11 shows a sample command file that displays the prompt

Do you wish to exit now? (Y/N)

If the user answers Yes, the program branches to the routine labelled Done, and control is returned to DOS. If the user answers No, all commands between the GOTO and LABEL commands are executed, rather than skipped over, and the Director report from the Mail database is displayed on the screen.

```
*(******************************** GOTEST.CMD)
*(---- Program to test the GOTO and LABEL commands)
NEWPAGE
SET VARIABLE YesNo TEXT
---- Ask if user wants to exit, rather than
---- continuing.  Branch to Done label.
FILLIN YesNo USING 'Do you wish to exit now? (Y/N) ' +
     AT 12,2
NEWPAGE
---- If exit requested, skip over all commands before
---- LABEL Done
IF YesNo = 'Y' THEN
     GOTO Done
ENDIF
---- If exit not requested, print Director report.
CONNECT MAIL
PRINT Director ORDER BY CustNo
DISCONNECT
QUIT    ---- Return to R> prompt
---- Routine to leave R:BASE and return to DOS
LABEL Done
EXIT    ---- Leave R:BASE
```

Figure 16.11: A sample program with GOTO and LABEL commands

Branching has the disadvantage of slowing down the speed of command file execution considerably, and in most cases a WHILE, IF, or SWITCH command can be used in place of the GOTO and LABEL commands. You should only resort to using a GOTO command when there appears to be no other way to accomplish a programming goal.

It is especially important to avoid using the GOTO command between a WHILE command and the corresponding ENDWHILE to branch to a label above the WHILE command. When R:BASE executes a WHILE command, it stores control information as well as an extra copy of the commands in the WHILE loop to make the WHILE loop faster to execute. If you leave the WHILE loop either by executing the corresponding ENDWHILE command or branching to a command below this ENDWHILE command, R:BASE decides that you are finished with the WHILE loop. However, if you branch to a command above the WHILE command, R:BASE will not assume you are finished with the WHILE loop. This means that the memory used to store the WHILE loop commands and control information will not be recovered. If you must leave a WHILE loop before the WHILE condition is satisfied, use the BREAK command to transfer to the command following the ENDWHILE command. Using the BREAK command to leave a WHILE loop will free the memory used to control the WHILE loop, since R:BASE will encounter the ENDWHILE command.

Although this problem is not as serious for the IF and SWITCH commands, you should also avoid branching above the IF or SWITCH command from between the IF and ENDIF or SWITCH and ENDSW commands.

If you do use a GOTO to branch backward from an IF, SWITCH, or WHILE group of commands, use the QUIT command at the end of your program. The QUIT command frees memory used for unfinished IF, SWITCH or WHILE commands and returns you to the R> prompt. Fortunately, you'll see that the GOTO command is rarely necessary as you learn more techniques in this book.

USING SUBROUTINES

Subroutines (sometimes called *procedures* or *macros*) are command files that can be accessed from other command files. They save programming effort by allowing you to perform a task that may require several commands with a single RUN command in a command file. Subroutines have the additional advantage of *parameter passing*. This technique leaves certain aspects of the routine open-ended so that it is more flexible.

Figure 16.12 shows a simple subroutine named Area.CMD, which calculates the area of a rectangle using the formula Area = Length × Width. The command

        SET VARIABLE Area = .%1 * .%2

calculates the area by multiplying the first (%1) and second (%2) parameters passed to the subroutine and stores the result in a variable named Area.

Be sure to place the RETURN command at the end of every subroutine. This ensures that control is returned either to the R> prompt or to a calling command file after the subroutine is done. Be

```
*(***************************************** Area.CMD
                      Subroutine to calculate area)
SET VARIABLE Area REAL
SET VARIABLE Area = .%1 * .%2
RETURN                              ---- Return to calling program
```

Figure 16.12: The Area.CMD subroutine

sure to place the RETURN command at the bottom of the subroutine (and *not* in the middle of an IF, SWITCH, or WHILE clause).

After creating and saving a subroutine, using the same technique that is used for creating command files, you can run it and pass parameters to it with the USING option of the RUN command.

For example, to calculate the area using a length of 5 and a width of 10, you would enter the command

RUN Area.CMD USING 5 10

To see the results of the calculation, enter the command

WRITE .Area

You'll see that the Area variable contains 50.

You also can pass variables to subroutines. For example, if you create the variables LengthVar and WidthVar, as below:

SET VARIABLE LengthVar = 5.543
SET VARIABLE WidthVar = 6.1234

you can use the command

RUN Area.CMD USING .LengthVar .WidthVar

When you write the Area variable, it will contain the results of the appropriate calculation.

You can pass up to nine parameters to a subroutine. The parameters are assigned numbers (for example, %1, %2, %3, and so on) from left to right. Separate each parameter with a blank space.

In some cases, you might want to pass a parameter to a subroutine that has spaces in it. For example, the subroutine in Figure 16.13 displays a title, the date, and the time at the top of the screen. The title to be printed is passed as a parameter (%1).

```
*(********************************* Title.CMD
                  Subroutine to print a title)
NEWPAGE
WRITE .%1 AT 2,1
WRITE .#DATE AT 2,60
WRITE .#TIME AT 2,70
RETURN
```

Figure 16.13: A subroutine to print a title

To print the title Accounts-Receivable Main menu using the Title subroutine, you would need to enclose the title in quotation marks:

RUN Title.CMD USING 'Accounts-Receivable Main Menu'

If you use the SHOW VARIABLES command after you've passed parameters to subroutines, you'll notice that R:BASE adds a second digit to the parameters, as in the %1-0 and %2-0 variables below:

VARIABLE	= *VALUE*	*TYPE*
#DATE	= 11/05/90	DATE
#TIME	= 12:45:46	TIME
#PI	= 3.14159265358979	DOUBLE
SQLCODE	= 0	INTEGER
%1-0	= Accounts-Receivable Main Menu	TEXT
%2-0	= 6.1234	DOUBLE
Area	= 33.94201	REAL
LengthVar	= 5.543	DOUBLE
WidthVar	= 6.1234	DOUBLE

R:BASE performs this "housekeeping" task as a means of keeping track of the level at which a parameter was used. The parameters in this example have the extension − 0 because they were called from the R > prompt. If they had been called from a command file, the extension would be − 1. If they had been called from a command file that had been called from another command file, the extension would be − 2. However, you need not concern yourself with these extensions, and you definitely should not add them yourself.

TECHNIQUES FOR DEBUGGING COMMAND FILES

Quite often, when you first run a command file, it will not perform exactly as you had expected. Errors in programs are referred to as *bugs,* and removing them is called *debugging*. There are several techniques that you can use to help debug programs.

DEBUGGING WITH THE ECHO ON COMMAND

If the screen is cleared by a NEW-PAGE or CLS command before you can read it, you can place a PAUSE command in your program just before the screen is cleared.

By entering the command SET ECHO ON at the R > prompt before running a command file, you can see each line in the program as R:BASE processes it. This way, if an error causes the program to stop running, you'll be able to see the exact line that caused the error. Then, you can use RBEDIT to correct the program and try running it again. To disable the ECHO option, use the SET ECHO OFF command.

SETTING MESSAGES

R:BASE will display general-purpose messages, such as "Database exists," while the command file is running. You can suppress messages by entering SET MESSAGES OFF at the top of a command file. However, if you find that you are having problems getting a command file to run, remove the SET MESSAGES OFF command from the command file and enter SET MESSAGES ON at the R > prompt. After correcting your program, you can replace the SET MESSAGES OFF command.

SETTING ERROR MESSAGES

You can enter the command SET ERROR MESSAGES OFF at the top of a command file to suppress the display of R:BASE error messages. However, if your command file has a bug in it that causes control to be returned to the R> prompt, you won't see what the error was. To debug the program, remove the SET ERROR MESSAGES OFF command from the command file. From the R> prompt, enter SET ERROR MESSAGES ON before you run the command file again. After you find and correct any bugs, you can put the SET ERROR MESSAGES OFF command back into the command file if you wish.

TRACKING VARIABLES

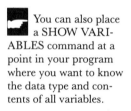 You can also place a SHOW VARI-ABLES command at a point in your program where you want to know the data type and contents of all variables.

You can enter the command SHOW VARIABLES at any time from the R> prompt. If your program uses variables, look closely at the variables displayed. Make sure that all of the variables your program needs have been created and that they are the appropriate data type. If you find that some variables have the incorrect data type, use explicit data typing near the top of your program to specify what type they should be. For example, enter a command like

SET VARIABLE YourName TEXT

Remember to use the CTXT function to display the contents of a variable that does not have the TEXT data type in a WRITE command.

To see the value of just one variable, use a WRITE command or a SHOW VARIABLES command with the variable name.

STOPPING A PROGRAM BEFORE IT FINISHES

Sometimes you will want to stop a program before it finishes. For example, you would want to stop it if you made a mistake and included a loop in your program that never stops (called an *infinite loop*), or if you noticed a bug in your program that made the rest of the program output meaningless. How do you tell your program that you want it to stop? If your program is running and not asking for input,

1. Press **Ctrl-Break** or **Ctrl-C**.

2. When R:BASE instructs you to ''press Esc to abort, anything else to continue,'' press **Esc**.

3. When R:BASE instructs you to ''press Esc to switch INPUT to KEYBOARD, Enter to continue,'' press **Esc**.

4. To clean up any loose ends, type **QUIT** and press ◄─┘; type **CLOSE** and press ◄─┘; and type **RETURN** and press ◄─┘.

Although the QUIT, CLOSE, and RETURN commands in step 4 will usually not be necessary, it doesn't hurt to enter them as insurance. The QUIT command cleans up unfinished business that R:BASE might have if you happened to stop the program between an IF and ENDIF, a SWITCH and ENDSW, or a WHILE and ENDWHILE command. The CLOSE command closes any cursors that you were using. The RETURN command will return you to the menu or program from which the program was called, in the event that this return needs to be completed.

If you want to stop your program when you are being asked to enter input with a FILLIN or PAUSE command, you have to answer the question (pressing Esc or ◄─┘) and then press Ctrl-Break or Ctrl-C while the program is executing other instructions. You can then continue with steps 2 to 4 above.

MAKING A PRINTED COPY OF A COMMAND FILE

Another method that will help you debug a command file is to make a printed, or hard, copy of it. Use the OUTPUT PRINTER and TYPE commands at the R> prompt. For example, to print a copy of the IO5.CMD command file, enter the commands

```
OUTPUT PRINTER WITH SCREEN
TYPE IO5.CMD
```

at the R> prompt. Enter the OUTPUT SCREEN command after printing the program to return to normal screen mode.

If your program contains WHILE, IF, or SWITCH commands, you might want to use a pen or pencil to draw connecting lines between all the WHILE and ENDWHILE commands, the IF and ENDIF commands, and the SWITCH and ENDSW commands, as shown in Figure 16.14. Make sure that each WHILE, IF, and SWITCH command has an associated ENDWHILE, ENDIF, and ENDSW command.

```
*(***************************** SAMPLE2.CMD)
*(--------- Program to test the SWITCH command)
---- Create variable to hold answer
CLEAR ALL VARIABLES
SET VARIABLE YesNo TEXT
---- Loop until a valid answer is entered
NEWPAGE
WHILE (.YesNo IS NULL) THEN
     ---- Display prompt and get answer
     FILLIN YesNo USING 'Send message to the printer? (Y/N) ' +
          AT 12,2
     ---- Decide whether to use printer or just screen
     SWITCH (.YesNo)
          CASE 'Y'      -- Printer
               OUTPUT PRINTER WITH SCREEN
               BREAK
          CASE 'N'      -- Screen
               OUTPUT SCREEN
               BREAK
          DEFAULT       -- Error  --  Get another answer
               SET VARIABLE YesNo = '-0-'
               NEWPAGE
               WRITE 'Please answer Y or N' AT 11,2
     ENDSW
ENDWHILE
---- Display message
WRITE 'Here is the message'
OUTPUT SCREEN     -- Back to normal screen display
QUIT
```

Figure 16.14: A sample program with connecting lines drawn in

Missing and misplaced ENDWHILE, ENDIF, and ENDSW commands will definitely cause problems in a program. Drawing connecting lines can help find them, as well as help you see more clearly the commands contained within the WHILE, IF, and SWITCH clauses.

AVOIDING BUGS WITH STRUCTURED PROGRAMMING

One of the best debugging techniques is to try to avoid bugs in the first place. The technique of *structured programming* can help accomplish this feat, and it will greatly aid in the process of debugging, as well as in making future modifications to a program.

The two basic rules of thumb for structured programming are quite simple:

- Use highly visible programmer comments in the command file to make it easy to locate commands that perform a specific task.

- Indent program lines within WHILE loops, IF clauses, SWITCH clauses, and CASE clauses so that you can easily see the beginning and ending points of these specific routines.

The programs we've developed in this chapter have adhered to these basic rules of thumb. Note that the program shown in Figure 16.15 does not follow the basic rules of structured programming. There are no comments and no indentations in the programming. To figure out what the program is supposed to do, you need to read every line in the command file.

```
SET VARIABLE Counter = 1
SET VARIABLE Done INTEGER
NEWPAGE
FILLIN Done USING 'How high shall I count?: ' AT 9,5
NEWPAGE
WHILE Counter <= .Done THEN
SET VARIABLE Progress = ('Loop Number' & CTXT(.Counter))
WRITE .Progress
SET VARIABLE Counter = (.Counter + 1)
ENDWHILE
QUIT
```

Figure 16.15: An unstructured program

As shown in Figure 16.16, the same command file can be made much easier to understand by inserting comments that describe the various tasks that the program performs. Furthermore, the indented lines between the WHILE and ENDWHILE commands make it easy to see the starting and ending points of the loop, as well as which commands are repeated within the loop. Indenting the program lines between the IF and ENDIF, the WHILE and ENDWHILE, and the SWITCH and ENDSW commands is especially beneficial because many program

```
*(******************************* Loop2.CMD)
*(------------ Program to test the WHILE loop)
-------------- Create Counter and Done variable
SET VARIABLE Counter = 1
SET VARIABLE Done INTEGER
-------------- Ask how high to count
NEWPAGE
FILLIN Done USING 'How high shall I count?: ' AT 9,5
NEWPAGE
-------------- Repeat loop until Counter > Done
WHILE Counter <= .Done THEN
       -------- Create a prompt and display it
       SET VARIABLE Progress = ('Loop Number' & CTXT(.Counter))
       WRITE .Progress
       -------- Increment Counter variable by 1
       SET VARIABLE Counter = (.Counter + 1)
ENDWHILE  ---   Bottom of WHILE loop
-------------- End of program
QUIT
```

Figure 16.16: A structured program (compare this to Figure 16.15)

errors are caused by leaving out the necessary ENDIF, ENDWHILE, and ENDSW commands. If you use indentations, a missing ENDIF, ENDWHILE, or ENDSW command will be more noticeable.

WHY LEARN PROGRAMMING?

You may be wondering why you need to know about R:BASE programming. The sample programs you've created and run in this chapter aren't necessarily the sort of programs you'll want to run on your own. We have used them to introduce the R:BASE programming language to you, and to show you the kinds of situations in which the different programming commands prove useful.

Generally, you'll want to incorporate the R:BASE programs you write into an application. In Chapter 15, when you worked with Applications EXPRESS, you may have wondered about the Custom and Macro options on the Applications EXPRESS Action menu. These refer to command files that you want to use at a particular point in your application. When you select Custom, R:BASE presents you with RBEDIT and allows you to write your own programs "on the fly" from within Applications EXPRESS. Although experienced programmers sometimes select this option, its disadvantage is that you won't be able to test the program on its own, outside of Applications EXPRESS. To see if it works, you'll have to run your application.

A command file added to an application as a macro in Applications EXPRESS should end with a RETURN command that will return to the application menu.

If you select Macro, on the other hand, R:BASE asks for the name of the program file you have created. Presumably, you've already tested the program on its own to make sure it works properly.

In the next chapter, we'll show you how powerful command files can be used to keep an accounts-receivable system up-to-date. You'll create several command files, test them, and then insert them into an accounts-receivable application.

Chapter 17

An Accounts-Receivable
Application

IN THIS CHAPTER, WE'LL DISCUSS SOME ADVANCED programming techniques with the R:BASE programming language and methods for integrating custom routines with applications developed by using the Applications EXPRESS feature. As we learn these new techniques we'll develop a complex accounts-receivable system with monthly billing.

DESIGNING ACCOUNTS-RECEIVABLE SYSTEMS

Before you begin developing a large system, write down your basic goals on paper. Sometimes an overall goal—such as developing an accounts-receivable/billing system—is too vague for a starting point. An outline allows you to break down your overall goal into smaller, more manageable ones. For example, consider how the goals below have been broken down into outline form.

I. Develop an accounts-receivable/billing system

    A. Maintain a customer list with accounts-receivable balances

    B. Maintain an inventory list of items in stock

    C. Maintain a history of individual charge transactions

    D. Maintain a history of payments

    E. Print monthly bills

From this point, define which tasks you'll need to do to attain each main goal under the overall goal.

I. Develop an accounts-receivable/billing system

    A. Maintain a customer list with accounts-receivable balances

        1. Add, edit, and delete customers

        2. Print customer list

B. Maintain an inventory list of items in stock

    1. Add, edit, and delete inventory items

    2. Print inventory list

C. Maintain a history of individual charge transactions

    1. Add, edit, and delete charges

    2. Print charge transactions

D. Maintain a history of payments

    1. Add, edit, and delete payments

    2. Print payment transactions

E. Print monthly bills

    1. Print the bills

    2. Update customer billing history

Looking at the project from this perspective makes designing the system easier to understand. Most tasks simply require you to manage data and print reports from tables. Once you've written down the basic goals of the project, you can begin designing the database structure.

DATABASE DESIGN

To meet the goals we've just defined, we'll need several tables in our accounts-receivable system databases. First, we'll need a table to record basic customer information, including the current, and 30-, 60-, 90-, and 120-day balances, as well as other relevant information. We'll name the database "ARSYS," and name the table for recording customer information "ARMain." The ARMain table will have the structure shown in Figure 17.1.

Next, we'll develop an inventory table for storing product numbers, product names, prices, and so forth. The purpose of this table is to speed up data entry in the accounts-receivable system. All the user will have to do is enter a product number, and R:BASE will automatically fill in the rest of the information for each charge transaction.

```
TABLE: ARMAIN
CUSTOMER INFORMATION

COLUMN DEFINITIONS
                                                          TEXT
   # Name      Description              Type       Length

   1 CustNo    Customer number          INTEGER
   2 L_Name    Last name                TEXT          12
   3 F_Name    First name               TEXT          15
   4 Company                            TEXT          20
   5 Address   Street address           TEXT          20
   6 City                               TEXT          15
   7 State                              TEXT           2
   8 Zip_Code  ZIP code                 TEXT          10
   9 Phone     Phone number             TEXT          13
  10 Curr_Bal  Current balance          CURRENCY
  11 Bal_30    30-day balance           CURRENCY
  12 Bal_60    60-day balance           CURRENCY
  13 Bal_90    90-day balance           CURRENCY
  14 Bal_120   120-day balance          CURRENCY
  15 Curr_Chr  Last total charge amount CURRENCY
  16 Curr_Pay  Last payment amount      CURRENCY
  17 BillDate  Last billing date        DATE
```

Figure 17.1: The structure for the ARMain table

We'll call the inventory table "Inventry." Its structure is shown in Figure 17.2.

We'll also need a table to record individual charge transactions. It's structure will be similar to the Charges table in the Mail database. In fact, let's call the table "Charges." Its structure is shown in Figure 17.3.

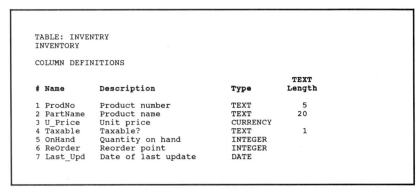

```
TABLE: INVENTRY
INVENTORY

COLUMN DEFINITIONS
                                                     TEXT
   # Name      Description            Type     Length

   1 ProdNo    Product number         TEXT         5
   2 PartName  Product name           TEXT        20
   3 U_Price   Unit price             CURRENCY
   4 Taxable   Taxable?               TEXT         1
   5 OnHand    Quantity on hand       INTEGER
   6 ReOrder   Reorder point          INTEGER
   7 Last_Upd  Date of last update    DATE
```

Figure 17.2: The structure of the Inventry table

```
TABLE: CHARGES
CHARGE TRANSACTIONS

COLUMN DEFINITIONS
                                                        TEXT
     # Name        Description              Type       Length

     1 CustNo      Customer number          INTEGER
     2 ProdNo      Product number           TEXT          5
     3 Qty         Quantity purchased       INTEGER
     4 U_Price     Unit price               CURRENCY
     5 Taxable     Taxable?                 TEXT          1
     6 T_Price     Total price              CURRENCY
     7 P_Date      Purchase date            DATE
```

Figure 17.3: The structure of the Charges table

Accounts-receivable systems typically revolve around a monthly billing cycle, so let's move all transactions that have been billed to a new table at the end of each billing period. We'll call the new table "CHistory" to remind ourselves that it contains past charge transactions. This table's structure will be identical to the structure of the Charges table. Only the table description will be different: "Charge transactions—history."

As for individual payment transactions, we'll store them in a table called "Payments." The structure of the Payments table is shown in Figure 17.4.

As with the Charges table, let's move payments that have already been recorded on a bill at the end of each month to a history table named "PHistory." This table's structure is identical to the structure of the Payments table, except the table description is "Payment transactions—history."

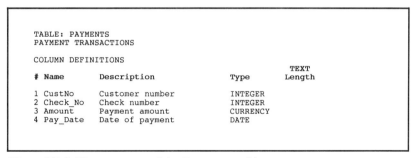

```
TABLE: PAYMENTS
PAYMENT TRANSACTIONS

COLUMN DEFINITIONS
                                                        TEXT
     # Name        Description              Type       Length

     1 CustNo      Customer number          INTEGER
     2 Check_No    Check number             INTEGER
     3 Amount      Payment amount           CURRENCY
     4 Pay_Date    Date of payment          DATE
```

Figure 17.4: The structure of the Payments table

We'll explain the purpose of the BillTemp table later in this chapter.

Finally, to simplify the printing of bills, we'll create a special table named "BillTemp" to hold records of both the Charges and Payments transactions. The structure of the BillTemp table is shown in Figure 17.5.

The hierarchical relationship among the ARMain, Charges, Payments, and the two History tables is shown in Figure 17.6. In our accounts-receivable system, the ARMain table is the *master table*: it maintains an ongoing balance of each customer's credit activities. The Charges and Payments tables are *transaction tables*: they record individual transactions during the month. In order to keep each customer's balance up-to-date, the ARMain master table receives data from the transaction tables. The job of the PHistory and CHistory tables is to record "old" transaction data that have already been through the entire monthly billing cycle.

```
TABLE: BILLTEMP
TEMPORARY BILLING INFORMATION

COLUMN DEFINITIONS
                                               TEXT
   # Name       Description          Type      Length

   1 CustNo     Customer number      INTEGER
   2 ProdNo     Product number       TEXT      5
   3 Qty        Quantity purchased   INTEGER
   4 U_Price    Unit price           CURRENCY
   5 Taxable    Taxable?             TEXT      1
   6 T_Price    Total price          CURRENCY
   7 P_Date     Purchase date        DATE
   8 Check_No   Check number         INTEGER
   9 Amount     Payment amount       CURRENCY
  10 Pay_Date   Date of payment      DATE
```

Figure 17.5: The structure of the BillTemp table

If you'd like to follow along and create an accounts-receivable system, display the R > prompt and enter the RBDEFINE command to create the ARSYS database. Create the ARMain, Inventry, Charges, Payments, and BillTemp tables as well using the structures shown in the Figures 17.1 through 17.5. Don't bother defining index columns for any of the tables at this point.

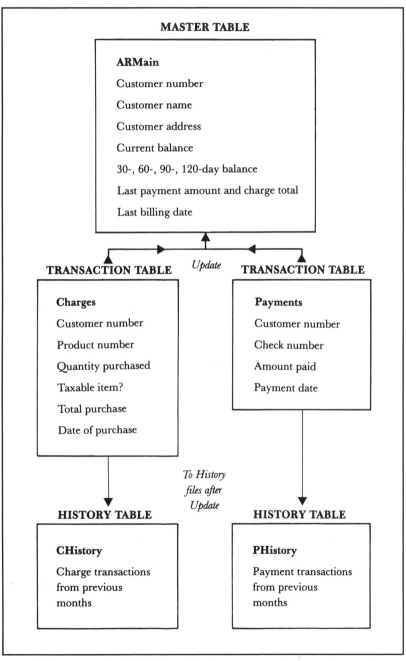

Figure 17.6: The relationship among the tables in the accounts-receivable system

To access the Tables pull-down menu, highlight Info and select create/modify on the R:BASE Main menu, or issue the RBDEFINE command at the R> prompt.

After you've created all five tables, use the Copy option in the Tables pull-down menu to copy the Charges table to the CHistory table and to copy the Payments table to the PHistory table. Then use the Modify option in the Tables pull-down menu to add

    –history

to the table descriptions for the history tables. Now you can begin developing forms for entering and editing data.

FORMS FOR YOUR ACCOUNTS-RECEIVABLE SYSTEM

Remember, you can access the Form Generator by entering the FORMS command at the R> prompt.

After you've created your accounts-receivable system tables, it's time to begin developing forms for entering and editing data. Bring up the Form Generator and connect to the ARSYS database, if necessary.

THE CUSTOMER FORM

For a review of how to create forms, see Chapters 8 and 13.

In the Form Generator, create a form for entering and editing customer information. Make "Main" the name of the form and "Customers" the description. Next, attach the form to the ARMain table. You don't need to customize the table, form, or field characteristics on this form. Nor do you need to define any variables for this form. Figure 17.7 shows one way to design a format for the Main form.

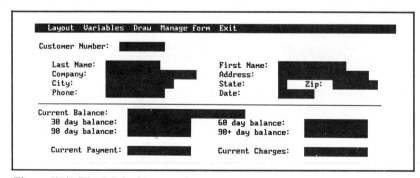

Figure 17.7: The Main form on the screen

Don't leave the Curr_Bal column empty (null) because we'll soon be developing a report that needs a value in this column. Enter values for the balances on the bottom half of the screen.

Now that you've created the form, give it a preliminary test with the Run option in the Manage form pull-down menu. For practice data, enter one or two rows of customer numbers that are easy to remember, such as 1001 and 1002. Later in this chapter you will develop a program to calculate the balances on the bottom half of the screen. Although you can fill in zeroes for these balances, it is a good idea to enter non-zero balances for at least one customer. This way, you can see what non-zero values look like on the report you will be creating. Keep this test data—it will be useful for testing other forms and reports.

THE INVENTORY TABLE FORM

You can use the Form Generator to create a form for entering and editing items in the inventory table. Name this form "InvForm," enter the description "Inventory," and attach it to the Inventry table. You don't need to define any variables or customize any table or form characteristics for this form. Figure 17.8 shows a suggested format for the form.

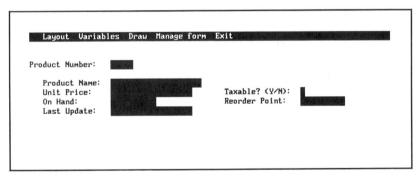

Figure 17.8: The InvForm form on the screen

See Chapter 8 for a review of how to add a default value to a data column.

For added convenience, you may want to customize the field characteristics for the Taxable and Last_Upd fields, adding a default of 'Y' for Taxable and .#DATE for Last_Upd. Give your form a quick test when you are finished, adding a sample row with an easy-to-remember part number like A-111. You'll be able to use this data when you test other parts of the accounts-receivable system.

THE CHARGES FORM

The form for entering and editing charges will be fancier than the Main and InvForm forms. For convenience, this form will automatically look up the customer name and company from the ARMain table whenever the user enters a customer number. These data will be displayed on the form so the user can verify that the correct customer number was entered.

As soon as the user enters a product number for the transaction, the form will look up the product name, unit price, and tax status on the Inventry table. These data will appear on the form immediately and will also be entered into the Charges table automatically. The user only needs to enter the quantity purchased, and the form will calculate and display the total sale.

Use the Form Generator to create the form. Assign the name "ChrgFrm" and the description "Charges" to the form, and attach it to the Charges table. Define the following variables:

```
Name1 = F_Name IN ARMain WHERE CustNo = CustNo
Name2 = L_Name IN ARMain WHERE CustNo = CustNo
VName = (.Name1 & .Name2)
VComp = Company IN ARMain WHERE CustNo = CustNo
VPartNm = PartName IN Inventry WHERE ProdNo = ProdNo
U_Price = U_Price IN Inventry WHERE ProdNo = ProdNo
Taxable = Taxable IN Inventry WHERE ProdNo = ProdNo
T_Price = (IFEQ(Taxable,'N',Qty*U_Price,(Qty*U_Price)*1.06))
```

Notice that the first four expressions look up information in the ARMain table based on the customer number entered onto the form. The customer name and company from the ARMain table are stored in the variables named VName and VComp.

The last four variables look up information in the Inventry table. The part name is stored in the variable named VPartNm. The unit price and taxable status are stored directly in the Charges table (because of the column names Taxable and U_Price, which are the actual column names in the Charges table). The total price (T_Price) is calculated using the IFEQ function to determine whether the item is taxable. T_Price is also a column name in the Charges table, which means that the results of this calculation are stored directly on the Charges table.

After you've defined the variables for the form, place the text and fields on the form. Figure 17.9 shows a format you might use for the ChrgFrm form. You don't need to customize any table or form characteristics for this form.

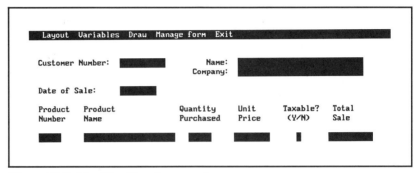

Figure 17.9: The ChrgFrm form on the screen

For your convenience, you can customize the field characteristics for the P_Date column and specify #DATE as the default value for the field. You can also customize the field settings for the CustNo and ProdNo columns to help users choose valid customer and product numbers. When you are entering data with the form, you will be able to press Shift-F3 when the highlighter is in the CustNo or Prod-No column to make a pop-up menu display the available choices. To provide a pop-up menu at row 4, column 35 for the CustNo column on this form that displays the contents of the CustNo column in the ARMain table, follow these steps on the Form Generator screen:

1. Display the Field Settings menu for the CustNo field by moving the cursor on the CustNo field, pressing **F6**, and answering **Yes** to customizing field settings.

2. Press **PgDn** to display the second page of the Field Settings menu.

3. Change the answer to the question "Do you want a pop-up menu for this field?" to **Yes** and press ↵.

4. Enter **ARMain** for the table name, **CustNo** for the column name, **Select a customer number** for the title, **4** for the upper-left corner row, and **35** for the upper-left corner column.

The title for this menu, "Select a customer number," will appear as a prompt in the status lines at the bottom of the screen.

5. Press **F2** to return to the Form Generator screen.

Using similar steps, provide a pop-up menu for the ProdNo column on this form that will display the contents of the ProdNo column in the Inventry table at row 12, column 13 with the title "Choose a product number."

After you've created the ChrgFrm form, enter a Charge transaction to give your form a quick test. Be sure to use only valid customer numbers and product numbers that you've already entered on the ARMain and Inventry tables. Later you'll add rules to ensure that the customer numbers and product numbers are on file. Of course, try pressing Shift-F3 and selecting a value from the pop-up menus for these fields.

THE PAYMENTS FORM

The payments form lets the user enter and edit data on the Payments table. Use the Form Generator as usual to create the form. Assign the name "PayForm" and the description "Payments" to the form, and attach the form to the Payments table.

On the Form Generator screen, create the following variables:

```
Name1 = F_Name IN ARMain WHERE CustNo = CustNo
Name2 = L_Name IN ARMain WHERE CustNo = CustNo
VName = (.Name1 & .Name2)
VComp = Company in ARMain WHERE CustNo = CustNo
```

Note that these variables look up customer information in the ARMain table based on the customer number entered onto the form. The form will display this information for the user's convenience when it is used to record or edit payment transactions.

After defining the variables, lay out the form format. Figure 17.10 shows a suggested format for the PayForm form.

For additional convenience, you can customize the field characteristics for the Pay_Date column by entering #DATE as the default date for the column. As well, you can customize the field characteristics of the CustNo column to define the same pop-up menu you defined for the CustNo column on the ChrgFrm form. For a quick

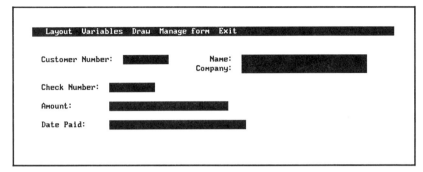

Figure 17.10: The PayForm form on the screen

test of this form, enter a payment. Once again, try choosing the customer number from the pop-up menu displayed when you press Shift-F3. After you've created all four forms, exit from the Form Generator and return to the R> prompt.

RULES FOR YOUR ACCOUNTS-RECEIVABLE SYSTEM

To display the Modify Table menu from the R> prompt when you are connected to the ARSYS database, issue the RBDEFINE command.

Chapter 10 tells how to create and modify rules. To modify the error message of a rule, highlight Rules, select Modify, select the rule, press ◄— three times, edit the message, and press ◄—.

Let's create a few rules to ensure that data entered in this system is consistent. You need to ensure that there are no duplicate customer numbers in the ARMain table and duplicate product numbers in the Inventry table. Also, you should make sure that the customer numbers entered in the Charges and the Payments table are in the ARMain table, and that the product numbers entered in the Charges table are in the Inventry table. Go to the Modify Tables menu to add rules.

Remember, the easiest way to create a rule that prevents a duplicate customer or product number is to create the rule by highlighting **R**ules, selecting **C**reate, and selecting the **R**equire a unique value option. After you've selected the appropriate table and column name, you can modify the rule's error message if you want to.

For the rule that doesn't allow duplicate customer numbers in the ARMain table, change the error message to "Duplicate Customer Number!" Change the error message for the duplicate product number rule in the Inventry table to "Duplicate Product Number!"

To ensure that each customer and product number entered in the Charges and Payments tables is on file, create two rules by highlighting **R**ules, selecting **C**reate, and selecting the **V**erify a value option.

Once again, you can customize the error messages for these two rules if desired.

For the rules that disallow a customer number which is not in the ARMain table, change the error message to "Customer Number not on file!" Change the error message for the rule that disallows a product number not in the Inventry table to "Product Number not on file!" Once you have created these rules, exit to the R> prompt.

REPORTS FOR YOUR ACCOUNTS-RECEIVABLE SYSTEM

You can create whatever reports you wish for the accounts-receivable system. We suggest that you develop reports similar to the Labels, CaLetter, Director, and Sales reports that you developed for the Mail database. Also, simple reports displaying data from the Payments and Inventry table would be useful.

THE AGING REPORT

To review the procedures for creating reports, see Chapters 7 and 12.

One of the primary reports for the accounts-receivable system will be the "Aging" report, which is shown in Figure 17.11. This report summarizes how much each customer owes by displaying the amounts that have been owing for 30, 60, 90 and 120 days. Create this report with the Report Generator, making "Aging" the name and "Aging Receivables" the description. Attach this report to the ARMain table.

```
                    ACCOUNTS RECEIVABLE AGING REPORT
    Date:   09/11/90                                    Page:  1

    Current Balance    30 Days      60 Days    90 Days   120+ Days   Paym

    Customer Number:  1001        Stewart Smith
          $1,171.02     $56.50     $256.27     $0.00     $203.00     $35

    Customer Number:  1002        Wanda Watson
            $283.82     $70.65      $80.38     $0.00     $296.47     $26

    Customer Number:  1003        Zeppo Magillicuddy
            $318.96     $50.12      $85.53     $0.00       $0.00     $25
```

Figure 17.11: A sample Aging report from the accounts-receivable system

When the Report Generator screen is displayed, define the variable as

VName = (F_Name & L_Name)

Then place the text, columns and variables on the screen, using Figure 17.12 as a suggested format. In the detail section, place the CustNo column and VName variable beside "Customer Number." In the middle of the detail section, place the columns Curr_Bal, Bal_30, Bal_60, Bal_90, Bal_120, and Curr_Pay. Left-justify the page number and customer number fields by adding a picture format of [<]9999 for #PAGE and [<]99999 for CustNo. When you test the report, you should see the aging of the customers you entered in previous testing.

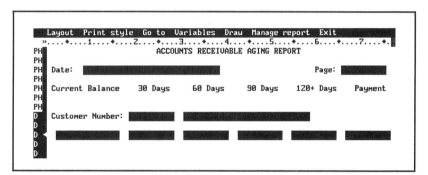

Figure 17.12: The Aging report layout on the Report Generator screen

THE BILLS REPORT

The "Bills" report prints monthly statements like the one in Figure 17.13. Create the Bills report with the description "Customer Bills" for the BillTemp table. Create the report variables listed below:

Name1	= F_Name in ARMain WHERE CustNo = CustNo
Name2	= L_Name in ARMain WHERE CustNo = CustNo
VName	= (.Name1 & .Name2)
VComp	= Company IN ARMain WHERE CustNo = CustNo
Addr	= Address IN ARMain WHERE CustNo = CustNo
C	= City IN ARMain WHERE CustNo = CustNo
S	= State IN ARMain WHERE CustNo = CustNo
Z	= Zip_Code IN ARMain WHERE CustNo = CustNo

```
CSZ       = (.C + ',' & .S & .Z)
B_Date    = .#DATE
D_Date    = (.B_Date + 30)
PartNm    = PartName IN Inventry WHERE ProdNo = ProdNo
            AND ProdNo IS NOT NULL
Prev_Bal  = Curr_Bal IN ARMain WHERE CustNo = CustNo
ChrgTot   = SUM OF T_Price
PayTot    = SUM OF Amount
Sub_Bal   = (.Prev_Bal + .ChrgTot)
Balance   = (.Sub_Bal - .PayTot)
```

```
Stewart Smith
ABC Co.
123 A St.
Los Angeles, CA 12345

┌─────────────────────────────────────────────────────────────────────┐
│ Customer Number: 1001     Billing Date: 09/11/90  Due Date: 10/11/90  │
└─────────────────────────────────────────────────────────────────────┘

Product   Product Name      Qty   Unit Price  Taxable?     Total    Payment

A-111   Semiconductor       10       $1.56       Y        $16.54
B-222   A/D Module           7      $89.00       Y       $660.38
C-333   RF Modulator         9      $34.56       Y       $329.70
                                                                    $550.00


Previous Balance:                  $673.16
Total Charges:                   $1,006.62
Total Payments:                    $550.00
                                  ─────────
Current Balance:                 $1,129.78
```

Figure 17.13: A sample bill printed by the accounts-receivable system

To review lookup expressions, see Chapter 12.

Several of these variables warrant discussion. First, note that the name, company, address, city, state, ZIP code, and current balance are obtained with lookup expressions that access the ARMain table. Similarly, the product name is taken from the Inventry table using a lookup expression.

The B_Date (billing date) variable is assigned the current date (.#DATE), and the D_Date (due date) variable is calculated by adding 30 days to the billing date variable (.B_Date + 30).

Balances for each bill are calculated by summing the total charges (ChrgTot = SUM OF T_Price), summing the total payments (PayTot = SUM OF Amount), and then adding the total charges to the current balance (Sub_Bal = (.Prev_Bal + .ChrgTot)) and subtracting the total payments (Balance = (.Sub_Bal - .PayTot)).

After you've typed in all the variables, define a breakpoint on the CustNo column for each subtotal—and hence for each invoice, since one invoice is printed for each customer. To do so, make CustNo the Break column for the Break1 point. Change the Variable Reset column to Yes, and select the following variables to reset: ChrgTot, PayTot, Sub_Bal, and Balance. Also, to ensure that each invoice is printed on a separate page, change the FORM FEEDS Before Header column to Yes.

Now lay out the text and fields on the report, using the suggested report format in Figure 17.14 as a guide. At the top of break header 1 (section H1), place the customer name, company, and address using variables VName, VComp, Addr, and CSZ. In the box, place the column CustNo, the variable B_Date, and the variable D_Date. In the detail section, place the column ProdNo, the variable PartNm, and then the columns Qty, U_Price, Taxable, T_Price, and Amount. In break footer 1 (section F1), place the variables PrevBal, ChrgTot, PayTot, and Balance. As you did in the Aging report, you could add a picture format to the customer number so that it is printed left-justified in the field.

If your printer does not do a good job of printing the lines made with the Draw menu option, such as the single-line box in the Break1 header or the line above the total in the Break1 footer, try making the horizontal lines with dashes (-) and leave out the vertical lines.

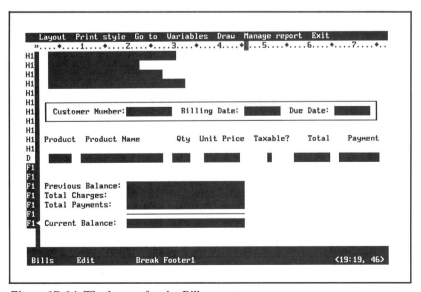

Figure 17.14: The layout for the Bills report

Since the Bills report gets its data from the BillTemp table, which is empty, you can't test it yet. In the next section we'll develop the appropriate command file for printing the bills.

COMMAND FILES FOR YOUR ACCOUNTS-RECEIVABLE SYSTEM

You can create most of the command files for the accounts-receivable system with the Applications EXPRESS menu. However, a few custom programs and subroutines will help refine the system. In this section, we'll develop these command files and subroutines, and we'll learn some advanced programming techniques along the way.

END-OF-MONTH PROCEDURES

Most accounting systems are based on a monthly schedule, whereby transactions are posted to a ledger at the end of each month. Our accounts-receivable system is no exception. The tasks performed at the end of each month can be summarized as follows:

1. Print monthly statements (bills or invoices).

2. Shift all current and 30-, 60-, 90-, and 120-day balances back one month.

3. Add new charges to the current balance.

4. Subtract new payments from the current balance.

Notice that blank lines are used to separate sections of the program. This makes the program easier to read.

We can write a single command file to handle all of these tasks; the user will be able to perform them simply by selecting one item in the menu. The command file to perform these tasks is named "End-Month.CMD," and is displayed in Figure 17.15.

First, this command file displays the message

Bills are to be printed once a month only
Monthly updates are automatically performed after Billing
Proceed with billing? (Y/N)

```
*(******************************* EndMonth.CMD)
-------------- Perform monthly billing and update
NEWPAGE
DISPLAY Bills.MSG
CLEAR ALL VARIABLES
SET VARIABLE YesNo TEXT
WHILE (.YesNo IS NULL) OR (.YesNo <> 'Y') THEN
     FILLIN YesNo=0 AT 22,1
     SWITCH .YesNo
         CASE 'Y'
             BREAK
         CASE 'N'
             GOTO Bailout
         DEFAULT
             BEEP
     ENDSW
ENDWHILE -- (.YesNo IS NULL) OR (.YesNo <> 'Y')

NEWPAGE
WRITE 'Prepare printer, then press any key to continue'
PAUSE

---- Set up the BillTemp Table
NEWPAGE
WRITE 'Working...'
SET RULES OFF
SET MESSAGES OFF
SET ERROR MESSAGES OFF
DELETE ROWS FROM BillTemp WHERE COUNT > 0
INSERT INTO BillTemp +
  (CustNo ProdNo Qty U_Price Taxable T_Price P_Date) +
   SELECT ALL FROM Charges
INSERT INTO BillTemp (CustNo Check_No Amount Pay_Date) +
   SELECT ALL FROM Payments

---- Print the Bills
SET NULL ' '
SET DATE FORMAT 'MM/DD/YY'
OUTPUT PRINTER
NEWPAGE
PRINT Bills
NEWPAGE
OUTPUT SCREEN
SET NULL '-0-'

---- Perform the update
---- First, shift back Current, 30, 60, and 90 day balances
UPDATE ARMain SET Bal_120 = (Bal_120 + Bal_90), +
                  Bal_90 = Bal_60, +
                  Bal_60 = Bal_30, +
                  Bal_30 = Curr_Chr +
   WHERE CustNo IS NOT NULL

---- Set current charges and payments to zero

UPDATE ARMain SET Curr_Chr = 0, +
                  Curr_Pay = 0 +
   WHERE CustNo IS NOT NULL

---- Next, update current balance from Charges and Payments
RUN Update.MAC USING ARMain CustNo Curr_Chr Charges CustNo T_Price PLUS
RUN Update.MAC USING ARMain CustNo Curr_Pay Payments CustNo Amount PLUS

UPDATE ARMain SET Curr_Bal = (Curr_Bal+(Curr_Chr-Curr_Pay)), +
                  BillDate = .#DATE +
   WHERE CustNo IS NOT NULL
```

Figure 17.15: The EndMonth.CMD command file

```
---- Now move transactions to history files
INSERT INTO CHistory SELECT ALL FROM Charges
DELETE ROWS FROM Charges WHERE COUNT > 0
INSERT INTO PHistory SELECT ALL FROM Payments
DELETE ROWS FROM Payments WHERE COUNT > 0

---- Now age the balances using the Age.CMD command file
RUN Age.CMD

---- Update complete
NEWPAGE
SET MESSAGES ON
SET ERROR MESSAGES ON
WRITE 'End of month procedures completed...'
SET RULES ON
RETURN

---- Bailout routine for immediate exit
LABEL Bailout
WRITE 'Returning to Main Menu without Update'
RETURN
```

Figure 17.15: The EndMonth.CMD command file (continued)

The purpose of this message is to give users a chance to change their minds, since the procedure is only to be performed once a month. The message is stored in a separate file named Bill.MSG. To create this file, enter

RBEDIT Bills.MSG

at the R> prompt and type in the message exactly as it appears above. Save the file in the usual way.

Now let's look at the EndMonth.CMD command file. The first lines include programmer comments and the NEWPAGE command to clear the screen. The DISPLAY command displays the Bills.MSG file we just created with RBEDIT. The condition in the WHILE command means that the WHILE loop will be executed if you have just created the YesNo variable (.YesNo IS NULL) or if the user has entered an invalid response (.YesNo < > 'Y'). Inside the WHILE loop, the FILLIN command waits for the user to respond and say whether to proceed with the end-of-month procedures. The YesNo = 0 in the FILLIN command means that the keystroke made by the user will be placed in the YesNo variable but not displayed on the screen. If the user answers Y, control breaks out of the SWITCH

You have to test the YesNo variable in the WHILE condition to see if it is NULL because a NULL value cannot be compared to any other value in R:BASE. You cannot depend on a NULL value to be equal, less than, or greater than any other value, whether the second value is NULL or not.

group of commands and the WHILE loop. If the user answers N, control is passed to a routine named Bailout at the bottom of the command file. Finally, if the user presses a key other than Y or N, the computer beeps and gives the user another chance to enter a response:

```
*(* * * * * * * * * * * * * * * * * * * * * * * * * * * EndMonth.CMD)
-------------- Perform monthly billing and update
NEWPAGE
DISPLAY Bills.MSG
CLEAR ALL VARIABLES
SET VARIABLE YesNo TEXT
WHILE (.YesNo IS NULL) OR (.YesNo < > 'Y') THEN
      FILLIN YesNo = 0 AT 22,1
      SWITCH .YesNo
            CASE 'Y'
                  BREAK
            CASE 'N'
                  GOTO Bailout
            DEFAULT
                  BEEP
      ENDSW
ENDWHILE -- (.YesNo < > 'Y') OR (.YesNo IS NULL)
```

If users choose to go ahead with the monthly procedure, the command file displays the prompt below, which reminds them to prepare the printer and waits for them to press any key to continue.

```
NEWPAGE
WRITE 'Prepare printer, then press any key to continue'
PAUSE
```

Next, the command file clears the screen and displays the message "Working..." The R:BASE rules and messages are then set off.

```
---- Set up the BillTemp Table
NEWPAGE
WRITE 'Working...'
SET RULES OFF
SET MESSAGES OFF
SET ERROR MESSAGES OFF
```

We chose to keep the charges and payments in separate files because charge transactions and payment transactions have different data fields. Charge transactions include data not stored with payment transactions, such as the product number, quantity, unit price, and taxable status. On the other hand, payment transactions store the check number, which is not part of charge transactions.

Next, the command file prepares the BillTemp table for printing bills. The BillTemp table consists of both charges and payments. The two tables are combined into BillTemp for printing reports, because R:BASE only allows a single transaction table in a report. We could have used a single table like BillTemp to record both charges and payments throughout the system; but for general data management, it may be preferable to keep the two tables separate, as we have done in this example.

First, the command file deletes any rows currently in the BillTemp table, since any rows there are no doubt from last month's billings. The DELETE ROWS command below performs the deletions:

```
DELETE ROWS FROM BillTemp WHERE COUNT > 0
```

Next, the command file inserts rows from the Charges and Payments tables onto the BillTemp table:

```
INSERT INTO BillTemp +
    (CustNo ProdNo Qty U_Price Taxable T_Price P_Date) +
    SELECT ALL FROM Charges
INSERT INTO BillTemp (CustNo Check_No Amount Pay_Date) +
    SELECT ALL FROM Payments
```

Because we are inserting the charges before the payments into the BillTemp file, the invoices will show the charges for each customer first and then display the payments below.

Next the command file prints the invoices. To keep null fields from being displayed as –0– symbols, the command file uses the command

```
SET NULL ' '
```

to display all null values as blanks. The date format is set to the MM/DD/YY format, and output is channeled to the printer. The NEWPAGE command starts the printing on a new page, and the PRINT Bills command prints the invoices using the report format named Bills. After the invoices are printed, NEWPAGE again ejects the paper in the printer, OUTPUT sets the output back to the screen, and SET resets the null character to –0–, as follows:

```
---- Print the Invoices
SET NULL ' '
SET DATE FORMAT 'MM/DD/YY'
```

```
OUTPUT PRINTER
NEWPAGE
PRINT Bills
NEWPAGE
OUTPUT SCREEN
SET NULL '-0-'
```

Once the bills are printed, an UPDATE command is used to shift the 90-day, 60-day, 30-day, and current balances back one month, as shown below:

The command was written using several lines with each update on a separate line to make it easier to see the updates being performed.

```
---- Perform the update
---- First, shift back Current, 30, 60, and 90 day balances
UPDATE ARMain SET Bal_120 = (Bal_120 + Bal_90), +
                  Bal_90 = Bal_60, +
                  Bal_60 = Bal_30, +
                  Bal_30 = Curr_Chr
WHERE CustNo IS NOT NULL
```

Since this is the start of a new month, the current charges (Curr _Chr) and current payments (Curr_Pay) are reset to zero in all the rows in the ARMain table, using an UPDATE command as follows:

```
---- Set current charges and payments to zero
UPDATE ARMain SET
                  Curr_Chr = 0, +
                  Curr_Pay = 0
WHERE CustNo IS NOT NULL
```

Next, a custom macro named Update.MAC (which we'll develop later) adjusts the current charges (Curr_Chr) and current payments (Curr_Pay) columns in the ARMain table to reflect charges and payments currently in the Charges and Payments tables:

```
---- Next, update current balance from Charges and Payments
RUN Update.MAC USING ARMain CustNo Curr_Chr Charges +
    CustNo T_Price PLUS
RUN Update.MAC USING ARMain CustNo Curr_Pay Payments +
    CustNo Amount PLUS
```

Next, an UPDATE command updates the current balance and the billing date in the ARMain table. The current balance (Curr_Bal) column is updated to reflect the previous month's balance, plus the current charges minus the current payments. The billing date (BillDate) column is updated to contain the date of the invoices just printed (which is the same as the system date, .#DATE):

```
UPDATE ARMain SET Curr_Bal = (Curr_Bal + (Curr_Chr-Curr_Pay)), +
                  BillDate = .#DATE
        WHERE CustNo IS NOT NULL
```

Once all of the updating is done, current transactions from both the Charges and Payments tables are inserted at the end of the CHistory and PHistory tables and deleted from the Charges and Payments tables. This keeps the Charges and Payments tables small, which helps speed general processing.

```
---- Now move transactions to history files
INSERT INTO CHistory SELECT ALL FROM Charges
DELETE ROWS FROM Charges WHERE COUNT > 0
INSERT INTO PHistory SELECT ALL FROM Payments
DELETE ROWS FROM Payments WHERE COUNT > 0
```

The next step is to age the existing balances by incrementally subtracting the current payment from the current aged balances. This task is handled by a command file named Age.CMD, which we'll develop soon. The EndMonth.CMD calls upon Age.CMD to age the balances in the line below:

```
---- Now age the balances using the Age.CMD command file
RUN Age.CMD
```

At this point, the end-of-month processing procedures are finished. The command file sets the normal messages back on, displays a prompt, and returns control to the calling program, as follows:

```
---- Update complete
NEWPAGE
SET MESSAGES ON
```

```
SET ERROR MESSAGES ON
WRITE 'End of month procedures completed...'
SET RULES ON
RETURN
```

One last routine in the EndMonth.CMD command file is the Bailout routine, which is called if the user does not wish to perform the procedures. The Bailout routine is shown below:

```
---- Bailout routine for immediate exit
LABEL Bailout
WRITE 'Returning to Main Menu without Update'
RETURN
```

AGING THE ACCOUNTS

The EndMonth.CMD command file already performed one aspect involved in aging the accounts receivable, that of shifting all the 30-, 60-, 90-, and over-90-day balances back one month (because, presumably, another 30 days have passed when the End-Month.CMD command file is run). The EndMonth.CMD command file did so with an UPDATE command, as discussed earlier.

The Bal_120 column actually records (and accumulates) all balances over 90 days past due. In other words, balances in the Bal_120 column are not shifted off to the right into oblivion. However, for a true picture of aged receivables, one should subtract the current payment from the aged balances, starting at the oldest period (Bal_120 in this casc) and working toward the Bal_30 balance. Incrementally subtracting the current payment from the aged balances is a large job and hence is handled separately in a command file named Age.CMD. Recall that EndMonth.CMD "calls" Age.CMD to perform this task with the command RUN Age.CMD.

The entire Age.CMD command file is shown in Figure 17.16. You can use the RBEDIT editor to key in this command file exactly as shown in the figure.

Let's briefly discuss how Age.CMD incrementally subtracts the current payment from the existing aged balances. First, numerous

```
*(------------------------------ Age.CMD
         Ages accounts receivable balances
         by incrementally subtracting current
         payment from existing balances.)

---- Set up variables
SET VARIABLE Remain CURRENCY
SET VARIABLE NextBal INTEGER
SET VARIABLE VCurrPay CURRENCY
SET VARIABLE VBal120 CURRENCY
SET VARIABLE VBal90 CURRENCY
SET VARIABLE VBal60 CURRENCY
SET VARIABLE VBal30 CURRENCY

---- Set up cursor for loop through table
DECLARE Cursor1 CURSOR FOR SELECT Bal_30 Bal_60 Bal_90 +
  Bal_120 Curr_Pay FROM ARMain
OPEN Cursor1

---- Get first row
FETCH Cursor1 INTO VBal30 INDICATOR I1, +
  VBal60 INDICATOR I2, VBal90 INDICATOR I3, +
  VBal120 INDICATOR I4, VCurrPay INDICATOR I5

WHILE (SQLCODE <> 100) THEN
    SET VARIABLE NextBal TO 1   -- 0 is "false", 1 is "true"
    SET VARIABLE Remain TO .VCurrPay

    ---- 90+ day balance
    IF .VBal120 > 0 THEN
        SET VARIABLE Remain = (.Remain - .VBal120)
        IF .Remain > 0 THEN
            UPDATE ARMain SET Bal_120 = 0 WHERE CURRENT OF Cursor1
        ELSE
            UPDATE ARMain SET Bal_120 = (.Remain * -1) +
              WHERE CURRENT OF Cursor1
            SET VARIABLE NextBal = 0
        ENDIF
    ENDIF

    ---- 90 day balance
    IF .NextBal = 1 AND .VBal90 > 0 THEN
        SET VARIABLE Remain = (.Remain - .VBal90)
        IF .Remain > 0 THEN
            UPDATE ARMain SET Bal_90 = 0 WHERE CURRENT OF Cursor1
        ELSE
            UPDATE ARMain SET Bal_90 = (.Remain * -1) +
              WHERE CURRENT OF Cursor1
            SET VARIABLE NextBal = 0
        ENDIF
    ENDIF

    ---- 60 day balance
    IF .NextBal = 1 AND .VBal60 > 0 THEN
        SET VARIABLE Remain = (.Remain - .VBal60)
        IF .Remain > 0 THEN
            UPDATE ARMain SET Bal_60 = 0 WHERE CURRENT OF Cursor1
        ELSE
            UPDATE ARMain SET Bal_60 = (.Remain * -1) +
              WHERE CURRENT OF Cursor1
            SET VARIABLE NextBal = 0
        ENDIF
    ENDIF
```

Figure 17.16: The Age.CMD command file

```
         ---- 30 day balance
         IF .NextBal = 1 AND .VBal30 > 0 THEN
            SET VARIABLE Remain = (.Remain - .VBal30)
            IF .Remain > 0 THEN
               UPDATE ARMain SET Bal_30 = 0 WHERE CURRENT OF Cursor1
            ELSE
               UPDATE ARMain SET Bal_30 = (.Remain * -1) +
                  WHERE CURRENT OF Cursor1
               SET VARIABLE NextBal = 0
            ENDIF
         ENDIF

         ---- Get next row
         FETCH Cursor1 INTO VBal30 INDICATOR I1, +
            VBal60 INDICATOR I2, VBal90 INDICATOR I3, +
            VBal120 INDICATOR I4, VCurrPay INDICATOR I5

   ENDWHILE

   DROP CURSOR Cursor1
   RETURN
```

Figure 17.16: The Age.CMD command file (continued)

variables are created with predefined data types. The lines below set
up the variable data types:

```
---- Set up variables
SET VARIABLE Remain CURRENCY
SET VARIABLE NextBal INTEGER
SET VARIABLE VCurrPay CURRENCY
SET VARIABLE VBal120 CURRENCY
SET VARIABLE VBal90 CURRENCY
SET VARIABLE VBal60 CURRENCY
SET VARIABLE VBal30 CURRENCY
```

A cursor is declared and opened, as below, to move through the
ARMain table one row at a time.

```
---- Set up cursor for loop through table
DECLARE Cursor1 CURSOR FOR SELECT Bal_30 Bal_60 Bal_90 +
   Bal_120 Curr_Pay FROM ARMain
OPEN Cursor1
```

Then the first FETCH command is issued, starting the "cursor"
at the first row in the table and extracting the column values from the

The INDICATOR variables I1, I2, I3, I4, and I5 in this FETCH command ensure that R:BASE does not display messages when the FETCH command encounters null values. R:BASE sets the INDICATOR variables to − 1 if the corresponding data variable is null or 0 otherwise.

row. The variables VBal30, VBal60, VBal90, VBal120, and VCurr-Pay receive the values from this row of ARMain in the columns Bal_30, Bal_60, Bal_90, Bal_120, and Curr_Pay:

```
---- Get first row
FETCH Cursor1 INTO VBal30 INDICATOR I1, +
    VBal60 INDICATOR I2, VBal90 INDICATOR I3, +
    VBal120 INDICATOR I4, VCurrPay INDICATOR I5
```

Then a WHILE loop is set up to access each row in the table, repeating the loop until the last row is processed (at which point the SQLCODE variable will equal 100):

```
WHILE (SQLCODE < > 100) THEN
```

The variable NextBal determines whether the next balance needs to be adjusted. If NextBal is one, then the next balance needs to be adjusted. If NextBal is zero, the next balance does not need to be adjusted. The Remain variable keeps track of the remainder of the current payment that needs to be subtracted from the next aged balance. These two variables receive their initial values in the commands below:

```
SET VARIABLE NextBal TO 1  -- 0 is "false", 1 is "true"
SET VARIABLE Remain TO .VCurrPay
```

Now the command file begins incrementally subtracting the current payment from the aged balances, starting at the Bal_120 (or over-90-day) balance. If there is a balance in the over-90-day category (that is, the Bal_120 column is greater than zero), then the Remain variable is set to the remaining payment (which is equal to the current payment) minus the amount of the Bal_120 balance, as below:

```
---- 90 + day balance
IF .VBal120 > 0 THEN
    SET VARIABLE Remain = (.Remain − .VBal120)
```

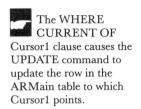
The WHERE CURRENT OF Cursor1 clause causes the UPDATE command to update the row in the ARMain table to which Cursor1 points.

If this remainder is greater than zero, then the balance in the Bal_120 column is set to zero:

```
IF .Remain > 0 THEN
    UPDATE ARMain SET Bal_120 = 0 WHERE CURRENT OF Cursor1
```

If the remainder is not greater than zero, then the over-90-day balance (Bal_120) is set to the absolute (positive) value of the Remain variable, and the NextBal indicator is set to zero ("false"), as follows:

```
    ELSE
        UPDATE ARMain SET Bal_120 = (.Remain * − 1) +
            WHERE CURRENT OF Cursor1
        SET VARIABLE NextBal = 0
    ENDIF
ENDIF
```

The same basic logic is used for the remaining aged balances. If the "Next Balance" indicator is "true," and there is a value greater than zero in the Bal_90 column, as below, then the command file can apply the payment remaining (in Remain) to the 90-day balance.

```
---- 90 day balance
IF .NextBal = 1 AND .VBal90 > 0 THEN
    SET VARIABLE Remain = (.Remain − .VBal90)
```

Now the command file decides what to do with the remaining payment amount. If this amount is greater than zero, then the 90-day balance is set to zero, as below:

```
IF .Remain > 0 THEN
    UPDATE ARMain SET Bal_90 = 0 WHERE CURRENT OF Cursor1
```

Otherwise, the 90-day balance is set to the absolute value of the remainder, and the NextBal indicator is set to zero ("false"), as follows:

```
    ELSE
        UPDATE ARMain SET Bal_90 = (.Remain * − 1) +
```

```
                WHERE CURRENT OF Cursor1
                SET VARIABLE NextBal = 0
            ENDIF
        ENDIF
```

The same process is repeated for the 60- and 30-day balances.

The command below moves the cursor to the next row in the ARMain table and extracts the values from the desired columns.

```
---- Get next row
FETCH Cursor1 INTO VBal30 INDICATOR I1, +
      VBal60 INDICATOR I2, VBal90 INDICATOR I3, +
      VBal120 INDICATOR I4, VCurrPay INDICATOR I5
```

If the FETCH command found another row, the ENDWHILE command loops back to repeat the process for this row in the ARMain table.

After all the aged balances in the ARMain table have been aged, the command

```
DROP CURSOR Cursor1
```

drops the cursor, and the command file returns control to the End-Month.CMD command file with the RETURN command.

There is one more command file (which is actually a procedure or macro) that needs to be written to complete the end-of-month procedures. This macro, named Update.MAC, updates the current charges and payments in the ARMain table from charges and payments in the Charges and Payments tables. Since updating is applicable to many databases (inventory, general ledger, and accounts payable, to name a few), we'll create this command file as a general-purpose macro that can easily be used in a variety of applications.

GENERAL-PURPOSE MACRO

You can use the macro that we'll develop in this section for any type of update. The syntax for using the Update.MAC macro is

```
RUN Update.MAC USING <master table name> +
+> <master table common column> <master table update +
```

```
+> column> <transaction table name> <transaction +
+> table common column> <transaction table +
+> update column> <type of update>
```

For example, to increment the current charges in the ARMain table by the T_Price amounts in the Charges table, you would use the command

```
RUN Update.MAC USING ARMain CustNo Curr_Chr +
+> Charges CustNo T_Price PLUS
```

where ARMain is the name of the table to be updated, CustNo is the name of the common column on which to base the update, and Curr_Chr is the name of the column in the ARMain table to be updated. Charges is the name of the transaction table, CustNo is the common column, and T_Price is the column to add to the Curr_Chr column. The PLUS option tells the macro to add the quantities from the Charges table to the current balance.

To update the ARMain table from the Payments table, use the command

```
RUN Update.MAC USING ARMain CustNo Curr_Pay +
+> Payments CustNo Amount PLUS
```

where, once again, ARMain, CustNo, and Curr_Pay are the table name, common column, and column to be updated, respectively. Payments, CustNo, and Amount are the table name, common column, and column to perform the update from, respectively. The PLUS option tells the macro to add the amounts in the Payments table to the current balance in the ARMain table.

The Update.MAC macro is shown in Figure 17.17. Enter the command

```
RBEDIT Update.MAC
```

to create and save the macro, just as you would any standard command file.

Looking at the macro line by line, we see that it begins with many comments. When you're writing general-purpose macros, it's a good idea to list the meaning of the various parameters passed to the macro

```
*(***************************************** Update.MAC)
------ Update a master table from a transaction table

*( Parameters are:  %1: Master table name
                    %2: Master table common column
                    %3: Master table update column
                    %4: Transaction table name
                    %5: Transaction table common column
                    %6: Transaction table update column
                    %7: PLUS MINUS or REPLACE)

NEWPAGE
CLEAR VARIABLES PassVal, Compare, CurrVal, NewVal

---- Make sure option %7 is valid
IF (%7 = 'PLUS') OR (%7 = 'MINUS') OR (%7 = 'REPLACE') THEN
    WRITE 'Performing update... Please wait'
ELSE
    WRITE 'Invalid update option'
    WRITE 'Must be PLUS, MINUS, or REPLACE'
    WRITE 'Press any key to try again...' AT 20 1
    PAUSE
    GOTO BailOut
ENDIF -- %7 option valid

SET MESSAGES OFF
SET ERROR MESSAGES OFF

---- Set up CURSOR for transaction table
DECLARE Cursor1 CURSOR FOR SELECT &%5 &%6 FROM &%4 +
  ORDER BY &%5
OPEN Cursor1

---- Get first row
FETCH Cursor1 INTO Compare INDICATOR I1, PassVal INDICATOR I2

WHILE (SQLCODE <> 100) THEN
    IF .Compare IS NOT NULL THEN
        SWITCH (.%7)
            CASE 'PLUS'  --  Prepare for update using PLUS
                SET VARIABLE CurrVal = &%3 IN &%1 +
                  WHERE &%2 = .Compare
                SET VARIABLE NewVal = (.CurrVal + .PassVal)
                BREAK

            CASE 'MINUS'  --  Prepare for update using MINUS
                SET VARIABLE CurrVal = &%3 IN &%1 +
                  WHERE &%2 = .Compare
                SET VARIABLE NewVal = (.CurrVal - .PassVal)
                BREAK

            CASE 'REPLACE'  --  Prepare for update using REPLACE
                SET VARIABLE NewVal = .PassVal
        ENDSW
        UPDATE &%1 SET &%3 = .NewVal WHERE &%2 = .Compare
    ENDIF

    ---- Get next row
    FETCH Cursor1 INTO Compare INDICATOR I1, PassVal INDICATOR I2
ENDWHILE

DROP CURSOR Cursor1
WRITE 'Update successful' AT 20 1
SET MESSAGES ON
SET ERROR MESSAGES ON
RETURN
```

Figure 17.17: The Update.MAC macro

```
---- Error encountered at outset -- Return
LABEL BailOut
CLEAR VARIABLE %7
RETURN
```

Figure 17.17: The Update.MAC macro (continued)

(%1 through %7 in this example), so that you can remember how to use the macro later.

```
*(******************************** Update.MAC)
------ Update a master table from a transaction table
*( Parameters are:  %1: Master table name
                    %2: Master table common column
                    %3: Master table update column
                    %4: Transaction table name
                    %5: Transaction table common column
                    %6: Transaction table update column
                    %7: PLUS MINUS or REPLACE)
```

The first commands in the macro clear the screen and then erase the variables PassVal, Compare, CurrVal, and NewVal. Since the data type these variables contain from the most recent update may be incorrect for the current update, they are re-created later with the appropriate data type.

```
NEWPAGE
CLEAR VARIABLES PassVal, Compare, CurrVal, NewVal
```

Next, the command file checks to make sure that the last parameter passed is a valid one. The parameter must be the word PLUS, MINUS, or REPLACE. If it is valid, the command file displays a prompt. If not, the command file displays an error message and branches to a routine named Bailout, as follows:

```
---- Make sure option %7 is valid
IF (%7 = 'PLUS') OR (%7 = 'MINUS') OR (%7 = 'REPLACE') THEN
        WRITE 'Performing update... Please wait'
```

```
ELSE
    WRITE 'Invalid update option'
    WRITE 'Must be PLUS, MINUS, or REPLACE'
    WRITE 'Press any key to try again...' AT 20 1
    PAUSE
    GOTO BailOut
ENDIF -- %7 option valid
```

Next, to prepare for updating, the command sets error messages off:

```
SET MESSAGES OFF
SET ERROR MESSAGES OFF
```

Now the command file begins the actual updating procedure. First, it sets up a cursor for the transaction table (parameter %4) sorted by the common column (parameter %5).

```
---- Set up CURSOR for transaction table
DECLARE Cursor1 CURSOR FOR SELECT &%5 &%6 FROM &%4 +
    ORDER BY &%5
OPEN Cursor1
```

Macro substitution is discussed in Chapter 11.

Notice when variables are used to represent column names, you must precede them with an ampersand (&). The ampersand tells R:BASE to access the values of the variables with macro substitution. Preceding the variable with an ampersand lets you use the contents of the variable as a part of a command. On the other hand, we have been using *dotted variables* (variables preceded with a dot). Preceding a variable with a dot lets you use the contents of the variable as a value in an expression used in an assignment command (when a variable is set equal to an expression) or a decision command (such as IF, WHILE, and SWITCH).

Then the cursor is placed at the first row in the transaction table and the PassVal and Compare variables are set to the appropriate column values.

```
---- Get first row
FETCH Cursor1 INTO Compare INDICATOR I1, PassVal INDICATOR I2
```

As long as the SQLCODE variable is not equal to 100, we know that there are still rows left to process in the transaction table and the command file performs the tasks in the WHILE loop below:

```
WHILE (SQLCODE < > 100) THEN
```

The next command, the IF command, ensures that no updating is done if the common column in the transaction table is null:

```
IF .Compare IS NOT NULL THEN
```

The SWITCH command interrogates parameter %7 since the type of update performed depends on whether PLUS, MINUS, or REPLACE was specified as parameter %7.

```
SWITCH (.%7)
```

Inside the SWITCH group of commands, the variable NewVal is set to the new value for the column to be updated in the master table. If the user specified PLUS, the variable NewVal is set to the value of the appropriate column in the master table (%3), incremented by the amount stored in the PassVal variable, where the common column in the master table (%2) matches the common column in the transaction table (Compare).

The name of the master table is obtained from the %1 parameter variable by macro substitution.

```
CASE 'PLUS' -- Prepare for update using PLUS
    SET VARIABLE CurrVal = &%3 IN &%1 +
        WHERE &%2 = .Compare
    SET VARIABLE NewVal = (.CurrVal + .PassVal)
    BREAK
```

If the user specified MINUS in the parameter list, the PassVal value is subtracted from the appropriate column in the master table. Then the result is stored in the variable NewVal, as below:

```
CASE 'MINUS' -- Prepare for update using MINUS
    SET VARIABLE CurrVal = &%3 IN &%1 +
        WHERE &%2 = .Compare
    SET VARIABLE NewVal = (.CurrVal - .PassVal)
    BREAK
```

If the user specified REPLACE, the NewVal variable is set to the PassVal value, as follows:

```
CASE 'REPLACE' -- Prepare for update using REPLACE
    SET VARIABLE NewVal = .PassVal
```

After the ENDSW command and before the ENDIF command, we have determined the new value for the update. The appropriate column in the master table is set to the value of NewVal, where the common column in the master table (%2) matches the common column in the transaction table (.Compare).

```
    ENDSW
    UPDATE &%1 SET &%3 = .NewVal WHERE &%2 = .Compare
ENDIF
```

Next, the cursor is moved to the next row in the transaction table, and the procedure is repeated until all rows from the transaction table have been processed.

```
---- Get next row
FETCH Cursor1 INTO Compare INDICATOR I1, PassVal INDICATOR I2
```

When the macro is done, it drops the cursor, displays a message and returns to the calling command file, as below:

```
    DROP CURSOR Cursor1
    WRITE 'Update successful' AT 20 1
    SET MESSAGES ON
    SET ERROR MESSAGES ON
    RETURN
```

The last routine in the Update.MAC macro is the BailOut routine, which is called in the event of an error at the beginning of the program. Before returning to the calling program, the routine clears the faulty update option (%7) from memory, as follows:

```
    ---- Error encountered at outset -- Return
    LABEL BailOut
    CLEAR VARIABLE %7
    RETURN
```

The Update.MAC macro is flexible, and it can be used for inventory-system updating, as well as for updating our accounts-receivable system. For example, to subtract the items that have been sold in the Charges table from the OnHand quantities in the Inventry table, you could simply enter the command

> RUN Update.MAC USING Inventry ProdNo OnHand Charges +
> +> ProdNo Qty MINUS

That's the real benefit of a general-purpose macro. You need only write the macro once, and then you can use it repeatedly, just as though it were a regular R:BASE command.

TESTING THE ACCOUNTS-RECEIVABLE SYSTEM

Before you use menus to integrate all the parts of the accounts-receivable system, you should do a thorough check from the R> prompt to see that all parts work as you want them to. You briefly tested the forms and one of the reports when you created them, but you need to test them again to ensure that the rules work as intended and that the reports and command files process transactions properly.

You should also use the Report Generator to create whatever additional reports you want for your various tables. You might want to add a directory listing, mailing labels, and perhaps form letters for the ARMain table, similar to the Director, Labels, and CaLetter report formats we developed in Chapters 7 and 14. You might also develop reports for displaying information from the Charges, Payments, and Inventry tables. Follow these general steps at the R> prompt to test your accounts-receivable system.

1. Type **CONNECT ARSYS** and press ← to be sure you are connected to the ARSYS database.

2. Enter **EDIT USING Main** and check the customers you entered earlier for test data. Press F7 and F8 to check additional customers. Change the balance to zero of each customer you entered with a non-zero balance, since the command files you created will take care of those values. When

you are finished looking at existing customers, exit to the
R > prompt.

3. Enter the command **ENTER Main** to add new customers.
As you did earlier, use customer numbers that are easy to
remember, such as 1001, 1002, 1003, etc. You don't have
to enter the last billing date, but set the balances in the bottom half of the screen to zero. Try entering a duplicate customer number to check the rule we created. When you are
finished, exit to the R > prompt.

4. Enter the command **ENTER InvForm** to add a few new
inventory records. Once again, use part numbers that will
be easy to remember for practice data, such as A-111,
B-222, C-333, and so on. Try entering a duplicate part
number to test the rule disallowing duplicates. After you've
entered a few new records, exit to the R > prompt.

5. Use the command **ENTER ChrgFrm** and add a few new
charge transactions for each customer. After you've entered
some valid charges, try entering customer numbers that are
not in the ARMain table and product numbers that are not
in the Inventry table. This way, you can test the rules that
the customer and product numbers have to be on file. Exit
to the R > prompt when you are finished.

If you have trouble
remembering the
customer or product
numbers you entered in
the ARMain and Inven-
try table, remember that
you can press Shift-F3 to
display a pop-up menu of
choices.

6. Enter the command **Enter PayForm** and add some payment
transactions. In addition to adding valid payments, check
the rule that the customer number has to be on file by
entering a customer number that is not in the ARMain
table. Again, exit to the R > prompt when you are done.

7. Use the command **RUN EndMonth.CMD** to test the End-
Month.CMD, UpDate.MAC, and Age.CMD command
files. The files should print the invoices and then take a few
minutes to perform all of the updating. If all runs smoothly,
you'll be returned to the R > prompt without any error
messages.

8. Enter the commands

    SELECT ALL FROM Charges
    SELECT ALL FROM Payments

to verify that the Charges and Payments tables are empty, ready for the next month's transactions.

9. Enter the commands

   SELECT ALL FROM CHistory
   SELECT ALL FROM PHistory

   to verify that the old transactions originally in the Charges and Payments tables were copied to the history tables.

10. Enter the command **PRINT Aging** to print the Aging report. Verify that the Current Balance now has the values printed on the bills.

Remember, you can print a hard copy of a command file with the commands OUTPUT PRINTER, TYPE *cmdfile*, and OUTPUT SCREEN, where *cmdfile* is the name of your command file.

If the Charges, Payments, and history tables do not contain the data you expected, perhaps there is an error in the EndMonth. CMD, UpDate.MAC, or the Age.CMD command file. Make sure you've keyed in the command files exactly as described in this chapter. You'll want to be sure to remove all the bugs from the command files if there are any, as well as from any forms or reports, before proceeding to the final step of integrating the accounts-receivable system through Applications EXPRESS.

INTEGRATING THE ACCOUNTS-RECEIVABLE SYSTEM

See Chapter 16 for a review of the steps involved in creating applications.

The final step in creating our working accounts-receivable system is to link all the modules together through menus generated by Applications EXPRESS. In this section, we will outline the major steps involved in creating this application.

1. Enter the **EXPRESS** command at the R > prompt to display the Applications EXPRESS menu.

2. Create an application called "AR" for the ARSYS database by highlighting **Create**, selecting **New** application, selecting **ARSYS** (if you are not already connected to the ARSYS database), typing **AR** and pressing ↵ for the name of the application.

THE ACCOUNTS-RECEIVABLE MAIN MENU

Figure 17.18 shows a suggested format for the Accounts-Receivable Main menu. The following steps outline how to specify the appearance and functionality of this menu.

1. Confirm **Main** as the suggested name for the Main menu.

2. To define the appearance of the Main menu, select **V**ertical menu type, choose **N**o to customized menu colors, fill in the menu title and options shown in Figure 17.18, and press **F2**.

3. Choose **Y**es to letting Esc exit the menu and **N**o to a help screen.

4. Define (1) Manage Customer List as a **M**enu called **Cust-Menu**, **V**ertical type, **N**o customized colors. Enter the menu title and options shown in Figure 17.19 and press **F2**. Answer **N**o to another action.

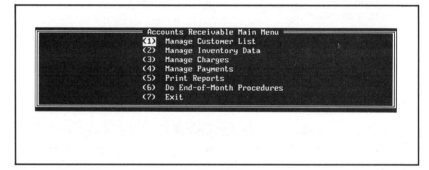

Figure 17.18: The accounts-receivable Main menu

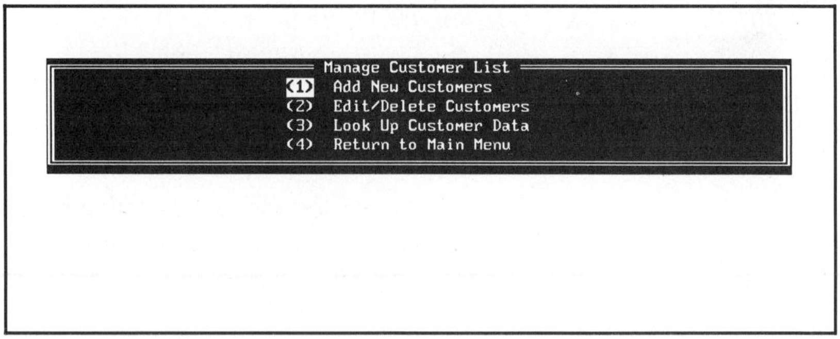

Figure 17.19: The CustMenu submenu

5. Define (2) Manage Inventory Data as a **M**enu called **InvMenu**, **V**ertical type, **N**o customized colors. Enter the menu title and options shown in Figure 17.20 and press **F2**. Answer **N**o to another action.

6. Define (3) Manage Charges as a **M**enu called **ChrgMenu**, **V**ertical type, **N**o customized colors. Enter the menu title and options shown in Figure 17.21 and press **F2**. Answer **N**o to another action.

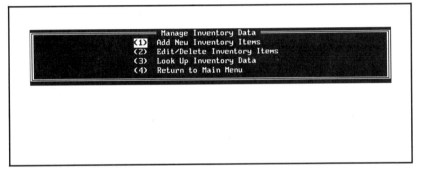

Figure 17.20: The InvMenu submenu

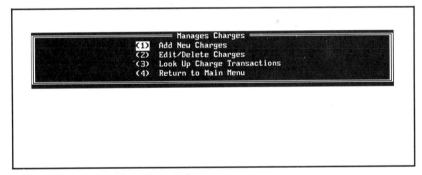

Figure 17.21: The ChrgMenu submenu

7. Define (4) Manage Payments as a **M**enu called **PayMenu**, **V**ertical type, **N**o customized colors. Enter the menu title and options shown in Figure 17.22 and press **F2**. Answer **N**o to another action.

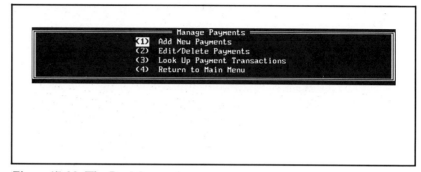

Figure 17.22: The PayMenu submenu

8. Define (5) Print Reports as a **Menu** called **ReptMenu**, Vertical type, **No** customized colors. Enter the menu title and options to access the various reports that you've created for your accounts-receivable system (except for printing invoices, which are printed automatically by the EndMonth. CMD command file). Figure 17.23 shows suggested options for the ReptMenu menu. When you are finished entering option descriptions, press **F2**. Answer **No** to another action.

9. Define (6) Do End-of-Month Procedures as a **Macro** with the file name **EndMonth.CMD**. Answer **No** to another action.

10. Define (7) Exit as an **Exit** option.

```
═══════════════════ Print Reports ═══════════════════
        <1>  Print Customer Directory
        <2>  Print Mailing Labels
        <3>  Print Form Letter
        <4>  Print Inventory List
        <5>  Print Aging Report
        <6>  Return to Main Menu
```

Figure 17.23: The ReptMenu submenu

CUSTOMERS SUBMENU ACTIONS

Having finished defining the Main menu, we are now asked to define the actions for each of the submenus. We will start by defining the actions for CustMenu, the customers submenu.

1. Choose **Yes** to letting Esc exit the menu and **No** to a help screen.

2. Define (1) Add New Customers as **L**oading the **AR**Main table using the **Main** form. Answer **No** to editing the form and **No** to another action.

3. Define (2) Edit/Delete Customers as **E**diting the **AR**Main table using the **Main** form. Answer **No** to editing the form. Press **F2** to skip sorting. Select a record where **C**ustNo is = EQUAL and answer **Yes** to a comparison value entered by the user, with prompt "**Enter customer number**", and select (Done). Answer **No** to another action.

4. Define (3) Look Up Customer Data as a **S**elect of the **AR**Main table. You can choose any columns that you like (or ALL columns) to display, but for this example, select **C**ustNo, **L_**Name, **F_**Name, and **C**urr_Bal, and press **F2**. Press **F2** to skip sorting. Select a record where **C**ustNo is = EQUAL and answer **Yes** to a comparison value entered by the user, with prompt "**Enter customer number**", and select (Done). Answer **No** to another action.

5. Define (4) Exit as an **E**xit option.

INVENTORY SUBMENU ACTIONS

Now that we've finished defining the actions for the customers submenu, R:BASE asks us to define the actions for InvMenu, the Inventory submenu.

1. Choose **Yes** to letting Esc exit the menu and **No** to a help screen.

2. Define (1) Add New Inventory Items as **L**oading the Inventry table using the **Inv**Form form. Answer **No** to editing the form and **No** to another action.

3. Define (2) Edit/Delete Inventory Items as **E**diting the Inventry table using the InvForm form. Answer **N**o to editing the form. Press **F2** to skip sorting. Select a record where **P**rodNo is = EQUAL and answer **Y**es to a comparison value entered by the user, with prompt "**Enter product number**", and select (Done). Answer **N**o to another action.

4. Define (3) Look Up Inventory Data as a **S**elect of the Inventry table. Select columns to display, say **P**rodNo, PartName, **U**_Price, and **O**nHand, and press **F2**. Press **F2** to skip sorting. Select a record where **P**rodNo is = EQUAL and answer **Y**es to a comparison value entered by the user, with prompt "**Enter product number**", and select (Done). Answer **N**o to another action.

5. Define (4) Exit as an **E**xit option.

CHARGES SUBMENU ACTIONS

Now, we will define the actions for PayMenu, the Payments submenu.

1. Choose **Y**es to letting Esc exit the menu and **N**o to a help screen.

2. Define (1) Add New Charges as **L**oading the **C**harges table using the ChrgFrm form. Answer **N**o to editing the form and **N**o to another action.

3. Define (2) Edit/Delete Charges as **E**diting the **C**harges table using the ChrgFrm form. Answer **N**o to editing the form. Specify sorting in **P**rodNo Ascending order and press **F2**. Select a record where **C**ustNo is = EQUAL and answer **Y**es to a comparison value entered by the user, with prompt "**Enter customer number**", and select (Done). Answer **N**o to another action.

4. Define (3) Look Up Charge Transactions as a **S**elect of the Charges table. Select whatever columns you would like to display and press **F2**. Choose any sort to your liking, and press **F2**. Select a record where **C**ustNo is = EQUAL and

answer **Yes** to a comparison value entered by the user, with prompt "**Enter customer number**", and select (Done). Answer **No** to another action.

5. Define (4) Exit as an **Exit** option.

PAYMENTS SUBMENU ACTIONS

Now that we've finished with the Charges submenu, we are ready to define the actions for PayMenu, the Payments submenu.

1. Choose **Yes** to letting Esc exit the menu and **No** to a help screen.

2. Define (1) Add New Payments as **Loading** the **Payments** table using the **PayForm** form. Answer **No** to editing the form and **No** to another action.

3. Define (2) Edit/Delete Payments as **Editing** the **Payments** table using the **PayForm** form. Answer **No** to editing the form. Press **F2** to skip sorting. Select a record where **CustNo** is = EQUAL and answer **Yes** to a comparison value entered by the user, with prompt "**Enter customer number**", and select (Done). Answer **No** to another action.

4. Define (3) Look Up Payment Transactions as a **Select** of the **Payments** table. Select all columns to display and press **F2**. Press **F2** to skip sorting. Select a record where **CustNo** is = EQUAL and answer **Yes** to a comparison value entered by the user, with prompt "**Enter customer number**", and select (Done). Answer **No** to another action.

5. Define (4) Exit as an **Exit** option.

You can press Shift-F6 to select all columns for display.

REPORTS SUBMENU ACTIONS

Next we will define the actions for the last submenu, ReptMenu, the Reports submenu.

1. Choose **Yes** to letting Esc exit the menu and **No** to a help screen.

2. For each option on the Reports submenu, select the Print action (except for the Exit option), and select the appropriate report name for each menu option. Select sort and search criteria for each report as you wish.

3. For the last menu option, define the action as **Exit**.

FINISHING UP

Now that we've defined all the submenus, we have just a couple more questions to answer.

1. Reply **No** to changing the default settings. R:BASE now prepares the programs to run this application.

2. Reply **No** to creating a startup file.

From this point, you'll be returned to the Applications EXPRESS menu. Highlight and select **Exit** twice to leave Applications EXPRESS.

PUTTING THE ACCOUNTS-RECEIVABLE SYSTEM TO WORK

To use the accounts-receivable system in the future, enter the command

RUN AR IN AR.APX

at the R > prompt or highlight Applications and select AR. You'll see the Accounts-Receivable Main menu.

At any time during the month, you can enter new data or edit existing data. Before you assign charges or payments to a customer, make sure the customer is entered onto the customer list with a unique customer number. To do so, select option 1, Manage Customer List, from the Accounts Receivable Main menu and option 1, Add New Customers, from the Customers submenu. You should enter zeros in all the balances on the bottom half of the screen when you enter a new customer.

You also need to add products to the inventory table before you enter charges for each product. To enter or edit products, select option 2, Manage Inventory Data, from the Main menu and option 1, Add New Inventory Items, from the inventory submenu. Each item you enter must have a unique product number.

As customers charge items and make payments, record each transaction on the Charges and Payments tables. To record charges, select option 3, Manage Charges, from the Main menu and option 1, Add New Charges, from the submenu. To record payments, select option 4, Manage Payments, from the Main menu and option 1, Add New Payments, from the submenu.

You can make changes and corrections to the Charges and Payments tables any time *prior to performing the end-of-the-month procedures.* The Charges and Payments submenus each have options for editing and deleting transactions. Now we need to discuss techniques for editing after the end-of-the-month procedures.

END-OF-MONTH PROCEDURES

At the end of the month (or whenever you send bills), you can select option 6, Do End-of-Month Procedures, from the Main menu to print the invoices and update all of the balances in the ARMain file. Be sure you have plenty of paper in the printer and that the printer is ready. Then select option 6 from the Main menu, and wait until the Main menu reappears. If you add a report format for mailing labels, you can print mailing labels for the invoices as well.

Once the end-of-the-month procedures are complete, you cannot change the information on the Charges and Payments tables, because those transactions have now moved to the history files to make room for next month's charges and payments. The Inventry file is unchanged, and the ARMain table has updated balances for the start of the new month.

ADJUSTMENT TRANSACTIONS

An audit trail is a series of transactions that provide a step-by-step explanation of how a situation developed or how a mistake was corrected.

Of course, errors will sneak through the end-of-month procedures from time to time. To fix those, you can add *adjustment transactions,* which not only correct the error, but also leave an *audit trail* to explain the change. For example, if you overcharge a customer or a customer returns some merchandise for which he or she has already been billed, you can simply enter a payment transaction to credit the account. (In fact, you could add a "comment" column to the Payments table to add comments to each transaction to explain the reason for the adjustment.)

Suppose you overcharged the customer $200.00 or the customer returned $200.00 worth of merchandise. Just add a payment transaction in the amount of $200.00. The next time the end-of-month procedures are performed, the $200.00 will automatically be credited to the customer's account, and it will appear on the next invoice as a credit and be stored in the history file for future reference.

We've covered much advanced material in this chapter, and unless you are already a programmer who is fluent in some other database-management language, the techniques we discussed will probably take some study and practice to master. The time and effort you invest will be worthwhile—the techniques that we've used in this chapter are similar to ones that you'll be using to develop your own custom applications.

Part IV

Advanced Application Techniques

Chapter 18

Advanced Programming Techniques

IN THIS CHAPTER, WE'LL DISCUSS SEVERAL ADVANCED programming techniques that help you make your programs more professional-looking and easier to use. Thanks to these advanced facilities, the user can provide information to a program or macro that you create. In fact, your program can even present menus of options to the user just like the menus R:BASE presents.

We'll also look at an R:BASE module called *CodeLock,* which converts ASCII command files into *binary format* and makes your programs run faster. Unlike ASCII files, which are stored in the format that you used to create the command file, *binary files* are stored using special codes that the computer can read easily. One of the advantages of storing command files in binary format is that they run faster. When a computer runs binary files, it does not have to convert the program from "English" (ASCII) to computer language (binary). Besides converting ASCII files to the binary format, CodeLock allows you to bring together several pieces of a program in a single file. Being able to bring more than one piece of a program into memory at one time means that R:BASE does not have to look on disk as often to find screen files, menu files, or macros that your program may be using, all of which saves time.

CREATING MENU FILES

Menus allow the user to choose from a set of options. The purpose of a *menu file* is to list the choices, title, and format of the menu. You must build a program that accesses the menu file, displays the menu, and receives the user's choice.

Chapter 15 discusses how to create applications with Applications EXPRESS that include pull-down, pop-up, vertical, or horizontal menus by which users choose programs or commands to execute.

You create menu files with the RBEDIT text editor (or your favorite ASCII word processor). You can make a menu file for just about every type of menu that you have seen in R:BASE. In addition to the pull-down, pop-up, vertical, and horizontal menus that are available in Applications EXPRESS, you can also create

- *Bar menus,* in which the options are arranged along a bar running across the screen.

- *Check box menus,* which look similar to pop-up menus and allow you to select several options at once. A check mark (✓) appears beside each option you select.

- *Sort check box menus,* which are similar to check box menus except that they let you establish priorities. The order of selection as well as the letter *A* or the letter *D* (representing Ascending or Descending sorting order) appear beside the selections to mark your choices.

These three types of menus are shown in Figure 18.1.

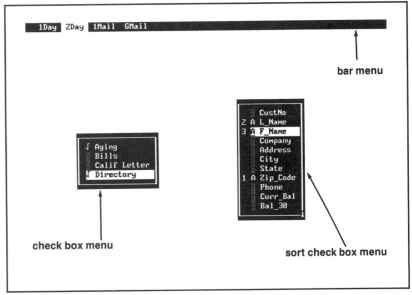

Figure 18.1: A bar menu, check box menu, and sort check box menu

VERTICAL, HORIZONTAL, POP-UP, AND BAR MENU FILES

The vertical bar is ASCII code 124, usually entered by pressing Shift-\ on the keyboard. To type a vertical bar using its ASCII code, hold down the Alt key, type 124 on the numeric keypad, and release the Alt key.

Vertical, horizontal, pop-up, and bar menus are the simplest types of menu files and all have the same format. Figure 18.2 shows an example of a menu file for a pop-up menu. Notice that this menu file starts with the name of the menu, ShipPop, on the first line. A menu name no more than eight characters long without spaces or punctuation marks must always be in the first line of the file, starting in the far left column. On the second line of the menu file you'll see that POPUP is the menu type for a pop-up menu. In this menu file format, the menu type could also be COLUMN (for a vertical menu),

ROW (for a horizontal menu), or BAR (for a bar menu). To the right of the menu type is the menu title, "Choose Shipping Method," placed between vertical bars (|). Beginning with the third line, four options—1Day, 2Day, 1Mail, and GMail—have been defined for this menu. Each of the options on this menu has a prompt beside it. The options, like the prompts, are enclosed in vertical bars. You don't have to provide prompts for the options, but they help explain the options, which is usually necessary when the options are abbreviated. The last line in a menu file is always ENDC.

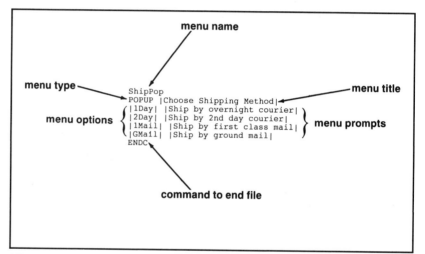

Figure 18.2: A sample pop-up menu file

ACCESSING MENU FILES WITH THE CHOOSE COMMAND

To display a menu that receives the user's choice, R:BASE provides the CHOOSE command. The general format for the CHOOSE command is

CHOOSE *choice variable name* FROM *menu file* AT *row, column*

where *menu file* defines the menu displayed with the top-left corner at position *row, column* on the screen, and *choice variable name* contains the option chosen by the user. The *column* variable is only required for pop-up menu files, since the rest of the menus cover the entire width of the

In the CHOOSE command format shown here, the *column* variable has been included because this is the format for a pop-up menu file. The other menu types don't require this variable.

screen. The choice variable records the user's choice in different ways, depending on the type of menu you are displaying. In POPUP, ROW, and BAR menu files, the choice variable will always be a TEXT variable that contains the name of the option chosen by the user. In COLUMN menu files, the choice variable will always be an INTE-GER variable that contains the number of the option chosen. Since the choice variable has to have a data type suitable to the type of menu being accessed, it is often convenient to leave the choice variable undefined. Instead, let the CHOOSE command create the variable with the correct variable type.

The CHOOSE command returns a choice automatically when the user presses the Esc key or the F1 (Help) key. For menus that return a TEXT choice, the choice variable will contain [Esc] if the user presses Esc, or HELP if the F1 key is pressed. On a COLUMN menu, pressing Esc sets the choice variable to 0 and pressing F1 sets it to -1.

Let's test the sample pop-up menu file we created earlier with a CHOOSE command. Figure 18.3 shows a program with a CHOOSE command in a loop that receives and displays a choice from the pop-up menu. The program stops when the Esc key is pressed. Follow these steps now to try out the sample menu file:

1. Use RBEDIT to type in the pop-up menu file in Figure 18.2. Call the file ShipPop.MNU.

```
--------------------------------- TestPop.ASC
------------------------- Testing a pop-up menu
CLS
CLEAR VARIABLE Done
SET VARIABLE Done = 'N'
WHILE (.Done = 'N') THEN
     ---- Display menu and receive user's choice
     CLEAR VARIABLE MChoice
     CHOOSE MChoice FROM ShipPop.MNU AT 10, 20
     ---- Clear the row where we will display choice
     CLS FROM 5 TO 5
     ---- Display choice
     WRITE .MChoice at 5, 20
     ---- If user presses Esc, end the program.
     IF .MChoice = '[Esc]' THEN
          SET VARIABLE Done = 'Y'
     ENDIF
ENDWHILE
QUIT
```

Figure 18.3: Program to access the sample pop-up menu file

2. Use RBEDIT to type in the test program in Figure 18.3. Call this file TestPop.ASC.

3. Type **RUN TestPop.ASC** and press ⏎ to start the program.

4. Notice the menu title in the lower-left corner of the screen and the option prompts in the lower-right corner. The option prompts change as you move the highlighter to different options.

5. Try selecting each of the options and try pressing **F1**. Note the value of the MChoice variable displayed above the menu.

6. When you are finished experimenting, press **Esc** to leave the program.

PULL-DOWN MENU FILES

Creating a pull-down menu file is more complicated than creating a pop-up, bar, vertical, or horizontal menu file. Because pull-down menus have a bar along the top and a submenu under each option on the bar, a pull-down menu file is like a combination of a bar menu file (the bar on top) and pop-up menu file (the submenus under each choice on the bar). Figure 18.4 shows a sample pull-down menu file. Once again, the first line lists the name of the menu and the second line the menu type and title. The next three lines define the options on the menu bar, and the ENDC that follows marks the end of the section of the menu file defining the menu bar. The POPUP sections below define the contents of the submenus beneath each corresponding option on the menu bar. The first POPUP section defines the submenu beneath PickUp, the first menu bar option; the second one defines the submenu beneath Courier, the second menu bar option; and so on.

The CHOOSE command format for accessing a pull-down menu is similar to the format for assessing pop-up, column, row, and bar menus. Because making a choice on a pull-down menu involves both highlighting an option on the menu bar and selecting an option in the submenu beneath, the choice variable in pull-down menus contains additional information. To accommodate both the menu bar option

```
ShipPull
PULLDOWN |Choose Shipping Method|
|PickUp|
|Courier|
|Mail|
ENDC
POPUP
|Factory| |Pick up at factory|
|Warehse1| |Pick up at warehouse #1|
|Warehse2| |Pick up at warehouse #2|
ENDC
POPUP
|1Day| |Ship by overnight courier|
|2Day| |Ship by 2nd day courier|
ENDC
POPUP
|1Mail| |Ship by 1st class mail|
|2Mail| |Ship by 2nd class mail|
ENDC
```

Figure 18.4: A sample pull-down menu file

and the submenu option, the choice variable must contain the number of the option highlighted on the menu bar as well as the text of the option chosen from the submenu. The number and option text are separated by a comma.

See Chapter 11 for more information about the SLOC function.

In order to test the pop-up menu we will have to use a modified version of the program shown in Figure 18.3. A suitable program to test the pull-down menu file in Figure 18.4 is shown in Figure 18.5. When you press Esc on a pull-down menu, the choice variable will contain the number of the bar option you have highlighted, followed by a comma and [Esc]. The program in Figure 18.5 tests to see if the choice variable contains the string [Esc] using the SLOC function.

```
------------------------------------ TestPull.ASC
------------------------ Testing a pull-down menu
CLS
CLEAR VARIABLE Done
SET VARIABLE Done = 'N'
WHILE (.Done = 'N') THEN
    ---- Display menu and receive user's choice
    CLEAR VARIABLE MChoice
    CHOOSE MChoice FROM ShipPull.MNU AT 10
    ---- Clear the row where we will display choice
    CLS FROM 5 TO 5
    ---- Display choice
    WRITE .MChoice at 5, 20
    ---- If user presses Esc, end the program.
    IF SLOC(.MChoice, '[Esc]') > 0 THEN
        SET VARIABLE Done = 'Y'
    ENDIF
ENDWHILE
QUIT
```

Figure 18.5: A program to access the sample pull-down menu file

As you did before, you may want to use RBEDIT to type in the sample pull-down menu file shown in Figure 18.4 into Ship-Pull.MNU, and type the sample test program in Figure 18.5 into TestPull.ASC. Then, to see the value of the MChoice variable when you press various keys, run the test program. Press Esc when you are finished with your testing.

CHECK BOX AND SORT CHECK BOX MENU FILES

Check box and sort check box menu files have a simple format similar to column, row, pop-up, and bar menus, but the choice variable can return many selections, separated by commas. Figure 18.6 shows a sample check box menu that allows a user to select one or more reports for printing in a batch, one after another without stopping. A user of an application might choose several reports to print overnight with this facility.

```
RepChkBx
CHKBOX |Select Reports to Print (Press F2 to accept, Esc to abort)
|Aging| |Aged Receivables Report|
|Bills| |Customer Bills|
|Calif Letter| |Form letter for California residents|
|Directory| |Directory of Customers|
ENDC
```

Figure 18.6: A sample check box menu file

To test this menu, we could use the test program we used to test the pull-down menu (see Figure 18.4), with a couple of changes. To create and run the new test file,

1. From the R > prompt, type **COPY TestPop.ASC TestChkB.ASC** and press ↵ to make a copy of the file.

2. Edit the file TestChkB.ASC using RBEDIT.

3. Change the comments in the first two lines to refer to the program file TestChkB.ASC and check box menus.

4. In the CHOOSE command, change the name of the menu file from ShipPop.MNU to **RepChkBx.MNU**.

5. Save the file in the usual way.

6. Use RBEDIT to type in the check box menu file in Figure 18.6 and save this file in **RepChkBx.MNU**.

7. Type **RUN TestChkB.ASC** and press ← to test this menu.

8. Press **Esc** to return to the R > prompt when you are finished testing.

It is also possible to make the column names in a table options on a menu. For example, you would do this to make it easier to sort a table. To make column names into menu options, you use the #COLUMNS feature of menu files, which has the format

#COLUMNS IN *tablename*

Although you can use the #COLUMNS feature in any menu file, it is most useful in a sort check box menu file. The sort check box menu file called ARMnChkS.MNU in Figure 18.7 allows you to enter sorting criteria for the ARMain table in the ARSYS database. Follow the directions below to create a test file called TestChkS.ASC and test the menu file ARMnChkS.MNU.

```
ARMnChkS
CHKSORT |Enter sorting criteria for the ARMain table|
#COLUMNS IN ARMain
ENDC
```

Figure 18.7: A sample sort check box menu file

1. Make a copy of the TestChkB.ASC file and call it **TestChkS.ASC**, and then modify TestChkS.ASC to refer to the ARMnChkS.MNU menu file. Do this by using the same technique you used to create the TestChkB.ASC test file.

2. Using RBEDIT, enter the sort check box menu file **ARMnChkS.MNU** shown in Figure 18.7.

3. Type **CONNECT ARSYS** and press ← to connect to the ARSYS database.

4. Type **RUN TestChkS.ASC** and press ◄─┘ to test the menu file.

5. Press **Esc** to return to the R > prompt when you are finished testing.

Now that you have seen how to use menu files to offer choices to the user, let's see how you can use the R:BASE module CodeLock to bring together menu files and other parts of a program and make the program run faster.

USING CODELOCK TO CONVERT YOUR FILES

The ASCII files can be created with RBEDIT or any other text editor that stores files in ASCII format.

With CodeLock, you can do five types of conversions:

- Command files and macros into binary command files
- ASCII command files into binary procedure files
- Menu files into binary procedure files
- Screen files into binary procedure files
- ASCII Application files into binary procedure files

In the last chapter, you learned how command files can use screen files, such as the Bills.MSG file we created in the last chapter, to display screens.

You can also combine up to 42 different files in a single procedure file using CodeLock. In this chapter, we'll experiment with converting the various types of files.

Before you can use CodeLock, make sure it is installed on your system. If you elected to install the entire R:BASE package, it will be in the directory with the other R:BASE files. If you bypassed installing CodeLock, you will need to go back and reinstall that part of R:BASE in order to follow along on-line in this section.

See Appendix A for more information about installing R:BASE.

CONVERTING COMMAND FILES

The simplest use of CodeLock is to convert a command file to binary format. In Chapter 16, we created a command file named Loop2.CMD to test the WHILE and ENDWHILE commands. Figure 18.8 shows the Loop2.CMD command file. Let's convert this program to a binary file using CodeLock from the R > prompt.

```
*(****************************** Loop2.CMD)
*(------------ Program to test the WHILE loop)
-------------- Create Counter and Done variable
SET VARIABLE Counter = 1
SET VARIABLE Done INTEGER
-------------- Ask how high to count
NEWPAGE
FILLIN Done USING 'How high shall I count?: ' AT 9,5
NEWPAGE
-------------- Repeat loop until Counter > Done
WHILE Counter <= .Done THEN
        -------- Create a prompt and display it
        SET VARIABLE Progress = ('Loop Number =' & CTXT(.Counter))
        WRITE .Progress
        -------- Increment Counter variable by 1
        SET VARIABLE Counter = (.Counter + 1)
ENDWHILE  ---   Bottom of WHILE loop
```

Figure 18.8: The Loop2.CMD command file

You can also start CodeLock from the DOS prompt by typing **CodeLock** and pressing ←┘.

1. Type CODELOCK and press ←┘ to display the CodeLock Main menu, as shown in Figure 18.9. Notice that this menu offers five types of ASCII to binary file conversions, as well as two selections for displaying directories and ASCII files.

```
                           CODELOCK
              Copyright (C) 1983-1990 by Microrim, Inc.

        ┌─────────────────────────────────────────────────────┐
        │ Convert an ASCII command file to a binary command file│
        │ Add an ASCII command file to a procedure file         │
        │ Add an ASCII screen file to a procedure file          │
        │ Add an ASCII menu file to a procedure file            │
        │ Convert an ASCII application file to a binary procedure file│
        │ Display directory                                     │
        │ Display the contents of an ASCII file                 │
        │ Exit                                                  │
        └─────────────────────────────────────────────────────┘
```

Figure 18.9: The CodeLock Main menu

2. Select the first option, **C**onvert an ASCII command file to a binary command file. A box with three prompts appears on the screen asking for information.

3. Under the "Name of the ASCII command file to convert" prompt, type **Loop2.CMD** and press ←┘.

The backup file Loop2.ASC is given the extension ASC because it is an ASCII file.

4. Under the "Name of the backup file" prompt, type **Loop2.ASC** and press ←┘. This is the file that will contain the original, unconverted command file.

5. Under the "Name of the binary command file" prompt, type **Loop2.CMD** and press ◄──┘. As CodeLock converts the command file, it displays each line on the screen. When it's done, you are prompted to press any key to continue.

6. Press a key to return to the CodeLock Main menu.

7. Select **Exit** to return to the R > prompt.

To run the converted command file, type the command **RUN Loop2.CMD** and press ◄──┘. You may not notice a major increase in speed when you're running this small command file, but as you begin converting larger command files, you will notice a significant improvement in your processing time.

Always fully test and debug a command file before converting it. However, if you need to make changes to a command file, be sure to use the unconverted backup. In this example, you would modify the Loop2.ASC command file with RBEDIT. Then, when reconverting with CodeLock, enter Loop2.ASC as the ASCII file to convert, Loop2.ASC as the backup file, and Loop2.CMD as the name of the binary file.

Remember, if you must make changes, edit the ASCII file and then reconvert it into a revised binary file.

If you need to check which version of a command file is the ASCII version and which is the converted version, you can enter the TYPE command from either the DOS prompt or the R > prompt, or select CodeLock's "Display the contents of an ASCII file" option. For example, after you've converted a command file, if you enter the command

TYPE Loop2.ASC

you'll see the ASCII file in its normal state. However, if you enter the command

TYPE Loop2.CMD

you'll see the binary file, which appears as a group of strange-looking characters including happy faces and umlauts (¨). You can see why you cannot edit the binary file.

PROCEDURE FILES

A *procedure file* is one that contains a group of previously separate files in a single binary file. The files within the procedure file can be command files, screen files, menu files, or macros. In this section, we'll develop a procedure file named TestProc.CMD that will contain all these types of files.

Adding Command Files to Procedure Files

Let's add the Loop2.CMD command file to our new procedure file TestProc.CMD. Display the CodeLock Main menu again with the CODELOCK command and proceed as follows:

1. Select the second option on the CodeLock Main menu, **A**dd an ASCII command file to a procedure file. A box with two prompts appears on the screen asking for information.

2. Under the "Name of the ASCII command file to add" prompt, type **Loop2.ASC** and press ←┘.

3. Under the "Name of the procedure file" prompt, type **TestProc.CMD** and press ←┘. The screen is cleared and a new prompt is displayed.

4. Beside the "Name of the binary command block" prompt, press ←┘ to accept the suggested name "Loop2." Code-Lock displays the command file as it converts the file and adds it to the procedure file. When it's done, you are prompted to press any key to continue.

5. Press a key to return to the CodeLock Main menu.

Before we try out the procedure file, let's add a screen file and a menu file to it.

Be sure to enter the name of the ASCII backup file if you've previously converted the command file.

Since the command file will be contained within a procedure file, you do not want to use file-name extensions.

Adding Screen Files to Procedure Files

In the last chapter, you created a screen file named Bills.MSG. Let's add that screen file to the TestProc.CMD procedure file.

1. Select the third option on the CodeLock Main menu, **Add an ASCII screen file to a procedure file.**

2. Under the "Name of the ASCII screen file to add" prompt, type **Bills.MSG** and press ←⏎.

3. Under the "Name of the procedure file" prompt, type **TestProc.CMD** and press ←⏎.

The screen is cleared and two information boxes appear. The top box is titled "Current blocks in the procedure file," and it contains "Loop2." Since each block in a procedure file must have a unique name, CodeLock displays the names of the blocks already in the file. As before, CodeLock suggests the name of the ASCII file being added, without the extension, as the name of the new block in the procedure file.

> If you enter the name of a command or screen file you have already added to this procedure file, CodeLock will replace the old command or screen file with the new one.

4. Beside the "Name of the binary screen block" prompt, press ←⏎ to accept the suggested name "Bills." You'll see the screen file displayed on the screen, and then you'll be prompted to press any key to continue.

5. Press a key to return to the CodeLock Main menu.

We'll see how to access the screen in the procedure file shortly. First, let's try adding a menu file to the procedure file.

Adding Menu Files to Procedure Files

Just like screen files, you can access menu files in ASCII format or you can add them to a procedure file. Figure 18.10 shows the COLUMN menu file we will add to the TestProc.CMD procedure

```
Menu1
COLUMN |Sample menu|
|Add New Data| |Add new customers|
|Edit/Delete Data| |Edit/delete customers|
|Print Report| |Print Directory report|
ENDC
```

Figure 18.10: A sample COLUMN menu file

file we are building. Add this file with the following steps:

1. Select **Exit** on the CodeLock Main menu to return to the R> prompt.

2. With **RBEDIT**, enter the **Menu1.MNU** menu file shown in Figure 18.10. Save the file and return to the R> prompt when you are done.

3. Type **CODELOCK** and press ◄── to display the CodeLock Main menu again.

4. Select the fourth option on the CodeLock Main menu, **A**dd an ASCII menu file to a procedure file.

5. Under the "Name of the ASCII menu file to add" prompt, type **Menu1.MNU** and press ◄──.

6. Under the "Name of the procedure file" prompt, type **TestProc.CMD** and press ◄──. The "Current blocks in the procedure file" box displays two names, "Loop2" and "Bills." CodeLock suggests the name of the ASCII file being added, without the extension, as the name of the new block in the procedure file.

7. Beside the "Name of the binary menu block" prompt, press ◄── to accept the suggested name "Menu1." You'll see the menu file displayed on the screen, and then you'll be prompted to press any key to continue.

8. Press a key to return to the CodeLock Main menu.

ACCESSING PROCEDURES

Now that you've created a procedure file, we can look at ways to access the procedures within it. First, you'll need to return to the R> prompt. Then, use the RUN command with the procedure block name and the procedure file name in the syntax

RUN *command file block* IN *procedure file name*

To run the Loop2 procedure, enter the command

RUN Loop2 IN TestProc.CMD

The Loop2 command file will run its course, and you'll be returned to the R> prompt.

To display a screen block in a procedure file, use the DISPLAY command with the syntax

> **DISPLAY** *screen block name* **IN** *procedure file name*

For this example, type the command

> **DISPLAY Bills IN TestProc.CMD**

and press ←┘. You'll see the screen display appear, and then you'll be returned to the R> prompt.

To access the menu in the procedure file, use the CHOOSE command with the syntax

> **CHOOSE** *variable name* **FROM** *menu block name* +
> +> **IN** *procedure file* **AT** *row, column*

▓ If you were accessing this screen from within another command file, you'd probably use the NEWPAGE command before the DISPLAY Bills IN TestProc.CMD command to clear the screen prior to displaying the screen block.

Let's see how to use the CHOOSE command to access the Menu1 menu block in the TestProc.CMD procedure file.

1. Type **CLEAR ALL VARIABLES** and press ←┘.

2. Type **NEWPAGE** and press ←┘ to clear the screen.

3. Type **CHOOSE MChoice FROM Menu1 IN TestProc.CMD AT 5** and press ←┘. You should see the menu appear on the screen.

4. Make a selection from the menu. You will be returned to the R> prompt.

5. Type **SHOW VARIABLES** and press ←┘ to see the type and value of the MChoice variable. Notice that the MChoice variable has the INTEGER data type.

▓ Because all variables have been cleared, the CHOOSE command will create the variable MChoice with the appropriate data type.

▓ When you press Esc to leave a COLUMN menu, the choice variable will be set to 0. Pressing F1 (Help) to leave a COLUMN menu sets the choice variable to −1.

▓ We have not created a screen file called MenuHelp.SCN. If you want to test the Menu-Test.CMD file fully, use RBEDIT to create a screen file named Menu-Help.SCN.

Figure 18.11 shows a sample command file, named Menu-Test.CMD, that can be used to respond to a user's menu choice. Looking at Figure 18.11, you can see that if the user presses F1, the command file displays a screen named MenuHelp.SCN. Also, the WHILE loop repeats as long as the MChoice variable does not

```
--------------------------------------------- MenuTest.CMD
---- Test the Menu1 block in the TestProc.CMD procedure file

---- User will enter the password
CONNECT MAIL IDENTIFIED BY

---- Set up loop for displaying menu
CLEAR VARIABLE MChoice
SET VARIABLE MChoice TO 1
WHILE (.MChoice <> 0) THEN

    ---- Clear screen and display menu.  Store choice in MChoice.
    NEWPAGE
    CHOOSE MChoice FROM Menu1 IN TestProc.CMD

    ---- Respond to menu selection
    SWITCH .MChoice
        CASE 1
            ENTER NamesFrm
            BREAK
        CASE 2
            EDIT ALL FROM Names
            BREAK
        CASE 3
            Print Director
            BREAK
        CASE -1    ---- Display help screen if F1 pressed
            NEWPAGE
            DISPLAY MenuHelp.SCN
            PAUSE
    ENDSW
ENDWHILE

NEWPAGE
WRITE 'Exit selected'
```

Figure 18.11: The MenuTest.CMD command file

equal zero. This means that the menu will be redisplayed until the user chooses to exit by pressing the Esc key.

If you develop the MenuHelp.SCN and MenuTest.CMD files, these, too, can be converted in the procedure file. You'll just need to change the line in the MenuTest.CMD command file that reads

DISPLAY MenuHelp.SCN

to the following:

DISPLAY MenuHelp.SCN IN TestProc.CMD

If you add the MenuTest.CMD command file to the TestProc.CMD procedure file and you want to run it, enter this command at the R> prompt:

RUN MenuTest IN TestProc.CMD

CONVERTING APPLICATION FILES

When you create an application file like the MailSys application you created in Chapter 15, R:BASE generates three files with the extensions .APP, .API, and .APX:

```
MailSys.APP
MailSys.API
MailSys.APX
```

When you're converting with CodeLock, use the .APP file as the name of the ASCII application file to convert.

To practice converting the MailSys application with CodeLock, follow these steps from the R> prompt:

1. Type **CODELOCK** and press ◄─┘ to display the CodeLock Main menu.

2. Select the fifth option on the CodeLock Main menu, **Con**vert an ASCII application file to a binary procedure file.

3. Under the "Name of the ASCII application file to convert" prompt, type **MailSys.APP** and press ◄─┘.

4. Under the "Name of the procedure file" prompt, type **MailSys.CMD** and press ◄─┘. Although you can add the application file to an existing procedure file, we are creating a new application file named "MailSys.CMD." CodeLock will display each line of the application file as it converts, and then you'll be prompted to press any key to continue.

5. Press a key to return to the CodeLock Main menu.

From the R> prompt, use the syntax

RUN *application name* **IN** *procedure file*

to run the converted application. In this example, you would enter the command

RUN MailSys IN MailSys.CMD

to run the converted MailSys application.

Since CodeLock and Applications EXPRESS generate the same binary code, the above command is equivalent to the command you typed in Chapter 15:

RUN MailSys IN MailSys.APX

You may be puzzled about the need to convert application files generated with Applications EXPRESS. In fact, you'll rarely need to go through the procedure outlined above, because Applications EXPRESS automatically creates binary files for you.

As we said above, Applications EXPRESS generates three files every time you use it to create an application. The .APX binary file is the one that is actually run. The .APP file is the "English" ASCII file that contains all the procedure blocks that Applications EXPRESS creates for you, as well as any macros or custom sections you may have added. In essence, it's a long command file, which can be run by typing

RUN *appname*.APP

The .API file is the one that R:BASE uses to generate a new .APP file if you use Applications EXPRESS to modify your application. In that sense, the .API file is the only one that Applications EXPRESS cares about.

Remember that without the .API file, you can't use Applications EXPRESS to modify your application.

What if you wanted to make some changes in your application but had lost or damaged its .API file? Since you wouldn't be able to use Applications EXPRESS, the easiest solution would be to make changes in your .APP file and then use CodeLock to convert the existing .APP file to a binary procedure file. Since a binary procedure file is the same as an .APX file, the end result would be the same as if Applications EXPRESS had generated the .APX file itself.

Finally, there will be those of you who like to do a lot of custom programming (working with ASCII files), but prefer to bypass Applications EXPRESS; you will need to use CodeLock if you want your application to run faster.

CONVERTING MACROS

Macros are particularly good candidates for procedure files. By combining (or *compiling*) macros, you can develop a library of general-purpose routines, stored together in a single file, that are readily accessible when you need them.

Figure 18.12 shows a macro named Summary.MAC, which you can use with the following syntax to summarize the data in a table:

RUN Summary.MAC USING *source table name* +
+> *break column column to sum destination* +
+> *table name*

```
------------------------------------- Summary.MAC
---------------------- Summarizes a table column
*(Parameters:       %1: Name of table to summarize
                    %2: Key field to summarize on
                    %3: Column to total
                    %4: Name of summary table
                    %5: Name of master table )

NEWPAGE
SET MESSAGES OFF
SET ERROR MESSAGES OFF
WRITE 'Summarizing... Please wait' AT 1,1
CLEAR VARIABLE Vsubtot, Thisno

---- Create empty table for summary data
DROP TABLE &%4
PROJECT &%4 FROM &%5 USING &%2 ORDER BY &%2
ALTER TABLE &%4 ADD Subtot CURRENCY
---- Set up a cursor for the new table
DECLARE SumCurs CURSOR FOR SELECT &%2 FROM &%4
OPEN SumCurs

---- Loop through the rows one customer at a time
FETCH SumCurs INTO Thisno INDICATOR I1
WHILE (SQLCODE <> 100) THEN
    COMPUTE Vsubtot AS SUM &%3 FROM &%1 WHERE &%2 = .Thisno
    ---- Update the new table's column for subtotal
    UPDATE &%4 SET Subtot = .Vsubtot WHERE CURRENT OF SumCurs
    FETCH SumCurs INTO Thisno INDICATOR I1
ENDWHILE  -- SQLCODE <> 100

DROP CURSOR SumCurs
WRITE 'Finished summarizing...' AT 21,1
SET MESSAGES ON
SET ERROR MESSAGES ON
NEWPAGE
RETURN
```

Figure 18.12: The Summary.MAC macro

For example, Table 18.1 shows some sample data from the Mail database in the Charges table. The Summary.MAC macro can create a table from these data that displays the sum of the Total column for each customer. In this example, the *source table name* is Charges, the *break column* is CustNo (since we're summarizing for individual customers), and the *column to sum* can be any numeric column. We'll use the Total column in this example. The table that you are creating for the summary (the *destination table name* portion of the command) can have any table name. However, if a table with the same name already exists, it will be overwritten—so be sure to use a unique table name unless you want to replace an existing table.

Table 18.1: Sample data in the Charges table

CUSTNO	PRODNO	QTY	U_PRICE	TAXABLE	TOTAL
1001	A-111	12	$10.00	Y	$127.20
1001	B-222	5	$12.50	Y	$66.25
1001	C-434	2	$100.00	Y	$212.00
1004	A-111	5	$10.00	Y	$53.00
1004	Z-128	10	$12.80	N	$128.00
1007	A-111	10	$10.00	Y	$106.00
1007	Z-128	10	$12.80	N	$128.00
1002	B-222	12	$12.50	Y	$159.00
1002	A-111	10	$10.00	Y	$106.00

Let's do this summary using the Summary.MAC macro with the following steps:

1. Use RBEDIT to enter the Summary.MAC macro in Figure 18.12.

2. Connect to the Mail database.

3. Enter the command

    RUN Summary.MAC USING Charges CustNo Total SumTable +
    +> Names

    to create a table named SumTable that summarizes the totals for each customer.

4. Type **SELECT ALL FROM SumTable** to view the output of the macro. With the sample charges listed in Table 18.1, you would see the data below:

CUSTNO	*SUBTOT*
1001	$405.45
1002	$265.00

In SumTable, a –0– will appear in the Subtot column for any customers in the Names table who don't have any charges in the Charges table.

1004	$181.00
1007	$234.00

Now suppose that you wish to put the Summary.MAC macro and the Update.MAC macro that you created in the last chapter into a single procedure file called "GenProcs.CMD." Piece of cake, right? Refer to these steps if you get stuck:

1. Type **CODELOCK** and press ◄── to display the CodeLock Main menu.

2. Select the second option on the CodeLock Main menu, **A**dd an ASCII command file to a procedure file.

3. Enter **Summary.MAC** as the command file to add, and **GenProcs.CMD** as the procedure file.

4. Press ◄── to accept the suggested command block name "Summary."

5. After the command file is displayed, press a key to return to the CodeLock Main menu.

6. Again select the **A**dd an ASCII command file to a procedure file option.

7. Enter **Update.MAC** as the command file to add and **GenProcs.CMD** as the procedure file. R:BASE reminds you that the GenProcs.CMD procedure file contains a block called Summary.

8. Press ◄── to accept the suggested command block name of **Update**.

9. After the command file is displayed, press a key to return to the CodeLock Main menu.

Once you've added the macros to the GenProcs.CMD procedure file, they can be accessed from the R > prompt using the syntax

RUN *block name* IN *procedure file name* USING *parameter list*

For example, if you wanted to run the Summary.MAC macro in the GenProcs.CMD procedure file to summarize the Total column by customer number in the Charges table, thereby creating a new table named SumTable, you would enter the command

> RUN Summary IN GenProcs.CMD USING Charges CustNo +
> +> Total SumTable Names

To run the Update.MAC macro in the GenProcs.CMD procedure file, you would enter a command such as

> RUN Update IN GenProcs.CMD USING ARMain CustNo +
> +> Curr_Bal Payments CustNo Amount MINUS

Of course, the parameters will vary depending on the tables involved and the type of update (PLUS, MINUS, or REPLACE). Also, be sure the appropriate database is open before you run the macro.

Remember, you can add up to 42 blocks to a procedure file, so you could develop a good collection of general-purpose macros and have them all readily accessible from a single file.

MODIFYING PROCEDURES

Never use RBEDIT (or any other editor) to modify a binary procedure file that was produced by CodeLock. To modify a block in a procedure file, always modify the original ASCII file and then use CODE-LOCK to add the ASCII file to the procedure file again.

At some point, you may need to make changes to a file that has already been converted into a procedure file. To do so, use RBEDIT to change the *original* file. Then, use CodeLock to add the file to the procedure file once again. When you specify the name of the modified file, CodeLock will display the warning

> Duplicate name—overwrite?

If you answer Yes, the modified file will be added to the end of the procedure file, and the existing copy of the block in the procedure will not be used if you access the command, screen, or menu block in the procedure file. However, even though the old block will no longer be used, it will continue to occupy space in the procedure file. If you have made many modifications to the blocks in the GenProcs.CMD procedure file, you can recover the wasted space by creating a new procedure file with the same blocks, as follows:

1. Use CodeLock to create a new procedure file called "Gen-Procs.UPD," adding up-to-date copies of all of the blocks in the GenProcs.CMD procedure file.

2. Use the ERASE command at the R > prompt to erase the GenProcs.CMD procedure file.

3. Use the RENAME command at the R > prompt to rename the GenProcs.UPD procedure file to Gen-Procs.CMD.

DISPLAYING THE DIRECTORY

The sixth option on the CodeLock Main menu, Display directory, allows you to view the files stored on disk. When you select this option, you'll see the prompt

Enter drive and subdirectory:

You can also specify a filename, including the DOS wildcards * and ?, to display a list of only some files in a directory.

Press ◄┘ to display the files on the current drive and directory. To view the files on a separate drive or directory, include the drive specification and directory name; for example, enter B:\Newdbs or C:\Newdbs.

DISPLAYING THE CONTENTS OF ASCII FILES

To view the contents of a file before you compile it, select the seventh option from the CodeLock Main menu, Display the contents of an ASCII file. CodeLock will display the prompt

Name of the file to be displayed:

Enter the name of the file (and the drive specification and directory name if necessary). For example, enter Loop2.ASC to display the contents of the Loop2.ASC file on the current drive and directory. Enter the file name B:Loop2.ASC to look for and display the Loop2.ASC file on drive B.

In this chapter, you've seen how to use menus in your programs to make them easier to use and look more professional, and how to make your programs run faster using CodeLock. Keep in mind that CodeLock provides an additional bonus, since it effectively encrypts your program. Binary files, for all practical purposes, can't be read by inquisitive humans. R:BASE does have excellent facilities for sharing data. In Chapter 19, we'll focus on Gateway and using dBASE files, two marvelous tools for sharing data with other programs on your computer.

Chapter 19

Adding the Versatility
of Other Programs
to R:BASE

R:BASE 3.1 COMES WITH COMMANDS AND PROGRAMS that allow you to translate data to and from a variety of formats and interface with other software systems. With two programs called DBCONV-3.EXE and APCONV-3.EXE, as well as Applications EXPRESS, you can convert R:BASE System V and R:BASE for DOS databases and programs to the new R:BASE 3.1 format. You also have the Gateway program to help you import data from and export data to a variety of packages. In particular, this chapter focuses on methods for providing information that WordPerfect and Microsoft Word can use in form letters. We'll also discuss exchanging data with d:BASE III and d:BASE III Plus, and how R:BASE 3.1 can obtain and change information in d:BASE III and d:BASE III Plus databases.

CONVERTING R:BASE SYSTEM V AND R:BASE FOR DOS TO THE R:BASE 3.1 FORMAT

You don't have to convert R:BASE 3.0 databases, applications, and command files to use them in R:BASE 3.1. To convert programs or data from R:BASE 4000, R:BASE 5000, or any other version of R:BASE older than R:BASE System V and R:BASE for DOS, first you will have to convert the old programs and data to R:BASE for DOS, and then convert the resulting programs and data from R:BASE for DOS to R:BASE 3.1.

If you are upgrading to R:BASE 3.1 from R:BASE System V or R:BASE for DOS, you can connect to your old databases, examine data, and even make changes to data in tables. However, you have to convert your original databases to the new R:BASE format if you want to use reports, forms, views, and rules. Command files, macros, and applications have to be changed to run under R:BASE 3.1. Because some commands and database names, tables, columns, and variables that were valid in previous versions of R:BASE are no longer valid, conversions can involve many changes. Fortunately, R:BASE supplies several tools to make converting easier. You can use the DBCONV-3.EXE program to convert databases, tables, forms, and reports; the APCONV-3.EXE to convert command files and applications program; and Applications EXPRESS to convert complete applications from R:BASE V and R:BASE for DOS to R:BASE 3.1.

CONVERTING DATABASES TO R:BASE 3.1 FORMAT

Let's suppose that you have an R:BASE System V or R:BASE for DOS database that you want to convert to the new R:BASE format. First, you have to prepare your database for the conversion.

Always back up your database before you make structural changes to it.

1. Back up the database you wish to convert.

2. Make sure that the database you are converting does not have the same name as an R:BASE 3.1 database you made already and that its name is not an R:BASE 3.1 reserved word. If necessary, change the name of the database.

See "Reserved Words" in the Command Dictionary section of the *Reference Manual* that came with your R:BASE package for a list of reserved words.

3. In R:BASE for DOS or R:BASE System V, open the database you wish to convert. Be sure to enter the owner password if any of the tables are password-protected.

4. From the R > prompt, use the following commands to print the details of the structure of your database. You have to wait for the printer to finish after each LIST command.

    ```
    OUTPUT PRINTER
    LIST TABLES
    LIST COLUMNS
    LIST ALL
    LIST FORMS
    LIST REPORTS
    LIST RULES
    LIST VIEWS
    LIST ACCESS
    OUTPUT SCREEN
    ```

    By examining the output of these LIST commands, you can make sure you have not forgotten to check any part of the database in your conversion.

Each database can have a maximum of 800 columns, but because R:BASE creates some columns in system tables, you still have to make sure that the database you are converting has fewer than 763 columns.

5. Examine the list of tables and columns at the beginning of your output. Make sure that you do not have more than 72 tables and 763 columns in your database. If necessary, delete some tables and columns.

6. Leave R:BASE for DOS (or R:BASE System V) and return to the DOS prompt.

Now it's time to use the DBCONV-3 program to perform the conversion.

7. Change to the directory that contains the database you wish to convert.

8. Type **DBCONV-3** and press ← to run the conversion program.

9. Select your database from the menu of databases in the current directory. If the database is password-protected, you will have to enter the owner password.

If the database you want to convert does not appear in the menu, press **Esc** to leave DBCONV-3 and change to the directory that does contain the database you want.

The DBCONV-3 program starts converting your database. As the conversion proceeds, you will see progress messages and messages about the changes you have to make to the database. When DBCONV-3 finishes, it prompts you to press any key to continue.

10. Press a key. DBCONV-3 displays the menu of databases again in the current directory.

11. Press **Esc** to leave DBCONV-3 and return to the DOS prompt.

DBCONV-3 writes more information about the changes you still have to make and stores it in a file called *dbname*.err, where *dbname* is the name of the database you are converting. To clean up the remaining details in the conversion process,

As you modify each part of the database, avoiding reserved words and making other adjustments, mark off the appropriate parts of the listing you created with the LIST commands in step 4, as well as the *dbname*.err listing.

12. Print the file *dbname*.err. Usually, you can do this with a DOS command such as **COPY** *dbname*.**err LPT1:**.

13. Examine the *dbname*.err file and identify any R:BASE 3.1 reserved words you used in the names of columns, variables, etc., in your databases.

14. Start R:BASE, connect to the converted database, and display the R > prompt.

A quick way to start R:BASE in Command mode is to enter the command RBASE -C at the DOS prompt.

15. Issue the RENAME command and change any names identified as reserved words in the *dbname.*err listing. Remember that you can rename tables, views, columns, forms, and reports, as well as change the owner password and the modify and read passwords. On the listing you created with the LIST commands, make a note of the new names you chose for tables, columns, etc.

16. Modify your rules, making sure that

   - column names are consistent with the changes you made to avoid reserved words,

   - variable names do not conflict with reserved words,

   - all text strings in rules have single quotes (') around them, and

   - comparisons with wildcard characters use the operators LIKE or NOT LIKE.

17. In each form and report, change the variable names to avoid using reserved words if you have to. Also, change the definitions of variables that include reserved-word variables or columns, if necessary.

18. Issue the GRANT and REVOKE commands to change any user passwords that happen to be reserved words.

Another way to modify R:BASE passwords is to enter the RBDEFINE command at the R > prompt and use the options in the Access rights pull-down menu.

19. Drop and re-create all views, being careful to use any new column and table names you have chosen and to avoid reserved words. If you are converting R:BASE for DOS views, you can use a shortcut to re-create views:

   a. Create an ASCII representation of the view with the following commands:

   ```
   OUTPUT viewtext
   UNLOAD STRUCTURE FOR oldview
   OUTPUT SCREEN
   ```

   where *oldview* is the name of the view you are converting.

   b. Use RBEDIT (or your favorite text files editor) to edit the *viewtext* ASCII file and change column and table names to the new values you have chosen. Make sure they do not conflict with reserved words. Also, add single quotes around text strings in WHERE clauses and use LIKE and NOT LIKE in conditions with wild-card characters.

c. Create the new view with the following commands:

DROP VIEW *oldview*
INPUT *viewtext*

20. Use the DROP TABLE command to drop the following tables (which are not needed for R:BASE 3.1): COMP-COLS, FORMS, PASSTAB, REPORTS, RULES, VIEWS, and VIEWWHER. You can also drop the VIEWCOND table if you are converting an R:BASE System V database.

21. Check the hard copy listings you made earlier to see that you haven't missed converting anything.

22. Test your data to make sure everything is working. Use the Edit screen to examine tables and views and to test your rules. Try all the forms and reports to make sure they are working properly. Check the variables particularly carefully to make sure they are producing the correct results.

23. Copy the converted database files to the directory where you store your data files. Remember that you will be copying three files. For example, in the case of a database named MyData, you would copy the files MyData1.RBF, MyData2.RBF, and MyData3.RBF.

After you've converted a database, you will probably want to convert all the program files and applications that work with it as well. Read on—the following sections explain how to do this.

Unless you have defined at least one form, password, report, rule, and view in your database, you will not have the FORMS, PASS-TAB, REPORTS, RULES, VIEWS, and VIEWWHER tables in your database.

CONVERTING COMMAND FILES TO R:BASE 3.1 FORMAT

Some R:BASE 3.1 commands have different formats from their R:BASE System V and R:BASE for DOS predecessors. Also, some of the defaults are different. Fortunately, R:BASE includes the APCONV-3.EXE program to assist with converting command files—as well as the .APP source files for applications—to R:BASE 3.1 format.

When you use the APCONV-3.EXE program to convert command files, the source file you are converting is saved in a subdirectory called OLDAPPS. As the file is converted, a line of dots is displayed to show the progress of the APCONV-3.EXE program. At the beginning of the source file, the defaults used in older versions of R:BASE are restored as follows:

The setting of AND determines the order of evaluation when AND and OR are used in IF and WHERE clauses. When AND is set ON (the R:BASE 3.1 default), conditions separated by AND are evaluated before conditions separated by OR. Older versions of R:BASE operated as though AND was set to OFF, with all conditions evaluated from left to right regardless of whether they were separated by AND or OR.

```
SET AND OFF
SET MANY = *
SET QUOTES = "
SET SINGLE = ?
```

Commands that can be converted to R:BASE 3.1 format are converted. All command line changes are *flagged* by special comment lines to make it easy for you to find them in the text file. These flags are summarized below.

*(*Original line:	The original line is displayed before the changed line.
*(*Done:	This command has significant changes.
*(*To do:	You have to make changes (such as the name of variables that are reserved words).

Status messages displayed on your screen during the conversion are stored in a file called APCONV-3.ERR.

To use the APCONV-3.EXE program to convert a command file,

1. Make sure the command file you want to convert does not contain any SET commands for QUOTES, SINGLE, MANY, and AND. You have to remove these commands from the command file so that the APCONV-3.EXE program produces the correct results.

2. At the DOS prompt, change to the directory containing your command file.

3. Make sure you have created an OLDAPPS subdirectory in the current directory to hold the backup versions of the command files you convert.

4. Type in the command APCONV-3 *command.fil* and press ↩, where *command.fil* is the name of your command file.

You have some cleanup work to do after the conversion program does its work. Use RBEDIT (or another text editor if you prefer) to examine each line of the converted file and perform the following tasks:

5. Check the *(*Done: comments to make sure that the changes are correct. Once you've made any necessary adjustments, and you are happy with the R:BASE 3.1 command generated, remove each comment line.

6. For commands flagged *(*To do:, convert the commands as required and remove the corresponding comment.

7. If you want to eliminate the AND, MANY, QUOTES, and SINGLE settings that differ from the R:BASE 3.1 defaults, delete the SET lines at the beginning of the program and make the corresponding changes in the program.

8. It is a good idea to improve on the conversions that the APCONV-3.EXE program makes for some commands. For example, the CHANGE command, an R:BASE 2.0 command, is not documented as part of R:BASE 3.1 and may be phased out in future releases. APCONV-3.EXE converts the CHANGE command to a version that works in R:BASE 3.1, but it is better to use the SQL standard UPDATE command, which is part of R:BASE 3.1. Similarly, you may want to convert the SET POINTER, SET VAR IN #, and NEXT # commands to OPEN CURSOR and FETCH commands.

9. Check to see if the APCONV-3.EXE program made any conversion mistakes, such as putting quotes around a variable that does not have a dot (.) or ampersand (&) in front of it.

10. Remove any remaining comment lines added by APCONV-3.EXE.

11. Copy the converted program to the directory containing your programs and test it.

You can also use the CodeLock program to translate your converted program to a binary command file, but CodeLock has one quirky feature. If you convert a file with a SET QUOTES command, CodeLock remembers the QUOTES setting until it encounters another SET QUOTES command or you select the Exit option to leave CodeLock. So, if you are converting files with a SET QUOTES command in them, put a SET QUOTES command at the beginning of each file you convert.

CONVERTING APPLICATIONS FOR USE UNDER R:BASE 3.1

As mentioned above, you can use the APCONV-3.EXE program to convert the .APP source file for an R:BASE System V or an R:BASE for DOS application to the R:BASE 3.1 format. However, if you have the .API file, it is better to use Applications EXPRESS to convert the application. Here's how to do it:

1. Change to the directory containing the .API file and start R:BASE.

2. Display the Applications EXPRESS menu.

3. Highlight Modify and select the application you want to convert.

4. Highlight Manage application and select Save changes.

5. Reply No to creating a startup file.

6. Highlight and select Exit from the Applications EXPRESS menu.

7. If your application contains custom programs or macros, convert those functions using the methods discussed above in the section called "Converting Command Files to R:BASE 3.1 Format."

8. Test your application.

IMPORTING AND EXPORTING DATA WITH GATEWAY

The Gateway program can copy data from tables to a variety of formats, as well as import data from external formats into R:BASE tables. To run Gateway, either select Import/export on the Tools pull-down menu or enter the command Gateway at the R > prompt or the DOS prompt. The Gateway menu will appear on the screen, as in Figure 19.1. As the menu shows, you can import data, export data, perform disk management functions, and change some settings.

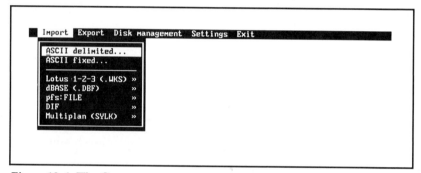

Figure 19.1: The Gateway menu

In the Import pull-down menu displayed in Figure 19.1, you can see the options for importing data into R:BASE:

Delimited and fixed ASCII files are discussed in more detail in the next section, "A Note on ASCII Files."

ASCII delimited	lets you import data in which fields are enclosed in quotes and separated by commas.
ASCII fixed	lets you import data in which fields are not marked by special characters but are fixed lengths.
Lotus 1-2-3 (.WKS)	lets you import spreadsheet data from Lotus 1-2-3 version 1.0 or 2.0, or Symphony.
dBASE (.DBF)	lets you import databases from dBASE II, III, and III Plus.
pfs:FILE	lets you import data from pfs:FILE or pfs:REPORT.

DIF	lets you import DIF format files, which can be produced by Visicalc and most other spreadsheet programs.
Multiplan (SYLK)	lets you import data from spreadsheets created by the Multiplan spreadsheet program.

The options for exporting data are the same as those for importing data, except that you can't export data in pfs:FILE or dBASE II format. The Disk management pull-down menu has the same options as the Disk management menu displayed by selecting Disk management in the Tools pull-down menu (found on the R:BASE Main menu).

The Settings pull-down menu has the following options:

Set rules	lets you decide whether to check the data against the data-entry rules you defined for the table that is receiving the data.
User password	lets you enter a user password.
Autonumbering	lets you decide whether to number the rows automatically in columns which are set up as autonumber columns.
Exceptions	lets you decide whether to save rows containing data that is the wrong data type or that violates data-entry rules.

As in all R:BASE modules, you can press F1 anywhere on the Gateway menu for help, and Shift-F1 for a description of available function keys.

Autonumber columns generate row numbers automatically whenever a new row is added to a table. You can designate a column as an autonumber column with the Autonumber pull-down menu on the tables menu. Access the tables menu with the RBDEFINE command at the R > prompt, or by selecting the Create/ modify option in the Info pull-down menu (on the R:BASE Main menu).

A NOTE ON ASCII FILES

Before discussing specific file transfer techniques, you should become familiar with basic ASCII file structures. Many software systems accept data that are stored in ASCII format. In fact, you can accomplish almost any data transfer imaginable, including many minicomputer and mainframe transfers, with some knowledge of ASCII file formats. Let's discuss those now.

ASCII (american standard code for information interchange) data files are generally stored in one of two formats: *delimited* or *fixed*.

Delimited ASCII Files

The most common format is the delimited ASCII file, also called the *sequential access* file. In this file, individual fields, or columns, are separated by commas (or another delimiting character). Character (text) fields are usually surrounded by quotation marks. Many data files passed from minicomputer and mainframe computers to microcomputers are stored as delimited ASCII files. Figure 19.2 shows a sample delimited ASCII file.

Fixed ASCII Files

Fixed ASCII files (also called *structured* or *random access* files) store data with fixed *field* (column) and *record* (row) lengths, with no delimiting characters between the fields. Often, information captured from other computers via a modem is stored in the fixed format. Figure 19.3 shows a sample fixed ASCII data file.

```
1003,"Tape Backup",1,1250.00,"7/8/91"
1000,"Ram Disk",1,1100.00,"7/8/91"
1001,"Floppy Disks",10,22.11,"7/9/91"
1001,"VGA Card",1,201.00,"7/9/91"
1001,"Video Cable",2,16.00,"7/9/91"
1001,"12 Mhz Clock",2,16.39,"7/9/91"
1002,"Tape Backup",1,1250.00,"7/9/91"
```

Figure 19.2: A sample delimited ASCII file

```
1003 Tape Backup     1    1250.00   07/08/91
1000 Ram Disk        1    1100.00   07/08/91
1001 Floppy Disks   10      22.11   07/09/91
1001 VGA Card        1     201.00   07/09/91
1001 Video Cable     2      16.00   07/09/91
1001 12 Mhz Clock    2      16.39   07/09/91
1002 Tape Backup     1    1250.00   07/09/91
```

Figure 19.3: A sample fixed ASCII data file

The format of the TYPE command is TYPE *ASCII.fil*, where *ASCII.fil* is the name of the ASCII file you want to display. If the ASCII file is not in the current directory, you can include a volume and subdirectory before *ASCII.fil*.

ASCII files generally contain only data and delimiters, with no special formatting codes or header information. Therefore, you can use the DOS or R:BASE TYPE command, or select the Show a file option on the Disk management menu to see the file displayed on the screen. Usually, displaying the contents of the file is an easy way to see whether the file is fixed or delimited.

TECHNIQUES FOR TRANSFERRING FILES

The section called "Importing and Exporting Files" in Chapter 8 of the R:BASE *Users Manual* discusses all the details of transferring files using Gateway. Rather than repeat all of that information here, we'll look at specific examples of transferring R:BASE table data. We'll look at some creative ways to perform transfers with ASCII files that are not discussed in the R:BASE manuals. In particular, we'll focus on exporting information to two common word processing packages, Microsoft Word and WordPerfect.

CREATING A FORM
LETTER WITH MICROSOFT WORD

Microsoft Word (like most other word processors) has a merge option that allows you to print form letters using data stored in delimited ASCII data files. You can easily create such files from any R:BASE table using Gateway.

For example, suppose you want to print form letters with Word using names and addresses from the Names table in the MAIL database that we created earlier in this book. You can create the ASCII delimited file with Gateway by following these steps:

1. At the DOS prompt in the \RBFILES\LEARN directory, type **Gateway** and press ←⏎. This displays the Gateway menu.

2. Highlight **E**xport and select **ASCII** delimited.

3. Type **WORD.DAT** and press ←⏎ for the name of the file to receive the data.

If you already had a
WORD.DAT file in
your directory, you would
be asked if you wanted to
append the exported data
to the end of WORD-
.DAT or overwrite it.

The order that the
columns are selected
determines the order that
they will appear in the
exported ASCII file. In
the form letter, the last
name will appear first,
the first name will appear
second, the company will
appear third, and so on.

4. Select **MAIL** as the database and enter the owner password **MYMAIL** when asked for a new user identifier.

5. Select **N**ames as the table.

6. Select columns **L_Name**, **F**_Name, **C**ompany, **A**ddress, **C**ity, **S**tate, and **Z**ip_Code and press F2.

7. Press **F2** three times to bypass sorting and selection criteria and finish defining the export query.

8. Choose **Y**es to exporting all rows.

9. Press ◄┘ to confirm the comma as the character to separate the columns in your output file.

10. Choose **Y**es to adding a carriage return/line feed at the end of each row. As R:BASE writes the data to the WORD-.DAT file, it displays a count of the number of rows exported.

11. When R:BASE asks you to press any key to continue, press a key to return to the Gateway menu.

12. Highlight and select **E**xit to leave Gateway and return to the DOS prompt.

The WORD.DAT file you just created has the correct format for producing form letters with word processors other than Microsoft Word, such as Wordstar, without requiring any changes. However, before you can use WORD.DAT as a merge file with Microsoft Word, you need to add a header line at the beginning of the file. The header line will provide a name for each field in the file. Prepare the merge file and produce the form letters by following these steps:

1. To prepare the merge file, start Word and load the file \RBFILES\LEARN\WORD.DAT. Adjust the margins so that all the data for each customer fits on one line. Type in a new first line with the field names of the data, as shown in Figure 19.4. Save the file to \RBFILES\LEARN\WORD-.DAT, which will be the default name when you choose Transfer and then Save.

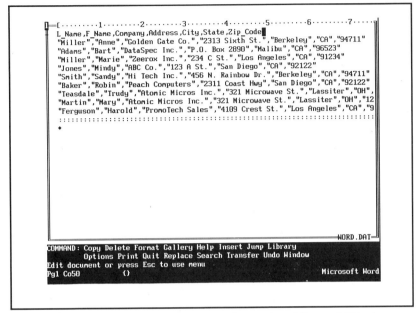

Figure 19.4: The WORD.DAT file ready for use in a Microsoft Word merge

2. Create the master form letter. Note that the name of the data file must be entered on the first line inside the chevron symbols («»). You create the left and right chevrons by entering Ctrl-[and Ctrl-] respectively. Now enter the field names, also within chevrons, at the locations shown in Figure 19.5. When the fields for the inside address have been positioned, type in the rest of the letter.

3. You could save this master form letter now if you wanted. To produce the form letters, leave the form letter on the screen, and select Print, and select Merge.

Tips for Interfacing with Microsoft Word

You can send R:BASE reports to Microsoft Word for further editing or inclusion in other documents. To do so, use the OUTPUT and PRINT commands to print the report to a file and load or merge the file into your Word document. For example, you could include the Sales

```
=[·········1········2········3········4········5········]········7····
«DATA WORD.DAT»

March 1, 1991

«F_Name» «L_Name»
«Company»
«Address»
«City», «State» «Zip_Code»

Dear «F_Name»:

Remember the next meeting on March 7th!  We have many
important items to discuss and we hope to see you there.

Sincerely,


Johnny Comearly
█


                                                    =FORMLET.DOC=
COMMAND: Copy Delete Format Gallery Help Insert Jump Library
         Options Print Quit Replace Search Transfer Undo Window
Microsoft Word Version 5.0
Pg1 Co1           {}                              Microsoft Word
```

Figure 19.5: The master form letter for the Microsoft Word mail merge

report in a Word document called "Quartrly.DOC" using the following steps:

1. Start R:BASE and display the R> prompt.

2. Place the Sales report in an ASCII file and leave R:BASE by entering the commands

   ```
   CONNECT MAIL IDENTIFIED BY MYMAIL
   OUTPUT Transfer.TXT
   PRINT Sales
   OUTPUT SCREEN
   EXIT
   ```

3. Start Word. Load Quartrly.DOC and move the cursor where you would like to include the Sales report.

4. Merge the file \RBFILES\LEARN\TRANSFER.TXT into your document. You may have to adjust the margins or edit the document to remove some of the information

merged from the TRANSFER.TXT document to make the report fit on the page.

5. Save the Quartrly.DOC document.

You can also use Word to create and edit R:BASE command files. Just be sure to save the files in Text-only mode.

CREATING A FORM LETTER WITH WORDPERFECT

Those of you who use WordPerfect will want to know how to transfer R:BASE data into WordPerfect format. The technique we just described for sending R:BASE reports to a file for subsequent editing in Microsoft Word works with WordPerfect as well. You'll use Ctrl-F5 (Text In/Out) and the DOS Text option to read in the R:BASE report.

However, if you want to take advantage of WordPerfect's Merge feature for multiple mailings, things are a bit more complex. Word-Perfect works well with ASCII-delimited files, but expects special field and record delimiters that are not produced by Gateway.

The simplest approach to creating a WordPerfect Merge file is to create an ASCII delimited file with Gateway and then use Word-Perfect's Search and Replace feature to make the appropriate changes in the ASCII delimited file.

Let's try creating a WordPerfect merge file called WP.DAT for our form letter.

1. At the DOS prompt in the \RBFILES\LEARN directory, type **Gateway** and press ← to display the Gateway menu.

2. Highlight **E**xport and select **A**SCII delimited.

3. Type **WP.DAT** and press ← for the name of the file to receive the data.

4. Select **MAIL** as the database and enter the owner password MYMAIL when asked for a new user identifier.

5. Select **N**ames as the table.

6. Select columns **L_Name**, **F_Name**, **C**ompany, **A**ddress, **C**ity, **S**tate, and **Z**ip_Code and press F2.

7. Press **F2** three times to bypass sorting and selection criteria and confirm the export specifications.

8. Choose **Y**es to exporting all rows.

9. Type \ and press ◄─┘ when asked to enter the character to separate the columns in your output file.

10. Choose **Y**es to adding a carriage return/line feed at the end of each row. As R:BASE writes the data to the WP.DAT file, it displays a count of the number of rows exported.

11. When R:BASE asks you to press any key to continue, press a key to return to the Gateway menu.

12. Highlight and select **E**xit to leave Gateway and return to the DOS prompt.

13. Start WordPerfect.

14. To begin editing the WP.DAT file we just created, press **Shift-F10** (Retrieve); type **\RBFILES\LEARN\WP.DAT** and press ◄─┘.

15. To change the carriage return/line feed at the end of each line to a record delimiter, press **Alt-F2** (Replace); choose **N** for confirm; press the **spacebar**, ◄─┘, and **F2** for the search string; and press **Shift-F9** (Merge Codes), **E**, **Ctrl-◄─┘**, and **F2** for the replace string.

16. Press **Home**, **Home**, and ↑ to return the cursor to the beginning of the document.

17. To change all backslashes to field delimiters, press **Alt-F2** (Replace); choose **N** for confirm; press \ and **F2** for the search string; and press **F9** (End Field), ◄─┘, and **F2** for the replace string.

18. Press **Home**, **Home**, and ↑ to return the cursor to the beginning of the document.

19. To remove the double quotes that enclose each field, press **Alt-F2** (Replace); choose **N** for confirm; press " and **F2** for the search string; and press **F2** for the replace string.

We chose the backslash character (\) as the delimiter separating columns because it does not appear in the columns we are exporting. We could have chosen other characters not found in our data, such as the tilde (˜), caret (^), or vertical bar (|).

The WordPerfect figures in this section were created with WordPerfect 5.1. If you have a different version of WordPerfect, your screen may differ from Figures 19.6 and 19.7.

20. Press **Home**, **Home**, and ↑ to return the cursor to the beginning of the document. Your screen should now look like Figure 19.6.

21. To save the document, press **F7** (Exit); choose **Yes** to save document; press ↵ to accept document name of \RBFILES\LEARN\WP.DAT; choose **Yes** to replace the file; and choose **No** to leaving WordPerfect.

```
Anne{END FIELD}■
Miller{END FIELD}■
Golden Gate Co.{END FIELD}■
2313 Sixth St.{END FIELD}■
Berkeley{END FIELD}■
CA{END FIELD}■
94711{END RECORD}■
=================================================================
Bart{END FIELD}■
Adams{END FIELD}■
DataSpec Inc.{END FIELD}■
P.O. Box 2890{END FIELD}■
Malibu{END FIELD}■
CA{END FIELD}■
96523{END RECORD}■
=================================================================
Marie{END FIELD}■
Miller{END FIELD}■
Zeerox Inc.{END FIELD}■
234 C St.{END FIELD}■
Los Angeles{END FIELD}■
CA{END FIELD}■
91234{END RECORD}■
=================================================================
C:\RBFILES\LEARN\WP.DAT                          Doc 1 Pg 1 Ln 1" Pos 1"
```

Figure 19.6: The secondary (Merge) file after the WordPerfect edits

The WP.DAT file is now ready to be used by WordPerfect as a merge or secondary file. Into the empty document you now have on the screen, type in the primary file (form letter) as shown in Figure 19.7. You can place a field from the Merge file in your form letter document as follows:

1. Position the cursor where you want the field to go.

2. Press **Shift-F9** (Merge Codes) and **F**.

3. Type the number of the field you want to appear at this position and press ↵. For example, to place the first name, you would type 1 and press ↵.

```
        March 1, 1991

        {FIELD}2~ {FIELD}1~
        {FIELD}3~
        {FIELD}4~
        {FIELD}5~, {FIELD}6~ {FIELD}7~

        Dear {FIELD}2~:

        Remember the next meeting on April 7!  We have many important
        items to discuss and we hope to see you there.

        Sincerely yours,

        Johnny Comearly
```

Figure 19.7: Entering a primary file for WordPerfect's Merge routine

The field number is the position of the field in each record in the secondary file: field 1 is the last name, field 2 is the first name, field 3 is the company, and so on. When you are finished typing in the form letter, save it in a file called RBFRMLET.WP as follows: press **F7** (Exit); choose **Yes** to save the document; type **RBFRMLET.WP** and press ←; and choose **No** to leaving WordPerfect. Merging the form letter in RBFRMLET.WP with the Merge file WP.DAT is easy.

1. Press **Ctrl-F9** (Merge/Sort) and **M** for Merge.

2. Type **RBFRMLET.WP** and press ← for the primary file.

3. Type **\RBFILES\LEARN\WP.DAT** and press ← as the name of the secondary file.

WordPerfect assembles all of the form letters in the document you are editing, starting a new page at the beginning of each one. As with any document, you can print your form letters using the Print (Shift-F7) function. When you are finished printing the form letters, leave WordPerfect and start R:BASE.

The exercises for exchanging information with Microsoft Word and WordPerfect give you an idea of the power and flexibility of Gateway. As you know from looking at the Gateway menu, the program can also be used to exchange files with dBASE III and dBASE III Plus. In the next section, you'll see how you can do more than just use Gateway to exchange files with dBASE—you can use R:BASE commands and menu functions to obtain information from and change information in a dBASE III database.

ACCESSING DBASE III AND DBASE III PLUS DATABASES

R:BASE has special facilities for accessing dBASE III and dBASE III Plus databases directly. With them, you can create *file-tables*, dBASE database files that appear as R:BASE tables. With a few exceptions, you can treat a file-table just as you would an R:BASE table, using the same menu functions and commands to display and change data. You can even have R:BASE keep as many as seven dBASE indexes up-to-date with your changes.

R:BASE will only maintain existing dBASE index files for a file-table. R:BASE cannot create a dBASE index file.

Before you can make a dBASE database become a file-table in an R:BASE database, you have to issue the ATTACH command to associate the dBASE database file with an R:BASE database. The ATTACH command has the syntax

ATTACH *dBASE file* USING *list of indexes*

where *dBASE file* is the name of a dBASE .dbf database file and *list of indexes* is a list of up to seven .ndx index files, separated by commas. The USING part of the command is optional, but if it is included, R:BASE will keep all index files up-to-date as you make changes to the data stored in the file-table.

Alternatively, you can attach a file-table by selecting the Attach file option on the dBASE files menu, which is displayed by highlighting Databases on the R:BASE Main menu and selecting dBASE files. To have R:BASE maintain a dBASE .ndx index file, choose the Select index option on the dBASE files menu. You will be asked to select an attached file-table and an index file name. As with the ATTACH command, you can attach a maximum of seven index files for one file-table, and all index files must already exist.

Suppose the name of the dBASE database is a reserved word in R:BASE or is the same as another table in the R:BASE database. R:BASE will not attach it—you will have to use the RENAME command at the DOS prompt to change the name of the database before you can attach it. When R:BASE attaches a file-table, it takes the first eight characters of the dBASE field name for the R:BASE column name. Before R:BASE finishes attaching a file-table, you will be asked to change any column names which are invalid in R:BASE, either because they are reserved words or the column names match another column name in use. These revised names are used only by R:BASE to access the file-table; they do not affect the field names in the dBASE database. Because dBASE field names can be longer than eight characters and R:BASE uses only the first eight characters of a field name as a column name, field names that have the same first eight characters will be treated as duplicates.

Once you have attached a file-table to an R:BASE database, the file-table remains part of the R:BASE database until you detach it using the DETACH command (or the Detach file option on the dBASE files menu). Once you connect to a database that contains file-tables, R:BASE prepares the file-tables in that database for access, searching for the file-tables in the current directory and in the directories in the DOS *path*.

If you connect to a database that contains file-tables that are not in the current directory and not on the DOS path, R:BASE will display a message telling you that it cannot find these file-tables. Although you could move all of these file-tables into the same directory as your R:BASE files, it is usually easier to add the directories containing these file-tables to the DOS path. To see what directories are in the DOS path, type **PATH** and press ← at the DOS prompt. The current DOS path will be displayed on your screen. If the directories for all of the file-tables you are using are in the DOS path, you do not have to change the path. However, if you find that some file-table directories are not in the path, you can add these directories to the path. To make sure that the changes you make to the path are available the next time you start your computer, you should change the PATH command in your AUTOEXEC.BAT file.

The AUTOEXEC-.BAT file contains commands which are executed every time you start your computer. By adding these directories to the PATH command in this file, you ensure that these directories become part of the DOS path each time you start your computer.

To edit your AUTOEXEC.BAT file, don't use the RBEDIT text editor since RBEDIT will lose the end of any line longer than 80 characters. Use another editor that allows you to edit ASCII files, such as the EDLIN editor that comes with DOS, as follows.

1. Edit the **C:\AUTOEXEC.BAT** using the editor of your choice.

2. Find the line starting with the word "path" (in uppercase or lowercase letters).

3. Move the cursor to the end of this line.

4. For each directory containing a file-table that is not in this path command, type a semicolon (;) followed by the volume and name of the directory. For example, if the file-table is in the DBPLUS directory on drive C, you would add ;C:\DBPLUS to the end of the path command.

5. Save the file and leave the editor.

6. Press **Ctrl-Alt-Del** to reboot your computer.

7. Before starting R:BASE, type **PATH** and press ←┘ to make sure that the path includes the new directories you added.

MAKING A RULE USING A DBASE DATABASE

It may be easier to understand how to use dBASE databases after we look at an example. Suppose that another division of your company had an accounts-receivable application written with dBASE III Plus. If this application maintained a database called BADCRED containing a list of customers that were bad credit risks, you might want to make sure that you didn't accept any orders from customers that appeared on this list. Let's make a rule in the MAIL database that a charge will not be accepted if the customer is found in the BADCRED dBASE database. For the sake of simplicity, we'll assume that BADCRED has a field which contains customer numbers that match the CustNo column in the Charges table. The dBASE definition for BADCRED is found in Figure 19.8. If you have a copy of dBASE III or dBASE III Plus, define the BADCRED database as shown in Figure 19.8.

Our first task in this example is to attach the BADCRED dBASE database to the MAIL R:BASE database. Although the database

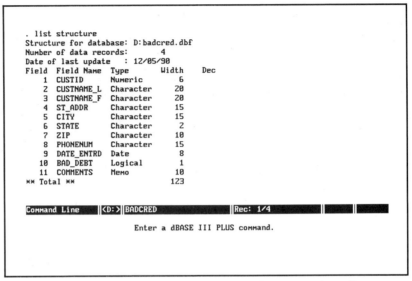

```
. list structure
Structure for database: D:badcred.dbf
Number of data records:      4
Date of last update    : 12/05/90
Field  Field Name  Type       Width    Dec
    1  CUSTID      Numeric        6
    2  CUSTNAME_L  Character     20
    3  CUSTNAME_F  Character     20
    4  ST_ADDR     Character     15
    5  CITY        Character     15
    6  STATE       Character      2
    7  ZIP         Character     10
    8  PHONENUM    Character     15
    9  DATE_ENTRD  Date           8
   10  BAD_DEBT    Logical        1
   11  COMMENTS    Memo          10
** Total **                    123


Command Line    <D:> BADCRED                    Rec: 1/4

            Enter a dBASE III PLUS command.
```

Figure 19.8: The dBASE definition for the BADCRED database file

name BADCRED is not a reserved word and does not have to be changed, you can see in Figure 19.8 that the names of several columns will have to be changed. The field names CUSTNAME_L and CUSTNAME_F are unique in dBASE but the first eight characters are not unique, so R:BASE will ask you to rename one of the corresponding columns in the file-table. The fields City and State have the same name as columns in the Names table, so you might expect that you will have to rename these columns in the file-table. In fact, since the City field has an equivalent data type (Character field, 15 characters long) as the City column in the Names table (TEXT field, 15 characters long), you won't have to rename this column in the R:BASE file-table. However, the State field is only two characters long in the dBASE database, so you will have to rename this column in the file-table. Since Zip is a reserved word, you will have to rename this column in the file-table also.

Let's attach the BADCRED dBASE database to the MAIL database and look at the structure of the file-table with the following steps from the Main menu:

1. Connect to the MAIL database, entering the owner password MYMAIL.

From the R>
prompt, you could
attach the BADCRED
database on drive D in
directory DBPLUS with
the command ATTACH
D:\DBPLUS\BADCRED.
After entering this
DETACH command,
R:BASE would ask you
to rename the CUST-
NAME, STATE, and
ZIP columns.

2. On the R:BASE Main menu, highlight **D**atabases, select dBASE files, and select **A**ttach file. Since there are no dBASE files in the current directory (\RBFILES\LEARN), the only choice which appears in the next pop-up menu is Other.

3. Select **O**ther.

4. Type the volume, directory, and name of the dBASE file, such as **D:\DBPLUS\BADCRED.DBF**, and press ↵. R:BASE now tells you that you have to rename the column that starts with CUSTNAME.

5. Press **1** to change CUSTNAME to CUSTNAM1 and press ↵. You are now asked to rename the STATE column.

6. Press **1** again to change STATE to STATE1 and press ↵. You are now asked to rename the ZIP column.

7. Press **1** to change ZIP to ZIP1 and press ↵. After working for a while, R:BASE returns you to the Main menu.

8. To look at the structure of the file-table we have just attached, highlight **E**xit and select **R**> prompt to display the R> prompt; and type **LIST badcred** and press ↵ to display the structure of the file-table, as shown in Figure 19.9.

After the initial re-
lease of R:BASE 3.1,
Microrim, Inc. (the
makers of R:BASE)
created a second version
of release 3.1 that cor-
rected some problems
involved in accessing
dBASE databases. If you
are going to be accessing
dBASE databases from
R:BASE, contact
Microrim Technical
Support at (206) 649-
9551 to obtain this
updated version of
release 3.1.

Looking at Figure 19.9, several points are worth noting. First, you can see near the bottom of the display that the number of rows is shown as DBF. The LIST command will not display the number of rows in a file-table. Near the top of the display, you can see that the name of the file-table is "badcred." Although you might want to change the name of the file-table to BadCred or BadCredt, you are not allowed to change the name of an R:BASE file-table, since this would require changing the name of the dBASE database file as well.

Also notice that in the dBASE database (see Figure 19.8) the second field is the last name (CUSTNAME_L) and the third field is the first name (CUSTNAME_F). However, in the R:BASE file-table (see Figure 19.9), the second column has been given the name CUSTNAME_F and the third column was renamed CUSTNAM1. Since R:BASE did not do a very good job assigning column names after you

```
R>LIST Badcred

    Table: badcred
    Read Password: No
    Modify Password: No

    Column definitions
    #  Name              Type          Index Expression
    1  CUSTID            INTEGER
    2  CUSTNAME_F        TEXT      20
    3  CUSTNAM1          TEXT      20
    4  ST_ADDR           TEXT      15
    5  CITY              TEXT      15
    6  STATE1            TEXT       2
    7  ZIP1              TEXT      10
    8  PHONENUM          TEXT      15
    9  DATE_ENTRD        DATE
   10  BAD_DEBT          TEXT       1
   11  COMMENTS          NOTE

    Current number of rows:       DBF

R>
```

Figure 19.9: The structure of the badcred file-table

renamed a column with a duplicate name, you should change the names of these columns to avoid any confusion. From the R > prompt,

1. Type **RENAME COLUMN CUSTNAME_F TO CustLName** and press ←⏎.

2. Type **RENAME COLUMN CUSTNAM1 TO CustFName** and press ←⏎.

3. Type **LIST badcred** to check your changes. The CustL-Name column should be the second column (matching the CUSTNAME_L field) and the CustFName column should be the third (matching the CUSTNAME_F field).

Now that the badcred file-table can be accessed just like an R:BASE table, let's make a rule that a transaction in the Charges table will not be accepted if the CustNo column in the Charges row is equal to a value in the CUSTID column in the badcred file-table. The easiest way to do this is to make a rule that the value in the CustNo column has to be found in the CUSTID column in the bad-cred file-table, change the requirement that the condition SUC-CEEDS to FAILS, and change the error message displayed to read

"This customer has an unacceptable credit rating!" Let's give it a whirl with these steps at the R > prompt:

1. Type **RBDEFINE** and press ◄┘ to display the R:BASE menu that allows us to create rules.

2. Highlight **R**ules, select **C**reate, and select **V**erify a value.

3. Select **C**harges for the Rule Table and **C**ustNo for the Rule Column.

4. Select **b**adcred for the Verification Table and **CUSTID** for the Verification Column.

5. With Rules still highlighted, select **M**odify, and select the last rule, "Charges—Value for CustNo must exist in."

6. Select **F**AILS to reverse the Succeeds/Fails selection.

7. Press ◄┘ to confirm the Charges table.

8. Press ◄┘ again to keep the same WHERE clause.

9. Type **This customer has an unacceptable credit rating!** and press ◄┘ to change the error message.

10. Highlight and select **E**xit to return to the R > prompt.

If you get an error message similar to "Data type changed on a keyed dBASE column after the table was ATTACHED," you have the original release of R:BASE 3.1. This release did not work very well with dBASE files. We suggest calling Microrim Technical Support at (206) 649-9551 to get an updated version of release 3.1.

To test our rule, we have to enter a charge in the Charges table for a customer in the badcred file-table. Since the badcred file-table is empty, you might want to add the first row to the file-table with the EDIT command. When you use the EDIT command to edit an empty table, R:BASE confirms that you want to add an empty row and then lets you change the null values in every column to the values you want. However, the EDIT command does not provide you with an opportunity to add an empty row to an empty file-table. An alternative technique is to add a row with the INSERT command, which is particularly easy since we need only fill in the customer number (CUSTID) for our example. Once we have a customer number in the badcred file-table, we can then enter a transaction in the Charges table to test our rule. Try adding the row to the badcred file-table and testing our rule as follows:

This INSERT command adds a row to the badcred file-table with 1001 in the CUSTID column and null values in all other columns.

1. Type **INSERT INTO badcred (CUSTID) VALUES (1001)** and press ◄┘.

2. Type **ENTER USING ChrgFrm** and press ⏎.

3. Enter a charge with a customer number **1001**, product number **A-111**, taxable status **Y**, quantity **5**, unit price **10.00**, and date of sale defaulting to today's date.

4. Highlight **A**dd/discard and select **A**dd row. The error message "This customer has an unacceptable credit rating!" is displayed at the bottom of the screen and you are prompted to press any key to continue.

5. Press a key to return to editing this charge.

6. Highlight and select **E**xit to return to the R> prompt.

Now that the badcred file-table is no longer empty, let's flesh out the fields after CUSTID 1001 in the first row and add some more rows. Give this a try with the following steps at the R> prompt:

1. Type **EDIT ALL FROM badcred** and press ⏎.

2. Enter values for the empty fields in the rest of the first row and add a few additional rows of information.

3. Highlight and select **E**xit to return to the R> prompt.

4. Type **EXIT** and press ⏎ to leave R:BASE.

5. Start dBASE.

6. Type **USE badcred** and press ⏎.

7. Type **LIST** and press ⏎ to verify that the data you entered in the R:BASE file-table is really in the dBASE database.

8. Type **QUIT** and press ⏎ to leave dBASE.

PITFALLS OF WORKING WITH FILE-TABLES

Because dBASE and R:BASE were designed with different features, it is inevitable that some features of R:BASE don't work in the usual way with file-tables and some features of dBASE are not duplicated in R:BASE. Here are some pitfalls to be aware of when you are working with file-tables:

- A dBASE Logical field becomes an R:BASE TEXT column one character long. If you want to be sure that data entered into this column from R:BASE is valid in a dBASE logical field, you have to add an R:BASE rule to ensure that only a Y, N, T, or F is valid in that column.

- You can't use the R:BASE BACKUP and RESTORE commands on a file-table. To back up the data in the file-table, enter the commands

  OUTPUT *backfile*
  UNLOAD DATA FOR *file-table* AS ASCII
  OUTPUT SCREEN

  This backs up only the data in *file-table* to the DOS file called *backfile*. To restore the data in *backfile* to *file-table*, you would use the command

  LOAD *file-table* FROM *backfile* AS ASCII

  To back up the details of how the file-table is attached, you have to back up the database containing the file-table in the usual way.

- R:BASE will not respect any dBASE passwords which have been set up. However, you can use the GRANT and REVOKE functions of R:BASE's system of table passwords to limit access to data in file-tables.

- R:BASE will not let you rename a column in a file-table which is used as an index column.

- A dBASE MEMO field is accessed in a file table as an R:BASE NOTE column. However, dBASE MEMO fields can be up to 64K bytes long, while R:BASE NOTE columns have a maximum length of only 4K bytes. If a dBASE MEMO field is too big for the corresponding R:BASE NOTE column, R:BASE will not record any changes you make to the information in this column and will show four asterisks in the field (****) to indicate that the field is too big for R:BASE to handle.

WHERE DO I GO FROM HERE?

R:BASE is a large and powerful database-management system for microcomputers. A single book on the subject can hardly do justice to its many capabilities. However, you've covered the basic concepts using practical examples, and we hope that these examples have helped you to understand the basic workings of R:BASE and enabled you to manage your own databases.

If you bought this book because the manuals that come with R:BASE seem too technical or abstract, this tutorial text should have given you sufficient practical background to make the more technical material in the manuals understandable. The *User's Manual* that comes with the R:BASE package provides more information about R:BASE menus, and the *Reference Manual* that should help you understand the programming language. Almost all of the information about using dBASE files is in the *R:BASE 3.1 Enhancements* that comes with R:BASE.

But perhaps the most important element in mastering any software package, including R:BASE, is practice. Hands-on experimentation (with some printed material nearby to back you up) will provide the experience that leads to complete mastery. Experimenting and working in a comfortable place will make your learning experience enjoyable and productive.

Appendix

Installing and Customizing R:BASE 3.1

APPENDIX

AS YOU INSTALL R:BASE 3.1 ON YOUR COMPUTER FOR the first time, your most obvious source of information will be the R:BASE documentation. You'll find the R:BASE *Installation Guide* very helpful, especially if you are installing the multi-user R:BASE system on a network server. Take the time to read through it.

However, for those of you who are allergic to manuals, here is a quick overview of the installation process for the single-user R:BASE package, as well as some tips and techniques for customizing R:BASE to meet your needs.

RUNNING THE INSTALL PROGRAM

The R:BASE package includes an installation program called INSTALL that guides you through the installation process. In fact, you can't just copy the files onto your hard disk from the diskettes that come with the R:BASE package, because most of the files on the diskettes are stored in compressed format to reduce the number of diskettes included in the package. Before you can copy the files, you have to use the INSTALL program to decompress them. To start the INSTALL program,

1. Put the diskette labelled "System Disk 1" in a diskette drive.

2. Make the drive containing System Disk 1 the default drive. If you put the diskette into drive A, type **A:** and press ←┘.

3. Type **INSTALL** and press ←┘.

The INSTALL program instructions are pretty easy to follow. If you want, you can press the Esc key to leave the INSTALL program and return to DOS at any point when INSTALL is asking a question. The INSTALL program asks you to make a few choices about where and how you want to install R:BASE (these choices are explained below). After your choices are made, R:BASE copies the information from the diskettes to the hard disk, and finally it decompresses the files and assembles the R:BASE system. INSTALL will ask you to make the following choices:

1. Choose the drive where R:BASE will be installed. The default is drive C.

2. Choose the directory where R:BASE will be installed. The default is \rbfiles.

3. Choose whether to install the entire R:BASE system (the default) or selected parts.

Remember that you need at least 7.5 million bytes available on disk if you want to install the entire R:BASE system.

If you have enough room to install the entire system, select this choice. You will have all of the R:BASE utilities, additional sample programs, and an on-line tutorial. If you don't have enough disk space, you'll have to choose which parts to install. You can safely leave out the sample programs and the on-line tutorial, since neither is required to run R:BASE or to follow the exercises in this book. Eliminating the sample programs and the tutorial saves between 1.4 and 1.9 million bytes on the hard disk.

4. If you are installing parts of R:BASE; on the menu that appears; place a Y beside each part of R:BASE that you want to install. You can use the ↑ and ↓ to move between the choices. Press ↵ when you have marked all of your choices on the menu.

5. Choose where to put the sample programs and the on-line tutorial, assuming you chose to install them. The default directories are \rbfiles\samples and \rbfiles\tutorial.

If your printer is not in the list, place a Y beside the first item, NONE, and press ↵. See the section below, "Installing Printers that Are not Supported by R:BASE" for information on how to make your printer available for use.

6. Select which printers you will use by placing a Y beside each of the corresponding printers on the list. Press ↵ when you have made your choices.

7. Choose whether you want to have INSTALL update your autoexec.bat file. If you choose Yes, the default, INSTALL will add the directory containing the R:BASE system files to the PATH command in your autoexec.bat file. If INSTALL changes your autoexec.bat file, it saves a copy of

your old autoexec.bat file in a file called "autoexec.bak." You can choose No if you are comfortable making this change yourself.

8. Choose whether to have INSTALL update your config.sys file. If you choose Yes, the default, INSTALL will make sure that the FILES setting is at least 20 and the BUFFERS setting is at least 16. Either the existing FILES or BUFFERS command will be changed or new ones added, if changes are required. When INSTALL changes your config.sys file, it saves a copy of your old config.sys file as "config.bak." If you want to make these changes yourself, choose No.

After you have made these choices, the INSTALL program asks you to insert the diskettes you need in order to assemble the parts of the R:BASE system you chose. Along the way, INSTALL will tell you if it has made changes to your autoexec.bat or config.sys file. When the installation is complete, compare the autoexec.bat and config.sys files with their .bak file counterparts to see exactly what changes were made. If R:BASE made changes to the autoexec.bat file and you are comfortable editing this file, you may want to put the directory containing the R:BASE files closer to the beginning of the PATH statement. This will make starting R:BASE go faster, because your computer will have to search fewer directories before it finds the R:BASE files.

ADDING TO R:BASE AFTER THE INSTALLATION

Suppose you've installed R:BASE but you need to add part of the program you did not install the first time. For example, suppose you started using a different printer. You would have to add the R:BASE support file for your new printer in order to use special print styles in the R:BASE Report Generator.

The INSTALL program lets you add parts of R:BASE after you have already installed the program. The procedure involved is very similar to the procedure for installing R:BASE.

1. Put the diskette labelled "System Disk 1" in a diskette drive.

2. Make the drive containing System Disk 1 the default drive.

3. Type **INSTALL** and press ←┘.

4. Choose the drive where R:BASE is installed.

5. Choose the directory where R:BASE is installed.

6. Choose to install selected parts of R:BASE.

7. Place a Y beside each part of R:BASE that you would like to add. Press the ↑ and ↓ to move between the choices. Press ←┘ when you have made your choices.

8. Follow INSTALL's instructions, inserting the diskettes in the drive as prompted.

INSTALLING PRINTERS THAT ARE NOT SUPPORTED BY R:BASE

What do you do if your printer is not on the list of supported printers? Your first step is to contact your printer's manufacturer or the dealer who sold you the printer. Find out if your printer is compatible with one of the printers R:BASE supports. A list of printers that R:BASE supports is found in Appendix C of the *Installation Guide* that came with your R:BASE package. If you find a compatible printer, you can make R:BASE support it by following the instructions outlined in the previous section, "Adding to R:BASE after the Installation."

Instructions for using the RBEDIT editor are found in Chapter 16.

If your printer is not compatible with any of the printers on the list, you can develop a custom printer definition file for your printer by using RBEDIT (or any editor that can save files as ASCII text). Here's how:

1. Put the file in the directory containing the R:BASE program files and choose a name for the file that has the extension .PRD, such as CUSTOM.PRD.

2. On the first line of the file, place a line that begins with a semi-colon (;) followed by the manufacturer and model of your printer. In a printer definition file, lines that begin with a semi-colon are ignored and can be used for comments.

APPENDIX

3. Starting with the second line of the file, enter one line for each feature of your printer with the syntax

#Code_Name <list of ASCII codes>

Here, *#Code_name* is the name you give to this print style— it will appear in the Print Styles menu in the Report Generator. The *list of ASCII codes* is a list of numeric ASCII codes that activate this feature, separated by spaces.

To find out which features your printer has and the codes that activate these features, look in the manual or guide that came with your printer, or contact your printer's manufacturer or dealer. In your manual, you may find that one of the codes is called ESC (or Escape). The ESC code is often used at the beginning of a group of codes. The ASCII equivalent of the ESC code is 27.

For example, if your printer manual says that sending the characters ESC, 45, and 1 will start underlining, you would include the following line in your printer definition file:

#Underline <27 45 1>

Don't forget to define a corresponding print style to turn off the feature, adding _off to the name of the print style that turns on the feature. For example, if sending ESC, 45, and 0 will stop underlining, you would include this line in your printer definition file:

#Underline_off <27 45 0>

When you are finished entering the control codes for your printer, save the file in the usual manner.

CHOOSING A PRINTER SETTING

R:BASE allows you to use the special features that come with your printer, such as compressed or expanded print, in reports. When you ran the INSTALL program, you chose to add printer support for one or more printers from the list. For each printer you chose, the INSTALL program copied the appropriate printer definition file to the directory containing the R:BASE program files. You can also

Angle brackets (<>) are included when you type in a control code in a printer definition file.

The R:BASE Report Generator is discussed in detail in Chapters 7 and 12.

create custom printer definition files, as described in the previous section. Still, even though the printer definition files are now in the directory that contains your R:BASE programs, the Report Generator will not offer you a choice of print styles for your reports unless you choose one of the printer definition files with the Settings menu. To do this, display the Settings menu, select Printer on the Configuration pull-down menu, and select the printer definition file for your printer. Remember to make the change to the RBASE.CFG file, either by saving your configuration on the R:BASE Settings menu or by editing the RBASE.CFG file directly.

See "Changing the Default Settings" later in this appendix for information on how to save your settings and edit the RBASE.CFG file.

CUSTOMIZING R:BASE 3.1

There are several ways to customize R:BASE defaults and specifying what happens when you start R:BASE.

- Change the default settings in the RBASE.CFG file.

- Specify settings in options on the RBASE command line. These settings override the settings in the RBASE.CFG file.

- Create a startup file which will execute as soon as R:BASE starts, and have this startup file run an application.

CHANGING THE DEFAULT SETTINGS

Save the settings on the Settings menu to the RBASE.CFG file by selecting the Save settings to option in the Configuration pull-down menu.

You can change most of the settings in the RBASE.CFG file with the Settings menu. When you save the settings on the Settings menu, the RBASE.CFG file is updated with the new settings. Alternatively, you can edit the RBASE.CFG file directly. RBASE.CFG is an ASCII file in the same directory as the R:BASE program files. You can edit this file with RBEDIT or any other ASCII text file editor.

You'll recognize most of the settings at the beginning of this file—they are available on the Settings menu, or accessible with the SET command. The settings for DIALOG and MENU following the line

; (See Command Dictionary for SET Keywords(COLOR))

set the colors for dialog boxes and menus in the same way that the DIALOG and SET MENU commands do. On the lines that begin COLOR, DIALOG, and MENU, the first color is the foreground color and the second is the background color. The color names for these settings (and the equivalent codes used in R:BASE command options) are listed in Table A.1.

Table A.1: Color Codes and Names

COLORS USED IN FOREGROUND OR BACKGROUND	
COLOR CODE	**COLOR**
0	Black
1	Blue
2	Green
3	Cyan
4	Red
5	Magenta
6	Brown
7	Light Grey
COLORS USED IN FOREGROUND ONLY	
COLOR CODE	**COLOR**
8	Grey
9	Light Blue
10	Light Green
11	Light Cyan
12	Light Red
13	Light Magenta
14	Yellow
15	White

Lines that start with CASEP, COLLATE, FOLD, EXPAND, and LCFOLD are character tables. You should be careful not to change these lines.

OPTIONS OF THE RBASE COMMAND

You can also create a startup program by creating a command file with the name RBASE.DAT. If there is a command file called RBASE.DAT in the current directory when you start R:BASE, it will be executed after any other startup programs you have specified.

When you start R:BASE, there are several options you can use after the RBASE command. These options, listed in Table A.2, can override the options specified in the RBASE.CFG file. If you specify both a startup program in the RBASE.CFG file and on the R:BASE command line, the program named in the RBASE.CFG file is executed before the program given on the R:BASE command line.

Table A.2: RBASE Command Line Options

OPTION	ACTION
–C	Bypasses the menus and leaves you at the R> prompt.
–P	Starts R:BASE in PBE Mode.
–R	Bypasses the Microrim logo screen.
–Bn	Sets the default background color to code n (see Table A.1).
–Fn	Sets the default foreground color to code n (see Table A.1).
–Mn	Enhances the clarity of screen displays on systems with a color graphics adapter and monochrome display (use –M1 for a clearer screen display).
–Tn	Specifies a type of monitor: –T0 indicates color, –T1 indicates monochrome, and –T2 is used for some compatibles, such as Tandy.
strtfile	Specifies a startup file.

Index

A

Selections from The SYBEX Library

DATABASES

The ABC's of dBASE III PLUS
Robert Cowart
264pp. Ref. 379-1
The most efficient way to get beginners up and running with dBASE. Every 'how' and 'why' of database management is demonstrated through tutorials and practical dBASE III PLUS applications.

The ABC's of dBASE IV
Robert Cowart
338pp. Ref. 531-X
This superb tutorial introduces beginners to the concept of databases and practical dBASE IV applications featuring the new menu-driven interface, the new report writer, and Query by Example.

The ABC's of Paradox
Charles Siegel
300pp. Ref. 573-5
Easy to understand and use, this introduction is written so that the computer novice can create, edit, and manage complex Paradox databases. This primer is filled with examples of the Paradox 3.0 menu structure.

Advanced Techniques in dBASE III PLUS
Alan Simpson
454pp. Ref. 369-4
A full course in database design and structured programming, with routines for inventory control, accounts receivable, system management, and integrated databases.

dBASE Instant Reference
SYBEX Prompter Series
Alan Simpson
471pp. Ref. 484-4; 4 ¾" × 8"
Comprehensive information at a glance: a brief explanation of syntax and usage for every dBASE command, with step-by-step instructions and exact keystroke sequences. Commands are grouped by function in twenty precise categories.

dBASE III PLUS Programmer's Reference Guide
SYBEX Ready Reference Series
Alan Simpson
1056pp. Ref. 508-5
Programmers will save untold hours and effort using this comprehensive, well-organized dBASE encyclopedia. Complete technical details on commands and functions, plus scores of often-needed algorithms.

dBASE IV Programmer's Instant Reference
SYBEX Prompter Series
Alan Simpson
544pp. Ref. 538-7, 4 ¾" × 8"
This comprehensive reference to every dBASE command and function has everything for the dBASE programmer in a compact, pocket-sized book. Fast and easy access to adding data, sorting, performing calculations, managing multiple databases, memory variables and arrays, windows and menus, networking, and much more. Version 1.1.

dBASE IV User's Desktop Companion
SYBEX Ready Reference Series
Alan Simpson
950pp. Ref. 523-9
This easy-to-use reference provides an exhaustive resource guide to taking full advantage of the powerful non-programming features of the dBASE IV Control Center. This book discusses query by example, custom reports and data entry screens, macros, the application generator, and the dBASE command and programming language.

dBASE IV User's Instant Reference SYBEX Prompter Series

Alan Simpson

349pp. Ref. 605-7, 4 3/4" × 8"

This handy pocket-sized reference book gives every new dBASE IV user fast and easy access to any dBASE command. Arranged alphabetically and by function, each entry includes a description, exact syntax, an example, and special tips from Alan Simpson.

Mastering dBASE III PLUS: A Structured Approach

Carl Townsend

342pp. Ref. 372-4

In-depth treatment of structured programming for custom dBASE solutions. An ideal study and reference guide for applications developers, new and experienced users with an interest in efficient programming.

Mastering dBASE IV Programming

Carl Townsend

496pp. Ref. 540-9

This task-oriented book introduces structured dBASE IV programming and commands by setting up a general ledger system, an invoice system, and a quotation management system. The author carefully explores the unique character of dBASE IV based on his in-depth understanding of the program.

Mastering FoxPro

Charles Seigel

639pp. Ref. 671-5

This guide to the powerful FoxPro DBMS offers a tutorial on database basics, then enables the reader to master new skills and features as needed -- with many examples from business. An in-depth tutorial guides users through the development of a complete mailing list system.

Mastering Paradox (Fourth Edition)

Alan Simpson

636pp. Ref. 612-X

Best selling author Alan Simpson simplifies all aspects of Paradox for the beginning to intermediate user. The book starts with database basics, covers multiple tables, graphics, custom applications with PAL, and the Personal Programmer. For Version 3.0.

Mastering Q & A (Second Edition)

Greg Harvey

540pp. Ref. 452-6

This hands-on tutorial explores the Q & A Write, File, and Report modules, and the Intelligent Assistant. English-language command processor, macro creation, interfacing with other software, and more, using practical business examples.

Power User's Guide to R:BASE

Alan Simpson
Cheryl Currid
Craig Gillett

446pp. Ref. 354-6

Supercharge your R:BASE applications with this straightforward tutorial that covers system design, structured programming, managing multiple data tables, and more. Sample applications include ready-to-run mailing, inventory and accounts receivable systems. Through Version 2.11.

Quick Guide to dBASE: The Visual Approach

David Kolodney

382pp. Ref. 596-4

This illustrated tutorial provides the beginner with a working knowledge of all the basic functions of dBASE IV. Images of each successive dBASE screen tell how to create and modify a database, add, edit, sort and select records, and print custom labels and reports.

Understanding dBASE III

Alan Simpson

300pp. Ref. 267-1

dBASE commands and concepts are illustrated throughout with practical, business oriented examples—for mailing list handling, accounts receivable, and inventory design. Contains scores of tips and techniques for maximizing efficiency and meeting special needs.

SYBEX

TO JOIN THE SYBEX MAILING LIST OR ORDER BOOKS
PLEASE COMPLETE THIS FORM

NAME _____ COMPANY _____

STREET _____ CITY _____

STATE _____ ZIP _____

☐ PLEASE MAIL ME MORE INFORMATION ABOUT **SYBEX** TITLES

ORDER FORM (There is no obligation to order)

PLEASE SEND ME THE FOLLOWING:

TITLE	QTY	PRICE
_____	____	____
_____	____	____
_____	____	____
_____	____	____

TOTAL BOOK ORDER ____ $____

CUSTOMER SIGNATURE _____

SHIPPING AND HANDLING PLEASE ADD $2.00 PER BOOK VIA UPS _____

FOR OVERSEAS SURFACE ADD $5.25 PER BOOK PLUS $4.40 REGISTRATION FEE _____

FOR OVERSEAS AIRMAIL ADD $18.25 PER BOOK PLUS $4.40 REGISTRATION FEE _____

CALIFORNIA RESIDENTS PLEASE ADD APPLICABLE SALES TAX _____

TOTAL AMOUNT PAYABLE _____

☐ CHECK ENCLOSED ☐ VISA
☐ MASTERCARD ☐ AMERICAN EXPRESS

ACCOUNT NUMBER _____

EXPIR. DATE _____ DAYTIME PHONE _____

CHECK AREA OF COMPUTER INTEREST:

☐ BUSINESS SOFTWARE

☐ TECHNICAL PROGRAMMING

☐ OTHER: _____

THE FACTOR THAT WAS MOST IMPORTANT IN YOUR SELECTION:

☐ THE SYBEX NAME

☐ QUALITY

☐ PRICE

☐ EXTRA FEATURES

☐ COMPREHENSIVENESS

☐ CLEAR WRITING

☐ OTHER _____

OTHER COMPUTER TITLES YOU WOULD LIKE TO SEE IN PRINT:

_____

_____

OCCUPATION

☐ PROGRAMMER   ☐ TEACHER

☐ SENIOR EXECUTIVE   ☐ HOMEMAKER

☐ COMPUTER CONSULTANT ☐ RETIRED

☐ SUPERVISOR   ☐ STUDENT

☐ MIDDLE MANAGEMENT   ☐ OTHER:

☐ ENGINEER/TECHNICAL _____

☐ CLERICAL/SERVICE

☐ BUSINESS OWNER/SELF EMPLOYED

CHECK YOUR LEVEL OF COMPUTER USE

☐ NEW TO COMPUTERS

☐ INFREQUENT COMPUTER USER

☐ FREQUENT USER OF ONE SOFTWARE

   PACKAGE:

   NAME _____

☐ FREQUENT USER OF MANY SOFTWARE

   PACKAGES

☐ PROFESSIONAL PROGRAMMER

OTHER COMMENTS:

_____

_____

_____

_____

_____

_____

_____

PLEASE FOLD, SEAL, AND MAIL TO SYBEX

SYBEX, INC.
2021 CHALLENGER DR. #100
ALAMEDA, CALIFORNIA USA
94501

SYBEX

SEAL

Quick Reference Guide to R:BASE Commands

Task/Topic		R> Commands
Edit data	•**I**nfo→*tablename* **F4**	EDIT
Edit data through a form	•**F**orms	EDIT USING
Enter user password	•**T**ools→**U**ser password	CONNECT
Exit to DOS	•**T**ools→**A**ccess to DOS	ZIP ROLLOUT COMMAND ZIP
Exit R:BASE	•**E**xit→**L**eave R:BASE	EXIT
Export data	•**T**ools→**I**mport/export •**E**xport	GATEWAY •**E**xport
Format for dates—output	•**T**ools→**S**ettings •**F**ormat →**D**ate output format	SET DATE FORMAT
Format for dates—input	•**T**ools→**S**ettings •**F**ormat→**D**ate input sequence	SET DATE SEQUENCE
Format for times—output	•**T**ools→**S**ettings •**F**ormat→**T**ime output format	SET TIME FORMAT
Format for times—input	•**T**ools→**S**ettings •**F**ormat→**T**ime input sequence	SET TIME SEQUENCE
Frequency distribution	•**I**nfo→*tablename* •**C**alculate→**T**ally	TALLY
Help	**F1**, **Shift-F1**	**F1**, **Shift-F1**
Join two tables	•**T**ools→**R**elational tools •**J**oin	JOIN
List forms	•**F**orms→**C**reate/modify •**L**ist	LIST FORMS
List reports	•**R**eports→**C**reate/modify •**L**ist	LIST REPORTS
Merge two tables	•**T**ools→**R**elational tools •**J**oin, •**I**ntersect	JOIN, INTERSECT
Multiple tables (view)	•**V**iews→**C**reate/modify	CREATE VIEW
Open (connect) a database	•**D**atabases	CONNECT
Password protection	•**I**nfo→**C**reate/modify •**A**ccess rights	GRANT, REVOKE

• means to highlight the menu item on the menu bar.
→ means to select the option in the pull-down or pop-up menu.